**Breadth and Depth
in Economics**

Fritz Machlup

Photo by Frederic Hinshaw

Breadth and Depth in Economics

Fritz Machlup-The Man and His Ideas

Edited by

Jacob S. Dreyer

Lexington Books
D.C. Heath and Company
Lexington, Massachusetts
Toronto

Library of Congress Cataloging in Publication Data
Main entry under title:

Breadth and depth in economics.

Bibliography: p.
1. Machlup, Fritz, 1902–   2. Economists–United States–Biography–
Addresses, essays, lectures. 3. Economics–Addresses, essays, lectures.
I. Dreyer, Jacob S.
HB119. M25B73   330'.092'4 [B]   77–238
ISBN 0–669–01430–3

Published simultaneously in Canada

Printed in the United States of America

International Standard Book Number: 0–669–01430–3

Library of Congress Catalog Card Number: 77–238

Contents

Preface

One can easily imagine an undergraduate economics student, assigned to study articles written by Fritz Machlup in every single course he is taking, becoming curious about this man who displays such extraordinary versatility in economics. If the budding economist stumbles upon the latest edition of the *Directory of Members* of the American Economic Association, he will find out that Fritz Machlup was born in 1902 in Wiener Neustadt, Austria. His dissertation *Die Goldkernwährung,* completed at the age of twenty-one, earned him the degree of Doctor Rerum Politicarum. Between 1935 and 1947 he was Professor of Economics at the University of Buffalo, from 1947 to 1960 at Johns Hopkins University, from 1960 to 1971 at Princeton, and since 1971 he has been teaching at New York University. The young researcher will also learn from the short sketch that Fritz Machlup authored three books: *International Trade and the National Income Multiplier* in 1943, *The Economics of Sellers' Competition* in 1952, and *The Production and Distribution of Knowledge in the United States* in 1960. Further scanning of the *Directory of Members* of the A.E.A. will lead to a discovery that Machlup served as Vice-President and President of the American Economic Association and also as President of the International Economic Association.

Most probably, the undergraduate economics major, satisfied that the man whose ideas have begun to influence his own outlook had a distinguished professional career, will desist from further search. If, however, he chooses to consult other recent biographical and bibliographical sources he will find out that Fritz Machlup wrote more than two dozen books, co-authored another eleven volumes, published an incredible number—about two hundred and fifty— articles in various journals and collective works, not counting book reviews, reports, and memoranda, had an honorable wartime record of public service, held innumerable positions on various professional committees, was called many times to give his expert advice to the U.S. Congress, Federal agencies, and international organizations, lectured in dozens of universities on all continents, taught hundreds of economists, many of whom have become prominent in their own right, and was accorded numerous honors reserved by the profession for its most distinguished members.

Yet, even this record, impressive as it may be, is quite deceiving, for it barely gives the reader an idea either of the caliber of Fritz Machlup as a person or of the quality of his scholarly accomplishments.

Those who have been intimately associated with Fritz Machlup for years, and even those who have known him less well, must have been most impressed with three of his attributes: rock-solid personal integrity, unconditional intellectual honesty, and genuinely superhuman capacity for work, in that order. These qualities of Fritz Machlup's mind and character have been recognized not only by those who share his views and values. His colleagues and students who consider themselves to be at the opposite end of the philosophical spectrum from the position occupied by Fritz Machlup, could not help admiring him for the consistency of his convictions and acceptance of their logical consequences.

I can recall his outrage when he learned about one of his assistants' participation in the disruption of a lecture on race and genetics given by William Shockley. I suppose he would have been equally outraged learning about attempts to prevent even Idi Amin from stating his most repulsive views, for his staunch opposition to restrictions on the freedom of expression would not be weakened by the recognition that pernicious consequences may conceivably result from dissemination of dangerous opinions in (or, for that matter, outside) the classroom. The logic of his libertarian *Weltanschauung,* and especially his unswerving commitment to academic freedom, compels him to defend the right to speak even by those who call for restrictions on the right to speak by others. The quest for freedoms (which, of course, he did not fail to catalogue[1]) is for Fritz Machlup a logical imperative as much as a philosophical or a moral one. This stand is reflected in many of his writings, especially those dealing with problems of economic policy or with social issues. It is even more apparent in Fritz Machlup's relations with his friends, associates, and students, in his respect for their views (as long as they are coherently stated), his tolerance for their preferences, and his patience with their idiosyncrasies. This is the image of the humanist that emerges from the opening essay of this volume by Robert Eisner.

Nowhere are Machlup's qualities as a person more apparent than in dealings with his numerous students. All who were fortunate enough to study under Professor Machlup, and I am one of them, would vouch that his image as a teacher drawn by Burton Malkiel is not exaggerated in the slightest. I have known students who failed his courses (and Machlup is a stern grader) complaining about excessive amounts of required reading, too many questions on the exam, excessive attention to the location of commas, semicolons, and parentheses, and many other things. But I still have to meet even one student who would contest his fairness or devotion. Fritz Machlup has become a truly great educator not only, perhaps even not mainly, because of his incomparable ability to explain, clarify, and expound. In my opinion, his success as a pedagogue stems from strict observance of what is to him an article of faith: my first duty is to my students. No matter what his other obligations may be, his lectures are always meticulously prepared, exams promptly graded (by him, not his teaching assistants), term papers carefully read. I know of few teachers who are as accessible to their students as Professor Machlup is. They can always call upon him for help in understanding details of his lectures or assigned readings, air their grievances, or just have a chat about anything ranging from abuse of econometrics to latest opera performances.

I have never succeeded in figuring out completely how Fritz Machlup does

it, how he manages to find enough time for all his activities. Neither his un-
diminishing capacity to absorb new knowledge quickly nor his proficiency in
writing can explain the output, both tangible and intangible, he has been
producing. Over the years I have known him, he has been carrying on huge
research projects one after another, publishing on average a book plus several
articles a year, delivering perhaps two dozen lectures abroad during the winter
and spring recesses, organizing and participating in numerous conferences, and
engaging in other professional activities—including, of course, teaching and
serving on departmental committees. Everybody around Fritz Machlup knows
that his working day consists of two shifts and that he is not following the
Biblical admonition to rest on Sabbath. But even when the pressure of dead-
lines lengthens the number of working hours in a week to three digits, his
students are not allowed to suffer.

Professor Machlup's devotion to his students attains greatest depth when
he is supervising their master's theses or doctoral dissertations. I had the
privilege to write my dissertation under him and so had several of my former
classmates. In later years, on a few occasions, Fritz Machlup and myself jointly
supervised master's theses and served on disseratation committees. My sample
of observations of his performance as an advisor is thus large enough to draw
statistical inferences. First, Professor Machlup would not accept the responsibility for guiding a student who appears unwilling to comply with his exacting
standards of scholarship. The main reason for this uncompromising stance is, I
suspect, to spare the student disappointment and frustration in the future.
Second, Machlup would place no limits on the time required of him to digest
several consecutive drafts of the study. The weaker the student and the lower
the quality of his or her work, the more effort Machlup would be prepared
to expend to render the scholarship of the thesis or dissertation respectable.
Third, he would create the ambiance of a joint enterprise, of a partnership set
up to investigate a certain problem, of an intellectual voyage in which his
student and himself are fellow sailors on equal footing even though they are
assigned different tasks.

His own tasks, as Fritz Machlup sees them (in addition to the obvious
duty of a dissertation supervisor), consist of sharing his insights and knowledge, but more preciously of using his keen instinct, given by Nature, and his
broad experience, acquired by life-long study and research, to steer the ship
away from shallow waters of triviality, submerged rocks of faulty reasoning,
and drifting glaciers of unsolvable problems. Fritz Machlup is a skipper of
unsurpassable skill, found only in the chosen few who have succeeded in
exploring both the surface of the seas and their depths.

These loose personal impressions and recollections of Fritz Machlup as a
man shed, of course, only a very dim light on his rich and complex personality.
At best, they may help those who have not had the opportunity to become
acquainted with him to see what the shape of his personality is. I cannot

expect the reader to learn anything about its texture, let alone its inner layers. If I have tried to paint my own picture of Fritz Machlup, it was mainly to supplement his better-known picture as a scholar.

I shall not even attempt to provide the customary comment on the scientific accomplishments of the person honored. The most superficial overview of Machlup's writing would take more space than I can afford. More important, the task of surveying, let alone assessing, his work would require an entire committee of scholars, for there is hardly an economist alive who would have the requisite competence in all fields affected by Machlup's touch. I would venture to say that as far as the versatility of his contributions to economics is concerned Fritz Machlup has no equal among his peers, and this book mirrors partially his extraordinary catholicity as an economist.

The volume is divided into eight parts, each one containing articles on subjects explored by Machlup himself at one point or another during his fruitful scholarly career. Part I, containing the articles by Eisner and Malkiel, is entitled "The Man" because it reflects on Fritz Machlup's personal qualities to a greater extent than other contributions to this volume. But additional glimpses of his personality can be gained from reading other essays in this collection, for instance those by Robert Triffin and Alfred Coats.

The essay by Coats, together with that by Mark Perlman, constitutes Part II: "The Methodologist"—a tribute to Machlup's outstanding contributions to the philosophy of science in general, and to economic methodology in particular. In the early stages of planning this volume I hoped to include another part, "The Semanticist." It turned out, however, that there are no economists of repute among his associates and friends who felt competent enough to write on this subject. My suspicion is that Machlup's advantage over his colleagues in exploring the meaning of words used by the profession is so overwhelming that it resulted in his virtual monopolization of the field.

Part III, "The Theoretician," includes two studies that are extensions of Machlup's theoretical work undertaken in earlier years. The article by John Chipman elaborates the elasticities approach to the analysis of devaluation defended by Machlup in the famous debate with Sidney Alexander. Paul Samuelson amplifies Machlup's analysis of commodity and factor substitution set out in his well-known article published in 1935.[2]

To see how limited the coverage herein is of Fritz Machlup's contributions to economic theory, it is enough to recognize that no essays in this volume are related to the theory of the firm or to the theory of inflation, to mention just two areas of economic theory that still carry the indelible marks of Machlup's incursions into them.

Part IV, "The Expert in International Finance," is included in recognition of Fritz Machlup's position as a doyen of international economists. The first article in this part, by myself, refers to his numerous writings on international reserves and their role in the process of adjustment of balance of payments disequilibria. The second article, by Walter Salant, is related to Machlup's classical work on the concept of balance of payments.[3]

Part V of this volume, entitled "The Initiator of Reform," acknowledges Machlup's endeavors in promoting needed modifications in the international monetary order. Efforts to reform the latter were undertaken by Machlup in the early 1960s, when the Bretton Woods system began to come under increasing strain. The stakes were high, and the maintenance of momentum towards reform required from its proponents more than just first rate intellectual justification for their position. To overcome deeply ingrained psychological inhibitions of the international financial community, distrust of monetary authorities, and political opposition of various pressure groups in different countries, Fritz Machlup and his associates had to summon all their managerial, diplomatic, and public relations skills. Robert Triffin's assessment of the impact of the Bellagio Group on the progress toward reform of the international monetary system adds one more talent to the known inventory of Machlup's gifts: that of an excellent organizer. The remaining two essays in Part V are evaluations of the final product of his labors. Machlup himself expressed disappointment with the outcome of reform efforts.[4] It is of interest to compare his comments with the evaluation of the emerging international monetary system provided by John Williamson and Otmar Emminger.

Apart from the intellectual challenge, Fritz Machlup's interest in international monetary reform is very much in line with his predilection for rationality in conducting any economic and social policy. He was variously labeled as an "economic liberal," "monetary conservative," or "fiscal disciplinarian," which in itself is enough to draft up a bill of accusation against labeling. But be that as it may, his drive for rationality does not mean that he regards policies derived from philosophical orientation different from his own as necessarily irrational. Machlupian rationality has its origins in unemotional semantics, positive economics, and objective gauging of political and institutional realities, all of which should be independent of one's ideological inclinations, ethical views, or political biases. This posture leaves more than enough room for differences of opinion but at the same time introduces a measure of discipline into discussions on ends and means of economic policy.

During his long career Fritz Machlup has been a much sought after formal and informal advisor to various policy makers. Even more influential than his testimonies before legislative organs, participation in advisory committees, and informal exchanges with central bankers and ministers of finance were his numerous articles dealing with a great variety of current policy issues. Part VI of this volume contains contributions dealing with one such broadly defined issue: macromanagement of an open economy under the regime of floating exchange rates. Gottfried Haberler and George Halm discuss in their articles several problems in the theory of economic policy against the background of current policy issues. Yasukichi Yasuba provides an insight into the policy making process of a permanent surplus country—Japan.

Part VII of this volume is a token appreciation of Fritz Machlup's monumental work in the fields of economics of knowledge, education, and technical progress. So varied and numerous are his writings in these fields that, given constraints of time and space, a painful choice had to be made as to which particular field of his endeavors should be represented in the volume. "The Student of Technical Progress"—the title of Part VII—refers to, among many others, two seminal articles written by Machlup almost twenty years ago.[5] Two contributions forming Part VII extend Machlup's original analysis in two different directions. The first, by William Baumol and Dietrich Fischer, is concerned with the derivation of conditions under which the rate of innovation is optimal. The second article, by Gerhard Prosi, considers the practical relevance of schemes supposed to render protection afforded to inventors and innovators optimal from society's point of view.

The eighth and last part of this volume is a reminder that Fritz Machlup's unbounded energy carried him also into exploration of the past. Occasionally he tried his hand at economic history, and in a much more systematic way he ventured into the history of economic thought. Machlup's interests in economic history are reflected in the article by Basil Moore, who attempts to resolve the still unsettled questions concerning the contribution of stock market speculation to the Great Depression. The closing article, by Charles Kindleberger, dissects Machlup's perception of the evolution of the concept of economic integration expounded in his recent book.[6]

Volumes of essays contributed by colleagues of a prominent scientist are usually meant to be a monument to his scholarly excellence, implicitly to his past scholarly excellence. In the case of Fritz Machlup, however, this interpretation of such a tribute would be totally unfounded. He is a man who at the age of seventy-five, instead of contemplating with melancholy the twilight of his career or basking lazily in the soft rays of fading glory of past triumphs, is laboring busily in the bright light of unweakened intellectual prowess. Quite strong correlation between Fritz Machlup's age and the rate of his scholarly output, although of the entirely unexpected sign—plus, is nonetheless statistically very significant. This volume is not a retirement gift. If anything, it is a congratulatory message sent to the man at the peak encouraging him to remain there for the years to come.

Fritz Machlup's amazing mental vitality was humorously described by Kenneth Boulding introducing him as the guest speaker at a banquet held at the University of Colorado in 1970.

Oh, happy is the man who sits
Beside, or at the feet of, Fritz
Whose thoughts, as charming as profound

Travel beyond the speed of sound,
All passing, as he speeds them up,
Mach 1, Mach 2, Mach 3, Machlup.
With what astonishment one sees
A supersonic Viennese,
Whose wit and vigor, it appears,
Are undiminished by the years.

Despite being treated by Calliope less generously than Professor Boulding is, I shall preserve his cadenza in reporting further progress that has occurred during the last seven years.

Maintaining their impressive lead
His thoughts kept racing at great speed.
But Fritz felt Mach is not enough.
He wanted more exciting stuff.
Defying Nature, tempting Fate
He made them to accelerate
Until they reached—oh yes, he dared!—
The speed of c (from mc^2).

Jacob S. Dreyer
Washington, D.C., August 1977

Notes

1. "Liberalism and the Choice of Freedoms," in *Roads to Freedom: Essays in Honour of Friedrich A. von Hayek,* Erich Streissler, Gottfried Haberler, Friedrich Lutz, and Fritz Machlup, eds. (London: Routledge and Kegan Paul, 1969).

2. "The Commonsense of the Elasticity of Substitution," *Review of Economic Studies,* Vol. 2 (1935), pp. 202-213.

3. Various articles on this subject written between 1938 and 1963 form Part One of *International Payments, Debts, and Gold* (New York: Charles Scribner's Sons, 1964; second edition, New York: New York University Press, 1976).

4. "Between Outline and Outcome the Reform Was Lost," in *Reflections on Jamaica,* Edward M. Bernstein et al., Essays in International Finance No. 115 (April 1976), (Princeton, N.J.: Princeton University), pp. 30-38.

5. "The Supply of Inventors and Inventions," *Weltwirtschaftliches Archiv,* Vol. 85 (1960), pp. 210-254, and "The Optimum Lag of Imitation Behind Innovation," *Festskrift til Frederik Zeuthen,* (Copenhagen: Nationaløkonomisk Forening, 1958), pp. 239-256.

6. *A History of Thought on Economic Integration* (London: Macmillan, 1977).

Part I:
The Man

1

Machlup on Academic Freedom

Robert Eisner

One hot summer day in 1948 a young man appeared in the office of a distinguished economist to discuss the possibility of work toward a doctorate. He had most recently worked as an organizer for a left wing union and then undertaken to return to a professional position in the United States Civil Service.

This pre-McCarthy year was already the year of the Truman loyalty program in which considerable numbers of government workers were discharged on grounds of presumed membership in or association with Communist or Communist front organizations. While the young man's civil service status was presumably clear and no such charges of "subversive" affiliations had been made against him, after a significant period of job search he discovered that all openings seemed to close. He was finally advised the nature of the problem by one friendly potential employer. It would prove very difficult if not impossible at that time to find anyone in the Federal government willing to go on record as having promoted the hiring of one who had worked for such a left wing union. If subsequently charges were to be raised and the new employee proved to have had unacceptable political affiliations, the career and position of his promoter would in turn be jeopardized. (Almost three decades later the reluctance of Soviet scientists to offer positions to young Jewish graduates was somewhat similarly explained. If they turned out to be would-be emigrés, that would redound to the discredit of their employers.)

On that hot summer day in 1948, the background of this student did not seem to disturb the distinguished economist. The hints of heretical views seemed rather to evoke his particular interest. Was the professor recalling his own youth, the young man wondered. Did he, more essentially, thrive on the intellectual challenge of diverse ideas and the opportunity to bring them into the rigorous competition structured by the discipline of economic theory and science?

The student did go on to complete a doctorate with the distinguished economist and his colleagues. The haven of academic freedom and opportunity provided in 1948 had profound effects upon his thinking and his professional career. And over the years he had ample occasion to see articulated in word and deed the relevant, underlying, and unshakable principles of his sponsor.

In his writings on academic freedom, Fritz Machlup has been uncompromising in his commitment to fundamental principles and rigorously logical in their application, this through all of the dark years of the 1950s and their infringements upon freedom at his own university and throughout the American academic world. The article "Academic Freedom" published in the *International Encyclopedia of the Social Sciences* as late as 1968 could still speak critically of "unsupported accusations" and "arbitrary action to dismiss without a hearing professors against whom charges of Communist affiliation have been publicly made." But these were not the words of Fritz Machlup. For as he saw clearly, the issue of academic freedom should never have been whether accusations of political dissidence were "unsupported" or whether or not there was a hearing to ascertain the veracity of charges of Communist affiliation. How often the "enlightened" response to the hysteria of witchhunts was only that we must observe due process in the burning of witches. The major sin of McCarthyism, we were told, was the punishment inflicted upon the innocent. Academic freedom to some was the right of the college or university to "cleanse its own house," to punish its own.

Machlup came to grips with the fundamentals in an essay, "On Some Misconceptions Concerning Academic Freedom," published in the winter 1955 issue of the *Bulletin* of the American Association of University Professors. First, he pointed out that academic freedom is more than an incidental aspect of general freedom of speech. "The professor's work *consists* of his thought and speech . . . [F]reedom of speech has a very special function in the case of those whose job it is to speak." (p. 756)

But then Machlup explained why it is sometimes difficult to rally all faculty members to the vigorous support of academic freedom. For the fact may be that only three or four of every thousand professors, most of whom do not work in politically sensitive subjects, "would ever have occasion to say or write things that would bring them into conflict with the authorities." Yet the values of academic freedom are in its externalities, in the benefits to society at large. "Since academic freedom promotes intellectual innovation and, indirectly, material as well as intellectual progress, to safeguard it is in the social interest. It is important that the few potential trouble makers are encouraged to voice their dissent, because from such dissent, however unpopular, the advancement of our knowledge and the development of material, social or spiritual improvements may depend. . . . [A]cademic freedom is a right of the people, not a privilege of a few. . . ." (pp. 757-8)

While arguing that rules for academic tenure and protection against threats of dismissal are of major importance in the defense of academic freedom, a matter to which we shall return, Machlup would have us combat by all practicable means all pressures to restrict academic freedom, whether the instruments relate to tenure, promotions, salaries, teaching loads, security clearance for access to research documents, or the like.

Machlup warned, in the context of the repression of the 1950s, against uncritical application of the facile declaimer that the price of freedom was responsibility. He argued forcefully, ". . . [T]he idea of offering, as a substitute for the encroachments on academic freedom 'from the outside,' more tactful encroachments 'from the inside' must be rejected. If college and university faculties were to take it upon themselves suspiciously to watch their members, to investigate alleged 'security risks,' and to recommend the dismissal of those judged to espouse 'wrong' ideas or to be disloyal to the 'right' causes, academic freedom would be gone." (p. 764) "The faculty," Machlup concedes, "has a moral responsibility to initiate action against a scoundrel who fakes evidence in research experiments, forges records to support his alleged findings, deliberately gives false testimony as a paid expert witness in private litigation, fabricates reports and figures, or disseminates what he knows to be fabrications, for the purpose of deceiving." But ". . . the charges must not refer to his political, philosophic, or religious opinions, beliefs, and associations." (p. 765)

Machlup went further and warned against any kind of serious retributions as "usual consequences" of the expression of unpopular views. That men such as Christ and Galileo were prepared to sacrifice their lives for their ideals cannot mean that society should rely for its dissidents on those of similar courage. "Assuming as a fact that scholars may be timid or too 'realistic,' society has developed the institution of academic freedom in order to reduce the penalties on unpopular unorthodoxy or on unfashionable orthodoxy and to encourage scholars to say whatever they feel that they have to say." (pp. 766–767)

As to the frighteningly prevalent opinion "that academic freedom must not be granted to those who abuse it," Machlup had a succinct conclusion: ". . . the occurrence of so-called abuses of academic freedom, far from being incompatible with the existence of academic freedom, are the only proofs of its existence." (p. 768)

Machlup rejected as well the "restrictionist view" that a scholar should be free only in the area of his competence. He asks us to ". . . recall that almost all great thinkers, originators and developers of great ideas were polyhistors, not narrow specialists." (p. 770) Should Leibnitz have been kept from philosophy, mathematics, law, and theology, Newton from theological problems, Kant from law and politics, Cournot, Jevons, and Newcomb from economics?

But should freedom extend to the right to advocate or teach subversive ideas? Machlup quotes Thomas Jefferson in his inaugural address of 1801:

If there be any among us who would wish to dissolve this Union or to change its republican form, let them stand undisturbed as monuments of the safety with which error of opinion may be tolerated where reason is left free to combat it. (p. 773)

And Machlup further quotes from Abraham Lincoln's first inaugural address:

Whenever [the people] shall grow weary of the existing government, they can exercise their constitutional right of amending it or their revolutionary right to dismember or overthrow it. (p. 773)

If we find ourselves unable to tolerate such complete freedom we should at least distinguish, Machlup points out, between a teacher who organizes a violent uprising or directly urges his students to participate in revolutionary conspiracy, and teachers who describe the "need" or "desirability" of a violent overthrow of the government or are critical of our present system and full of praise for another, or show decided preference for radical changes. Machlup sees possibly legitimate application of the word subversion to the organization of violent uprisings or direct urging of participation in revolutionary conspiracies but concludes:

We all condemn communist countries for suppressing academic freedom when they silence the critics of communism and the friends of capitalism. In any case, academic freedom does not stop this side of "dangerous" beliefs. We must not, as cowards, allow ourselves to brand as "conspiracy violently to overthrow the government" the teaching of ideas that can be answered by reasoned argument. (pp. 774–775)

Machlup scoffs at the notion that academic freedom is "only for loyal citizens." For "thought knows no nation." The absurdity of obligations of loyalty is particularly obvious in the case of noncitizens in American universities (or Americans abroad). Ultimately, "Treason, espionage, or other criminal acts will be punished by the state, and the faculty may decide that a convicted felon, if his motives or methods were dishonorable, is not fit to hold a teaching position. But appraisals by university authorities or faculties of a professor's loyalty to the government should not enter into a determination of his academic tenure." (p. 777)

A familiar argument in the 1950s was that members of the Communist Party could not be allowed to teach because they had surrendered their own independence of thinking to some outside authority. Machlup pointed out that the scholar must build on findings reached by others and "must accept probably the bulk of his knowledge on the authority of others. Who can say that his faith in such authority is not genuine, not honest? Who can prove that a scholar's acceptance of truths pronounced by others indicates a surrender of independence?" (pp. 778–779) Machlup proceeds to reject categorically a scholar's affiliation or association as a criterion for judging fitness as a college or university teacher.

What of "freedom for those who would destroy freedom"? Many Communists, Machlup points out, did not necessarily believe in the destruction of freedom, whatever the party leadership may have desired. Some, Communists or others, may advocate institutions or policies incompatible with intellectual freedom but deny this incompatibility. But what of "avowed totalitarian communists [who] frankly admire the political institutions of the Soviet Union, and openly advocate the adoption in our country of these institutions, including the abolition or restriction of most political freedoms"? Machlup's answer, if such a person could be found: "If we silence him, *we* have *actually* abrogated freedom of speech, whereas *he* has merely talked about doing so." (p. 781)

On the matter of a prescribed oath for academic teachers, Machlup's objections are fundamental. He does not find refuge in the pragmatic argument that they are ineffective in their stated purpose. Rather, he asserts, "A thinker and teacher who has taken an oath binding him positively to allegience to, or negatively to renunciation of, any doctrine or system, is no longer a disinterested scholar." (p. 783) Even if he has no personal objection to the substance of the oath, he has limited his intellectual freedom to change. He has indeed vitiated the force of whatever he may have to say in areas affected by the oath in that his listeners may discount his expressions as those to which he has been compelled.

Machlup has come back to discussions of academic freedom in the last decade. In an article for *The Encyclopedia of Education* in 1971, he takes up the issue of freedom both for collective and academic bodies and for all of the individuals associated with them. He distinguishes between the professor's freedom to teach and the student's freedom to learn, noting some conflict, for example, on the matter of teacher evaluation of students. Machlup makes a forceful distinction "between the individual's freedom as a right to be left alone and protected from pressures and interferences on the one hand and as a right to participate in collective decision making on the other hand." (p. 10) He suggests that the participation by faculty members or students in the governance of an institution should be based on their competence in the matters to be decided.

In the light of student unrest and protests of the late sixties and early 1970s Machlup is moved to condemn destruction or violence by students that has prevented other students from attending classes, stopped lectures of professors and guest speakers, or vandalized classrooms and university buildings. "That some of the militants' causes and issues may be 'morally justified' is quite irrelevant; protectors of academic freedom must be blind as to color and deaf as to social, political, religious and moral arguments." (p. 11) Violations of academic freedom, Machlup reminds us, have over the centuries come not only from outsiders, such as the state, the church, the public, and donors, but insiders, including governing boards, administrations, professors, assistants, and students. They have stemmed from religious, nationalistic, and political motives. We can lament alike the universities of Paris, Marburg, and Leiden banning

Cartesian philosophy centuries ago and twentieth century students at the University of Prague preventing professors from lecturing in German, students at Louvain obstructing French-speaking professors, and militant students in Germany under the Nazis disrupting the lectures of "liberal" professors.

In "European Universities as Partisans," published in a 1971 *Bulletin* of the Carnegie Foundation for the Advancement of Teaching, Machlup offers a moving history of the running battle of never impartial universities with papal, episcopal, imperial, royal, ducal, municipal, and corporate authorities. Universities were frequently established on the basis of ideological or theological commitments, as the University of Toulouse in 1229 to combat and supress Albigensianism, the University of Marburg in 1527 to promote Lutheranism. The trials and tribulations of William of Occam, John Wyclif, and John Hus, including banning and burning of books, dismissal, exile, and execution, were expressive of the partisanship of academic institutions acting at the behest of crown and church on one side or another of the disputes of their era.

Machlup notes that, in modern times, some have deplored the alleged fact that German faculties did not act and speak out against the repression of the Nazis and have criticized their presumed neutrality in the face of evil. But Machlup notes ruefully, in fact, "At many German universities the academic senates, or various bodies of the faculties, did speak out, take official positions, make solemn pronouncements—in support of the *Führer* and his policies, endorsing measures to attain Aryan purity by means of academic purges." He warns of naiveté "in expecting that academic bodies, especially those composed entirely of professors, would always be on the side of the angels and would, by overwhelming majority if not unanimously, give their learned endorsements to resolutions in favor of the True, the Good, and the Beautiful." (p. 24)

Applying his views to the contemporary scene, particularly the passions engendered by the war in Indochina, Machlup argued, "that it is improper for a university or an institution and for a faculty as a collective body of the institution to express and publicize 'official' positions on scientific, philosophical, moral, social or political issues, no matter how strongly any members of the collective body may feel about these issues." ("The Faculty: A Body Without Mind or Voice," published in *Carnegie Bulletin No. 34,* 1971, p. 31.) By presuming to speak for the entire academic body, administrations or groups of their faculty infringe upon the academic freedom of dissenters. Machlup recalled judgments of the University of Paris that Joan of Arc was a witch and that the ideas of Descartes were unsound and must not be taught, along with the position of "Trinity College, Cambridge, in 1916 that loyalty to the war effort was imperative and disloyal teachers must be dismissed." He recalled the more recent action, in 1950, of the Senate of the University of California declaring membership in the Communist Party incompatible with holding a teaching position (a resolution rescinded twenty years later by the same faculty body).

And what of faculty resolutions expressing the substantial abhorrence among academic communities of the recent war in Vietnam? Are there perhaps some issues which seem of such overwhelming importance to the academic community that it should discard the otherwise useful principle of neutrality? Here Machlup warns persistently of the deception of expressing a corporate view when there is no corporate heart or brain, of implying unanimity of the faculty by any collective statement voted by a majority of those participating; there is a very simple and honest way in which any group, be it a majority or a minority of the faculty, can publicize its unanimous position on any issue: in a statement signed by its supporters.

The issue of academic freedom has loomed large in Machlup's consideration of the related matter of academic tenure. Recognizing that tenure provisions are likely to prove a substitute for higher faculty salaries and recognizing as well that they may prove of greatest attractiveness to those of lesser confidence and greater timidity, Machlup counts as crucial the value of tenure as an instrument of freedom. Machlup catalogued the items of that freedom: "to be uninhibited in criticizing, and in advocating changes of accepted theories, widely held beliefs, existing social, political and economic institutions, the policies and programs of the educational institution . . ., and the administration and governing board of the institution . . ., and . . . in coming to the aid of any . . . colleagues whose academic freedom is in jeopardy." On this last, "we need and want teachers and scholars who would unhesitatingly come to the defense of the 'oddball,' the heretic, the dissenter, the troublemaker. . . ." ("In Defense of Academic Tenure," *AAUP Bulletin,* Summer, 1964, p. 120.)

Machlup has been clear, logical, consistent, and courageous in his defense of the Academy from the explicit constraints that would be applied by the various curtailers of freedom. That battle is hardly fully won, perhaps will never be over, in the United States and in the rest of the world. In my own institution, as I prepared this piece, a furor developed over a book by an associate professor of engineering that undertook to depict the holocaust in which an estimated six million Jews (and millions of others) were destroyed by Nazi tyranny as a myth of Israeli politicians and Zionist propaganda. Protests mushroomed, from the community at large, from faculty, and from students. One presumably liberal trustee was quoted to the effect that as far as he was concerned the professor (who had tenure) should be fired. The president and provost of the university were criticized for failing to condemn the errant author, whose book had been published by a small extremist press in England, but was generally unavailable in the United States. The administration did quietly ascertain that no university funds or contracted time of the professor had been devoted to the book and, as the furor continued to rise, issued a statement making clear the university's opposition to and condemnation of antisemitism (of which the university was by then being accused!), but without attacking the faculty member. Large numbers of the faculty published a public statement "disassociating themselves" from the views of the offender. Passions subsided, one may hope, when the university sponsored a series of lectures by distinguished specialists on the history, nature, and implications of the tragic mass exterminations of World War II.

The faculty member at my institution continues to teach engineering. As far as is known, his professional performance has been fully satisfactory. One may however wonder what, in the light of all of our history, such a storm portends for the still delicate plant of academic freedom. In particular, why did so many of my colleagues consider it wise, or necessary or expedient to "disassociate themselves" from the views of the errant author. I had assumed that each of us in an academic institution expresses his own views and that no one else, whether colleague, administrator, or student, can express his views for him without his specific authorization. And I should also hate to see any precedent for the president of my university, an eminent economist, publicly condemning (or commending), in his role as university president any of my own economic heresies. Some direct application of Machlup's well-expressed views on the neutrality of academic institutions serves us well.

It is easy to look with comfort at progress in the United States within little more than a generation in the struggle against the deprivations of academic freedom known so well in the past. But many of us with memories of earlier times have noted with dismay the historical forgetfulness of a new generation. In causes whose righteousness many of us also believed, there seemed at times too little cognizance of the need for preserving freedom for dissent from dissenters as well as for dissenters, whether in speeches *defending* an unpopular war or expressions of views on race repugnant to majorities and minorities.

Recent times have raised further, stubborn issues that go beyond conventional rules of academic freedom. Should the campus be used for military training? Should freedom extend to all company recruiters regardless of the business for which they are seeking personnel? Should the laboratories and libraries and minds of the university be available to the body politic or the private profiteer? Can there be a meaningful free market place of ideas if particular kinds of ideas are financed and paid for by research grants that suit the purposes of governments or consulting contracts for private enterprise?

Are scholars lured inevitably into the kinds of work where money is available? Do habits of thought, modes of expression, choices of forum, basic mind sets become conditioned by the wider rewards of public and private purses?

It was notorious that few political scientists and others whose business involved them in relations with government were publicly conspicuous in criticism of the war in Indochina; larger numbers seemed disproportionately its apologists. Do economists with possibilities of lucrative business consulting arrangements speak and write as freely as they might on matters which may upset the business community? How many academic economists who have identified their persuasions with either of our two major political parties and have found themselves welcomed in administrative councils of one or the other have been fully free and candid in their public utterances, if not their thoughts?

The young man of the beginning of our story once contemplated a doc-toral dissertation on "Karl Marx and the Accumulation of Capital." At one point a senior social scientist at a friendly lunch urged this as an unwise topic for one looking to a promising career. The contemplated dissertation was abandoned.

How many young economists today are dissuaded, wisely or unwisely, from pursuing their research interests by the conviction, their own or of others, that these research interests will not "pay" in terms of professional recognition and advancement? Indeed, young radicals in the economics profession protest of discrimination in employment against those of their views and interests. The profession, through its Association, is committed to doing what it can, itself or with the American Association of University Professors, to combat overt polit-ical discrimination. But what can be said of the pervasive notions of conventional wisdom in economics—or in other fields—which treat new or different ideas as wrong and their proponents as incompetent?

Milton Friedman in private conversation once expressed to me the thought that the general liberal prejudice in the academic community was such that one could be confident that any conservative economist who survived must be very competent indeed. Hence, a university might be justified in regarding an econo-mist's conservative credentials as objective evidence of his quality of the same kind as a degree from a good rather than inferior graduate school. Was he wrong in either judgment, or both?

In the oft-quoted final passage of his *General Theory,* John Maynard Keynes suggested, "In the field of economic and political philosophy there are not many who are influenced by new theories after they are thirty years of age. . . ." (pp. 383-384) Should we be more actively promoting an academic climate in which new theories of the young or even, more hopefully of some of more advanced age, may have a cordial welcome?

And what after all should be the role of the Academy in society? That it should be free from political dictation is easy for most of us to agree. Most may also recognize that academic institutions should be politically neutral. But should academicians be free from the concerns of society? Should scientists be immune to particular contemporary interests in matters of nuclear physics? Should econ-omists not be encouraged to concern themselves with issues of unemployment, inflation, poverty, discrimination, economic development, or natural resources as society perceives these problems? Further, what should we do to assure that some intellectual capacities are devoted to looking for new solutions outside of the current system as well as to techniques to improve the workings of the sys-tem we know?

Machlup has distinguished aptly between "freedom from" and "freedom to" ("Liberalism and the Choice of Freedoms," Erich Streissler, ed., *Roads to Freedom,* London, Routledge, 1969, p. 123) or between freedom and oppor-tunity. "A university that has inadequate building and inadequate library facilities provides poor opportunities. A university that has forbidden certain subjects, books, or speakers violates freedom." (Encyclopedia of Education 1971, p. 21) The political struggle against the violation of freedom frequently lies on a clearer path, but may not efforts to broaden opportunities for the dissemination and exploration of ideas be sometimes of comparable importance? There is of course no presumption that unpopular ideas should be pressed on people, any more than that such ideas should be kept from them. In terms of a neatly enforceable principle it may be easier to stand on the freedom line. But is the effect different if the library is prohibited from ordering books with unpopular ideas or if its budget is restricted and it decides, on financial considerations alone, that there is too little interest in books with unpopular ideas to warrant their purchase? Do externalities in new ideas, which are unpopular precisely because they are new, perhaps justify subsidization?

We have the ultimate aim of maximizing a social welfare function of which academic freedom, most of us are convinced, is a critical argument. For we do have faith in the essential progress of ideas as long as they can move and develop and compete freely. Ideas can be wrong and can do social damage. But we take our chances on short run setbacks in the confidence that over the longer run the "better" ideas would triumph more often. For that, freedom from the traditional constraints on the Academy, of which Machlup has written and for which he has fought so well, is vital. But is it enough?

Neither Machlup nor I would want to jeopardize that still precarious traditional academic freedom. We would both, I would believe, be sensitive as well to the need to extend it as we can. We are all too painfully reminded by events at home and abroad that that first frontier of freedom is rarely reached and hardly secure. But we may reach it more broadly and maintain it more securely if we also search for new frontiers of intellectual diversity and the means of achieving them.

2

Fritz Machlup as a Teacher

Burton G. Malkiel

I am pleased to have this opportunity to write what is a very personal essay about Fritz Machlup as a teacher. I have had ample opportunity to observe him as a teacher in several contexts. When he first arrived in Princeton in 1960, I as a graduate student had seminars with him in international economics, price theory, and methodology. In 1963 and 1964 I served as his rapporteur during several conferences he organized on the international monetary system. Later I was his colleague at Princeton until his "retirement" in 1971. Thus, I was able to observe him as a teacher for over a decade, and I have drawn on both this experience and that of several of his former students in preparing this essay.

In an environment where graduate seminars were typically filled with highly mathematical presentations of complex theorems and sophisticated empirical analysis, Fritz was something of an anachronism. His reading lists did not contain the latest wrinkles on the conditions under which the factor-price equilization theorem would hold, or the most recent mathematical developments in general equilibrium theory. Yet I believe he imparted certain indispensable techniques of analysis and of model building, invaluable habits of clarity and consistency in the use of concepts and language, and most fundamentally, a love of truth and discovery that had a major influence on all the graduate students he knew. In this essay I will try to stress some of the characteristics of Fritz Machlup as a teacher: his vitality and love of teaching; his stress on precision and careful reasoning; his liberal values; his kindness, generosity, and openness with students; and the impact of his teaching on the world of affairs.

First of all, Fritz loved to teach. Although he gently corrected me when I once introduced him as a man whose first love was teaching (his *first* love was women), it was clear he had that compulsion to communicate—that irrepressible vitality, and that "touch of ham" that are the hallmarks of so many enthusiastic and successful teachers. An audience literally "turned him on."

I recall the evening of his presidential address before the American Economic Association. Fritz had undergone major surgery earlier in the month and, characteristically, he ignored his physician's advice that he should not make

13

the trip to the convention. Richard Lester introduced him by referring to the famous three ambitions of Joseph Schumpeter and portrayed Fritz as an economist in the "true Austrian tradition." Fritz, who was very weak and in considerable discomfort, literally staggered to the lectern. But, upon confronting an obviously sympathetic and friendly audience, his voice strengthened, his familiar smile returned, and I am sure that latecomers hearing a typically energetic Machlup presentation would never have guessed his true physical condition. His enthusiasm, vitality, and facility with language and exposition are now legendary. These qualities were best described by Kenneth Boulding, who once referred to Fritz as a man with an "anti-Midas touch"—"If he touched gold he would turn it to life."

Fritz's teaching was marked by precision. He brooked no careless reasoning in his seminars. When teaching price theory, he came to class with a large ruler, a blackboard compass, and protractor to insure that his diagrams were perfectly accurate. My recollections of Machlup seminars are filled with memories of extraordinarily adroit and precise diagrammatic presentations of elasticity of demand and its connection with marginal revenue; of Hicks's consumer surplus and the variety of equivalent or compensating income variations; and of the relationship between time preference, interest rates, and income expectations.

He especially insisted on the same precision in the use of language. His thesis advisees knew better than to turn in a sloppily written and carelessly thought-out draft. Students who used terms such as "international liquidity," "payments imbalances," or "structural disequilibria," would be forced to clarify their own thinking and sort out precisely what they meant. More often than not, this discipline would demonstrate to the student that his or her original notions were not clearly thought out. This insistence on precision was extended to the most minute grammatical detail. For example, I am sure none of his thesis advisees will ever forget the hyphen rule, which requires a hyphen between an adjective and a noun when both are used together to modify another noun. His well known example went: "There is nothing more disgusting than a high school teacher, be he a high-school teacher or an elementary-school teacher." Unfortunately, the rule appears to have gone out of fashion.

One of the hallmarks of Fritz Machlup's teaching was his consistent attention to the problems of economic semantics. This ran throughout his seminars and his advising, but was especially evident in his seminar on methodology—which regularly attracted not only economics students but those from many other disciplines as well. As Fritz himself wrote in the preface to the paperbound edition of *Essays in Economic Semantics,* his motivation was "to dispel semantic and conceptual fog and allow greater visibility in areas in which both the fog and the traffic have been dense."

Throughout his seminars he warned against "terminological promiscuity" and the use of "weaselwords" and "jargon" to avoid a commitment to definite and clear thought. He believed that terms with so many meanings that we never know what their users are talking about should either be dropped from our vocabulary or "purified" of confusing connotations. Thus, for example, he would subject terms such as "equilibrium" and "disequilibrium" to a thorough cleansing job. Where he believed sufficient confusion precluded such cleansing, as was the case with such terms as "pure competition," he used new ones, such as "perfect polypoly."[1]

Fritz would go to great pains to point out where confusion in the use of terms has produced serious misunderstanding, as well as fruitless controversy. As his student Merton Miller indicated, "By forcing ambiguities, sloppy reasoning, and implicit theorizing out in the open, Professor Machlup has alerted his own students and the profession at large to the tyranny of words."[2]

Fritz displayed an excellent sense of humor in his teaching, and was not averse to making himself the butt of his jokes. Fritz was extremely poor at remembering the names and faces of his students (especially if they were male) and would excuse himself with the following story: Apparently some years ago Fritz was to meet Professor Dewhurst, whom he had not seen in some time, in a hotel lobby at 1:00 P.M. for lunch. Fritz was punctual, of course, but it was not until 1:05 that he noticed his luncheon guest walking down the lobby. "Dewhurst," Fritz entoned, "how splendid to see you. It has been far too long." "Fritz," replied the man, "I am Harry Guthman. We occupied adjoining offices at Buffalo for several years."

"Of course, Guthman, please forgive me. I am so happy to see you." The two men chatted amicably for a few minutes and Fritz resumed his wait for Dewhurst. Some fifteen minutes later Fritz spotted his luncheon partner entering the lobby. "Dewhurst," Fritz exclaimed excitedly," I was so afraid we had missed connections—delighted to see you looking so well."

"Fritz," replied the gentleman, "I am still Harry Guthman."

I have spoken with many graduate students who wrote dissertations under Machlup's supervision. A universal sentiment among all Fritz's advisees was appreciation of the extraordinary amount of time he devoted to them. Quick reactions to drafts and consistent encouragement would be given to those whose theses were well in hand, a flood of ideas to those unable to find a suitable topic, and gentle proddings to the dilatory.[3] I would conjecture that he must have one of the most successful records of completed dissertations by students of anyone in the profession. In many cases these theses would not have been written without his help. The following "grateful student letter" is typical.

"On two occasions my spirits were especially low: first, in September 1959, when I convinced myself that a dissertation was beyond my capabilities; and second, in April 1960, when I despaired of meeting the May deadline. In each instance you talked me out of my despondency, encouraged—or prodded— me to continue and (against my better judgment) I did. As a result, I can today (May 16, 1960) look back upon a completed dissertation. Several times I have

heard you say that the only way to get anything done is to set oneself a deadline—in my case, I got something done largely because you took it upon your-
self to set a deadline for me and to see that I met it. For your help and guidance
during this period I will always be grateful."[4]

Every one of Fritz's former students stressed the extraordinary degree to
which he cared for his students and the unusual amount of time he devoted to
them. He was never too busy to see students, and would regularly go out of his
way to accommodate their needs. Fritz's approachability and generosity with
his students was often extended to his home. At Hopkins and at Princeton the
Machlup home was always open, and students often enjoyed an evening of
intellectual stimulation and uncommon hospitality. The warmth and charm of
Mitzi Machlup always made such occasions especially memorable.

Another common theme of Machlup's seminars was his strong belief in
"liberal values," in the sense in which the term was used by Locke. Machlup's
liberal values stressed individual freedom and favored the removal of coercive
restraints by the state. This made him a passionate defender of neoclassical
economics and the traditions of the Austrian school. Fritz would frequently
stress the nexus between economic and political freedoms—and the further
link between political and intellectual freedoms. His faith in economic freedoms
and free markets rested in his conviction that such freedom provided the most
efficient organization, not only for creating economic welfare but also for
maintaining political freedoms. I suspect none of his graduate students escaped
their association with Machlup without a very strong challenge to their own
values.

One of Fritz's great contributions to Princeton University was the institution of a "Seminar on Research in Progress," which was devoted exclusively
to helping graduate students develop publishable papers. Such a seminar had
existed for many decades at Johns Hopkins, and Fritz made the establishment
of such a seminar a condition for his coming to Princeton. The original format
of the seminar involved predistribution of a written paper and the assignment
of two "chief critics" to begin the discussion. The paper writer would make
some brief comments at the start of the seminar and then the chief critics
would each make ten-minute oral presentations before the general discussion
began. The seminars were taken very seriously by the students and were well
attended by faculty. Fritz always attended the seminars and would make a
characteristic Machlupian intervention near the end that seemed to put even
the most chaotic discussion into perfect focus. I have been unable to obtain full
records of the seminar papers to check how many of the papers were eventually
published. For the years I checked, however, I found that each year a substantial
number of the papers later appeared in major journals. My own first article[5] was
presented to the first Seminar on Research in Progress held at Princeton. I
benefitted enormously from the high quality of the discussion.

Fritz's teaching has never been confined to the formal classroom. He

continues to lecture extensively throughout the world. He regularly presents
between fifty and one hundred lectures outside his university each year. Moreover, he has not dwelt in the stratosphere of pure theory without reference to
the application of that theory to the outside world. He is keenly interested in
policy and has been enormously influential in shortening the "cultural lag"
between the discovery of academic ideas and their use in the world of reality.
For example, I think it is not an exaggeration to state that his teaching was a
significant factor in gaining worldwide acceptance for greater flexibility of
exchange rates.

At the annual Bank Fund meetings in 1963, Douglas Dillon, then Secretary
of the Treasury of the United States, announced the launching of two studies
on the functioning of the international monetary system. These studies were to
be conducted without academic economists who, according to a representative
of a national monetary authority, "had for years been spawning plans and
proposals, . . . had not come up with any new and practical ideas, and their
views were so much in disagreement that their advice was practically useless to
those in charge of decision making."[6] Fritz found his professional pride challenged and on the spot decided to organize a study by an international group
of nongovernmental economists—"designed to interpret their disagreements in
a form potentially useful to decision-makers."[7] Thus was born the "Bellagio
Group of Thirty-Two," whose report contained an extraordinarily lucid and
still amazingly up-to-date analysis of the issues involved. The report concluded
with the statement, "Exchange rates should be allowed to change more frequently than currently contemplated by major governments."[8]

The Bellagio report was, in fact, quite useful and relevant for government
officials. Indeed, in the fall of 1965, Dr. Otmar Emminger of the German
Central Bank suggested that officials and academics might join forces and "examine the possibility of formulating principles that could guide the national
authorities in their policies aiming at external balance."[9] There followed a
number of meetings—generally with roughly equal numbers of academics and
officials—which have continued up to the present time. I know of none of the
government officials who has not agreed that these meetings were enormously
valuable. By the time of the Bürgenstock Conference in 1969, a group of
thirty-eight academics and officials discovered "much common ground in their
criticism of" the then-present system of fixed but adjustable parities.[10] I think
it is generally agreed that these conferences played an important role in convincing government officials of the need for greater flexibility in exchange rate
movements.

Perhaps the most appropriate encomia to Fritz's abilities as a teacher
come from the scores of his graduate students who will feel forever in his debt.
On the occasion of his leaving Hopkins to come to Princeton to assume Jacob
Viner's chair (The Walker Chair in International Economics), one of his colleagues collected a set of letters from his former Hopkins graduate students,

which were assembled into a beautiful album and presented to him during a farewell dinner.[11] A few representative quotes from these letters can far better explain than I have done the warm feeling Fritz's students have for him, and the enormous value they place on his teaching.

The outstanding characteristic of your approach to your work has been the love of truth for its own sake.

Martin Bailey

If ever one man was the intellectual child of the other, that has been my relation-ship to you . . . . It will be difficult for me to live up to your standards, those of a painstaking and dedicated teacher.

John Chipman

Your patience and skill as a teacher, and wise and general counsel as an adviser, has been a continuing inspiration to me in my graduate teaching. Your high standards of scholarship continue to guide and stimulate me in an attempt to pass them on to future generations of graduate students.

Ralph Davidson

It was your example that convinced me that the truly great teacher does not stop there. He, unlike the average, entices the student to use his ability to the fullest; he sparks his curiosity and nurtures the flame; he has time for discussion, and patience with muddled questions; he exhibits a real interest in topic selec-tion, bibliographies and writing styles; above all, he challenges the student.

Edgar O. Edwards

Out of the ideas and discussion and argument of one of your classes I recall the conception of my first brief article, so important to a striving but uncertain graduate student. When I brought a draft of the manuscript to you, you encour-aged me to go ahead but pointed out that one section—which I of course de-leted—was quite wrong. You added, and I hope you will appreciate the humour of my story, that I was very lucky to have you read the draft because the editor would have accepted the paper without ever perceiving the error. I have no doubt you were right on both counts; I was very lucky.

Robert Eisner

First of all, you were the epitome of everything a good teacher should be— dramatic, forceful—clear and patient. Secondly, you furnished the image of what a good scholar should be and, therefore, what I should emulate. By example you taught me to value research highly, to perform it painstakingly, and attempt to express it clearly. . . . Last of all, in order but not in importance, you were my friend. I shall long remember the many kindnesses and courtesies extended by you to me and my family. The dinners at your home, the informal conversations in your office, the interest displayed by you in my future and the aid extended by you to help me realize what I wanted of life.

W. David Maxwell

It was no until I have been out on my own for several years and understood how hard the job of teaching really was—you always made it look so easy—that I could fully appreciate how privileged I was to have been one of your students.

Merton Miller

Your insistence on precision and clarity in exposition, has been a great blessing in my teaching and research work. I have always felt some guilt for consuming so much of your time and energy; but it may be a small reward for you to know that I feel that whatever qualities I possess in my work are largely your creation.

Michael Michaely

Perhaps your chief contribution to all of us was your rigorous insistence on clarity of thought and expression; and I am sure all of those for whose graduate work you were primarily responsible will always carry the stamp of your influence on their professional activities. Through your students your influence will continue to extend, in both an oral and written tradition, far into the future.

Edith Penrose

It is in large part through your unselfish devotion to us, the graduate students, that . . . we became what we are today. I, for one, have found that the value of your teaching and guidance grows with each passing year.

Marc Nerlove

And so have we all! The professional world is full of Fritz Machlup's ex-pupils, who owe much of their habits to his training in method and approach and who will long remember his example and stimulus with gratitude and affection. I am delighted that Fritz did not retire at the calendar age of sixty-eight but instead accepted an appointment at New York University. There he has continued the same schedule of teaching, outside lecturing, and scholarship with undiminished vitality and acuity. Indeed, if anything, the pace of his activities has accelerated. The profession is grateful that Fritz Machlup continues to teach us, and to contribute to our discipline. We wish him many more years of providing both students and colleagues with so distinguished an example of what a dedicated scholar and lover of truth and humanity can be.

Notes

1. See Fritz Machlup, *The Economics of Sellers' Competition,* (Baltimore: The Johns Hopkins Press, 1952).

2. Merton Miller et al., eds., preface to Fritz Machlup, *Essays in Economic Semantics,* (New York: New York University Press, 1975) p. 1.

3. Fritz is a meticulous record keeper. If a student promised a draft by the first of the month and had not delivered, a gentle reminder would be forthcoming on the second day of the month.

4. This letter was taken from an album presented to Fritz Machlup by his former students on the occasion of his leaving Johns Hopkins University.

5. Burton G. Malkiel, "Expectations, Bond Prices, and the Term Structure of Interest Rates," *Quarterly Journal of Economics,* May 1962, pp. 197–218.

6. *International Monetary Arrangements: The Problem of Choice, Report on the Deliberations of an International Study Group of 32 Economists* (International Finance Section, Princeton University, 1964), p. 6.

7. Ibid., p. 6

8. Ibid., p. 102.

9. William Fellner, Fritz Machlup, Robert Triffin, et al., *Maintaining and Restoring Balance in International Payments* (Princeton, N.J.: Princeton University Press, 1966), p. viii.

10. C. Fred Bergsten, George N. Halm, Fritz Machlup and Robert V. Roosa, *Approaches to Greater Flexibility of Exchange Rates: The Bürgenstock Papers,* (Princeton, N.J.: Princeton University Press, 1970).

11. I am grateful to Mitzi Machlup for making this album available to me.

Part II:
The Methodologist

3

Methodology and Professionalism in Economics: A Subordinate Theme in Machlup's Writings

Alfred Coats

1.

The history of economics currently appears to be undergoing a modest revival both among teachers and researchers. Nevertheless some of its important aspects and themes are still seriously neglected. This chapter is designed to link together two of those themes—methodology and professionalism—and to illustrate their interrelationships by reference to some of Fritz Machlup's writings.

The tentative and provisional character of this exercise must be emphasized at the outset, for a variety of reasons. The existing literature on these two topics is very different in size and character. The volume of general works on the methodology of economics is enormous, but it has hitherto been little used by historians of the subject, for much of it is not readily susceptible to historical analysis and interpretation.[1] By contrast there has been little or no serious effort to examine the history of the economics profession, and one of the aspects of that subject most pertinent to the present discussion—the formation and development of professional standards—is still virtually uncharted territory.

To explore these matters is no easy task, and in addition to the intrinsic difficulties of the undertaking there are the additional hazards involved in analyzing the works of the formidable analyst whose achievements constitute the *raison d'être* of this volume. Such a task can be inviting only to a member of that species which proceeds precipitately in advance of the proverbial angels; and it is to be hoped that in this instance at least the master will not be held responsible for the follies of his former students.

2.

The title of a short Machlup article published over forty years ago, "Why Bother with Methodology?"[2] provides a convenient starting point for this inquiry. The question is apt, for many distinguished economists have invested time and energy in this subject, despite the fact that methodology has usually been held in low esteem by their professional peers. What irresistible force has drawn them,

23

seemingly against their better judgment, into this treacherous morass from which few reputations have emerged entirely unsmirched? In this, as in so many other matters, the motivations have usually been mixed, and not always pure. Individual self-interest, the desire to defend or assert the superiority of a specific method, approach, doctrine, school, or even a policy or ideology, has often been present; but there has also been a perennial desire to establish or to maintain and defend certain approved procedures or standards of professional practice. For this reason a study of the sociological aspects of methodological controversy can be enlightening. And it is also worth noting—on this occasion only in passing—that the spatial and temporal distribution of methodological discussion in economics is also a subject of considerable interest, one that still awaits systematic investigation.[3]

Methodological writings in economics usually have two distinct dimensions: the cognitive and the regulative. From the cognitive standpoint they are concerned, whether explicitly or implicitly, with such questions as: what is knowledge in economics and what are its limitations? How is it attained? What are the criteria and tests of valid knowledge? From a regulative standpoint, however, somewhat different questions arise, such as: how can correct standards of scientific practice be established and maintained? How are knowledge-seeking processes best organized and controlled? How is knowledge most efficiently accumulated, preserved, and disseminated? While many writers on the methodology of economics have recognized the existence of both the cognitive and the regulative aspects of their discipline, and have appreciated that methodological debates usually raise questions of professional values and standards as well as questions of logic and scientific method, they have rarely chosen to consider the regulative aspects directly or in depth.

From the professional standpoint, values and standards are invariably involved when methodological discussion occurs. If, as is usually claimed, economics is a science, it must be acknowledged that science is a "moral enterprise," one that is deeply influenced by the individual scientist's personal aims and interests as well as those of the society to which he belongs.[4] Like other human activities, science cannot be value free in any absolute sense: in addition to the supreme "end" or value of scientific endeavor—the pursuit of "truth"—there are also subordinate procedural ideals or rules, some of which are purely instrumental (i.e., positive means to the pursuit of scientific knowledge, such as freedom of inquiry), while others are aesthetic.[5] These procedural ideals, such as "certainty," "universality," "simplicity," "system," are necessarily general in character, and their interpretation and their applicability to particular circumstances and cases is accordingly liable to dispute. Moreover, "all formal rules of scientific procedure must prove ambiguous, for they will be interpreted quite differently according to the particular conceptions about the nature of things by which the scientist is guided."[6]

This does not, of course, mean that the results of scientific work are purely arbitrary, for in principle at least these results are

subject to the self-corrective mechanisms of science as a social enterprise. . . .
It would be absurd to claim that this institutionalised mechanism for sifting
warranted beliefs has operated or is likely to operate in social enquiry as effectively as it has in the natural sciences. But it would be no less absurd to conclude
that reliable knowledge of human affairs is unattainable merely because social
enquiry is frequently value orientated.[7]

In economics, however, where the authority of tradition is strong, where well-
defined standards of technical competence are lacking, and where it is exceedingly difficult to devise conclusive empirical tests of the validity of economic
hypotheses or statements, there are serious obstacles to the smooth functioning
of the "self-corrective mechanisms of science as a social enterprise." As this is
so, the scope for the individual economist's personal judgment is much greater
than in disciplines where technical and professional standards are more rigorous
and uniform.

3.

The foregoing remarks suggest the possibility of viewing methodological discussion as part of the overall process of scientific advance, a process which has
a number of facets: logic; personality; human interaction; the formation,
preservation, and development of scientific standards and traditions; the interaction of one set of standards or tradition with another; and the interaction of
the members of the scientific community with the wider society of which they
form a part. Against this background the concept of professionalization falls
into place.

The attempt to define a profession and the process of professionalization
has in the past absorbed a considerable amount of scholarly time and energy.
For the present purpose, however, it is sufficient to mention certain characteristics or traits that seem especially relevant to the present discussion.[8] To a
greater or lesser extent the members of a profession possess a common sense of
identity and purpose; a set of shared values and standards; a high degree of
generalized, systematic knowledge; a common language, which is understood
only partly by outsiders; a measure of control over the selection and training of
recruits, which is also a socialization process; and a system of rewards, both
monetary and honorary, which primarily symbolize work achievement. There
are, of course, in any profession various subcommunities or subspecialisms and
there is never perfect unanimity or harmony, if only because the individual
members usually possess a high degree of personal independence and autonomy.

Nevertheless, even in a controversial and rapidly changing subject like economics, where there are no effective controls over entry and no accepted codes of ethics, it is not difficult to recognize many of the characteristic features of a professional community.

4.

It is now time to consider some aspects of the interrelationships between methodology and professionalism as revealed in some of Fritz Machlup's writings, even though limitations of space and the author's competence make it impossible to do justice to the subject.

To what extent do these issues appear in Machlup's work, and in what form? As is well known, Machlup has been an enormously prolific and wide-ranging author, and in addition to his career as an economist his role in professional matters has been prominent both within the American Economic Association and in the American Association of University Professors. Although the concept of professionalism does not appear as such in the methodological writings reviewed for the purposes of this chapter, it is nevertheless a recurrent underlying theme, for Machlup is an unusually self-conscious economist, highly sensitive to matters of language, method, and philosophy, and in addition concerned with economic theory and its applications to policy. Consequently, his writings contain many revealing insights into his conception of professional standards and values. Much of Machlup's methodological writing has been motivated by dissatisfaction with "the scientific attitude of a generation of economists contemptuous of 'philosophical' reflection and impatient to get on with the business of measuring."[9] Economists should "bother with methodology" simply because it is both important and unavoidable. Admittedly, methodological discussion is usually inconclusive, for the issues in dispute "cannot be settled either by empirical tests or by formal logical demonstration."[10] But there is no easy way out. Reliance on "authority" is dangerous, while to imagine that methodology—or, for that matter, metaphysics—is avoidable is a delusion. Those who turn away from the subject are often unaware of the limitations of their own method and neglectful of the gap between their methodological prescriptions and their practice. Even if he makes no explicit reference to methodological or philosophical issues "the researcher in economics cannot avoid using a method and implicitly accepting an epistemological position on how to distinguish the knowable from the unknowable, the true from the false, the probable from the improbable."[11] Current standards of professional practice are frequently lax. "Too often researchers do not question the meanings of the terms with which they work; they are diving into third-rate statistical data which they believe, or assume, to be suitable proxies for the vague or ambiguous theoretical concepts with which their supposedly first-rate models are finished."[12]

Central to Machlup's own methodological position is his opposition to certain fashionable and influential currents in mid-twentieth century thought which threaten to create "a scientific orthodoxy which in turn (a) tends to block the development of new methods, (b) tends to exclude many problems from the jurisdiction of science, and (c) tends to make scientists 'safe' rather than 'daring'."[13] These tendencies can be summed up in the word "scientism"—the fundamental belief that natural science methods can be applied directly to the social sciences without due regard to the special characteristics of their subject matter and to the distinctive problems with which they are concerned. In economics scientism appears in a number of different guises—for example positivism, operationalism, behaviorism, mathematization, quantification—not all of which are inherently dangerous, but each of which is liable to be pushed to extremes by some of its proponents. Thus, while acknowledging that there are several varieties of empiricism, Machlup especially attacks what he terms radical empiricism or ultra-empiricism: the doctrine of those who "refuse to recognize the legitimacy of employing at any level of analysis propositions not independently verifiable".[14] His views on these matters have been the subject of considerable scholarly debate, which cannot be reviewed again here.[15] But while acknowledging an element of exaggeration in the statement of his views, which is deliberately designed to warn his fellow economists of the dangers of extremism, it is important to emphasize Machlup's profound and persistent antiauthoritarianism, whether in matters of terminology, philosophy, method, theory, or policy. Even in Machlup's methodological writings there is, of course, an unavoidably prescriptive element, for correct standards must be upheld and errors exposed and eliminated. Nevertheless, he has repeatedly stressed the need to preserve the analyst's freedom to choose his terms, problems, methods, and models as he deems appropriate. A few of his innumerable appeals for professional toleration will suffice to illustrate the point: "I shall not attempt to tell other people in which problems they should be interested or from which problems they should turn away"; "the semanticist may analyze, but not dictate"; "no theorist is appointed or ordained to speak in the name of theory."[16] To those who seek to make economics an exclusively mathematical discipline he has appealed on behalf of "polylingual scholarship," even though he concedes that reluctance to make "the serious effort required in learning new languages" may explain "the common preference for vague and ambiguous terms."[17]

So profound is Machlup's hostility to scientific orthodoxy, with its concomitant restrictions on the scientist's freedom of choice, that he sometimes appears to carry toleration to extremes, with the result that his methodological prescriptions seem vague or eclectic. For example, despite repeated pleas for precision of language he admits that catchall words like "model" are "a boon, not only for sloppy thinkers and writers, but also for thoughtful ones when they have a good reason for postponing commitment to a definite idea."[18] Hence, "without wishing to restrict the freedom of choice of those who formulate definitions, I submit that the choice should be appropriate to the purposes for which the concept is used"—an injunction which hardly provides specific guidance.[19] Somewhat similar difficulties arise from his statements that "models of different degrees of realism and complexity will be adequate for different problems"; that "any well constructed model furnishes precisely the results the constructor wants it to furnish"; or that as there are twenty-one different concepts of the firm to be found in the literature of business and economics it is "pointless" to argue "which is the most important or the most useful."[20]

As positive guides to correct methodological practice these observations can hardly be regarded as helpful, and it is easy to understand why they have been described as "conventionalist stratagems,"[21] given Machlup's persistent and persuasive arguments in favor of "the legitimacy and usefulness of abstract theorizing on the basis of unrealistic assumptions, or perhaps on the basis of assumptions regarded as 'reasonable' though not universally true."[22] His conception of the functions of economic theory strikes many economists as unduly modest. Its "sole purpose and value," he maintains, "is to deduce logically necessary conclusions"; contrary to widespread opinion its value "is not measured in terms of its immediate applicability to policy making but, instead, in terms of the improved insight and better understanding of complex relationships."[23] In an age dedicated to social engineering, both piecemeal and wholesale, Machlup's personal feelings are revealed in his remark that "there are instances, thank God, in which the investigator selects his project out of sheer intellectual curiosity and does not give 'two hoots' about the social importance of his findings. Still to satisfy curiosity is a value too, and indeed a very potent one."[24]

Machlup's reluctance to specify precise rules of procedure is perhaps best illustrated by his well-known essay on verification, a subject on which he admits that "my own views are so decided that I cannot see how intelligent people can still quarrel about them, and I have come to believe that all good men think as I do, and only a few misguided creatures think otherwise."[25] It is presumably the nature of the subject, rather than evasiveness, that leads him to say that his analytical machine helps us to select an "adequate" cause for an observed change, and to find the "probable" effect. Although we cannot get reliable figures, and our statistical concepts may not be exact counterparts of our analytical concepts, "we cannot be too fussy, and must be satisfied with what we can get." Any attempt to establish "a rigid verification requirement would be out of place"; nevertheless the analyst's judgment will usually be sufficient, "even if he cannot support it with more than the most circumstantial evidence or mere 'impressions'."[26]

Whether Machlup's treatment of verification is "adequate" for its purpose is a question beyond the scope of this essay, although it is appropriate to remark that there is much to be said in favor of methodological agnosticism, as against those who make excessive claims for their own methods and base dogmatic assertions on weak reasoning and unsubstantial evidence. More directly relevant to the present purpose, however, is the extent to which Machlup has acknowledged the role of personal judgment and values in scientific affairs, a matter that has been increasingly acknowledged in the recent literature of the logic and philosophy of science. In the course of a detailed discussion of the relationships between normative and positive economics, Machlup provided a list of a dozen different kinds of values and value references of concern to the economist, four of which—his own values as an analyst and as an adviser and persuader—are of direct relevance to this discussion.

1. Values of the economist as analyst that influence him in the choice of his research projects, of the problems to be analyzed and of the hypotheses to be entertained and examined.
2. Values of the economist as analyst that influence him in the choice of his research technique and analytical procedures, in the weights he attaches to various types of evidence, in the elegance of his logical demonstrations, and in his eagerness to subject his findings to suitable empirical tests.
3. Values of the economist as analyst that influence him in the choice of his terminology and in the acceptance of available statistical data as magnitudes adequately reflecting his theoretical constructs (such as national product at market prices, with the given distribution of income).
4. Values of the economist as adviser or persuader that influence him in substituting his own value judgments chiefly for those of his actual or symbolic clients but without deliberate falsifications of his data or conscious bias in his findings.[27]

Once again, a few examples must suffice to illustrate the recognition of personal values in Machlup's own work. In terminological matters, for example, while making strenuous efforts to awaken his professional colleagues to the need for linguistic precision and consistency he concedes that "standards of clarity are not uniform . . . I cannot be sure whether, when I complain about vagueness, my perception is too poor, my sense of discrimination too fine, my insistence on unambiguous expression too pedantic—or whether the writings in question were just too wooly."[28] Moreover, he acknowledges that his own biases may well influence his interpretations, for "my suspicion is aroused by the strange coincidence that I have found crypto-apologetic meanings of structure only in pleas for policies which I do not like: restrictions of competition, price and allocation controls, import barriers, exchange restrictions. Have I perhaps failed to notice similar aberrations in policies I happen to like? . . . to grasp an argument that leads to conclusions hitherto rejected is much more difficult than to grasp an argument supporting a preconceived conclusion. Where I do not like the results, I am more eager than otherwise to question the validity of the premises, the consistency of the argument, the clarity of the concepts. . . . Aware of these influences of one's political philosophy upon one's understanding of concepts, I must concede the possibility that my judgement has not attained the degree of fairness to which I aspire."[29]

Many economists have admitted the influence of value judgments on their views on policy matters. Few, however, have been as full and explicit as Machlup in acknowledging the influence of personal values on the selection of analytical methods and terms. In his analysis of the relationship between macro- and microeconomics, for example, Machlup denied that there is a *logical* link between methodological individualism and ethical or political individualism, but he conceded that "there are psychological associations between them. An economist who has become accustomed to assign great importance to individual choices as elements in the explanation of economic phenomena may easily have developed a bent of mind hospitable to ideas of individual freedom of choice in economic, political, and social affairs in general."[30]

Whatever the direction of the causal relationship in Machlup's own case, there is no denying the compatibility of his professional and his political beliefs. Is it surprising that this staunch and eloquent advocate of individual freedom in academic and political affairs should be so insistent upon the economist's right to individual freedom in the choice of assumptions, models, and theories? He has, admittedly, prescribed some moderate rules designed to limit freedom of choice in terminological matters; but it is no exaggeration to say that much of his methodological writing has been designed to assert the economic theorist's right to exist professionally. Machlup has expressed his preference for "daring" rather than "safety" in scientific work, and has defended the dissemination of "hunches and impressions" as a "necessary first step on the route to more securely warranted beliefs"[31] —presumably because he ultimately has faith in the ability of the scientific community to devise and apply the established "mechanism for sifting warranted beliefs."

This faith is, however, neither blind nor naive. His well-known reservations about the limitations of statistical data and empirical research stem from an acute awareness that overconfidence and dogmatism are seldom absent, even from the community of professional scholars. While enjoining honesty in the exposure of value judgments, and declaring that "as a rule we probably will indicate which value position we regard as the most 'reasonable.' Most of us will do this in a rather unmistakable way, since we are usually convinced that our own ethical values are more ethical than others"[32] —he is nevertheless only too well aware of the influence of unconscious bias. Moreover, in his "customs officer" analogy he recognizes not only the "norms" the peripatetic economist knows to be in his personal baggage, but adds that "he cannot declare those values that he will work out or develop only long after settling down, when he finds that he has to make choices for which none of the evaluations that he had ever thought about are relevant."[33]

Nevertheless, despite all his warnings and reservations, Machlup is not pleading that the economist should refrain from making policy statements—merely that he should express them with due caution and recognize their limitations. "For while economics can well serve to criticize policies, by showing that the reasoning on which they are based is faulty, inconsistent or woefully incomplete, economic analysis will rarely be complete enough to permit unambiguous conclusions from it to be drawn in the form of positive prescriptions for the governments of nations." This does not diminish the importance of economic theory, but "merely urges caution in its application."[34] More than one policy recommendation can be drawn from a given theory, if only because "economic theory is not derived solely from economics, but from a complex of considerations involving several fields of knowledge and also numerous value judgments." Beyond this, a fertile theorist can usually "think of countless alternatives in any problem of economic policy" as, for example, in Machlup's case, when he enumerated forty-one different types of measures "capable of removing or reducing the U.S. payments deficit."[35]

5.

Fritz Machlup's work forms part of a long and vigorous liberal-ideological tradition in economics dating back at least as far as Carl Menger and the late nineteenth century Austrian school. The term liberal is, of course, elusive, and in dealing with such a dedicated semanticist it is fitting to cite his own definition of the word, as "one who values liberty above all social goals and who will never consent to the restriction of any freedom, economic, political, or intellectual, except as the price to be paid for the fuller realization of other freedoms."[36] Although the foregoing review of his views on methodological and professional matters has been limited and selective, enough has been said to reveal the compatibility between his preaching and his practice. While he has not been loath to express his opinions on a wide range of issues of professional and public concern, he has displayed a remarkable tolerance of variety in scholarly matters. This toleration has not, however, been complete. He has been persistently hostile to abuses of scholarship whether in the form of dogmatism, obscurantism, or laxity of standards. As a persistent defender of abstract theory he has been especially impatient with loose reasoning, and has always insisted on the "demands of logic," distinguishing between "reasonable" and other theories, asserting that "analysis requires" that certain distinctions be explicated, and protesting that "it is hopeless to argue where one side flouts logic."[37] Describing himself as a "compulsive pedagogue" with a "love for language," "a fascination with matters of exposition, composition, style, rhythm, and sound," he has displayed an inveterate "propensity to sort things out, clarify terminology, and remove ambiguities."[38] Even if he had made no significant contributions to the advancement of economic theory or to the understanding of economic policy problems, this would in itself have been a significant contribution to the maintenance and elevation of professional standards.

As a persistent and eloquent spokesman for general economic theory—in line with such distinguished allies as Ludwig von Mises, Friedrich A. von Hayek, Frank H. Knight, and Milton Friedman—Machlup has been consistently swimming against the tide of mid-twentieth century empiricism in economics. While acknowledging the need for the hypotheses with empirically fertile implications, and recognizing the value of empirical research, he has nevertheless insisted that "the *chief condition* for improved research is a thorough understanding of the theories to be tested." Familiarity with the relevant technical and institutional conditions, and a grasp of the relevant research techniques employed are "supplementary" prerequisites.[39] Doubtless Machlup believes that given the preoccupations of the age these supplementary requirements are unlikely to be neglected. In an era dedicated to Beherrschungswissen (knowledge for the sake of control, power or action) he believes it is essential to preach the value of *Bildungswissen* and *Erlösungswissen* (knowledge for the sake of knowledge, and for the sake of salvation).[40] In the last analysis the basic values of professional scholarship are honesty and humility, for "the faster we learn, the more we appreciate the incompleteness of our knowledge, and the more doubtful we become of its definiteness."[41]

Notes

1. There have, however, been some valuable contributions to this subject. See, for example, T.W. Hutchison, *'Positive' Economics and Policy Objectives* (London: Allen and Unwin, 1964).

2. *Economica,* New Series Vol. 3 (1936), pp. 39-45;

3. For a preliminary study of one aspect of the field see the chapter author's unpublished Ph.D. thesis, *Methodological Controversy as an Approach to the History of American Economics, 1885-1930* (Johns Hopkins, 1953). Under the influence of nostalgia it seems appropriate to quote Machlup's remark that Johns Hopkins provided "what probably was the best climate for graduate study in economics that had existed anywhere," from an unpublished paper, "Reminiscences without Regrets," delivered at the American Economic Association Meetings in December 1974.

4. See Bernard Barber, *Science and the Social Order* (Glencoe, Ill: Free Press, 1952); also Michael Polanyi, *Personal Knowledge* (Chicago: University of Chicago Press, 1958).

5. For example, see Morris R. Cohen, *Reason and Nature: An Essay on the Meaning of Scientific Method* (New York: Harcourt, 1931) p. 83, also J.W.N. Sullivan, *The Limitations of Science* (New York: Viking Press, 1949),

chapter 7. On the role of aesthetic and ideological elements in economics see, for example, E. Ronald Walker, *From Economic Theory to Policy* (Chicago: University of Chicago Press, 1943); Joan Robinson, *Economic Philosophy* (Chicago: Praeger, 1963), p. 61.

6. Polanyi, *Personal Knowledge*, p. 167.

7. Ernest Nagel, *The Structure of Science, Problems in the Logic of Scientific Explanation* (London and New York: Routledge, Kegan, and Paul; Harcourt Brace, 1961), pp. 489–90.

8. See, for example, William J. Goode, "Community within a Community; the Professions," *American Sociological Review*, Vol. 22 (April 1957), p. 194; Bernard Barber, "Some Problems in the Sociology of Professions," *Daedalus,* Vol. 92 (1963), p. 672.

9. From the Introduction to *International Mobility and Movement of Capital,* Fritz Machlup, Walter Salant, and Lorie Tarshis, eds. (New York: National Bureau of Economic Research 1972), p. 4.

10. "Homo Oeconomicus and His Class Mates," in Maurice Natanson, ed., *Phenomenology and Social Reality. Essays in Memory of Alfred Schutz* (The Hague: Nühoff, 1970) p. 125.

11. "Operationalism and Pure Theory in Economics," in Sherman Roy Krupp, Ed., *The Structure of Economic Science: Essays in Methodology* (N.J: Prentice-Hall, 1966), p. 54; "Issues in Methodology,"*American Economic Review, Papers and Proceedings,* Vol. 42 (1952), p. 34.

12. Machlup, et al., *International Movement and Mobility of Capital*, p. 4.

13. Quoted, with approval, from Arnold M. Rose, *Theory and Method in the Social Sciences* (Minneapolis: University of Minneapolis Press 1954), p. 254, in *American Economic Review*, Vol. 65 (1955), p. 395.

14. "The Problem of Verification in Economics," *Southern Economic Journal,* Vol. 22, (July 1955), p. 7.

15. See, for example, T.W. Hutchison, "Professor Machlup on Verification in Economics," *Southern Economic Journal,* Vol. 22 (April 1956), pp. 476–83; Jack Melitz, "Friedman and Machlup on The Significance of Testing Economic Assumptions," *Journal of Political Economy,* Vol. 73 (February 1965), pp. 37–60; Spiro J. Latsis, "A Research Programme in Economics," in Latsis, ed., *Method and Appraisal in Economics* (Cambridge: Cambridge University Press 1976), especially pp. 9–14.

16. "Issues in Methodology," p. 70; "Positive and Normative Economics: An Analysis of the Ideas," in Robert L. Heilbroner, ed., *Economic Means and Social Ends, Essays in Political Economics* (Englewood Cliffs, N.J.:Prentice-Hall 1969), p. 100n.; "Concepts of Competition and Monopoly," *American Economic Review, Papers and Proceedings,* Vol. 45 (1955), p. 483.

17. "Issues in Methodology," p. 71; *Involuntary Foreign Lending* (Stockholm: Almguist and Wicksell, 1965), p. 81n.

18. "Operational Concepts and Mental Constructs in Model and Theory

Formation," in *Giornale Degli Economisti,* Vol 19 (September-October, 1960), p. 19.

19. *Essays on Economic Semantics* (Englewood Cliffs, N.J. : Prentice-Hall, 1963), p. 251.

20. "Issues in Methodology," p. 70. He added "To expect that one theory of the firm should serve all purposes is almost like expecting one all-purpose theory of man or a panacea that cures all ills from sore throats to broken noses." See also "Situational Determinism in Economics," *British Journal for the Philosophy of Science,* Vol. 25, (September 1974), p. 283; and "Theories of the Firm: Marginalist, Managerial, Behavioral," *American Economic Review,* Vol. 57 (March 1967), p. 28.

21. See, for example, Latsis, "A Research Programme in Economics"; also T.W. Hutchison, "History and Philosophy of Science and Economics," in Latsis, *Method and Appraisal in Economics,* especially pp. 195-6.

22. "Theories of the Firm: Marginalist, Managerial, Behavioral," p. 2.

23. "Operationalism and Pure Theory in Economics," p. 61; and *International Trade and The National Income Multiplier* (Philadelphia, Pa. : Blakiston, 1943), p. 218.

24. "On the Alleged Inferiority of the Social Sciences," in Leonard I. Krimerman, ed., *The Nature and Scope of Social Science. A Critical Anthology* (New York: Appleton-Century Crofts, 1969), pp. 171-2.

25. "The Problem of Verification in Economics," p. 5.

26. *Ibid.,* pp. 12, 13, 15.

27. "Positive and Normative Economics: An Analysis of the Ideas," p. 114.

28. *Essays on Economic Semantics,* p. 82. Nevertheless, on semantic questions Machlup has prescribed a number of procedural rules. For example, the unnecessary coining of new terms is to be "castigated" as a sign of lack of humility, and a practice liable to be positively confusing. Terms that have degenerated should be abandoned and the economist has a "moral duty" to distinguish the different meanings of terms and concepts, especially when they can be used either in an analytical, descriptive, or evaluative manner. Persuasive definitions are dangerous, because they can be used to convey the impression that logical necessity also implies political or moral necessity. Yet "the real ground for objection" to persuasive definitions—for example of "equilibrium"—is not so much the disguised politics but the fact that the concept itself "becomes less useful, if not useless in the analysis of most problems." This practice consequently involves the "sabotage of economic analysis." *Ibid.,* pp. 71-2.

29. *Ibid.,* p. 96.

30. *Ibid.,* p. 143.

31. "The Illusion of Universal Higher Education," in S. Hook, P. Kurtz, M. Todorovich, eds., *The Idea of A Modern University* (Buffalo, N.Y.: Prometheus Books, 1974), p. 10.

32. "Positive and Normative Economics: An Analysis of the Ideas," p. 124. Elsewhere he notes that value judgments, "even if they cannot be refuted, can be debated, defended, criticized." "The Illusion of University Higher Education," p. 16.

33. "Positive and Normative Economics: An Analysis of the Ideas," p. 129.

34. *International Trade and the National Income Multiplier*, p. 218. Earlier on the same page Machlup acknowledged that the policy of more generous foreign lending which he advocates "has not naturally grown out of the body of economic analysis contained in these passage, but was rather arbitrarily appended to it." However, he added, this is "common more or less to all policy recommendations." *Ibid.*

35. "Positive and Normative Economics: An Analysis of the Ideas," p. 127. Such intellectual refinement is, of course, wholly inappropriate when the economist is required to give specific advice on urgent policy problems, for example, as an adviser to government or business. Machlup is, however, well aware of this fact of life, having been actively involved in national and international policy-advising bodies.

36. "Liberalism and the Choice of Freedoms," in Erich Streissler, ed., *Roads to Freedom: Essays in Honour of Freidrich A. von Hayek* (London: Routledge and Kegan Paul, 1969), p. 145.

37. *Essays on Economic Semantics*, pp. 268, 287.

38. "That's the way it was—I think", pp. 4, 23.

39. *Essays on Economic Semantics*, p. 190 (emphasis supplied). This is from the conclusion to his famous essay, "Marginal Analysis and Empirical Research."

40. These terms are from Max Scheler. See Machlup, "Do Economists know Anything?" *The American Scholar*, Vol. 22 (Spring 1953), p. 179. This is one of several essays in which Machlup provides a persuasive case for the social sciences against those—including many social scientists—who consider them to be inferior to the natural sciences. See "On the Alleged Inferiority of the Social Sciences."

41. "Do Economists Know Anything?" p. 182.

4

Reflections on Methodology and Persuasion

Mark Perlman

It takes a degree of recklessness for an economist to let on that he is trying to say something about or even in defense of methodology. The word itself is so frequently misused that one has need initially to identify the sense in which it is used. I use it in the classical (philosophically conventional) sense.

Worse yet, the reason that methodology as a topic is mauled by most economists is because the need for its content is not perceived as "relevant." Several years ago I wrote an essay about the methodological problems of public health investment. A kindly critic suggested that I use the phrase, "the kritirology of public health investment" to suggest to readers that what I had in mind might be important. I then discovered the great truth. The problem was not the lack of euphony of the new phrase; the problem was that virtually nobody thought that anyone ought to be concerned about the *kinds* of reasons advanced for supporting public health programs. I gave up. Now I wonder if another attempt at indicating the critical role of methodology is worth making. How does one discuss the complexities (and particularly the subtleties) of chromatics to those blinded from birth? Perhaps entry occurs when it is explained as an exercise or as a game. And then, perhaps, consolidation will begin when some appetite has been developed.

On the other hand, I think that some methodologists may have given their subject a deservedly bad name because they have asserted a simplicity of approach that does credit neither to their audience nor to themselves. On this, more later.

As indicated previously, the current style among economists is to eschew discussions of methodology. It was not always so. John Cairnes, John Stuart Mill, John Neville Keynes, Alfred Marshall, Lionel Robbins, Gunnar Myrdal, Terence Hutchison, Milton Friedman, Paul Samuelson, and Fritz Machlup have at different times written, even written extensively, on the topic. Two purposes seem to me likely for their writing. They may have wished to achieve intellectual efficiency, and an essay or a book on "thinking straight" may be the best way to do it. Revelations are usually efficient things, certainly from the standpoint of those who accept them, and a straightforward book asserting what is wheat and what is chaff may seem to show the shortest distance. Not infrequently, this kind of advice is offered by way of analogue. This is how the physicists managed "to do so well," or the mathematicians, or the chemists, or the modern linguists, or. . . .

The other purpose seems to be a more limited teaching objective. It involves recognizing that "incremental remedial action" is needed from time to time. "Try a bit of this, for a change, rather than more of that." This kind of methodological advice seems perhaps to be a denial of what methodology is all about since it appears to suggest that discussion of the criteria for thinking is simply a means to some greater end, an end that is apparently not *simple truth* but the mechanism of learning. It is as though the methodologist were a lawyer arguing a case—first he uses one argument, then another—not in the least embarrassed by the plethora of incongruent (even contradictory) assumptions involved in the process. One perceptive friend once suggested to me that economists are like engineers, ask them a question and they will give you an answer. Physicists, by way of contrast, are different; ask them a question and they are likely to reply that they do not know the answer. Insofar as the point had validity, it explains why economists differ one from another; it is not intended to be a lesson in personal humility. Physicists do not *as physicists* have to ponder what seem to be immediate queries like allocation or growth decisions; economists and engineers do. Later in this chapter I will return to this view of economic methodology as an "incremental remedial" process, but it seems to me to explain a great deal about the work of Marshall and even of Robbins. It also explains much about Machlup and his influence.

1.

While in the strictest sense methodology is that branch of epistemology that deals with the selection of criteria for use in inquiry and discussion, I propose to rephrase (and perhaps loosen) the definition. What I have in mind is the thought that methodology is the study of the bases for critical (i.e., self-conscious) persuasion. My point is that the modern retitled intellectual discipline, "the history and philosophy of science," may not be broad enough to "do what I think has to be done." Or, perhaps, it is aimed in another direction. *Science,* as the phrase seems to be used, means either applied science (i.e., oriented toward particulars) or pure science (i.e., oriented toward universals). The cause of the difficulty is that learning does not, in my view, fall neatly into either of these two categories or—even if one allows for interaction—into a third indistinguishable category, which may be called science but which is not perceptibly individualizing or general at any particular stage of the process.

Thus, if we proceed by looking at the process as one involving the bases of persuasion, I think that we may make some progress. I must, however, restrict

this discussion to academic inquiry not only because of the inevitable space
limitations but also because there are a plethora of persuasion types irrelevant
to our immediate interest. What are some of them? Persuasion at a painful
moral cost—"guilty beyond a shadow of a reasonable doubt." Persuasion
based on subliminal resonances—"moonlight and roses." Two examples
may convince that there are others as well. Suffice it to assert that my
concern here focuses on academically critical persuasion and is therefore
squarely in the area of what I perceive as traditional (classical) methodology.

2.

In the preface to the *Selected Writings of Fritz Machlup,*[1] George Bitros notes
that there are three "fundamental characteristics" of Machlup's work: (1) a
taxonomic method of analysis; (2) a "relentless pursuit for clarity of concepts
and consistency in their use," and (3) a "pathos for individual liberties."
While I do not dispute that these are present, I suggest that there are at least two
more. They and their implications constitute what this essay offers. Moreover,
these two provide what I believe to be critical insights into past and current
controversies about formal methodology.

First, to my mind Machlup's work reflects an unusually wide tolerance
for different kinds of understanding. As such, it reflects what has become
something of an exception in the profession—a broad cross-cultural training
in history and epistemology in the basics of the humanities and in the applied
sciences. Madariaga once contrasted the tolerance stemming from indifference
with the tolerance stemming from conviction. Machlup's is of the latter type.
If he is intolerant of unnecessary semantic fuzziness, he nonetheless accepts for
serious discussion most other products of the mind. What permeates Machlup's
work in methodology is the omnipresent reflection of his having studied many
different kinds of knowledge. Some were essentially cognitive and in that
sense empirical or inductive. Others were deductive and in that sense capable
of that quality of rigor so much admired by pure scientists. Some involved moral
revelation—true, not of a particularly rabbinical mold, but which depended upon
related cultural definitions or priorities. Whewell called this last type intuition:
Whewell also appreciated whence it came. Some of the disciplines Machlup
studied and which are reflected in his general writings were clearly based on
his own cultural preferences (music and the theatre are ready examples). A
Gymnasium education shows. In Machlup's case, it is dominant. His enthusiasm
for Schumpeter's[2] catholicity of understanding of method is not feigned. In
that sense Schumpeter and he are more than kindred spirits, however different
their policy preferences. In fundamentals they were hammered on the same
forge.

A second aspect beyond those Bitros lists as fundamental is Machlup's effective preference for heuristics. Whatever else Machlup set out to be, he clearly succeeded as a teacher. And he succeeded as a teacher of others because he was geared to teach himself. In an essay, not included in the collection of *Selected Writings,* Machlup threw an intellectual punch at Terence W. Hutchison for excessive and destructive narrowness. Hutchison had asserted that there were only two kinds of statements—those that could be shown empirically to be false (but which were accepted as conditionally valid until that was done) and those that were simply definitions and were thus without empirical content. Machlup's point was that Hutchison knowingly or otherwise neglected the "category of propositions used in most theoretical systems: the heuristic postulates and idealized assumptions in abstract models of interdependent constructs useful in the explanation and prediction of observable phenomena." "What if?" says the conjecturing historian. "It is precisely because the dog didn't bark," remarked the perspective Sherlock Holmes. It is not only the usefulness of the "counterfactual" event that can give the "actual" event meaning; to the thinker both the "counterfactual" and the "actual" have real meaning, but there is also the catalytic kind of thinking (intuitive), which is absorbed, which does not seem to enter into the substance of the conclusion, but which is needed none the less. Again Whewell dealt with the point: so did others like Einstein and von Neumann. To the extent that we are all self-teaching, we must be cognizant of the role of disinterested (detached or seemingly unrelated) considerations in our ponderings.

It is the stress on the self-educational aspect of the discipline of economics that is basic to this essay. Methodology, clearly considered, is simply an analysis of how one becomes convinced by oneself as well as by others—the two processes are not the same, but are systematically related.

It can be argued that there are essential differences between heuristics and massive programs for whole disciplinary breakthroughs, just as there are essential differences between social economies and private economies or between macro-analysis and microanalysis. Perhaps it is the role of the genius that permits a single mind in the process of training itself to see the complexity of the system. Or perhaps it is the interaction of geniuses' roles—after all Newton did not see the cosmic (or at any rate the solar-system) implications of his laws of mechanics until Christopher Wren asked why the laws should not be so extended. But I am prepared to entertain the other hypothesis and settle for the view that systems writ small (heuristics) or large (concerted disciplinary creations) are essentially the same thing.

So how does one go about it? My method is essentially historical; that is, I tend to see how it has been done, what the problems seem to have been, and then speculate about what are the problems now.

While the current trend is to discuss recent thoughts on the topic, I feel that there is some advantage to going back a century or so in order to see what happened in our discipline, economics. Before doing so, however, let us recall the current state of the debate. In 1974 there was a conference at Nafplion in the Peloponnesus. Originally called by Imre Lakatos, the Hungarian revolutionary turned London School of Economics academic, the conference came into being after Lakatos's death and was run under the supervision of Spiro Latsis, an erstwhile Lakatos student. Two excellent volumes have been published within the past year by the Cambridge University Press based on the papers presented at these meetings. One,[3] with Colin Howson as editor, was written prior to the conference and is about the evolution of certain propositions in the natural sciences (what I earlier referred to as some of the applied sciences). It is historical in content, though the essay on Einstein and Lorenz seems quite modern. The other volume,[4] with Latsis as editor, contains papers presented at or written in response to the actual discussions.

The critical idea originally behind the conference was the pairing of Lakatos's theory of scientific methodological research programs with the ideas of Thomas S. Kuhn. In the Howson volume there is a definitive (in many senses) essay by Lakatos, in which he ultimately seems to come to the position that one perceives what is scientific (I would say, what is academically persuasive) by seeing what succeeds, rather than by discovering new basic ideas (*à la* Kuhn) or even by setting up (ex ante) detailed testing programs, that is, Methodological Scientific Research Programs (*à la* himself). I do Lakatos's views something of a minor injustice, but even so it seems clear to me that it is a departure from what I understood to be a clarion call for a MSRP, an ex ante program that is supposed to be convincing. What is supposed to persuade is never so impressive as what has persuaded: this is the ex ante/ex post distinction that has proven so important to our understanding of Wicksell and Myrdal (who posed it so neatly), as well as of Keynes and Shackle.

The Latsis volume is about economics and is addressed to improving its scientific (by which I also mean persuasive) content. But this he does largely by assertive argument.

Mark Blaug, nonetheless, presents a thoroughly useful, if somewhat loaded, essay summarizing the present state of the methodological confrontation in economics. For all his sharp rhetoric, Blaug is quite detached insofar as the Kuhn/Lakatos paradigm/MSRP issues are concerned. I infer that Blaug focuses most on the earlier, or Popperian phase of the subdiscipline's development. In my view, Blaug's assessment would have been more persuasive (to me, at least) if he had caught more of that part of Lakatos's anti-Popperian essay, to which I have alluded in the preceding paragraph. It is contained in Part C, *Against aprioristic and anti-theoretical approaches to methodology,* and entitled "History of science and its rational reconstructions."[5] Blaug is not one to muffle his views and it is evident that his sympathies lie most with the pre-Popperian analysts, particularly Lionel Robbins, *The Nature and Significance of the Economics Science.* And, in my view he is right (i.e., I share his view and was persuaded prior to reading his essay).

As one who was trained at Wisconsin in the atmosphere of the *Methoden-*

streit, but at the historical side of it, I came on Robbins's views first as an
alleged exposition in English of the other or Viennese side. Hogben's shrill
attack brought its own reaction.[6] And while I am prepared to concede that there
was some overstatement among many of the Viennese school (and I do not think
it trenchant to elaborate on this point), I found it hard to fault Robbins at
those points where he was most frequently assailed. One cannot assess what the
battle meant to Schmoller and his associates, on the one hand, or to Menger
and his, on the other, but those meanings need not be particularly relevant to
us except to point out how individuals interested in persuading others slip
into irreconcilable controversy. Southey put it all too plainly:

> "And everybody praised the Duke,
> Who this great fight did win."
> "But what good came of it at last?"
> Quoth little Peterkin.
> "Why that I cannot tell."
> "But 'twas a famous victory," said he.
>
> *After Blenheim*

Robbins's classic work is the kind of thing that attracts and then reattracts:
if the eighteenth century Scottish influence on London was a sort of tolerant
common sense, Robbins's influence on economics was much the same kind of
thing. (Perhaps this will be appreciated only by those who have read the book
with a modicum of attention to the adjectives, adverbs, and particularly to the
explicit qualifications—a nicety overlooked by Myrdal and many others who
have set the book and Robbins up as "straw men.")

Robbins is, I think, the latest in a series of British methodologist/economists.
That approach I have called the "incremental remedial action" type. Its content
is quite consistent with Robbins's primary occupation, which was as a man-of-
affairs. In his case, the approach was essentially a brief for clearer thinking
(persuasion, if you please). What he seems to have wanted to say is that there
is a professional side to economics (really political economy), which hinges
on the capacity to draw distinctions between processes and goals. It is quite
possible, indeed at times appropriate, for an economist to offer advice regarding
process without getting involved in selection of goals.

No one who knows Robbins's record as a salvager of the physical and
professional lives of refugee economists can possibly imagine that he was not
committed to a complex system of social goals. His capacity to reverse and even
then to reconsider his own views regarding the Keynesian goals certainly suggests
that he pondered not only arguments but also the secondary and tertiary implications of the processes, the goals, and, what is most difficult, their interactions.
To my mind Robbins (unlike his colleague at the London School of Economics,
Karl Popper) perceived the methodological need of economics as a need to use
the perspective offered by participation in public life (with the goal of persua-

siveness) to add depth of argumentation as in the separate parts of a lawyer's brief as well as a degree of intellectual power (even imagination) to the discipline. This depth element is important; it suggests a broad cultural understanding cannily applied to an established body of knowledge. While I am tempted to think that Robbins liked to believe that one could separate wheat from chaff (to use this metaphor once more), I rather suspect that he was more interested in including more in the topic than he was in casting out the "impurities" (as revealed by some verification or falsification test).

Erudition, integrity, and responsiveness to others' contributions are rather strong nouns. I suspect that Robbins would endorse them as the elements of the kind of persuasion that appealed to him. I believe them to be characteristic of most of Robbins's contribution and of Machlup's. Both men clearly believed that their judgments were at times flawed—yet, their appreciation of the flaws is essential to their methodological view. Advance consists of absorption of ideas involving compensatory adjustment when the new element seems to be ill-fitting or, alternatively, overpowering. Hence the tension between what has been absorbed and the next step.

Recently, I have been looking at the changes wrought in the discipline by Alfred Marshall, whose contributions were certainly the most self-conscious in the era of the turn of the century. Marshall's Methodological Appendix to his *Principles of Economics* is very revealing in as much as he advocated something that in retrospect seems somewhat different from his own forte.

3.

Marshall was brought back to Cambridge by the group around Henry Sidgwick, himself no mean intellectual leader. Marshall's predecessor as Professor of Political Economy had been Henry Fawcett, a man of great personal attainment (he had overcome a parentally caused blinding accident to go on to become a professor, a member of Parliament, and a Minister of the Crown). Fawcett was a devotee of the views, both substantive and methodological, of John Stuart Mill. I have elsewhere discussed the similarity of the negative reactions to Mill's economics at Cambridge and among the principal leaders of American Institutionalism (Veblen, Mitchell, and Commons).[7] In that essay I also take care to explain why I think that Marshall's parallel answer was in many ways superior to the work of the American three. Here I note only that Marshall's effort, as I understand it, was to decanonize deductionism and ethical utilitarianism and to stress the co-equal importance of empiricism as the necessary "incremental remedial action" (to use my own phrase again). There seems to be relatively little in Marshall's personal background that would have led him to advocate the need for empiricism—after all he was a successful Johnian Wrangler, and his Mathematical Appendix to the *Principles* certainly confirms his easy competence with abstract reasoning. Yet, it was the techniques of applied science that he stressed in his bit-at-a-time Methodological Appendix. My surmise is that the wind of empiricism blew on to the new economics tripos (which Marshall established at Cambridge) from the Cavendish (Applied Physics) Laboratory and from such other laboratories as biology and chemistry.

To my mind Marshall's contribution achieved heroic proportions because of its timing. It came when the Mill formulations pertaining to value (utilitarianism) and to method (deduction) needed corrective remedial action. Marshall provided it. Why he did so is an interesting speculation and suggests that he was "commissioned" to do the job by his Cantabrigian sponsors, who sensed whence came the new wind.

There was some time later a similar pressure in Oxford, but it did not take the form of developing a curriculum in economics; rather it was in a combination of politics, philosophy, and economics. It was not as self-consciously remedial for the economics discipline as the Cambridge reform was. Nor did it have the long term (fifty- to seventy-year) impact.

Nonetheless these two changes were profound redirections in the methodology of economics. It is said that Oxford is cosmopolitan and dilettantish, while Cambridge is provincial and professional. In a sophisticated world persuasion is achieved most directly when one manages to be cosmopolitan and professional. That was the goal of the traditional *Gymnasium* or *Realgymnasium* education. In our present emphasis on specialization perhaps the current methodological incremental remedial action is to become more aware of what goes on in other disciplines—much as Marshall (I believe) was "commissioned" to make economics more of an applied and less of a pure science. But how does one know where to turn? The answer is in doing what persuades—and experimentation and then critique of it are the methods to pursue.

In sum, I do not think that breakthroughs have or are going to occur just because we can plan to work on new basic ideas. Nor do I think that one can design ex ante an efficient Methodological Scientific Research Program. Ex post, both may have been seen to have occurred. But for those of us who want progress in the near future, there seems to be no better way than by assessing in a sophisticated manner what we have (and that is no small task, being eschewed by most of our students who—to use Santayana's observation— are self-condemned to rediscover that which has been known before) and then by taking small or somewhat larger steps to compensate for perceived defects.

It comes back to sophistication and heuristics, to persuasion and knowledge of methodological experience, and ultimately to our teachers and our capacity to teach ourselves and our students.

In many senses the lessons of empiricism have been memorized without being understood. Students run regressions as though the computer were a free good (which it may well be to them). "What do you expect to find?" is a worthwhile question for most of my students and colleagues—one worth putting long before they start examining data. Such a query leads to initial apriorism—to some kind of "reasoned" (as distinct from "behavioral") result. Then given an explicit expectation, and a next step of the discovery of empirical findings, the final exciting step of explaining the deviations of the one from the other is the payoff.

The point could be the venerable one that one needs both deduction and induction; such a view is right, but it is Marshall's (not my) point. It is also true that one is likely to need incremental remedial action at any point in time; that the balance between the two can get out of line just as can the balance between white and red blood cells, a balance essential to the physical survival of mammals. What I believe should be stressed is that the goal of methodology is far more complicated than laying out a "royal road"; it is the development of a foundation for heuristics. Someone has said that when we can argue, we will not need to fight. That is only a partial truth. When we learn what it takes to persuade reasonably (and argument is only one method for it) and when we stop insisting how others ought to be convinced, methodology will become a high priority part of the economics curriculum. I suspect that we are not far from that time.

Notes

1. *Selected Economic Writings of Fritz Machlup,* George Bitros, ed. (New York: New York University Press, 1976), pp. vii, *ff.*

2. "Schumpeter's Economic Methodology," *Review of Economics and Statistics* 33 (May 1951), 145–51.

3. Colin Howson, ed., *Method and Appraisal in the Physical Sciences; The Critical Background to Modern Science, 1800–1905* (Cambridge: The University Press, 1976).

4. Spiro Latsis, ed., *Method and Appraisal in Economics* (Cambridge: The University Press, 1976).

5. Spiro Latsis, ed., *Method and Appraisal.*

6. "Prolegomena to Political Arithmetic," in Lacelot Hogben ed., *Political Arithmetic: A Symposium of Population Studies,* (London: Allen & Unwin, 1938). See pp. 28–30.

7. "Orthodoxy and Heterodoxy in Economics: A Retrospective View of Experiences in Britain and the U.S.A.," *Zeitschrift für Nationalökonomie* 37, No. 1-2 (1977), 151-64.

Part III:
The Theoretician

5

A Reconsideration of the "Elasticity Approach" to Balance-of-Payments Adjustment Problems

John S. Chipman

Introduction

According to Hegelian dialectics, thought is supposed to progress by means of a process of thesis, antithesis, and synthesis. One would like to think, therefore, that those branches of economic theory that are most characterized by continued controversy are the ones making the most rapid progress, and that those fields in which theses are put forward with the greatest degree of dogmatism, and antitheses with the greatest amount of vehemence, are the ones in which our knowledge of the actual workings of the economy is the greatest. Unfortunately, however, the opposite seems to be true. Dogmatic self-assurance, coupled with ringing denunciation of the work of others, seems to be not an indication of knowledge, but rather a symptom of our deep ignorance of the actual facts.

The following thesis was put forward by John Stuart Mill in 1848 (Vol. 2, Book 3, Chapter 22, §3, p. 175): "It thus appears, that a depreciation of the currency does not affect the foreign trade of the country: this is carried on precisely as if the currency maintained its value." A century and a quarter later, essentially the same thesis—but with a subtle and significant difference—was put forward again in the following words (Dornbusch, 1975): "It is well known by now, and indeed may have been known to the attentive reader of Meade's work for twenty years, that an exchange rate change in and of itself will exert no real effects. It is rather because some other nominal variable is fixed that an exchange rate change represents a real change and can therefore be expected to affect other real variables, among them the trade balance."

Mill's thesis was stated in a form that was empirically refutable, at least in principle; and one of his most faithful followers, upon the conclusion of a number of painstaking empirical studies of the international adjustment mechanism, had this to say about it (Taussig, 1927, pp. 338-9):

The older writers assumed that the main currents of international trade were not

Work supported by Ford Foundation grant 750-0114. An earlier draft was completed while the author was a Fellow at the Center for Advanced Study in the Behavioral Sciences, Stanford, 1972-73.

49

affected by the substitution of paper money for metallic. . . . Differences between the monetary systems of the trading countries simply caused the counters
of exchange in each of them to be different, nothing more. . . .

It seems never to have occurred to these writers to inquire what would
happen if, under paper conditions, a *status quo* were disturbed.

Taussig went on to state (p. 345):

This then is our first proposition, and a fundamental one. In the absence of a
common monetary standard, the rate of foreign exchange depends on the mere
impact of the two quantities on hand at the moment.

There followed (pp. 346–358) an account that can be recognized today as containing the essence of what Machlup (1955, p. 172) has called the "relative-
prices approach"—but which is still commonly referred to as the "elasticity
approach"—to the theory of balance-of-payments adjustment under variable
exchange rates. Particularly noteworthy in Taussig's account—presented as a
description of a hypothetical course of events following a disruption of the
status quo by an autonomous capital movement—is his explicit assumption
(p. 350) that "nothing happens to change the quantity of money in either country, or to change the velocity of circulation, the use of credit substitutes, and so
on," from which follows "the fixity of the *total money income* of the population" and consequently "stability of domestic prices." In sum (p. 348): "Under
specie the level of domestic prices in each country will be changed. . . . But with
dislocated exchange, the level of domestic prices in each will remain as it was
before. . . . Under paper, . . . a new and different normal quotation for foreign
exchange will be established."

Taussig's theory is the antithesis of Mill's. On the face of it, the doctrine put
forward by Dornbusch in the above quotation would seem to be an admirable
synthesis. It affirms Mill's thesis—with the qualification that a change in the
exchange rate must be "an exchange rate change in and of itself." It proceeds to
adopt the Taussig antithesis—but couched as a theory of exchange rate change
not "in and of itself." Unfortunately, however, no method is furnished to help
us distinguish empirically between an exchange rate change that is and one that
is not "in and of itself." In effect, an exchange rate change "in and of itself" is
defined as one for which Mill's thesis is true. The synthesis has transformed the
thesis into a tautology.

Taussig had already elaborated his theory in 1917, and one among his many
illustrious students—Frank Graham—had subjected it to empirical test in 1922.
In this important paper Graham made a clear distinction between internationally
traded commodities and "domestic commodities"—i.e., those not entering international trade—and he found confirmation of Taussig's theory in the fact that in
periods of heavy borrowing, prices of domestic commodities in the United States
would rise relatively to international commodities, and the value of gold in

terms of dollars would fall. Graham reaffirmed this thesis in 1948 (p. 199), and in his final 1949 account was as explicit as he could be; referring to "the case of a currently debtor country of independent currency and freely mobile exchange rates" he said (Graham, 1949, p. 2): "The fall in the exchange value of the currency of any such country would raise the *domestic-currency* price of internationally traded commodities but would leave the prices of domestic commodities unchanged."

I have made a point of going into some of the background of the "relative-prices approach" to balance of payments theory in order to counter an impression that has recently been created that this approach, as exemplified, say, by the precise analytic statement to be found in Machlup's seminal paper on the foreign exchanges (1939, 1940), is no more than an historical aberration of the depression years.[1] In the words of Frenkel and Johnson (1976b, p. 29):

As documented in the next section, the monetary approach to balance-of-payments theory has a long, solid, and academically overwhelmingly reputable history. The continuity of its development, however, was reversed and the approach suppressed in international economic theory for upwards of a quarter of a century by the events of the 1930s.

It is not my aim to prove that the relative-prices approach has a longer, solider, or more overwhelmingly reputable history than the monetary approach. The proposition that relative prices have an important—in fact, essential—role in the adjustment process is one that can be defended quite well on its merits without reference to the length of its pedigree. However, recollection of the historical origins of the relative-prices approach is helpful as a reminder that it is not as narrowly based as its critics are wont to affirm, and that there is more to it than will be found in the caricature usually set up by its adversaries and indeed by some of its proponents.

That the "elasticity approach" should have come under fire is not surprising, for it does need defending. The problem with it is that it is, and has remained for far too long, just an "approach" and not a tightly-knit "theory." It has never been shown how it can be imbedded in a neoclassical general-equilibrium model. My aim in this chapter is to show how this can be done.

The formal framework of the "elasticity approach" goes back—not as early as Hume's time, I regret to say, but a good deal earlier than the Great Depression —to Bickerdike's verbal and geometric analysis of 1906, supplemented by his important algebraic analysis of 1907, greatly enriched by Edgeworth's masterly treatment of 1908, and capped by Bickerdike's 1920 contribution to the theory of foreign exchange. While the latter contribution was apparently buried in obscurity until unearthed by Metzler in 1948, the same cannot be said for the three earlier ones; on the contrary, being the analyses that gave birth to the theory of the optimal tariff, they were widely cited and the subject of lively discussion in the 1940s in Cambridge, by Kaldor (1940), Kahn (1947–48),

Graaff (1949-50), and others, and in particular were well known to Mrs. Robinson (1946-47, p. 107n).[2]

But then a curious thing happened. In her 1947 treatment of the theory of foreign exchange, Mrs. Robinson set forth her famous expression for the effect of a devaluation on the balance of trade in a brief footnote with the starkest of explanations (p. 142). Essentially the same formula was displayed by Metzler (1948, p. 226), with no explanation at all. These papers, together with Machlup's 1939-40 article, were required reading for a generation of graduate students, who demanded clearer explanations of the formulas and more precise clarification of the relations between the various demand and supply elasticities for imports and exports and the elasticities of supply and demand for foreign exchange. There ensued the well-known expositions of Haberler (1949), who acknowledged the assistance of Hyman Minsky; of Ellsworth (1950), with a mathematical appendix by Bronfenbrenner (1950); and of Allen (1954), with an appendix due largely to Lionel McKenzie. These were all within the kind of framework with which economists were most comfortable at the time—that of partial equilibrium—although these authors believed—correctly, as it turns out, but they were unable to show it—that their analyses could be given a valid general-equilibrium interpretation. The "elasticity approach" has come to be identified very largely with these types of expositions.

On the other hand, the original Bickerdike-Edgeworth analysis—despite a distressing gap which, by their own acknowledgment, they were unable to fill— is essentially a general-equilibrium one. My task is to show how the gap can be filled and the analysis made complete. The first important point to notice.is that, following in the tradition of Jevons and Marshall, they took prices to be the dependent variables and quantities (of imports and exports) as the independent variables; that is, they dealt with *inverse demand functions* (compare Samuelson, 1950, p. 377) rather than with the more familiar (to us) *direct demand functions* expressing quantities as functions of prices and income. This has three important implications in the analysis to be presented below: (1) income in this formulation, far from being neglected, becomes a dependent variable, along with expenditure ("absorption") and thus the balance of payments; (2) the natural adjustment process is one of Marshallian nontâtonnement type (Marshall, 1879, Samuelson, 1947, p. 266) as opposed to the Walrasian tâtonnement type as formalized by Samuelson (1947, p. 270) and Arrow, Block, and Hurwicz (1959); (3) the use of inverse demand functions allows one to handle the case (arising from flat or ruled production possibility surfaces) of multivalued excess demand functions with simple calculus methods.

The second point concerns the constant unit of measure in which prices of the import and export good are expressed in each country. With the benefit of hindsight it seems surprising that Bickerdike and Edgeworth found such difficulty justifying this assumption. In apologetic tones Bickerdike said (1906, p. 533): "it is implied that money can be regarded as a constant measure, which is not a legitimate supposition when we are considering the producers and consumers to belong to different 'nations'." Edgeworth suggested (1908, p. 542): "We might imagine the national money in Mr. Bickerdike's system to be an inconvertible (or at least unexportable) currency, regulated, as some theorists have proposed, so that its value should remain constant. Constancy of value might be secured by one of the methods of measuring the value of money which I have elsewhere described . . .", which *could* mean by stabilizing the average price level of other, nontraded, commodities, though Edgeworth does not say so explicitly. The obvious (to us) solution was suggested by Graaff (1949–50, p. 53n), of introducing a domestic good which plays the role of numéraire.

So formulated, the "elasticity approach" is simply a model of a neoclassical two-country world with two traded goods and one nontraded good in each country, the latter acting as numéraire in each case, this being made possible by inconvertible currencies, appropriate monetary policies, and a flexible exchange rate. These assumptions are essential, but no others. To reproduce the standard Robinson-Metzler formulas (and to furnish the traditional Haberler-Ellsworth diagrammatics with a correct general-equilibrium interpretation) one must make the rather artificial assumption of zero cross-elasticities of inverse trade demand functions; but this assumption is easily removed, resulting of course in still more fearful formulas (and in sacrificing the diagrammatics). The case of "infinite elasticity of supply of exports" becomes simply the case of a single factor of production and specialization in the export and domestic goods, yielding a flat (straight-line) Ricardian production transformation locus between these two goods. And finally, the demand and supply curves for foreign exchange, introduced by Haberler (1933) and Bresciani-Turroni (1934) and most fully elaborated and developed in the classic article by Machlup (1939–40), turn out to be equilibrium loci of precisely the same kind as Marshall's reciprocal demand curves; and they can be defined quite generally without the need to assume zero cross-elasticities.

So reconstructed, how well does the "elasticity approach" stand up to the "absorption approach" and to the "monetary approach" to balance-of-payments adjustment theory? I take this question up in the final section.

The Reconstituted Model

It will be assumed that there are two countries, each of which is capable of producing three commodities, the first two of which are tradable (with zero transport costs) and the third nontradable.

Let p_i^k denote the price of commodity i in country k, denominated in country k's currency, and q_i^k the same, denominated in gold; let r^k be the value of country k's currency in terms of gold. Then

$$p_i^k r^k = q_i^k \qquad (i = 1, 2, 3; k = 1, 2) \tag{5.1}$$

Let the exchange rate χ be defined as the price of a unit of country 1's currency in units of country 2's currency. Then, since $q_i^1 = q_i^2$ for $i = 1, 2$ (this equilibrium condition will be assumed to hold instantaneously), we have

$$\chi = \frac{r^1}{r^2} = \frac{p_1^2}{p_1^1} = \frac{p_2^2}{p_2^1} = \frac{p_3^2}{p_3^1} \cdot \frac{q_3^1}{q_3^2} \tag{5.2}$$

It will be convenient to introduce the parameter

$$\mu = \frac{p_3^1}{p_3^2} \tag{5.3}$$

so that (5.2) becomes

$$\mu\chi = \frac{q_3^1}{q_3^2} \tag{5.4}$$

Under a gold standard regime, χ is fixed; under an inconvertible paper currency regime with flexible exchange rates of the type specified by Taussig and Graham, it is μ that is fixed. Each regime carries with it specific implications about monetary policy and monetary behavior; in a complete model these should be brought in explicitly, as proponents of the monetary approach quite properly insist. This will not be done here, since my purposes are more limited. Suffice it to say that in all the analysis that ensues, it is the ratio q_3^1/q_3^2 of gold prices of the domestic goods in the two countries that is the important variable; as far as the model is concerned, there is nothing to distinguish the gold-standard and the flexible-exchange-rate regimes other than the trivial substitution of $1/\mu$ for χ in the dynamic adjustment process. Of course, this does not mean that there are not significant differences between such regimes in the real world, from which we are abstracting only a small part.

The rates of consumption and production of commodity i in country k will be denoted x_i^k and y_i^k respectively, and the excess of consumption over production by $z_i^k = x_i^k - y_i^k$, for $i = 1, 2, 3$ and $k = 1, 2$. Country k will be assumed to have a production possibility set (or "production block" in Meade's terminology) denoted $\mathcal{Y}^k(\varrho^k)$, where ϱ^k is a vector of factor endowments in country k; for example, if $y_i^k = f_i^k(v_i^k)$, where f_i^k is the production function in industry i in country k and v_i^k the vector of factor inputs in industry i, then under the usual Heckscher-Ohlin-Lerner-Samuelson assumptions of perfect factor mobility, cost minimization, and competitive factor markets, $\mathcal{Y}^k(\varrho^k)$ is the set of output vectors $y^k = (y_1^k, y_2^k, y_3^k)$ which can be obtained from these production functions subject to the constraint

$$\sum_{i=1}^{3} v_i^k \leqslant \varrho^k$$

(see for example Chipman, 1974a, p. 27).

I shall continue in the time-honored tradition of international trade theory and assume that individual preferences are identical and homothetic, so that an aggregate utility function $U^k(x^k) = U^k(x_1^k, x_2^k, x_3^k)$ exists which the community as a whole may be assumed to be maximizing (see Chipman, 1974b). It is more convenient to deal with consumption and production simultaneously and to express utility as a function of the excess of consumption over production, in the manner of Meade (1952). To obtain a formal counterpart of Meade's "trade indifference curves" we define country k's *trade utility function* (see Chipman, 1974a, p. 34n) by

$$\hat{U}^k(z^k; \varrho^k) = \max \left\{ U^k(x^k): x^k \in \mathscr{Y}^k(\varrho^k) + z^k \right\} \qquad (5.5)$$

We now introduce the concept of an *inverse trade demand function,* which is the straightforward counterpart of the inverse demand function (also called "indirect demand function") introduced by Samuelson (1950) (see also Katzner, 1970, p. 44):

$$P_i^k(z^k; \varrho^k) \equiv \frac{\hat{U}_i^k(z^k; \varrho^k)}{\hat{U}_3^k(z^k; \varrho^k)} \qquad (i = 1, 2)$$

$$P_3^k(z^k; \varrho^k) \equiv z_1^k P_1^k(z^k; \varrho^k) + z_2^k P_2^k(z^k; \varrho^k) + z_3^k$$

$\qquad (5.6)$

The first two functions define the "marginal trade rate of substitution" between commodities i and 3, or the "excess demand price of commodity i" in terms of commodity 3 (the numéraire). The third function defines the excess of desired expenditure (or "absorption" in Alexander's 1952 terminology) over the national income that will be forthcoming given the amounts by which consumption exceeds production.

We shall stipulate as one of the defining properties of "equilibrium" that there is no inventory accumulation or decumulation. In that case, the amount z_i^k must correspond in equilibrium to the quantity of commodity i imported into country k (if positive) or exported from country k (if negative); accordingly, in equilibrium we have

$$z_i^1 + z_i^2 = 0 \quad (i = 1, 2); \quad z_3^k = 0 \quad (k = 1, 2) \tag{5.7}$$

(We shall assume that, initially and throughout the analysis, country 1 exports commodity 1 to country 2 and imports commodity 2 from country 2; hence, z_1^2 are the (positive) exports of commodity 1 from 1 to 2, and z_2^1 the (positive) imports of commodity 2 into 1 from 2.) In equilibrium, therefore, the third function of (5.6) also stipulates the deficit in country k's *balance of payments on current account* (expressed in terms of country k's currency) as a function of the quantities exported and imported.[3] Just as we assumed above that the equilibrium condition $q_i^1 = q_i^2$ ($i = 1, 2$) holds instantaneously, henceforth the equilibrium conditions (5.7) will also be assumed to hold instantaneously.

Accordingly, defining country k's balance-of-payments deficit on current account (in terms of its own currency) as

$$d^k = p_1^k z_1^k + p_2^k z_2^k \quad (k = 1, 2) \tag{5.8}$$

the following six equations must be satisfied in equilibrium:

$$\frac{p_1^1}{p_3^1} = P_1^1(-z_1^2, z_2^1, 0; \ell^1) \qquad \frac{p_1^2}{p_3^2} = P_1^2(z_1^2, -z_2^1, 0; \ell^2)$$

$$\frac{p_2^1}{p_3^1} = P_2^1(-z_1^2, z_2^1, 0; \ell^1) \qquad \frac{p_2^2}{p_3^2} = P_2^2(z_1^2, -z_2^1, 0; \ell^2) \tag{5.9}$$

$$\frac{d^1}{p_3^1} = P_3^1(-z_1^2, z_2^1, 0; \ell^1) \qquad \frac{d^2}{p_3^2} = P_3^2(z_1^2, -z_2^1, 0; \ell^2)$$

Letting T denote an autonomous transfer from country 1 to country 2, if positive, or an autonomous transfer from country 2 to country 1, if negative, expressed (in either case) in terms of country 1's currency, we have

$$d^1 = -T \qquad d^2 = \chi T \tag{5.10}$$

To complete the system, we have from (5.2)

$$\chi = p_1^2/p_1^1 \qquad \chi = p_2^2/p_2^1 \tag{5.11}$$

For fixed p_3^1 and p_3^2, this is a system of ten equations in the nine unknowns $p_1^1, p_1^2, p_2^1, p_2^2, d^1, d^2, z_1^2, z_2^1$, and χ. The equations are not independent, since from the definition of P_3^k in (5.6), either one of the equations on the third line of (5.9) follows from the remaining nine equations. That is, an excess of absorption over income in one country is necessarily equal (when expressed in the same currency) to an excess of income over absorption in the other country—a point that we shall have occasion to stress later on. In order to make our results comparable to Machlup's 1939–40 analysis of the supply and demand for foreign exchange, it will be convenient to retain the sixth equation of (5.9).

Accordingly, eliminating the variables $p_1^1, p_1^2, p_2^1, p_2^2, d^1, d^2$ from (5.9), (5.10), and (5.11), setting $p_3^2 = 1$ for convenience, and recalling the definition of P_3^k in (5.6) as well as conditions (5.7), the system reduces to a system of three independent equations

$$\mu\chi = \frac{P_1^2(z_1^2, -z_2^1, 0; \ell^2)}{P_1^1(-z_1^2, z_2^1, 0; \ell^1)} \qquad \mu\chi = \frac{P_2^2(z_1^2, -z_2^1, 0; \ell^2)}{P_2^1(-z_1^2, z_2^1, 0; \ell^1)}$$

$$\chi T = z_1^2 P_1^2(z_1^2, -z_2^1, 0; \ell^1) - z_2^1 P_2^2(z_1^2, -z_2^1, 0; \ell^2) \tag{5.12}$$

in the three unknowns z_1^2, z_2^1, and χ (the variables ℓ^1, ℓ^2, $\mu = p_3^1$, and T being parameters).

Under certain conditions[4] the first two equations of (5.12) may be solved for z_1^2, z_2^1 to obtain functions

$$z_1^2 = F_1(\chi; \mu, \ell^1, \ell^2) \qquad z_2^1 = F_2(\chi; \mu, \ell^1, \ell^2) \tag{5.13}$$

For the case $T = 0$ we may now define the supply and demand functions for foreign exchange by substituting the functions (5.13) in the expressions in the third equation of (5.12):

$$S_2(\chi; \mu, \ell^1, \ell^2) = F_1(\chi; \mu, \ell^1, \ell^2)P_1^2[F_1(\chi; \mu, \ell^1, \ell^2), -F_2(\chi; \mu, \ell^1, \ell^2), 0; \ell^2]$$
$$\tag{5.14}$$
$$D_2(\chi; \mu, \ell^1, \ell^2) = F_2(\chi; \mu, \ell^1, \ell^2)P_2^2[F_1(\chi; \mu, \ell^1, \ell^2), -F_2(\chi; \mu, \ell^1, \ell^2), 0; \ell^2]$$

Except for the unimportant difference that Machlup (1939–40) defines the exchange rate as $1/\chi$ rather than χ, these may be identified precisely with his supply and demand curves for foreign exchange, the parameters μ, ℓ^1, ℓ^2 allowing for shifts in these curves. For example, if $T = 0$ then it is clear from (5.12) that an "inflation" in country 1, which we can identify with a rise in μ, leads to a proportional devaluation of country 1's currency, that is, an equal percentage reduction in χ.[5] This could be described in terms of a simultaneous shift in both curves of (5.14). Such an example was explicitly mentioned by Machlup (1939–40, p. 27).

Comparative Statics and Dynamics

As a simple dynamic adjustment process corresponding to (5.12) we may postulate

$$\dot{z}_1^2 = \kappa_1 \left\{ \frac{P_1^2(z_1^2, -z_2^1, 0; \ell^2)}{P_1^1(-z_1^2, z_2^1, 0; \ell^1)} - \mu\chi \right\}$$

$$\dot{z}_2^1 = \kappa_2 \left\{ \mu\chi - \frac{P_2^2(z_1^2, -z_2^1, 0; \ell^2)}{P_2^1(-z_1^2, z_2^1, 0; \ell^1)} \right\} \tag{5.15}$$

$$\dot{\chi} = \kappa_3 \left\{ z_1^2 P_1^2(z_1^2, -z_2^1, 0; \ell^2) - z_2^1 P_2^2(z_1^2, -z_2^1, 0; \ell^2) - \chi T \right\}$$

where the κ_i are positive speeds of adjustment. For example, the first equation of (5.15) ensures that if the marginal rates of transformation between commodities 1 and 3 in the two countries are such as to result in the cost of producing the domestic good in country 1 relative to the cost of producing the domestic good in country 2 being less than the corresponding price ratio (computed in any common currency at the prevailing exchange rate), exports of commodity 1 from country 1 to country 2 will increase.

If $T \neq 0$, say $T < 0$, then the "equilibrium" state $\dot{\chi} = 0$ of the third equation of (5.15) will in general be one in which there is a continually recurring transfer of funds (whether in the form of reparations, immigrants' remittances, foreign aid, or private investment) from country 2 to country 1. It will not, except in an interesting special case discussed in the final section, entail any movement of international reserves from country 1 to country 2, and will therefore not be a situation of "balance-of-payments deficit" in Johnson's (1958) sense. This is worth emphasizing, since it brings out the fact that the "elasticity approach" has been designed primarily to deal with phenomena (international capital movements) specifically ruled out by assumption by proponents of the "monetary approach" (Johnson, 1958, p. 54).

In the following development, it will be convenient to assume $T = 0$ in the initial state. This will enable us to reproduce the classical elasticity formulas, as well as to avoid inessential algebra.

Defining the elasticities of the inverse trade demand functions

$$\pi_{ij}^k = \frac{z_j^k}{P_i^k} \frac{\partial P_i^k}{\partial z_j^k} \qquad (i, j = 1, 2) \tag{5.16}$$

—termed "flexibilities" by Bronfenbrenner (1942), following Frisch—we may write the Jacobian matrix of (5.15), evaluated at $T = 0$, as $J = C_1 A C_2$ where

$$C_1 = \text{diag}\left\{\kappa_1/(z_1^2 P_1^1), \kappa_2/(z_1^1 P_2^1), 1\right\} \quad C_2 = \text{diag}\left\{P_1^2, P_2^2, \mu z_1^2 P_1^1\right\}$$

and

$$A = \begin{bmatrix} \pi_{11}^2 - \pi_{11}^1 & \pi_{12}^2 - \pi_{12}^1 & -1 \\ \pi_{21}^1 - \pi_{21}^2 & \pi_{22}^1 - \pi_{22}^2 & 1 \\ 1 + \pi_{11}^2 - \pi_{21}^2 & -1 - \pi_{22}^2 + \pi_{12}^2 & 0 \end{bmatrix} \qquad (5.17)$$

From (5.12) we find that

$$\frac{1}{\chi}\frac{d\chi}{dT} = \frac{1}{\mu z_1^2 P_1^1} \frac{\begin{vmatrix} \pi_{11}^2 - \pi_{11}^1 & \pi_{12}^2 - \pi_{12}^1 \\ \pi_{21}^1 - \pi_{21}^2 & \pi_{22}^1 - \pi_{22}^2 \end{vmatrix}}{\begin{vmatrix} \pi_{11}^2 - \pi_{11}^1 & \pi_{12}^2 - \pi_{12}^1 & -1 \\ \pi_{21}^1 - \pi_{21}^2 & \pi_{22}^1 - \pi_{22}^2 & 1 \\ 1 + \pi_{11}^2 - \pi_{21}^2 & -1 - \pi_{22}^2 + \pi_{12}^2 & 0 \end{vmatrix}} \qquad (5.18)$$

From Metzler's (1945, pp. 282–3) results, as amended by Arrow (1974, pp. 184–5), we know that a *necessary* condition for the system (5.15) to be dynamically stable for all positive speeds of adjustment κ_i is that the diagonal elements of A be nonpositive, the second order principal minors of A be nonnegative, and the determinant of A be negative. The latter condition is also necessary for stability given any positive speeds of adjustment (see Samuelson 1947, p. 431). The condition that a system be stable independently of the adjustment speeds may for convenience be described as "Metzler stability," and the necessary conditions just described as the "modified Hicks conditions." Metzler stability then implies that $d\chi/dT \leq 0$, that is, that a transfer from country 1 to country 2 will give rise to a devaluation of country 1's currency if it has any effect on the exchange rate at all.[6]

That there is a real possibility that a transfer will have no effect on the exchange rate at all follows at once from a previous result (Chipman, 1974a, Theorem 5) to the effect that if (i) production and utility functions are identical and homogeneous in both countries, (ii) all three commodities are produced in each country, and (iii) factor rentals are initially equalized between them (a virtual certainty under those conditions), a transfer will leave all prices unaltered. These conditions assure that the exchange rate will play a purely monetary role, that is, that it will be affected by μ but not by T.

Our analysis can also be used to examine the so-called "small-country case."

This may be given a finite interpretation by assuming that country 2 is endowed with only a single factor of production so that, with constant returns to scale, its production possibility surface will be a flat triangle. If country 2 is large enough relative to country 1, it will be a "focal country" in Graham's sense (1948, p. 58), its costs determining world prices. Then $\pi_{ij}^2 = 0$ for $i, j = 1, 2$, and $d\chi/dT < 0$ if and only if $\pi_{11}^1/\pi_{12}^1 > \pi_{21}^1/\pi_{22}^1$. If, now, we assume that country 1 also has a single factor of production, and specializes in commodities 1 and 3, then $\pi_{11}^1 = \pi_{12}^1 = 0$ and $d\chi/dT = 0$. Here, then, we have another interesting case in which the exchange rate plays only a purely monetary role.

The Separable Case

We now come to the special assumption that lies behind the "elasticity approach": additively separable trade utility functions. This is the condition that $\partial P_i^k/\partial z_j^k = 0$ for $i, j = 1, 2$ and $i \neq j$, which is characteristic of preferences that can be represented by (trade) utility functions of the form $\hat{U}(z) = \hat{u}_1(z_1) + \hat{u}_2(z_2) + \hat{u}_3(z_3)$. It is important to note that separability of the original utility function $U(x)$ does not imply that of $\hat{U}(z)$.[7]

Let us set $\pi_{12}^k = \pi_{21}^k = 0$ for $k = 1, 2$, and define the "supply flexibilities" σ_k and "demand flexibilities" δ_k by

$$\sigma_1 = \pi_{11}^1 \qquad \sigma_2 = \pi_{22}^2 \qquad \delta_1 = -\pi_{22}^1 \qquad \delta_2 = -\pi_{11}^2 \qquad (5.19)$$

A necessary condition for stability of the system (5.15) is that

$$|A| = (1 - \delta_1)(1 - \delta_2) - (1 + \sigma_1)(1 + \sigma_2) < 0 \qquad (5.20)$$

This condition was first obtained by Edgeworth (1908, p. 541n), via a different route (see the "Marshallian Offer Curve Analysis" section, below).

From the modified Hicks conditions mentioned in the last section, a necessary condition for Metzler stability of (5.15) is that both $\sigma_1 + \delta_2 \geq 0$ and $\sigma_2 + \delta_1 \geq 0$. If either one of these terms is zero, then from (5.18) we have $d\chi/dT = 0$. If, on the other hand, both $\sigma_1 + \delta_2 > 0$ and $\sigma_2 + \delta_1 > 0$, then necessarily $d\chi/dT < 0$, and (5.18) yields (putting $c = 1/\mu z_1^2 P_1^1$)

$$\frac{1}{\chi}\frac{d\chi}{dT} = c \cdot \frac{1}{\dfrac{1 - \delta_2}{\sigma_1 + \delta_2} + \dfrac{1 + \sigma_2}{\delta_1 + \sigma_2}} \qquad (5.21)$$

This is Bickerdike's original formula (1920, p. 120). A necessary condition for Metzler stability, when $\sigma_1 + \delta_2 > 0$ and $\sigma_2 + \delta_1 > 0$, is then

$$\frac{1 - \delta_2}{\sigma_1 + \delta_2} + \frac{1 + \sigma_2}{\delta_1 + \sigma_2} > 0 \tag{5.22}$$

If, following Bickerdike (1907, p. 100n) and Edgeworth (1908, p. 541n), we define the "elasticities of demand for country 1's imports and exports" and the "elasticities of supply of country 1's exports and imports" (to avoid confusion I shall refer to them as *indirect elasticities*) as the *reciprocals* (when they exist) of the corresponding demand and supply flexibilities of (5.19), that is, as

$$\iota_k = \frac{1}{\delta_k} \qquad \epsilon_k = \frac{1}{\sigma_k} \qquad (k = 1, 2) \tag{5.23}$$

then Bickerdike's "stability condition" (5.22) becomes[8]

$$\frac{\iota_1 \iota_2 (\epsilon_1 + \epsilon_2 + 1) + \epsilon_1 \epsilon_2 (\iota_1 + \iota_2 - 1)}{(\epsilon_1 + \iota_2)(\iota_1 + \epsilon_2)} > 0 \tag{5.24}$$

This is Metzler's famous formula (1948, p. 226), to which Joan Robinson's (1947, p. 142n) reduces when $T = 0$. However, it is not a correct stability condition unless $(\epsilon_1 + \iota_2)/\epsilon_1 \iota_2 > 0$ and $(\iota_1 + \epsilon_2)/\iota_1 \epsilon_2 > 0$. On the other hand, Edgeworth's stability condition (5.20) becomes

$$\frac{\iota_1 \iota_2 (\epsilon_1 + \epsilon_2 + 1) + \epsilon_1 \epsilon_2 (\iota_1 + \iota_2 - 1)}{\iota_1 \iota_2 \epsilon_1 \epsilon_2} > 0 \tag{5.25}$$

We now consider the case of "infinite elasticity of supply" of exports and imports, where $\epsilon_1 = \epsilon_2 = \infty$ (or $\sigma_1 = \sigma_2 = 0$). This means that the marginal trade rate of substitution between the export and domestic good is zero in both countries. The most natural condition leading to this result is the assumption that there is a single factor of production (say, labor) in each country, with each country specializing in its domestic and export goods. In this case, since the modified Hicks conditions require $\delta_k \geq 0$, provided these are both positive the Edgeworth and Bickerdike conditions both reduce to the notorious and misnamed "Marshall-Lerner condition"

$$\iota_1 + \iota_2 - 1 > 0 \tag{5.26}$$

But before we too quickly accept this result we must consider the question: is the assumption of "infinite supply elasticities" consistent with the hypothesis that the trade utility function $\hat{U}^k$ is separable? A moment's reflection will cause us to realize that the answer must be in the negative—except for an uninteresting freak case.

Let us assume that country 1 produces commodities 1 and 3 only, with a single factor of production (labor), by means of the production functions $y_i^1 = f_i^1(v_i^1) = b_i^1 v_i^1$, $i = 1, 3$, where $v_1^1 + v_3^1 = \ell^1$, ℓ^1 being country 1's endowment of labor. Country 1's production possibility set is then defined by

$$\mathcal{Y}^1(\ell^1) = \left\{ (y_1^1, y_2^1, y_3^1) \geqslant (0, 0, 0) : y_1^1/b_1^1 + y_3^1/b_3^1 \leqslant \ell^1, y_2^1 = 0 \right\} \quad (5.27)$$

Writing the production constraints in the form

$$\frac{x_1^1}{b_1^1} + \frac{x_3^1}{b_3^1} \leqslant \frac{z_1^1}{b_1^1} + \frac{z_3^1}{b_3^1} + \ell^1 \qquad x_2^1 = z_2^1 \qquad (5.28)$$

and noting that the first will hold with equality (i.e., there will be full employment) as long as U^1 is an increasing function, upon substituting (5.28) in the utility function we see from the definition (5.5) that the trade utility function $\hat{U}^1$ has the form

$$\max_{x_1} U^1 \left[x_1^1, z_2^1, b_3^1 \left(\frac{z_1^1}{b_1^1} + \frac{z_3^1}{b_3^1} + \ell^1 \right) - \frac{b_3^1}{b_1^1} x_1^1 \right] = V^1 \left(\frac{z_1^1}{b_1^1} + \frac{z_3^1}{b_3^1} + \ell^1, z_2^1 \right) \quad (5.29)$$

for some function V^1. Denoting its partial derivatives by V_1^1 and V_2^1 respectively, we have from (5.6)

$$P_1^1(z^1; \ell^1) = \frac{b_3^1}{b_1^1}$$

$$\qquad (5.30)$$

$$P_2^1(z^1; \ell^1) = b_3^1 \frac{V_2^1(z_1^1/b_1^1 + z_3^1/b_3^1 + \ell^1, z_2^1)}{V_1^1(z_1^1/b_1^1 + z_3^1/b_3^1 + \ell^1, z_2^1)}$$

Thus $\pi_{11}^1 = \pi_{12}^1 = 0$ and we have an "infinite elasticity of supply of exports." However, in order to have $P_{21}^1 \equiv \partial P_2^1/\partial z_1^1 \equiv 0$ we must require that the function V_2^1/V_1^1 depend only on its second argument, z_2^1. It is not hard to see that this implies that V^1 must have the "parallel" form $V^1(\zeta_1^1, z_2^1) = \psi(\zeta_1^1 + W(z_2^1))$, where ψ is an increasing function and W is an increasing concave function (see Samuelson, 1942, p. 85; Chipman and Moore, 1976, p. 89). From (5.29) it follows immediately that

$$\hat{U}^1(z^1; \ell^1) = \psi \left[\frac{z_1^1}{b_1^1} + \frac{z_3^1}{b_3^1} + \ell^1 + W(z_2^1) \right] \quad (5.31)$$

Now it can be shown that the original utility function U^1 is recoverable from the trade utility function $\hat{U}^1$ by *minimizing* the latter subject to the production constraints (5.28); accordingly, the utility function must have the form

$$U^1(x_1^1, x_2^1, x_3^1) = \psi \left(\frac{x_1^1}{b_1^1} + \frac{x_3^1}{b_3^1} + W(x_2^1) \right) \qquad (5.32)$$

This is what is implied by allowing ϵ_1 to approach infinity and requiring $\hat{U}^1$ to remain separable.

In words, (5.32) states that consumers in country 1 regard one labor-hour's worth of commodity 1 as a perfect substitute for one labor-hour's worth of commodity 3, and that this amount of labor time can be considered as a standard of value for all three commodities (i.e., taking ψ to be the identity function, the marginal utility of either of the produced commodities is equal to the constant amount of labor time required to produce a unit of it). This requires tastes to be completely tied to the technology. It is surely a freak possibility.

Given this result, is there any way to salvage the "stability condition" (5.26)? One way to accomplish this *partially* is the following. Let us assume "infinite elasticities of supply of exports" in both countries. That is, let us assume that the relative (to the domestic commodity) supply price of the export good is a constant, equal to $P_1^1(z^1; \varrho^1) = b_3^1/b_1^1$ for country 1, as in (5.30) above, and analogously, to $P_2^2(z^2; \varrho^2) = b_3^2/b_2^2$ for country 2. Then we have

$$\pi_{11}^1 = \pi_{12}^1 = 0 \qquad \pi_{22}^2 = \pi_{21}^2 = 0 \qquad (5.33)$$

Under these conditions a necessary stability condition for (5.15) is, from (5.17),

$$|A| = \pi_{22}^1 + \pi_{22}^2 \pi_{11}^1 + \pi_{11}^2 + \pi_{21}^2 - \pi_{21}^1 \pi_{12}^2 + \pi_{12}^2 < 0 \qquad (5.34)$$

The first three terms in this expression are equal to $-(\iota_1 + \iota_2 - 1)/\iota_1 \iota_2$, so that a *sufficient* condition for (5.34) to follow from (5.26) is that the ι_k be positive (as assumed in deriving (5.26)) and that $\pi_{21}^1 \leqslant 0$ and $\pi_{12}^2 \leqslant 0$, that is, that in each country the export good should be weakly relatively trade substitutable with the import good in relation to the domestic good (see Chipman 1974a, p. 71). From the above result would actually require $\pi_{21} < 0$ and $\pi_{12}^2 < 0$ almost everywhere, that is, that the export and import goods be strong relative trade substitutes in this sense. This would allow us to say that fulfillment of (5.26) guarantees fulfillment of (5.34). But (5.34) is only a necessary, not a sufficient, condition for stability.

We can conclude that the separability assumption constitutes the one principal and serious defect of the "elasticity approach" as formulated heretofore. As applied to a pure exchange model, for example to Haberler's (1950) short-run model, the assumption is innocuous enough, since as applied to the original utility function it is limiting but not far-fetched; but it leads only to trouble when extended to allow for production adjustments. But while it is a serious defect, it is by no means a fatal one; for it can easily be dispensed with, and there is no need to adopt it, as the above analysis has made clear.

The Supply and Demand for Foreign Exchange

In introducing the concepts of supply and demand for foreign exchange, Machlup (1939, p. 10) stated: "Every demand and supply curve must refer to a certain period of time which is allowed for the depicted changes and adjustments to take place," which he referred to as the "short period." He went on to state (p. 11):

> ... it shows, for example, how the quantities of foreign exchange supplied by exporters will react upon a rise in the price of foreign currency after the export industries have adapted their selling prices in dollars to the increase in business.
>   In other words, the short-period demand and supply curves of foreign exchange are not drawn on the basis of "given commodity prices" in the two countries, but on the basis of "given demand and supply conditions" in the commodity markets of the two countries.

This makes quite clear the *general-equilibrium* nature of Machlup's curves, showing that they are loci portraying equilibria in the commodity markets; they are thus of the very same nature as Marshall's reciprocal demand curves. This justifies the definition (5.14) given above.

From (5.12), (5.13), and (5.16) we may readily compute the elasticities of country 1's exports and imports with respect to the exchange rate:

$$
\zeta_1^2 \equiv \frac{\chi}{F_1} \frac{\partial F_1}{\partial \chi} = \frac{\begin{vmatrix} -1 & \pi_{12}^1 - \pi_{12}^2 \\ -1 & \pi_{22}^1 - \pi_{22}^2 \end{vmatrix}}{\begin{vmatrix} \pi_{11}^1 - \pi_{11}^2 & \pi_{12}^1 - \pi_{12}^2 \\ \pi_{21}^1 - \pi_{21}^2 & \pi_{22}^1 - \pi_{22}^2 \end{vmatrix}}
$$

$$
\zeta_2^1 \equiv \frac{\chi}{F_2} \frac{\partial F_2}{\partial \chi} = \frac{\begin{vmatrix} \pi_{11}^1 - \pi_{11}^2 & -1 \\ \pi_{21}^1 - \pi_{21}^2 & -1 \end{vmatrix}}{\begin{vmatrix} \pi_{11}^1 - \pi_{11}^2 & \pi_{12}^1 - \pi_{12}^2 \\ \pi_{21}^1 - \pi_{21}^2 & \pi_{22}^1 - \pi_{22}^2 \end{vmatrix}}
$$

(5.35)

The elasticities of supply and demand for foreign exchange are readily obtained from these by the formulas

$$
\varphi_S \equiv -\frac{\chi}{S_2} \frac{\partial S_2}{\partial \chi} = -(1 + \pi_{11}^2) \zeta_1^2 - \pi_{12}^2 \zeta_2^1
$$

$$
\varphi_D \equiv \frac{\chi}{D_2} \frac{\partial D_2}{\partial \chi} = (1 + \pi_{22}^2) \zeta_2^1 + \pi_{21}^2 \zeta_1^2
$$

(5.36)

(The signs appearing in these definitions are due to the fact that χ has been defined as the price of country 1's currency in terms of country 2's, rather than the other way around). In the separable case, in terms of the notations (5.19) and (5.23) these reduce to

$$\varphi_S = \frac{\epsilon_1(\iota_2 - 1)}{\epsilon_1 + \iota_2} \qquad \varphi_D = \frac{\iota_1(\epsilon_2 + 1)}{\iota_1 + \epsilon_2} \tag{5.37}$$

These are precisely the same as the expressions given in Haberler (1949) and Bronfenbrenner (1950). If the third equation of (5.12) is replaced by the equation corresponding to country 1's balance-of-payments deficit, we obtain analogous expressions for the elasticities of supply and demand for country 1's currency as opposed to country 2's by permuting the subscripts 1 and 2 in (5.37); these are just as in Haberler (1949) and Allen (1954).

If we think of the dynamic adjustment process as a two-stage one, with the commodity markets clearing first and the foreign exchange market second, then we can imagine that the speeds of adjustment of the first two equations of (5.15) are infinitely rapid by comparison with that of the third. The latter differential equation then becomes

$$\dot{\chi} = \kappa_3 \left\{ S_2(\chi; \mu, \ell^1, \ell^2) - D_2(\chi; \mu, \ell^1, \ell^2) \right\} \tag{5.38}$$

for the c: .e $T = 0$. In this case we can express the stability condition in terms of elastic dies rather than slopes (see Machlup, 1950, p. 53), namely in the form $\varphi_S + \varphi_D > 0$, and it is not hard to see that in the separable case the Metzler condition (5.24) results.[9]

Marshallian Offer-Curve Analysis

We could just as well adopt the converse assumption that the foreign exchange market adjusts infinitely rapidly by comparison with the commodity markets. An idealization of this kind leads to a variant of Marshallian offer-curve analysis.

If to (5.12) we add the redundant equation

$$-T/\mu = -z_1^2 P_1^1(-z_1^2, z_2^1, 0; \ell^1) + z_2^1 P_2^1(-z_1^2, z_2^1, 0; \ell^1) \tag{5.39}$$

we can subtract either one of the first two, say the second. Country 1's offer curve can now be defined as the set of points (z_1^2, z_2^1) satisfying (5.39), that is, as the implicit function

$$\Omega^1(z_1^2, z_2^1; \ell^1; \mu, T) \equiv T/\mu - z_1^2 P_1^1(-z_1^2, z_2^1, 0; \ell^1) + z_2^1 P_2^1(-z_1^2, z_2^1, 0; \ell^1) = 0$$

$$\tag{5.40}$$

Analogously, but with the substitution of the first equation of (5.12) in the third in order to eliminate the exchange rate, we may define the implicit function

$$\Omega^2(z_1^2, z_2^1; \ell^1, \ell^2; \mu, T) \equiv \frac{T \, P_1^2(z_1^2, -z_2^1, 0; \ell^2)}{\mu \, P_1^1(-z_1^2, z_2^1, 0; \ell^1)} - z_1^2 P_1^2(z_1^2, -z_2^1, 0; \ell^2)$$

$$+ z_2^1 P_2^2(z_1^2, -z_2^1, 0; \ell^2) = 0 \qquad (5.41)$$

Unfortunately, this is not a genuine Marshallian offer curve for country 2, since it is contaminated by the exchange rate term, which involves one of country 1's inverse trade demand functions. But this cannot be helped, and it simply shows that Marshallian offer curve analysis is not a very suitable tool for handling these problems, except in the special case $T = 0$. For our limited purposes, however, it will be enough to examine the stability conditions in the neighborhood of a point where $T = 0$; for that case, the definitions (5.40) and (5.41) reduce to Edgeworth's (1908, p. 544n), and they describe genuine Marshallian offer curves.

If, at an initial equilibrium with $T = 0$, $\partial \Omega^1 / \partial z_1^2 \neq 0$ and $\partial \Omega^2 / \partial z_2^1 \neq 0$, the offer curves in the neighborhood of the equilibrium point $(\bar{z}_1^2, \bar{z}_2^1)$ can be expressed in the form

$$z_1^2 = G_1(z_2^1; \ell^1) \qquad z_2^1 = G_2(z_1^2; \ell^2) \qquad (5.42)$$

with imports as a function of exports in each country. This is always possible (globally) when the $\hat{U}^k$ are strictly quasiconcave and separable, since then $\partial \Omega^1 / \partial z_1^2 = z_1^2 \partial P_1^1 / \partial z_1^1 - P_1^1 < 0$ and $\partial \Omega^2 / \partial z_2^2 = z_2^1 \partial P_2^2 / \partial z_2^2 - P_2^2 < 0$. Following Alexander (1951, p. 386), we may define the "elasticities of trade" α_k of the two countries as

$$\alpha_1 = \frac{z_2^1}{G_1} \frac{\partial G_1}{\partial z_2^1} \qquad \alpha_2 = \frac{z_1^2}{G_2} \frac{\partial G_2}{\partial z_1^2} \qquad (5.43)$$

As a dynamic adjustment process we may postulate as in Samuelson (1947, p. 266)

$$\dot{z}_1^2 = \kappa_1 \left\{ G_1(z_2^1; \ell^1) - z_1^2 \right\}$$

$$\dot{z}_2^1 = \kappa_2 \left\{ G_2(z_1^2; \ell^2) - z_2^1 \right\} \qquad (5.44)$$

Then it is readily verified that a necessary and sufficient condition for local stability is[10]

$$\alpha_1 \alpha_2 < 1 \qquad (5.45)$$

From (5.40) and (5.41) we find that the elasticities of trade (5.43) are related to the flexibilities (5.16) by

$$\alpha_1 = \frac{1 - \pi^1_{12} + \pi^1_{22}}{1 + \pi^1_{11} - \pi^1_{21}} \qquad \alpha_2 = \frac{1 + \pi^2_{11} - \pi^2_{21}}{1 - \pi^2_{12} + \pi^2_{22}} \qquad (5.46)$$

In the separable case these reduce to $\alpha_k = (1 - \delta_k)/(1 + \sigma_k)$, whence Edgeworth's stability condition (5.25) follows immediately from (5.45). In fact, it is in this way that the condition was originally obtained by Edgeworth (1908, p. 544n).

The condition (5.45) may also be stated in terms of the Marshallian elasticities of excess demand ω_k (Marshall, 1923, p. 337). As is well known (see Johnson, 1950–51, p. 29) these are related to the elasticities of trade by $\alpha_k = (\omega_k - 1)/\omega_k$, or

$$\omega_k = \frac{1}{1 - \alpha_k} \qquad (k = 1, 2) \qquad (5.47)$$

so that provided ω_1 and ω_2 are both positive (5.45) becomes

$$\omega_1 + \omega_2 - 1 > 0 \qquad (5.48)$$

This is the well-known Marshallian stability condition (Marshall 1923, p. 354).

The formal similarity between (5.48) and (5.26) has unfortunately given rise to considerable confusion. Condition (5.26) was attributed by Mrs. Robinson (1947a, p. 143n) to Lerner (1944, p. 377), who provided a verbal analysis of exchange stability, and subsequent writers (e.g., Haberler 1949, p. 203) have agreed with this attribution. And yet, Hirschman (1949, p. 52) has called (5.26) the "Marshall-Lerner condition"—a term which seems to have stuck despite the fact that they are quite different conditions except in the freak case discussed above of infinite supply elasticities.[11] Machlup—always a stickler for correct terminology—is almost alone in eschewing this expression, employing instead the somewhat awkward but at least unobjectionable phrase "the theorem of the 'critical value' of the sum of the demand elasticities in international trade" (Machlup 1950, p. 55). We verify readily that in the special case of separable trade utility functions (5.47) becomes $\omega_k = \iota_k(\epsilon_k + 1)/(\iota_k + \epsilon_k)$—quite similar in form to the expressions (5.37) for the elasticities of supply and demand for foreign exchange—and that (5.48) then reduces to

$$\omega_1 + \omega_2 - 1 = \frac{\iota_2 \iota_1(\epsilon_1 + \epsilon_2 + 1) + \epsilon_1 \epsilon_2(\iota_1 + \iota_2 - 1)}{(\iota_1 + \epsilon_1)(\iota_2 + \epsilon_2)} > 0 \qquad (5.49)$$

This looks like (5.24), but the denominators are different. Both formulas reduce (formally) to (5.26) in the special case $\epsilon_1 = \epsilon_2 = \infty$, because then $\omega_k = \iota_k$ for $k = 1$, 2. However, condition (5.48) is much more general, not requiring the assumption of separable trade utility functions, let alone the still more special assumption of infinite supply elasticities. It is not even clear that Lerner really had in mind (5.26) rather than (5.48)—in which case the linking of his name with Marshall's would at least be consistent, although still erroneous as a description of (5.26).

Devaluation and the Terms of Trade

It was pointed out by Machlup in 1955 (p 195) that there had been a "remarkable change of opinion" among economists during the preceding decade concerning the effects of a devaluation on the terms of trade, the earlier opinion having tended to be that a devaluation necessarily was accompanied by a deterioration in the terms of trade.[12] For the kind of reasoning underlying these earlier opinions we can do no better than quote Machlup himself (1939, p.10):[13]

A rise in the price of foreign currency makes imported commodities more expensive in terms of dollars (assumed here to be the domestic currency) and exported commodities cheaper in terms of the foreign currency.

One could read similar explanations in the newspapers during the 1971–73 period of successive devaluations of the dollar; and when, instead, it turned out that the prices of exportables rose as well, it was of course concluded by much of the public that this was proof of a conspiracy on the part of wicked speculators and profiteers. But the newspapers' analyses had lagged considerably behind those of at least the more perceptive economists, for already in 1950 Machlup had this to say (p. 55):

When an analyst, for example, assumes that a depreciation by ten per cent lowers the prices of export goods to foreigners by ten per cent, he implicitly assumes that the domestic prices remain unchanged. In postulating that these prices remain unchanged although the volume of exports is increased, he makes the implicit assumption that the elasticity of supply of these export goods is infinite.

To the extent that a transfer from country 1 to country 2 causes a devaluation of country 1's currency, the question is formally identical with that of the effect of a transfer on the terms of trade, that is, with the transfer problem. In terms of the model (5.12), this is readily determined. Expressing the solution values of (5.12) as functions of T, substituting these in the functions P_1^1 and P_2^1, and differentiating P_1^1/P_2^1 totally with respect to T, we obtain

$$\frac{1}{p_1^1/p_2^1} \frac{d(p_1^1/p_2^1)}{dT} = (\pi_{11}^1 - \pi_{21}^1) \frac{1}{z_1^2} \frac{dz_1^2}{dT} + (\pi_{12}^1 - \pi_{22}^1) \frac{1}{z_2^1} \frac{dz_2^1}{dT} \quad (5.50)$$

We find readily from (5.12) that

$$\frac{1}{z_1^2} \frac{dz_1^2}{dT} = \frac{X}{z_1^2 P_1^2} \frac{\Delta_{31}}{\Delta} \qquad \frac{1}{z_2^1} \frac{dz_2^1}{dT} = \frac{X}{z_1^2 P_1^2} \frac{\Delta_{32}}{\Delta} \quad (5.51)$$

where Δ is the determinant of the matrix A of (5.17), and Δ_{ij} is the cofactor of the element of the ith row and jth column of A. Substituting (5.51) in (5.50) we obtain

$$\frac{1}{p_1^1/p_2^1} \frac{d(p_1^1/p_2^1)}{dT} = \frac{X}{z_1^2 P_1^2} \frac{1}{\Delta} \begin{vmatrix} \pi_{11}^1 - \pi_{21}^1 & \pi_{12}^1 - \pi_{22}^1 \\ \pi_{11}^2 - \pi_{21}^2 & \pi_{12}^2 - \pi_{22}^2 \end{vmatrix} \quad (5.52)$$

From the stability condition $\Delta < 0$, we conclude that a transfer strongly worsens country 1's terms of trade if and only if

$$(\pi_{11}^1 - \pi_{21}^1)(\pi_{12}^2 - \pi_{22}^2) > (\pi_{11}^2 - \pi_{21}^2)(\pi_{12}^1 - \pi_{22}^1) \quad (5.53)$$

In the special case of additively separable trade utility functions (5.52) reduces to

$$\frac{1}{p_1^1/p_2^1} \frac{d(p_1^1/p_2^1)}{dT} = \frac{X}{z_1^2 P_1^2} \frac{\delta_1 \delta_2 - \sigma_1 \sigma_2}{(1 - \delta_1)(1 - \delta_2) - (1 + \sigma_1)(1 + \sigma_2)} \quad (5.54)$$

Since the denominator is negative by Edgeworth's stability condition (5.20), we obtain the criterion: the paying country's terms of trade deteriorate (strongly) if and only if

$$\delta_1 \delta_2 > \sigma_1 \sigma_2 \quad (5.55)$$

or, in terms of the "indirect elasticities" of (5.23), if and only if

$$\epsilon_1 \epsilon_2 > \iota_1 \iota_2 \quad (5.56)$$

This is Pigou's formula (1932), derived independently by Yntema (1932, p. 91). It is also the formula subsequently and apparently independently derived by Mrs. Robinson (1947b, p. 163n), in the form $\epsilon_1/\iota_1 > \epsilon_2/\iota_2$, for the conditions under which a devaluation would lead to a deterioration in the terms of trade of the devaluing country.[14]

In the special case of constant supply prices of exports, in which (5.33) holds, we may note from (5.52) and (5.18) that

$$\frac{1}{p_1^1/p_2^1} \frac{d(p_1^1/p_2^1)}{dT} = \frac{1}{\chi} \frac{d\chi}{dT} = \frac{c}{\Delta} \begin{vmatrix} \pi_{11}^2 & \pi_{12}^2 \\ \pi_{21}^1 & \pi_{22}^1 \end{vmatrix} \tag{5.57}$$

that is, the percentage deterioration in the terms of trade is the same as the percentage devaluation. This of course follows from the fact that, in the notation of (5.27) above, under the assumed conditions we have from (5.2) and (5.3)

$$\frac{p_1^1}{p_2^1} = \chi \mu \frac{b_3^1/b_1^1}{b_3^2/b_2^2} \tag{5.58}$$

This is the basic assumption adopted by Hirschman (1949) and underlying the models of Harberger (1950) and Laursen and Metzler (1950). It should be noted that the result holds independently of separability.

Elasticity Optimism, Pessimism, and Skepticism

Two different types of "elasticity" concepts emerged in the preceding analysis: an *indirect* elasticity, which is the *reciprocal* of an elasticity of an inverse or *indirect* demand function; and a Marshallian elasticity of excess demand with respect to the terms of trade. On the other hand, the elasticity concept that has been used for purposes of statistical estimation has almost invariably been an elasticity of a *direct* demand function (see for example Leamer and Stern 1970, pp. 9–12). Thus, we have three distinct concepts of "elasticity of demand for imports." How are they related? The case made by Orcutt (1950) against what Machlup (1950) has called "elasticity pessimism" was based entirely on the premise that the relevant elasticity concept was of the third, "direct" type, involving the quantity of imports as a dependent variable and the price of imports as an independent variable. This being assumed, he argued that the conventional direct least-squares estimator of the elasticity of demand for imports was biased downwards. But where does all this discussion lead us if it turns out that the wrong parameter has been estimated in the first place?

I shall not attempt to provide a general answer to this question, which seems to be difficult (and probably not worth pursuing), but will instead limit myself to providing a precise answer in a special case.

It should be observed first of all that there are difficulties involved in defining an aggregate, direct demand function for imports in a competitive economy. For one thing, once prices are specified in such an economy, the value of the national product is determined, since efficiency requires this value to be maximized at those prices over the production possibility set. This means that the only component of national income that is free to vary independently of prices is the deficit in the balance of payments on current account. Secondly, once the prices and the foreign deficit are given, there is no guarantee that the aggregate demand for the domestic, nontraded, good will be equal to the aggregate supply; in order to describe a general-equilibrium situation; therefore, it is necessary to assume that prices and the foreign deficit do not vary arbitrarily, but are so constrained in their variation that the market for domestic goods will be cleared.

Now suppose, at least provisionally, that we may regard the prices of a country's export and import goods (denominated in its own currency) as exogenous to that country. Then the above reasoning implies that the country's nominal national income and the price of its domestic commodity must be regarded as endogenous.[15] In general they cannot be assumed to be held constant even if the import price alone varies. For, unless the country produces no import-competing goods, a rise in the (domestic-currency) price of imports, by increasing the value of the domestic output of import-competing goods, will necessarily increase nominal national income. Further, if the price of the export good is held constant, then unless the price of the domestic good is tied to that of the export good by constant costs, a rise in the price of the import good will necessitate some adjustment in the price of the domestic good so as to permit the market for the latter to be cleared. These difficulties can be assumed away by postulating that production possibilities have the special form (5.27) analyzed in an earlier section. In that case, the direct elasticity of demand for imports coincides (as is easily verified) with the Marshallian elasticity.

How does the direct elasticity of demand for imports compare with the corresponding *indirect* elasticity? Since neither is constant in general, it does not seem possible to provide a straightforward answer that will cover all cases; however, we can provide one for the case in which the country's utility function is of the constant-elasticity-of-substitution (C.E.S.) type

$$U^k(x^k) = - \sum_{j=1}^{3} \theta_j^k (x_j^k)^{(\rho_k - 1)/\rho_k} \qquad \left(\theta_j^k > 0, \quad \sum_{j=1}^{3} \theta_j^k = 1 \right)$$
$$(5.59)$$

Assuming production possibilities to be given by (5.27) for country 1, and analogously for country 2, it is possible by carrying out the constrained maximization (5.5) to compute $\hat{U}^k$ explicitly,[16] and we find that the flexibilities (5.16) become

$$\pi_{kk}^k = - \frac{1}{\rho_k} \qquad \pi_{kj}^k = - \frac{1}{\rho_k} \frac{s_k}{1 - s_k} \qquad (j \neq k) \qquad j, k = 1, 2 \qquad (5.60)$$

where s_k is the share of imports in country k's national income, and ρ_k is the constant elasticity of substitution. Thus we have, from (5.19) and (5.23),[17]

$$\iota_k = \rho_k \qquad (k = 1, 2) \qquad (5.61)$$

Defining country k's direct demand function for commodity i, $x_i^k = h_i^k(p_1^k, p_2^k, p_3^k, I^k)$, by the condition that $h^k(p^k, I^k)$ maximizes $U^k(x^k)$ subject to the budget constraint $\Sigma_{i=1}^k p_i^k x_i^k \leqslant I^k$, where I^k is country k's nominal national income, if no import-competing goods are produced at home, so that consumption of importables coincides with imports, we may define the *direct elasticities of demand for imports* by

$$\eta_1 = -\frac{p_2^1}{h_2^1}\frac{\partial h_2^1}{\partial p_2^1} \qquad \eta_2 = -\frac{p_1^2}{h_1^2}\frac{\partial h_1^2}{\partial p_1^2} \qquad (5.62)$$

In the case of C.E.S. utility functions (5.59) we find readily that

$$\eta_k = (1 - s_k)\rho_k + s_k \qquad k = 1, 2 \qquad (5.63)$$

Combining this with (5.61) we have the result, under the special conditions (5.27): *the direct elasticity of demand for imports is in between the indirect elasticity of demand for imports and unity.* Under those same special conditions we also have $\eta_k = \omega_k$.

In making his case against "elasticity pessimism," Machlup stated (1950, p. 56): "a correct critical value of [the sum of the] demand elasticities for more realistic conditions, that is, for situations with lower supply elasticities, must lie *below* unity." He did not say that the correct elasticities would be higher. Thus, his concept appears to be closer to our ι_k than to the Marshallian ω_k. But (5.61) and (5.63) imply that if $\eta_k < 1$, then $\iota_k < \eta_k < 1$, so the "true" *indirect* elasticities are smaller than the *direct* ones being estimated; hence, even if the η_ks are underestimated, the statistical estimates of the η_ks need not underestimate the ι_ks. On the other hand, as we saw from (5.34) above, (5.26) is an incorrect stability condition; even with infinite supply elasticities the critical upper bound to $\iota_1 + \iota_2$ is below unity (under the above assumption $\pi_{ik}^k < 0$ for $i \neq k$). It is a wonder if anybody can draw firm conclusions out of this situation!

Let us consider now the allegation that the conventional least squares estimator of η_1 will tend to underestimate its true value. Orcutt's argument was based on geometric and intuitive considerations, but the following interpretation may be offered. Suppose we assume (and what this means will be discussed in the next paragraph) that world equilibrium at time t can be represented by the intersection of a demand and supply curve for country 1's imports, defined by the equations $z_2^1(t) = \alpha_i + \beta_i p_2^1(t) + \epsilon_i(t)$ for $i = 1, 2$ respectively, where the

$\epsilon_i(t)$ are random variables with zero means and covariances E $\epsilon_i(t)\epsilon_j(t) = \sigma_{ij}$. The least squares estimator of either one of the β_is is defined by

$$b = \frac{\sum_{t=1}^{n} [p_2^1(t) - \bar{p}_2^1] [z_2^1(t) - \bar{z}_2^1]}{\sum_{t=1}^{n} [p_2^1(t) - \bar{p}_2^1]^2} \tag{5.64}$$

where

$$\bar{p}_2^1 = \frac{\sum_{t=1}^{n} p_2^1(t)}{n} \qquad \bar{z}_2^1 = \frac{\sum_{t=1}^{n} z_2^1(t)}{n}$$

given a sample of observations at times $t = 1, 2, \ldots, n$. Solving the demand and supply equations it is not hard to see that

$$(\text{Plim}_{n \to \infty} b) - \beta_1 = \frac{(\beta_2 - \beta_1)(\sigma_{11} - \sigma_{12})}{\sigma_{11} - 2\sigma_{12} + \sigma_{22}} \tag{5.65}$$

If the demand curve is downward sloping ($\beta_1 < 0$) and the supply curve upward sloping ($\beta_2 > 0$), as explicitly assumed by Orcutt (1950, p. 127), then $|\beta_1|$ will be underestimated by $|b|$, in the sense that $|\text{Plim } b| < |\beta_1|$, if and only if $\sigma_{11} > \sigma_{12}$. In particular this will be the case if $\dot{\sigma}_{12} < 0$, that is, if shifts in supply and demand are *negatively* correlated. This appears to be what Orcutt meant by saying (1950, p. 123) that the "demand and supply schedules for imports . . . shift up and down together."[18] The result also follows if the shifts are *uncorrelated* ($\sigma_{12} = 0$). If $\sigma_{11} > \sigma_{12}$, note that the result still follows if the supply curve is backward sloping ($\beta_2 < 0$) provided it is steeper than the demand curve ($\beta_1 < \beta_2$), that is, *provided the equilibrium is stable.* To the extent that Orcutt's reasoning is used to argue that devaluation will be effective, because equilibrium is stable, it is worth noting that this conclusion has been assumed in advance.

In fact, it is illegitimate to assume, as Orcutt does, that the foreign supply curve is upward sloping. Under the special assumptions we have considered, the appropriate supply curve for country 1's imports is country 2's *reciprocal demand curve* as defined by Viner (1937, p. 539), which could be backward bending as

Viner noted.[19] There would then be nothing to prevent multiple intersections (alternately stable and unstable) of the two curves, and, if the premise is (at least provisionally) accepted that only equilibria are observed (and, obviously, this means that only *stable* equilibria are observed, since we could no more observe unstable ones than we could observe eggs standing on end) then we cannot in principle rule out the possibility that what we observe at different points in time are alternate stable intersection points of the same curves, rather than stable intersection points of shifted curves. In that case, the least-squares procedure would provide excellent estimates of the average slopes of *both* curves.

But it is of course very unreasonable to assume that we observe equilibria, as Machlup (1958) has argued with great perceptiveness. In fact, as he says (p. 122): "I cannot recognize an equilibrium in international trade no matter how hard I look." That being the case—and I agree—it is hard to be anything but skeptical concerning the correct values of the elasticities, however these might be defined.

Do Relative Prices Matter?

Judging by the long litany of accusations recited in Frenkel and Johnson's book (1976a), the relative-prices approach to the analysis of balance-of-payments adjustment problems is in terrible shape and in deep trouble. In fact, "it is hopelessly defective as an approach to devaluation" (Johnson 1977, p. 254). What are the charges with which this approach is faced? Here are some of the most oft-repeated ones:

1. It assumes that "all goods are traded" (Frenkel and Johnson 1976b, p. 27). On the contrary, the *essence* of the relative-prices or elasticity approach is the role of nontraded goods, as has been recognized from the beginning by Taussig (1927) and Keynes (1930), and quite explicitly by Machlup (1955, p. 183).
2. "Changes in the terms of trade . . . are the center-piece of the elasticity approach" (Frenkel and Johnson, 1976b, p. 27). On the contrary, this was specifically rejected by Taussig (1927), Pigou (1922, 1932), Graham (1948, 1949), Robinson (1947b), Haberler (1952), and Machlup (1950, 1955, 1956), and is instead the position associated with the originator of the "absorption approach" (Alexander, 1952).
3. It "implicitly assumes that changes in domestic income consequent on an increase in export earnings . . . have no further effects on demand," (Johnson 1976, p. 266) or "income is implicitly held constant" (Johnson 1977, p. 254). One need only consult the third equation of (5.6) and of (5.12) above, which provide the source of Machlup's (1939–40) supply and demand for foreign exchange (5.14), to see that this is not so.
4. It assumes "wage rigidity" and "mass unemployment" and is based on the

"implicit assumption of the existence of unemployed resources" (Johnson 1972, pp. 149–50). One will find not even the glimmer of a hint of wage rigidity and unemployment in the accounts of Taussig (1927), Keynes (1930), Graham (1948), and Machlup (1939–40). And rightly or wrongly, full employment has been assumed all along in this paper.

5. It "invariably uses partial-equilibrium real analysis concepts" (Johnson 1976, p. 262). It has been one of the main objects of this paper to disprove this contention.

6. It "provides no analysis . . . of the sources of increased production" (Johnson 1977, p. 254). An imperfect analysis, perhaps, by means of supply elasticities and the assumption of zero cross-flexibilities—but surely not "no analysis"!

A somewhat more substantial criticism arises in the course of Johnson's 1958 analysis of balance-of-payments deficits, which starts out with the acceptance of Alexander's (1952) view that it is more helpful to think of a balance-of-payments deficit as "an excess of aggregate payments by residents over aggregate receipts by residents" (Johnson, 1958, p. 49), than as an excess of international payments over international receipts. While the point may be accepted, the "absorption approach" has a pitfall of its own: it is all too easy to forget that, in equilibrium, an excess of payments over receipts in country 1 must be exactly offset by an equal excess of receipts over payments in country 2. Johnson asserted (1958, p. 51) that a country could not undergo a continuing balance-of-payments deficit (defined (Johnson, 1958, p. 49; 1976, p. 262) as a state in which official reserves were declining—presumably at a constant rate) unless it were sustained by continued credit creation. (This followed from an assumption, later made explicit (1958, p. 54), that he was "abstracting altogether from international capital movements (other than reserve transactions between foreign exchange authorities)".) But if it is true that country 1's deficit cannot be sustained unless the depleted cash balances are being constantly replenished by continued credit creation, then it must be equally true that country 2's equal and opposite surplus cannot be sustained unless country 2 insists on sterilizing the money inflow or offsetting it by continued credit contraction. The complete picture, then, is one of "involuntary foreign lending" from country 2 to country 1 (see Machlup 1965, p. 62–4). We need not go into (and could not possibly settle) the philosophical question of whether the onus for the deficit should be placed on country 1 for creating the situation or on country 2 for not allowing the upward price movements (the "imported inflation") to take place. But from the point of view of positive analysis, in terms of the present model we would have to characterize the situation described by Johnson as an autonomous (we need not say "voluntary" if this causes offense) capital movement from country 2 to country 1. In fact, in terms of our model no conceptual distinction is possible between "voluntary" and "involuntary" autonomous capital movements, yet only the second kind would give rise to a balance-of-payments deficit in Johnson's sense. The analysis of the relative-prices approach therefore confirms rather than rebuts Johnson's contention (1972, p. 150) that "a fully employed economy cannot use devaluation alone as a policy instrument for correcting a balance-of-payments deficit"; for it has surely never been alleged by proponents of the relative-prices approach that a devaluation brought about by an autonomous capital movement would succeed in choking off that capital movement itself!

Finally we may consider the criticism that "the familiar elasticity condition (sum-of-the-elasticities-of-demand-for-foreign-exchange-greater-than-unity[20]) for exchange market stability . . . is completely irrelevant to a monetary international economy . . . because it is the condition for stability of exchange in a barter economy" (Johnson, 1976, p. 281). The reasoning appears to be that if such conditions are not required in a monetary *model,* which "for simplicity" rules out relative price variations *by assumption* (Johnson, 1972, p. 154), then they are irrelevant to the *real world* in which money and relative prices both play a role. This is a good example of the fallacy of misplaced concreteness (Machlup, 1958, p. 122).

The basic idea of the monetary approach appears to be that the dichotomy between barter and monetary theory which unfortunately prevails in economic thinking is also a basic characteristic of the world that our imperfect theories try to describe; that there is one set of forces, or markets, that takes care of real or barter adjustments, and another that takes care of monetary ones, in complete isolation from one another. In a Walrasian (Cartesian?) world with n commodities, n prices surely suffice; an exchange rate is, according to this way of thinking, a superfluous $(n + 1)$th price—a fifth wheel—whose role must therefore be "purely monetary." But if spare tires are needed in real cars, might not spare prices be needed in real economies? In this chapter we have seen that exchange rates play an essential role if some prices (those of domestic goods) are *completely inflexible.* Might this not remain the case if they are only *somewhat inflexible?*

We have not answered this in the present chapter, but an answer suggests itself. Imagine that, over time, the adjustment process represented by the third equation of (5.15) takes place for a time; and that at a specified moment, the exchange rate becomes fixed and variations in the nominal price of the domestic commodity take its place. In the final equilibrium, relative gold prices would remain as before, but the final exchange rate would be "indeterminate" (to use the prevailing unfortunate expression). It would be "indeterminate" only in the sense that *we* are unable to come up with a theory of its determination with our static methods. A more complete analysis than we have been able to present here would probably lead us to the following conclusion:

No satisfactory theory of exchange rate determination is possible within the confines of the method of comparative statics.

Notes

1. Taussig and his students were not the only ones to have rejected Mill's thesis on the basis of empirical evidence accumulated before the Great Depression. Bresciani-Turroni (1924) did likewise. And not surprisingly, we can trace the Taussigian point of view at least back to Malthus (1811, esp. pp. 342-3).

2. Taussig's book was also cited by Mrs. Robinson in the same article (1946-47, p. 11), and his analysis was described as "the 'neoclassical' account of capital movements." In her 1947 treatment of the Foreign Exchanges (1947a, p. 134n), she stated: "It will be obvious that my main endeavour is to elaborate the hints thrown out by Mr. Keynes in his *Treatise on Money,* Chap. 21." If we consult this chapter (Keynes, 1930), which was written before the Great Depression, we find a neoclassical argument along Taussigian lines, in terms of relative price changes and resource reallocation, with not even the contemplation of unemployment. It is obviously and strongly influenced by Taussig, of whose work Keynes says (p. 334n): "his treatment of the influence of international investment on the price-levels in different countries is far in advance of any other discussion of the subject." There follows an analysis that is pure Taussig (Keynes, 1930, p. 358): "If the exchange-rate is altered so as to depreciate the local money to an appropriate extent, equilibrium is restored by *raising* the price of foreign-trade goods whilst leaving that of home-trade goods unchanged, thus attracting entrepreneurs towards an increased production of the former with the consequence of increasing the surplus production of foreign-trade goods." Essentially the same account is found subsequently in Meade (1951, p. 234), but without reference to Keynes: "The consequence . . . will be that the price in B of all B's foreign-trade products will tend to rise relatively to the price of B's home-trade products. . . . The process of readjustment of the balance of trade . . . can now be regarded as essentially a matter of the consequential shift of demand and supply between foreign-trade and home-trade products in A and B." It should be added that all these accounts owe much for their development to Ohlin (1928).

3. This formulation brings out a difference between the concepts employed here and the conventional accounting practices. In the usual formulation (see, for example, Alexander, 1952; Machlup, 1955; Johnson, 1958), involuntary inventory accumulation is (implicitly) included in investment and therefore in output and national income, so that the equality between the excess of income over expenditure and the balance of payments on current account is merely an accounting identity.

4. The requirement is that

$$\begin{vmatrix} \pi_{11}^2 - \pi_{11}^1 & \pi_{12}^2 - \pi_{12}^1 \\ \pi_{21}^2 - \pi_{21}^1 & \pi_{22}^2 - \pi_{22}^1 \end{vmatrix} \neq 0$$

where the π_{ij}^k are defined by (5.16). As will be clear from formula (5.18), this is equivalent to the condition that a transfer have *some* effect on the exchange rate, or that the supply or demand for foreign exchange be not infinitely elastic.

5. This example also brings out the importance of assuming $T = 0$ in order to obtain this purely "monetary" effect on the exchange rate. In fact, proponents of the monetary approach are well aware of this when they require stock-adjustment conditions that ensure $T = 0$ in equilibrium.

6. It is significant that this result depends on the particular dynamic adjustment process (5.15) postulated and on its assumed Metzler stability at the initial point. Under a different type of dynamic adjustment process, the corresponding result in terms of the relative gold prices of the domestic commodities in the two countries need not follow; see Chipman (1974a, p. 71).

7. Separability of $U(x)$ is innocent enough, and is satisfied by many utility functions (e.g., the functions in the constant-elasticity-of-substitution family—see (5.59) below) employed in econometric work. It should be emphasized that additive separability of $U(x)$ does *not* imply zero cross-elasticities of the *direct* demand function. On the contrary, if $U(x) = \Sigma\, u_i(x_i)$, zero cross-elasticities would imply $u_i'(x_i) + x_i u_i'' = 0$, and this can be satisfied only by $u_i(x_i) = a_i + b_i \log x_i$.

8. It was noted by Jones (1961, p. 209) that for this formula to make sense it was "necessary to introduce a third, nontraded commodity serving as *numéraire*." However, he added that the analysis leading to (5.24) was necessarily of a "*partial*-equilibrium nature." The above development shows that this is not the case.

9. Since the condition of note 4 is assumed to hold, and since under the assumption of separability we have $\pi_{kk}^k \geqslant 0$, $\pi_{ii}^k \leqslant 0$ for $i \neq k$, and $\pi_{ij}^k = 0$ for $i \neq j$, the four elasticities of (5.23) are all positive. Consequently the conditions (5.24) and (5.25) become equivalent. Under the dynamic process (5.38), the Edgeworth condition (5.25) is therefore necessary and sufficient in the separable case, whereas under the process (5.15) it is necessary but not sufficient. This may be what lies behind Machlup's doubts (1939, p. 12) as to whether it is legitimate "to transform operational time into clock time." Note that under (5.15), arguments to the effect that (5.24) or (5.25) is fulfilled (e.g., Machlup 1950, p. 56) do not in themselves provide sufficient grounds for "elasticity optimism," since (5.25) is not in general a sufficient condition for stability of exchange equilibrium.

10. The Jacobian matrix of (5.44) is the matrix product

$$\begin{bmatrix} \kappa_1 & 0 \\ 0 & \kappa_2 \end{bmatrix} \begin{bmatrix} -1 & \partial G_1/\partial z_2^1 \\ \partial G_2/\partial z_1^2 & -1 \end{bmatrix}$$

If its characteristic roots are complex or repeated, then $\alpha_1 \alpha_2 \leqslant 0$ and (5.45) is certainly satisfied; if they are real, they are both negative if and only if (5.45) holds.

11. According to Hirschman (1949, p. 50): "Marshall was first to point out that devaluation might produce an unfavorable effect on the balance of trade . . . on the condition that 'the total elasticity of demand of each country be less than unity, and on the average less than one half . . . .'" However, in the passage in question (Marshall, 1923, Appendix J, p. 354), Marshall makes no mention either of devaluation or of the balance of trade. Marshall was discussing the question of unstable and multiple equilibria, in terms of the dynamic movement of what he called the "exchange-index," which he defined (p. 340) as the point in his phase diagrams which we have here denoted (z_1^2, z_2^1); that is, he was discussing the properties of a system of differential equations which we have represented here (following Samuelson) by (5.44). The only price concepts mentioned by Marshall in his analysis are the "rate of interchange" (p. 353) and the "terms of trade" (p. 345), expressions which are defined as synonymous and presented with a warning (p. 161): "The phrase 'rate of exchange' is avoided; because it is already specialized, in connection with the Foreign Exchanges, to indicate the rate at which command over the currency of one country can be obtained in terms of the currency of another country." Taussig (1927, p. 9) also warned of this linguistic trap, which Hirschman apparently fell into.

12. While this is true, if we go back far enough—to Pigou (1922)—we find the emphatic statement that "the two are not connected with one another at all" (p. 150).

13. The citation follows the clarificatory 1964 rewording but is otherwise identical with the original 1939 passage.

14. It should be stressed that Pigou explicitly defined the elasticities in the *indirect* form (5.23), following Jevons (see also Pigou, 1947). The distinction between the direct and indirect elasticities was explicitly remarked upon by Kahn (1947–48, p. 17) and Graaff (1949–50, p. 54n). For the derivation of (5.56) see also Viner (1937, p. 341), Bronfenbrenner (1942), Pigou (1947, p. 180), and Johnson and Carter (1950). An analysis along Robinsonian lines was presented by Haberler (1952). Condition (5.56) is equivalent—in the case of the pure exchange model with separable preferences—to Samuelson's (1952, p. 286) well-known inequality expressed in terms of income propensities.

15. What this means is that instead of having one equation for each country we should have at least three, the import demand equation being supplemented by two additional equations indicating the dependence of income and the price of the domestic commodity on the export and import prices. (For a complete system one would also not want to ignore the market for country 1's export good.) This would be a system of "block recursive" type, and the least-squares method would be justified if one could assume that the random influences on consumption of importables were independent of those on national income and the price of the domestic commodity.

16. For country 1 the formula is (dropping country suffixes for notational convenience)

$$U^1(z_1^1, z_2^1, z_3^1; \ell^1) = -\theta_2(z_2^1)^{(\rho-1)/\rho}$$

$$- (\theta_1^\rho b_1^{\rho-1} + \theta_3^\rho b_3^{\rho-1})^{1/\rho} \left(\frac{z_1^1}{b_1} + \frac{z_3^1}{b_3} + \ell^1 \right)^{(\rho-1)/\rho}$$

17. This result depends critically upon the assumption that country k specializes in its export and domestic goods. If, say, we replaced (5.27) by a fixed-output production possibility set $\mathscr{Y}^1 = \{\bar{y}_1^1, \bar{y}_2^1, \bar{y}_3^1\}$ (which we could interpret as Haberler's 1950 short-run specific-factors technology, with the formal identity $\bar{y}^1 = \ell^1$), then it is not hard to see that in place of (5.61) we would obtain $\rho_1 x_2^1/z_2^1$ (for country 1), that is, the elasticity of substitution divided by the share of imports in the consumption of importables. With positive domestic production of imports this would yield $\iota_1 > \rho_1$.

18. One must be careful about the use of words here. On the assumption that the demand and supply curves have negative and positive slopes respectively, and that price is measured vertically and quantity horizontally, the curves "shift up and down together" if and only if they shift to the left and right in *opposite* directions.

19. This should not be interpreted as meaning that Viner's diagrams are valid only under these assumptions, but rather that it is only under these assumptions that they are applicable to the analysis of exchange rate determination—a purpose which there is no reason to believe Viner himself had in mind (*pace* Hirschman, 1949). For *his* purposes, Viner's curves had more general validity.

20. Johnson must have meant "greater than zero." See the discussion at the end of the section, "The Supply and Demand for Foreign Exchange." If we formally allowed ϵ_1 and ϵ_2 to approach infinity in (5.37), we would obtain $\varphi_s = \iota_2 - 1$ and $\varphi_D = \iota_1$, yielding (5.26). But as indicated in "The Separable Case," this procedure is not in general legitimate.

References

Alexander, Sidney S., "Devaluation Versus Import Restriction as an Instrument for Improving Foreign Trade Balance," International Monetary Fund *Staff Papers* 1 (April 1951), 379–396.

——, "Effects of a Devaluation on a Trade Balance," International Monetary Fund *Staff Papers* 2 (April 1952), 263–278.

Allen, William R., "Stable and Unstable Equilibria in the Foreign Exchanges," *Kyklos* 7 (Fasc. 4, 1954), 395–410.

Arrow, Kenneth J., "Stability Independent of Adjustment Speed," in *Trade, Stability, and Macroeconomics: Essays in Honor of Lloyd A. Metzler* (edited by George Horwich and Paul A. Samuelson), New York: Academic Press, 1974, pp. 181–202.

Arrow, Kenneth J., H.D. Block, and Leonid Hurwicz, "On the Stability of the Competitive Equilibrium, II," *Econometrica* 27 (January 1959), 82–109.

Bickerdike, C.F., "The Theory of Incipient Taxes," *Economic Journal* 16 (December 1906), 529–535.

——, Review of *Protective and Preferential Import Duties* by A.C. Pigou, *Economic Journal* 17 (March 190 /), 98–102.

——, "The Instability of Foreign Exchange," *Economic Journal* 30 (March 1920), 118–122.

Bresciani-Turroni, Costantino, "Il deprezzamento del marco e il commercio estero della Germania," *Giornale degli Economisti e Rivista di Statistica* [4] 64 (September 1924), 457–485. English translation: "The Depreciation of the Mark and Germany's Foreign Trade," in Bresciani-Turroni, 1937, Ch. 6, pp. 224–252.

——, "The 'Purchasing Power Parity' Doctine," *L'Égypte Contemporaine* 25 (January-February 1934), 433–464.

——, *The Economics of Inflation,* London: George Allen and Unwin Ltd., 1937. Translated from the Italian, *Le Vicende del Marco Tedesco,* Milan: Università Bocconi, 1931.

Bronfenbrenner, Martin, "International Transfers and the Terms of Trade: An Extension of Pigou's Analysis," in *Studies in Mathematical Economics and Econometrics* (edited by Oscar Lange, Francis McIntyre, and Theodore O. Yntema), Chicago: University of Chicago Press, 1942, pp. 119–131.

——, "Exchange Rates and Exchange Stability: Mathematical Supplement," *Review of Economics and Statistics* 32 (February 1950), 12–16.

Chipman, John S., "The Transfer Problem Once Again," in *Trade, Stability, and Macroeconomics: Essays in Honor of Lloyd A. Metzler* (edited by George Horwich and Paul A. Samuelson), New York: Academic Press, 1974, pp. 19–78 (1974a).

——, "Homothetic Preferences and Aggregation," *Journal of Economic Theory* 8 (May 1974), 26–38 (1974b).

Chipman, John S., and James C. Moore, "The Scope of Consumer's Surplus Arguments," in *Evolution, Welfare, and Time in Economics. Essays in Honor of Nicholas Georgescu-Roegen* (edited by Anthony M. Tang, Fred M. Westfield, and James S. Worley), Lexington, Mass.: Lexington Books, D.C. Heath and Company, 1976, pp. 69–123.

Dornbusch, Rudiger, "Alternative Price Stabilization Rules and the Effects of Exchange Rate Changes," *Manchester School of Economic and Social Studies* 43 (September 1975), 275–292.

Edgeworth, Francis Ysidro, "Appreciations of Mathematical Theories, III,"
    Economic Journal 18 (September, December 1908), 392-403, 541-556.
    Reprinted as "Mr. Bickerdike's Theory of Incipient Taxes and Customs
    Duties," in F.Y. Edgeworth, *Papers Relating to Political Economy,* Vol. II,
    London: Macmillan and Co., 1925, pp. 340-366.
Ellsworth, P.T., "Exchange Rates and Exchange Stability," *Review of Economics
    and Statistics* 32 (February 1950), 1-12.
Frenkel, Jacob A., and Harry G. Johnson, *The Monetary Approach to the Bal-
    ance of Payments.* London: George Allen & Unwin, 1976 (1976a).
Frenkel, Jacob A., and Harry G. Johnson, "The Monetary Approach to the
    Balance of Payments: Essential Concepts and Historical Origins," in
    Frenkel and Johnson, 1976a, pp. 21-45 (1976b).
Graaff, J. de V., "On Optimum Tariff Structures," *Review of Economic Studies*
    17 (1949-50), 47-59.
Graham, Frank D., "International Trade under Depreciated Paper. The United
    States, 1862-79," *Quarterly Journal of Economics* 36 (February 1922),
    220-273.
——, *The Theory of International Values,* Princeton, N.J.: Princeton University
    Press, 1948.
——, "The Cause and Cure of 'Dollar Shortage'," *Essays in International Finance*
    10 (January 1949), International Finance Section, Princeton University,
    Princeton, N.J., 15 pp.
Haberler, Gottfried, *Der internationale Handel,* Berlin: Verlag von Julius
    Springer, 1933. English translation: *The Theory of International Trade with
    Its Applications to Commercial Policy,* London: William Hodge & Company,
    1936.
——, "The Market for Foreign Exchange and the Stability of the Balance of
    Payments," *Kyklos* 3 (1949), 193-218.
——, "Some Problems in the Pure Theory of International Trade," *Economic
    Journal,* 60 (June 1950), 223-240.
——, "Currency Depreciation and the Terms of Trade," in *Wirtschaftliche
    Entwicklung und soziale Ordnung* (edited by Ernst Lagler and Johannes
    Messner), Vienna: Verlag Herold, 1952, pp. 149-158.
Harberger, Arnold C., "Currency Depreciation, Income, and the Balance of
    Trade," *Journal of Political Economy* 58 (February 1950), 47-60.
Hirschman, Albert O., "Devaluation and the Trade Balance: A Note," *Review
    of Economics and Statistics* 31 (February 1949), 50-53.
Johnson, Harry G., "Optimum Welfare and Maximum Revenue Tariffs," *Review
    of Economic Studies* 19 (1950-51), 28-35. Reprinted in Harry G. Johnson,
    International Trade and Economic Growth, London: George Allen &
    Unwin, 1958, pp. 56-61.
——, "Towards a General Theory of the Balance of Payments," in Harry G.
    Johnson, *International Trade and Economic Growth,* London: George Allen

& Unwin, 1958, pp. 153-168. Reprinted in Frenkel and Johnson, 1976a, pp. 46-63. Page references are to the latter.

——, "The Monetary Approach to Balance-of-Payments Theory," in Harry G. Johnson, *Further Essays in Monetary Economics,* London: George Allen & Unwin, 1972, pp. 229-249. Reprinted in Frenkel and Johnson, 1976a, pp. 147-167. Page references are to the latter.

——, "The Monetary Theory of Balance-of-Payments Policies," in Frenkel and Johnson, 1976a, pp. 262-284.

——, "The Monetary Approach to the Balance of Payments: A Non-Technical Guide," *Journal of International Economics* 7 (August 1977), 251-268.

Johnson, Harry G., and C.F. Carter, "Unrequited Imports and the Terms of Trade," *Economic Journal* 60 (December 1950), 837-839.

Jones, Ronald W., "Stability Conditions in International Trade: A General Equilibrium Analysis," *International Economic Review* 2 (May 1961), 199-209.

Kahn, R.F., "Tariffs and the Terms of Trade," *Review of Economic Studies* 15 (1947-48), 14-19.

Kaldor, Nicholas, "A Note on Tariffs and the Terms of Trade," *Economica,* N.S., 7 (November 1940), 377-380.

Katzner, Donald W., *Static Demand Theory,* New York: The Macmillan Company, 1970.

Keynes, John Maynard, *A Treatise on Money,* Vol. I, London: Macmillan and Co., 1930.

Laursen, Svend, and Lloyd A. Metzler, "Flexible Exchange Rates and the Theory of Employment," *Review of Economics and Statistics* 32 (November 1950), 281-299.

Leamer, Edward E., and Robert M. Stern, *Quantitative International Economics,* Boston: Allyn and Bacon, 1970.

Lerner, Abba P., *The Economics of Control,* New York: The Macmillan Co., 1944.

Machlup, Fritz, "The Theory of Foreign Exchanges," *Economica,* N.S., 6 (November 1939), 375-397, 7 (February 1940), 23-49. Reprinted in Machlup (1964), pp. 7-50. Page references are to the latter.

——, "Elasticity Pessimism in International Trade," *Economia Internazionale* 3 (February 1950), 118-137. Reprinted in Machlup (1964), pp. 51-68. Page references are to the latter.

——, "Relative Prices and Aggregate Spending in the Analysis of Devaluation," *American Economic Review* 45 (June 1955), 255-278. Reprinted in Machlup (1964), pp. 171-194. Page references are to the latter.

——, "The Terms-of-Trade Effects of Devaluation upon Real Income and the Balance of Trade," *Kyklos* 9 (Fasc. 4, 1956), 417-452. Reprinted in Machlup (1964), pp. 195-222. Page references are to the latter.

——, "Equilibrium and Disequilibrium: Misplaced Concreteness and Disguised

Politics," *Economic Journal* 48 (March 1958), 1–24. Reprinted in Machlup
(1964), pp. 110–135. Page references are to the latter.

——, *International Payments, Debts, and Gold,* New York: Charles Scribner's
Sons, 1964. Published in the U.K. under the title, *International Monetary
Economics,* London: George Allen & Unwin, 1966.

——, *Involuntary Foreign Lending,* Stockholm: Almqvist & Wiksell, 1965.

[Malthus, Thomas R.] , "Depreciation of Paper Currency," *Edinburgh Review,*
17 (February 1811), 339–372. Reprinted in Bernard Semmel, ed., *Occasional Papers of T.R. Malthus,* New York: Burt Franklin, Publisher, 1963,
71–104.

Marshall, Alfred, *The Pure Theory of Foreign Trade,* published privately, 1879.
Reprinted, together with *The Pure Theory of Domestic Values,* London:
London School of Economics and Political Science, 1930; third impression,
1949.

——, *Money, Credit, and Commerce,* London: Macmillan and Co., 1923.

Meade, James Edward, *The Theory of International Economic Policy.* Vol. I. *The
Balance of Payments,* London: Oxford University Press, 1951.

——, *A Geometry of International Trade,* London: George Allen & Unwin,
1952.

Metzler, Lloyd A., "Stability of Multiple Markets: The Hicks Conditions,"
Econometrica 13 (October 1945), 277–292.

——, "The Theory of International Trade," in *A Survey of Contemporary
Economics* (edited by Howard S. Ellis), Philadelphia: The Blakiston
Company, 1948, pp. 210–254.

Mill, John Stuart, *Principles of Political Economy, with Some of Their Applications to Social Philosophy* (in two volumes), London: John W. Parker, West
Strand, 1848.

Ohlin, Bertil, "The Reparations Problem," *Index* (Svenska Handelsbanken,
Stockholm), No. 28 (April 1928), 2–33.

Orcutt, Guy H., "Measurement of Price Elasticities in International Trade,"
Review of Economics and Statistics 32 (May 1950), 117–132.

Pigou, Arthur Cecil, "The Real Ratio of International Interchange," *Manchester
Guardian Reconstruction Supplement,* December 1922. Reprinted in
Arthur C. Pigou, *Essays in Applied Economics,* London: P.S. King & Son,
1923, pp. 149–155. Page references are to the latter.

——, "The Effect of Reparations on the Ratio of International Interchange,"
Economic Journal 42 (December 1932), 532–543.

——, *A Study in Public Finance,* Third (Revised) Edition. London: Macmillan
and Co., 1947.

Robinson, Joan, "The Pure Theory of International Trade," *Review of Economic
Studies* 14 (1946–47), 98–112.

——, "The Foreign Exchanges," in *Essays in the Theory of Employment,* 2nd ed.,
Oxford: Basil Blackwell, 1947, pp. 134–155 (1947a).

——, "Beggar-my-Neighbour Remedies for Unemployment," in Joan Robinson, *Essays in the Theory of Employment,* 2nd ed., Oxford: Basil Blackwell, 1947, pp. 156-170 (1947b).

Samuelson, Paul A., "Constancy of the Marginal Utility of Income," in *Studies in Mathematical Economics and Econometrics, In Memory of Henry Schultz* (edited by Oscar Lange, Francis McIntyre, and Theodore O. Yntema), Chicago: University of Chicago Press, 1942, pp. 75-91.

——, *Foundations of Economic Analysis,* Cambridge, Mass.: Harvard University Press, 1947.

——, "The Problem of Integrability in Utility Theory," *Economica,* N.S., 17 (November 1950), 355-385.

——, "The Transfer Problem and Transport Costs: The Terms of Trade when Impediments are Absent," *Economic Journal* 62 (June 1952), 278-304.

Taussig, Frank W., "International Trade under Depreciated Paper. A Contribution to Theory," *Quarterly Journal of Economics* 31 (May 1917), 380-403.

——, *International Trade,* New York: The Macmillan Co., 1927.

Viner, Jacob, *Studies in the Theory of International Trade,* New York: Harper & Brothers Publishers, 1937.

Yntema, Theodore O., *A Mathematical Reformulation of the General Theory of International Trade,* Chicago: University of Chicago Press, 1932.

6

Pseudo-Maximization to the Rescue of Derived Factor Demand of a Competitive Industry

Paul A. Samuelson

Exactly forty-two years ago, when I was an undergraduate taking Jacob Viner's first course in graduate economic theory, his celebrated 301 at the University of Chicago, a brilliant comet visited the seminar. Later I learned this was Fritz Machlup. I term him a comet because his was a strange and new face in the heavens; but actually Machlup twinkled like a star of the first magnitude. After Viner made some remarks, not completely complimentary, about Böhm-Bawerk's tedious discrete-horse markets, Machlup intervened with great courtesy and élan, pointing out that in the *Excursi* of later editions, Böhm had worked out the continuous-variable supply and demand intersections so beloved of Marshall's Anglo-Saxon readers.

That was the first of many benefits I received from Fritz's scholarship: like the dividends on consols, Machlup's contributions to modern economics continue to accrue, not with the long gaps of Haley's comet but fortunately with its predictable regularity.

Although I did not know it then, Machlup must already have written by the time of that Viner seminar his 1935 paper "The Common Sense of the Elasticity of Substitution." This article could serve as a model for any would-be scholar. It makes clear much that was murky. It is a *tour de force* of skillful exposition—unpretentious, modest, punctilious in its scholarly attributions. At the same time it had depth, pointing to problems still to be solved (some of which I found still waiting resolution a third of a century later when, for the Hicks *Festschrift*, I tackled Machlup's vital concept of *intercommodity* substitutions).

Now I hope to provide some simplification, clarification, and generalization (all Machlupian earmarks!) to one of the problems involved in the original discussions of the elasticity of substitution by Hicks (1932), Joan Robinson (1933), Kahn (1933, 1935), Meade (1934), Paul Douglas (1934), Pigou (1934), Tarshis (1933), Abba Lerner (1933, 1934, 1936), Paul Sweezy (1933), Machlup (1935, 1936), Champernowne (1935), Milton Friedman (1936), Mosak (1938), Roy Allen (1938), and others. (I invite the reader to savor the above names.) Aside

I owe thanks to the NSF for financial aid, and to Vicki Elms for editorial assistance.

from tackling the problems of (a) relative shares of factors in a one-product aggregative economy, and (b) their shares in a general equilibrium mode involving Machlup-Hicks intercommodity substitutions, these early writers hoped to employ the elasticity of substitution concepts (c) *to analyze a single competitive industry's demand for two or more factors of production.* This last venture had, by the late 1930s, bogged down in a swamp of hard-to-handle and inconclusive matrices. More recently, advances in duality theory by Shephard (1953, 1970), Samuelson (1947, 1953, 1960, 1962, 1965, 1968, 1972, 1974), Uzawa (1962), McFadden (1963), Diewert (1971a,b), Hicks (1936, 1963, 1970), Sato and Koizumi (1970, 1973a, b), Akerlof and Burmeister (1970), Silberberg (1971), Vázquez and Puu (1973), Sakai (1975), and others have provided some much needed simplification to the analysis.

However, the last word has by no means yet been said. It is a pleasure to use a concept near to Fritz Machlup's heart—that of *maximizing*—to yield some enormous simplifications and also some fresh, verifiable testings of the model.

A Frankenstein-Samuelson Monster

Machlup is of course famous for his 1940's defense of marginalism. He insists that firms *really do* try to maximize their profits and that we economists will have to recognize the validity of this instance of the "economic principle" even if it complicates our analysis (rather than enormously simplifying it, as is actually the case). Carl Menger, the Abraham of the Austrian School and Machlup's spiritual grandsire, had insisted a century ago in his polemics against the Historical School on the methodological dogma of rational individualism, upon which all sound economic analysis *must* be based. Machlup as Joseph has found no need to alter the faith of his forefathers. Far from it.

If I were to allege to Fritz that hydrogen molecules maximize utility or that salt economizes on love, he would regard these as pathetic examples of the "Pathetic Fallacy" (according to which rocks have broken hearts and willow trees weep) and he might urge me to go on the wagon. Or he might indulge my excursion into poetry as perhaps a sign of evolving senility. None the less, my serious proposal in the present effort is to fabricate (or "forge") a function to be maximized for an industry that is a collection of a multitude of independent and competitive firms. The magnitude that is thought of as being maximized will be found to be measurable in dollars[1] and is closest in concept to "net utility" or "consumers' surplus." One must warn, however, that there are no normative or welfare connotations implied by this mechanical construction.

Why do I construct such a monstrosity? Because scientists must be opportunists and exploit every advantage the data offer. As I explained in my Nobel Lecture, Samuelson (1971), enormous unification and simplification can be procured whenever an economic problem can, by serendipity, be formulated as a maximum or minimum problem. Voltaire said that if God had not existed, we would have had to invent Him. I say, "Since this competitive industry's comparative-statics can be shown to behave as if the industry had a soul and an integrable mind, expediency urges us to pretend it has. Pretend? Operationally speaking, in effect it does maximize—else we could not successfully pretend it does. Abraham, Isaac, and Jacob be hanged if they don't approve."

The Industry Problem

Returning to sobriety, consider with Hicks (1932) and Robinson (1933, ch. 22) the following one-industry situation.[2]

output = neoclassical production function of 2 or more inputs

$$q = Q(x_1, x_2, \ldots) = Q(\mathbf{x}) : \qquad \text{a monotone increasing function} \quad (6.1.1)$$

$$\equiv m^{-1} Q(mx_1, mx_2, \ldots): \qquad \text{1st-degree homogeneity} \quad (6.1.2)$$

$$Q(a+2b) - Q(a+b) \leqslant Q(a+b) - Q(a): \qquad \text{"diminishing returns"} \\ \text{or concavity} \quad (6.1.3)$$

$$\partial Q/\partial x_i = Q_i, \ \partial^2 Q/\partial x_i \partial x_j = Q_{ij} \qquad \text{is well-defined;} \qquad \text{smoothness} \\ (6.1.4)$$

$$p = P[q], \qquad P'[q] > 0: \qquad \text{Cournot-Marshall industry demand}$$

$$q = Q[p], \qquad Q'[\ ]P'[\ ] \equiv 1 \qquad \text{for equilibrium pairs} \quad (6.2)$$

where the warning in note 2 about the distinction between $Q(\ )$ and $Q[\ ]$ should be noted.

$$y_1, y_2, \ldots: \qquad \text{factor prices of } x_1, x_2, \ldots, \text{given to each firm}$$

$$0 = s_i(x_i, y_i; \ldots), (i = 1, 2, \ldots): \qquad \text{supply schedules of factors} \quad (6.3)$$

Except for the assumption in (6.1.4) of smooth differentiability, the above assumptions are sufficient (and, actually, necessary) for viable competition in this Hicks-Robinson industry. Darwinian competition will then impose the marginal productivity conditions:

$$y_i = P[Q(x_1, x_2, \ldots)] \ [\partial Q(x_1, x_2, \ldots)/\partial x_i] \qquad (i = 1, 2, \ldots) \ (6.4.1)$$

$$P[Q(\mathbf{x})]\,Q(\mathbf{x}) \equiv y_1 x_1 + y_2 x_2 + \ldots \tag{6.4.2}$$

So long as $P'[q] < 0$, it can be shown that (6.4) implies reduced form factor demand functions

$$x_i = X^i(y_1, y_2, \ldots) \qquad (i = 1, 2, \ldots) \tag{6.5}$$

These will be single valued functions for all positive (y_j) provided the conditions of (6.1.2)–(6.1.4) are strengthened so that the smooth iso-Q contours approach the axes asymptotically in Inada fashion.

So far, the properties of (6.5), such as the sign of $\partial X^i(\ )/\partial y_i$, have not been explored. And, thus far, no connection of (6.4) or (6.5) with a maximum problem has been exposed.

Consider now what would have replaced (6.4) if this Marshallian industry had been run by a "monopolist" (e.g., by a sole seller given exclusive rights to provide the product q to customers). The monopolist's maximum problem would have replaced (6.4) by

$$\begin{aligned}
&\mathrm{Max}_{x_i}\Big\{Q(\mathbf{x})P[Q(\mathbf{x})] - y_1 x_1 - y_2 x_2 - \ldots\Big\} \\
&\equiv \mathrm{Max}_{x_i}\Big\{R[Q(\mathbf{x})] - y_1 x_1 - y_2 x_2 - \ldots\Big\} \\
&\equiv R[Q(\mathbf{x}^*)] - y_1 x_1^* - y_2 x_2^* - \ldots \\
&\equiv -\mathrm{II}^*(y_1, y_2, \ldots)
\end{aligned} \tag{6.6.1}$$

where $(x_1^*, x_2^*, \ldots, q^*)$ are functions of $(y_1, y_2, \ldots)$ given by roots of the extremal conditions

$$R'[Q(x_1, x_2, \ldots)]\,[\partial Q(x_1, x_2, \ldots)/\partial x_i] - y_i = 0 \qquad (i = 1, 2, \ldots)$$
$$\tag{6.6.2}$$

$$R[q] \equiv qP[q] \qquad R'[q] \equiv P[q] + qP'[q] \qquad R''[q] < 0$$
$$\tag{6.6.3}$$

$$P[Q(\mathbf{x})]\,Q(\mathbf{x}) - y_1 x_1 - y_2 x_2 - \ldots = -Q(\mathbf{x})^2 P'[Q(\mathbf{x})] > 0 \tag{6.6.4}$$

In (6.6) I assumed that the monopoly is viable with positive output, upon which it is seen to necessarily earn a surplus profit.[3]

The problem in (6.6) is certainly a maximum problem: Menger and Machlup would not find it a camel hard to swallow. Its properties are by now old hat, as in Samuelson (1947, ch. 4) Thus, the relations (6.6.2) can be solved for the following reduced-form demands

$$x_i = \partial \Pi^*(y_1, y_2, \ldots)/\partial y_i \qquad (i = 1, 2, \ldots) \qquad (6.7.1)$$

$$\partial^2 \Pi^*(\ )/\partial y_i^2 < 0 \qquad (6.7.2)$$

$[-\partial^2 \Pi^*(\ )/\partial y_i \partial y_j]$ is positive definite with principal minors all positive.

Constructing The Industry's Maximand

We can reduce our (6.4.1) relations to the amenable maximization case of (6.6.2) once we realize that $P[q]$ in (6.4.1) can be the derivative of an existent function and can therefore play exactly the role that $R'[q]$ did in (6.6.2). Define

$$Y[q] \equiv \int_{q_0}^{q} P[v]\,dv : \qquad \text{the area under the demand curve} \quad (6.8.1)$$

$$Y'[q] \equiv P[q] \qquad (6.8.2)$$

$$\partial Y[Q(x_1, x_2, \ldots)]/\partial x_i \equiv P[Q(x_1, \ldots)][\partial Q(x_1, \ldots)/\partial x_i] \qquad (i = 1, 2, \ldots)$$

$$(6.8.3)$$

For

$$Y[Q(x_1, x_2, \ldots)] \equiv Y(x_1, x_2, \ldots)$$
$$\partial Y[Q(x_1, x_2, \ldots)]/\partial x_i \equiv Y_i(x_1, x_2, \ldots)$$
(6.8.4)

for short,

$$Y_i(x_1, x_2, \ldots) \equiv P[Q(x_1, x_2, \ldots)][\partial Q(x_1, x_2, \ldots)/\partial x_i]$$
$$[Y_{ij}(x_1, x_2, \ldots)] = [(P)(\partial^2 Q/\partial x_i \partial x_j) + (P')(\partial Q/\partial x_i)(\partial Q/\partial x_j)]$$
(6.8.5)

is negative definite.

Now the basic Hicks-Robinson industry equilibrium of (6.4) can be cast in the following maximizing form

$$\text{Max}_{x_i} \left\{ Y(x_1, x_2, \ldots) - y_1 x_1 - y_2 x_2 - \ldots \right\}$$

$$= Y(x_1^*, x_2^*, \ldots) - y_1 x_1^* - y_2 x_2^* > 0 \qquad (6.9.1)$$

$$= -X(y_1, y_2, \ldots) \qquad (6.9.2)$$

the industry's *dual* function; and where $(x_1^*, x_2^*, \ldots)$ are optimal values of (x_j^*) for given (y_j),

$$x_i^* = \partial X(y_1, y_2, \ldots)/\partial y_i \qquad (i = 1, 2, \ldots)$$

$$= X_i(y_1, y_2, \ldots) \qquad (6.9.3)$$

for short; and where (x_j^*) are the roots of the extremal first-order maximum conditions equivalent to (6.4.2):

$$y_i = Y_i(x_1, x_2, \ldots) \equiv P[Q(x_1, x_2, \ldots)] \frac{\partial Q(x_1, x_2, \ldots)}{\partial x_i}$$

$$\qquad (6.9.4)$$

$$[Y_{ij}(\mathbf{x})] \text{ and } [X_{ij}(\mathbf{y})] \equiv [Y_{ij}(\mathbf{x})]^{-1} \qquad \text{negative definite}$$

Under our strong regularity conditions on $Q(\mathbf{x})$, such that its contours are smooth and asymptotic to the axes, demands are unique and smooth.

There is an interesting moral from this rigorous model. It shows that maximization can be *simultaneously* postulated both for small firms *and* for the industry aggregate they belong to! This raises a question much debated in modern biology.

Is evolution a drama played out, as some writers insist, by the *selfish gene?* Or, does reciprocal altruism—among families, clans, parents, and the like—play a vital role so to be itself subject to selection and fitness survival? Our exact analysis shows that it need not always be a case of one or the other—the selfish gene *or* the selfish family. Both, or neither, might be involved. (Indeed, with a countable infinity of units one might, as in Samuelson (1968, Equations 17-20), construct an *endless* hierarchy of higher and lower stages, *each* of which involves maximization at its level.) In principle, revealed preference methods can be used to test and refute hypothesized models of maximization. Thus, econometricians or biometricians can measure whether observations on (6.5) do satisfy approximately the Maxwell reciprocity relations, $\partial X^1(\ )/\partial y_2 \equiv \partial X^2(\ )/\partial y_1$, that enable (6.5) to be written as (6.9.3).

Much of biology, like much of Parsonian sociology, impresses the experienced economist as empty talk about untestable tautologies of *extrema* language. The young science of economics has perhaps some good examples to set for some of the older sciences (and still has some stables of its own that need cleaning!).

Easy Fruits of Maximization

From the maximizing formulation, we at once infer some basic facts:

1. A rise in an input price will, when other input prices are constant (*or* where some other inputs' quantities rather than prices are held constant), lower the amount of it demanded by the industry:[4]

$$(\Delta x_1)(\Delta y_1) \leqslant 0 \qquad X_{11}(y) < 0 \tag{6.10}$$

2. A rise in one input's price may raise or lower the amount the industry demands of another input. Unlike the case where q is held constant, there is no presumption toward "substitutability" rather than complementarity. Robinson (1933) found this out the hard way, deriving the criterion for $n = 2$ that $\partial x_2/\partial y_1 \lessgtr 0$ depending on whether industry-product demand elasticity is absolutely greater than the Hicks-Robinson elasticity of substitution, $\eta \gtrless \sigma$ in Hicks notation. Since the sign of $\partial x_2/\partial x_1$ is opposite in the polar cases where q and where p are frozen, one infers without breaking $\partial x_2/\partial y_1$ down into scale-and-substitution effects that all sign patterns are possible. Whatever the sign pattern of $\partial x_2/\partial y_1$, one can assert from the maximizing formulation above the following:

The algebraic value of $\partial x_i/\partial y_j$ and $\partial x_j/\partial y_i$ must be equal. And likewise for the dimensionless elasticity expressions $k_i[\partial \log x_i/\partial \log y_j]$ or $[\partial \log x_i/\partial \log y_j]/k_j$:

$$X_{ij}(y) \equiv X_{ji}(y) \qquad k_i\frac{Ex_i}{Ey_j} \equiv k_j\frac{Ex_j}{Ex_i} \tag{6.11}$$

and so on, where $k_i = x_i y_i/\Sigma_1^n x_j y_j$ and Ez denotes $dz/z = d \log z$, as in $Eq/Ep = p[q]/p'[q]q = -\eta$, or in $Ex_i/Ey_j = \partial \log X_i(y)/\partial \log y_j$.[5]

This analysis dispells the "paradox" of Richard Nelson (1957), who thought it strange that a rise in the price of wheat farm labor could *raise* the wheat land rents of farmers. Nelson's case can be shown to be a simple variant of the problem solved in Robinson (1933), so that her criterion $\eta \gtrless \sigma$ is identical with Nelson's criterion $\eta \gtrless$ ratio of Average Variable Cost Curve's Elasticity to Marginal Cost Curve's Elasticity.[6] The methods of Samuelson (1960) can show the two problems' complete equivalence. Since *any* pattern of complementarity between two factors is possible, nothing should surprise us.

3. From the maximizing formulation alone, we know from Samuelson (1947) that the more comprehensive weak-axiom inequality holds:

$$(\Delta y_1)(\Delta x_1) + (\Delta y_2)(\Delta x_2) + \ldots \leqslant 0 \tag{6.12}$$

And all this holds even if we dispense with definable partial derivatives and marginal products. Thus, in the case of fixed proportions,

$$q = \text{Min}\,[x_1/a_1, x_2/a_2, \ldots]$$

$$p^* = a_1 y_1 + a_2 y_2 + \ldots$$

$$x_1^* = a_i q^* = a_i p^{-1} \left[\sum_1^n a_j y_j \right] = a_i X' \left[\sum_1^n a_j y_j \right]$$

$$\partial x_i^* / \partial y_i = a_i^2 X'' \left[\sum_1^n a_j y_j \right] < 0$$

as in (6.10) above. Similarly, $\partial x_i^* / \partial y_j = a_i a_j X''[\;\;] < 0$.

In terms of smooth derivatives, $[-X_{ij}(\mathbf{y})]$ and $[-Y_{ij}(\mathbf{x})]$ are positive definite with all their principal minors positive:

$$\partial x_i / \partial y_i < 0 \qquad (\partial x_i / \partial y_i)(\partial x_j / \partial y_j) - (\partial x_i / \partial y_j)^2 > 0 , \ldots, \text{ and so on.}$$

$$\tag{6.13}$$

4. A maximum problem like (6.9) or (6.6) is known to be subject to the Le Chatelier-Samuelson inequalities. Therefore, we get as a bonus the Marshall-Hicks principle of derived demand: "The demand for labor will be more elastic if the supply of land responds elastically to any change in its price induced by a rise in wage." That is:

$$0 > \left(\frac{\partial x_1}{\partial y_1} \right)_{x_2 = \bar{x}_2} \geqslant \left(\frac{\partial x_1}{\partial y_1} \right)_{y_2 = \bar{y}_2} \qquad n \geqslant 2 \tag{6.14}$$

If space permitted, the analysis of Samuelson (1960) could be used to derive various generalizations of these shorter run and "rationing" phenomena, only a sampling of which is provided in sections 6A-4 and 6A-5 of the mathematical appendix to this chapter.

Throughout the rest of this chapter, I shall derive various duality and equilibrium relations. The nonmathematical reader may wish to skim some of this material. Let me call the attention of any parting guests to the fact that this one-industry model could be easily generalized to the case of a cluster of industries that use the same inputs. Thus, replace $p = P[q(\mathbf{x})]$ by

$$p_s = Y_s[q_1, \ldots, q_m] \qquad (s = 1, \ldots, m)$$

$$= \partial Y[\mathbf{q}]/\partial q_s \qquad\qquad (6.15.1)$$

where $Y[\mathbf{q}]$ is a definable "payoff" function measured in utils.

$$q_s = Q^s(x_{1s}, x_{2s}, \ldots) \equiv m^{-1} Q^s(mx_{1s}, mx_{2s}, \ldots) \qquad (6.15.2)$$

and so on. Then (6.4.1) and (6.9) can be replaced by

$$\text{Max}_{x_{is}} \left\{ Y[Q^1(x_{11}, \ldots), Q^2(x_{12}, \ldots), \ldots] - y_1 \sum_{s=1}^{m} x_{1s} - y_2 \sum_{s=1}^{m} x_{2s} - \ldots \right\}$$

$$= -X(y_1, y_2, \ldots) \qquad (6.16.1)$$

$$x_i = x_{i1} + x_{i2} + \ldots = \partial X(y_1, y_2, \ldots)/\partial y_i \qquad (i = 1, 2, \ldots) \quad (6.16.2)$$

$$[X_{ij}(\mathbf{y})] \text{ negative definite} \qquad (6.16.3)$$

The function dual to $X(y)$ of (6.16.1) can be defined as $Y(\Sigma_1^m x_{1s}, \Sigma_1^m x_{2s}, \ldots)$, which is an aggregate function for the complex of industries.

Pursuing this line we shall reach the model of general equilibrium of Samuelson (1968), which tries to embrace the intercommodity substitutions of Machlup (1935) and achieves its greatest simplicity when all consumers have uniform homothetic tastes. (Those who skip the mathematical appendix to this chapter may perhaps still want to look at its concluding section.)

Methodological Caveats

To say, "Total revenue for a firm or industry rises when it raises price if and only if it has elasticity of demand less than unity in absolute value," is not to assert a true or false empirical proposition. Repeating the tautological *definition* of "Marshallian demand elasticity" in the above manner is useful, at best, in its *implicit* suggestion that Gregory King was correct in his noting that, "In the real world, demand may be *either in*elastic or *elastic* (and, in seventeenth-century England, tended for grain to be inelastic)."

In what sense is the following Robinson-Allen proposition useful or interesting?

"Cross-elasticity has algebraic sign of 'Elasticity of Substitution minus Industry Demand Elasticity.'"

$$Ex_2/Ey_1 = k_2(\sigma_{12} - \eta) \tag{6.17}$$

where k_2 is the proportion of *total* factor incomes going to the second factor. Or, for q held constant, we have

$$(Ex_2/Ey_1)_{\bar{q}} = k_2\sigma_{12} \tag{6.18}$$

It is illusory to say, "The sign of σ_{12} 'explains' the sign of $(Ex_2/Ey_1)_{\bar{q}}$." They are essentially the same thing, and it is no "explanation" to give a thing as a cause for itself. The proposition in (6.17) has at least this use (although the interpretation I am about to give is late in being recognized). Since it can be shown that σ_{12} must be positive for $n = 2$ (and, for $n > 2$, must "average out" positive), one is at least alerted to the fact that (6.17) is of mixed sign and *could* be anything. We are warned against false dogmatism!

A second use comes from the fact that we *might* have *separate* knowledge about industry technology and industry market structure. When we know that demand for q is *very inelastic,* we can be sure that at least one factor has positive cross-elasticity with any factor whose price has changed; and, by Marshall-Hicks reasoning, we can bet that a factor's own-elasticity is low.

But, as Pigou (1934, p. 240) noted[7] in realistic despair, taxonomy only sets out for the asking the questions whose answers we'd like to know.

Far more useful than deductive propositions (which merely nominate for questioning questions that could be asked of the data) are testable and refutable hypotheses that can be proposed as descriptions of the regularities of the economic observables. Examples are the hypotheses of (6.13) that $\partial X_i(y)/\partial y_i < 0$ and $[\partial X_i(y)/\partial y_j]$ is a symmetric negative-definite matrix and that the testable relation (6.12) holds.

I doubt that Fritz Machlup agrees with my viewpoint. But let me illustrate it on what Hicks in *Value and Capital* (1939, p. 311) calls the Fundamental Equation of Value Theory (his capital letters). If a person with income M, facing prices $(p_1, \ldots, p_n)$, buys goods $(x_1, \ldots, x_n)$ satisfying the demand relations, $x_i = D^i(M; p_1, \ldots, p_n)$, with $\partial D^i( )/\partial p_j = D^i_j( )$ and $\partial D^i/\partial M = D^i_0( )$, then Hicks's "fundamental" relations take the form:

$$[D^i_j(M; \mathbf{p}) + D^j(M; \mathbf{p})D^i_0] = [x_{ij}( )] \tag{6.19}$$

where $[x_{ij}(\ )]$ is a symmetric matrix of "substitution terms" defined by the final n rows and columns of the inverse of the bordered matrix

$$\begin{bmatrix} 0 & p_j \\ p_i & u_{ij} \end{bmatrix}$$

where, at equilibrium,

$$\lambda p_i = u_i(\mathbf{x}) \qquad \sum_1^n p_j x_j = M$$

The equalities of (6.19) merely *name* the substitution terms defined on their right. At most, one might be led from (6.19) to realize that $(\partial U/\partial p_j)$ $+ x_j(\partial U/\partial M)$ vanishes, so that a change in p_j alone accompanied by a change in income, $dM/dp_j = x_j$, is truly "compensatory." But that is not a fact of fundamental interest for its own sake. What is fundamental is not the relation (6.19), but rather the simplicity relations and the inequalities that the matrix in (6.19) satisfies: we should speak of the "fundamental inequalities and symmetries of the theory of ordinal maximizing by a consumer," namely[8] that

$$\sum_1^n \sum_1^n z_i x_{ij}(M; \mathbf{p}) z_j < 0 \tag{6.20}$$

for *all* $\mathbf{z}$ *not* proportional to $\mathbf{p}/M$. Hence, $x_{11} < 0$, and so on.

If one must speak of a "fundamental equality," the best single one might be the equality of marginal utility per dollar spent in every use, which Stigler (1965, p. 85) attributes to Gossen and which implies (6.19). In my notation, and with various modern adaptations (such as omitting Gossen's additive-independence), it would become

$$\frac{u_1(\mathbf{x})}{p_1} = \ldots = \frac{u_n(\mathbf{x})}{p_n} = \frac{\sum_1^n x_j u_j(\mathbf{x})}{M} \tag{6.21}$$

But (and this is the view that I would urge on Machlup), (6.21) is fundamental precisely to the degree that it does give us the revealed-preference hypotheses of the matrix of (6.19), implied inequalities of (6.20).

My same point can be made less technically in connection with the supply response of a competitive firm facing unchanged factor prices. If its total cost curve is $C(q)$ and is convex, then almost everywhere the MC equality holds, $p = C'(q)$; this equality is useful to the degree that it provides us with the testable knowledge on supply response, $dq/dp > 0$ or $\Delta q \Delta p \geqslant 0$—a conclusion implied by the fact that $C''(q) > 0$ holds almost everywhere where the above equality holds.

Mathematical Appendix

6A-1. Duality and Homotheticity

To save space I shall from now on use mathematics more freely: equations will be numbered by sections. Returning to the one-good industry of Cournot and Marshall, I call attention to one special feature of (6.4) or (6.8) and (6.9) that results from the first-degree homogeneity of $Q(\mathbf{x})$: the function $Y(x_1, x_2, \ldots)$ has *homothetic* contours, whose slopes are constant when the ratios of the xs, as denoted for example by $\mathbf{x}/x_1$, are constant. That is,

$$y_i/y_1 = Y_i(\mathbf{x})/Y_1(\mathbf{x}) \equiv M^i(\mathbf{x}/x_1) \qquad (i = 2, \ldots) \qquad (6A.1.1)$$

It can then be shown that the dual function defined in (6.9.2) must also have homothetic contours, namely

$$x_i/x_1 = X_i(\mathbf{y}) \equiv M^{*i}(\mathbf{y}/y_1) \qquad (i = 2, \ldots) \qquad (6A.1.2)$$

We see this by solving (6A.1.1) uniquely for $\mathbf{x}/x_1$ in terms of $\mathbf{y}/y_1$.

It follows that we are entitled to rewrite $X(\mathbf{y})$ in a canonical form dual to $Y(\mathbf{x}) \equiv Y[Q(\mathbf{x})]$, namely as

$$X(y_1, y_2, \ldots) \equiv X[P(y_1, y_2, \ldots)] \qquad (6A.1.3.1)$$

where again the distinction between brackets and parentheses in $X(\ )$ and $X[\ ]$ is to be noted.

$$X_i(y_1, y_2, \ldots) \equiv X'[P(y_1, y_2, \ldots)] P_i(y_1, y_2, \ldots) \qquad (6A.1.3.2)$$

$$\equiv Q[P(y_1, y_2, \ldots)] P_i(y_1, y_2, \ldots) \qquad (6A.1.3.3)$$

where

$$p = P[q] \equiv X'[q]$$

$$q = P^{-1}[p] \equiv Q[p] \equiv X'[p] \qquad (6A.1.3.4)$$

$$P'[\ ]Q'[\ ] \equiv X''[\ ]Y''[\ ] \equiv 1$$

and where $P(y_1, y_2, \ldots)$ is the *production dual* to $Q(x_1, x_2, \ldots)$, namely the homogeneous-first-degree, concave *minimum-unit-cost-of-production* function, defined by Shephard (1953) and others as

$$P(y_1, y_2, \ldots) \equiv \text{Min}_{x_i} \frac{y_1 x_1 + y_2 x_2 + \ldots}{Q(x_1, x_2, \ldots)} \qquad (6A.1.4.1)$$

$$Q(x_1, x_2, \ldots) \equiv \text{Min}_{y_i} \frac{x_1 y_1 + x_2 y_2 + \ldots}{P(y_1, y_2, \ldots)} \qquad (6A.1.4.2)$$

$$Q_i(x) = y_i/p \qquad P_i(y) = x_i/q \qquad (6A.1.4.3)$$

To exploit this production duality within the framework of overall industry duality, we note that (6.9) can be rewritten in a form more symmetric between quantities and prices, (x_j, q) and (y_j, p), namely

$$\text{Max}_{x_i} \left\{ Y[Q(x_1, x_2, \ldots)] - y_1 x_1 - y_2 x_2 - \ldots \right\}$$

$$= -X[P(y_1, y_2, \ldots)] \equiv - \int_{P[q^0]}^{P(y)} Q[p] \, dp$$

$$(6A.1.5.1)$$

$$\text{Max}_{y_i} \left\{ X[P(y_1, y_2, \ldots)] - x_1 y_1 - x_2 y_2 - \ldots \right\}$$

$$= -Y[Q(x_1, x_2, \ldots)] \qquad (6A.1.5.2)$$

where $P[q]$ and $Q[p]$ are the inverse and dual functions already noted in (6A.1.3.4).

Remark: For $n = 1$, and with $Q(x_1) \equiv x_1$, we trivially have in $Y[Q(x_1)]$ $\equiv Y[x_1]$ and $X[P(y_1)] \equiv X[y_1]$, respectively, the area vertically under the demand curve and the negative of the consumer-surplus area measured to the left of the demand curve.

The extremal first-order maximum conditions provide Legendre transformation relations of duality

$$Y[Q(x)] + X[P(y)] \equiv \sum_{1}^{n} y_j x_j \qquad (6A.1.5.3)$$

for

$$y_i = Y_i(x) = Y'[Q(x)] Q_i(x) \qquad x_i = X_i(y) = X'[P(y)] P_i(y)$$

$$(6A.1.5.4)$$

Also

$$\partial Y[\ ]/\partial\alpha + \partial X[\ ]/\partial\alpha \equiv 0 \qquad (6A.1.5.5)$$

if α is a parameter in $Y[Q(x;\alpha);\alpha]$ and $X[P(x;\alpha);\alpha]$.

Since $X_i(y)$ and $Y_i(x)$ are inverse functions, their Jacobians must be inverse matrices. For I, the identity matrix,

$$I = [\partial x_i/\partial y_j][\partial y_i/\partial x_j]$$

$$\equiv [X_{ij}(y)][Y_{ij}(x)] \qquad (6A.1.5.6)$$

$$\equiv [X'[P]P_{ij} + X''[P]P_iP_j][Y'[Q]Q_{ij} + Y''[Q]Q_iQ_j]$$

where, as indicated in (6A.1.3.4),

$$X''[\ ]Y''[\ ] = 1 \qquad (6A.1.5.7)$$

for (p, q) equilibrium pairings. Also,

$$[\partial x_i/\partial y_j] \equiv [X_{ij}(y)] \equiv [X_{ij}(y)]^T \qquad (6A.1.5.8)$$

and so on; where A^T is the transpose of the matrix A. Of course, in (6A.1.5.7), a similar symmetry holds for $[\partial y_i/\partial x_j]$. In (6A.1.5.6), $[\partial \log x_i/\partial \log y_j]$ and $[\partial \log y_i/\partial \log x_j]$ must also be inverses; but these last dual elasticity matrices, which it is often convenient to write as $[Ex_i/Ey_j]$ and $[Ey_i/Ex_j]$, will obviously not be symmetric.

6A-2. Duality and Elasticities-of-Substitution-or-Complementarity

For $n \geqslant 2$, the Allen (1938, pp. 503-9) *partial elasticities*, $[\sigma_{ij}]$, are useful. Exploiting duality theory, Sato and Koizumi (1973a) give appropriate modification to the related $[s_{ij}]$ definitions suggested in Hicks (1970). In my notation, which uses σ_{ij}^* for the 1973 c_{ij} coefficients, we have the dual families of coefficients:

$$\sigma_{ij}(y/y_1) = \frac{P(y)P_{ij}(y)}{P_i(y)P_j(y)} = \sigma_{ji}(y/y_1) \qquad (6A.2.1)$$

$$\sigma_{ij}^*(x/x_1) = \frac{Q(x)Q_{ij}(x)}{Q_i(x)Q_{ij}(x)} = \sigma_{ji}^*(x/x_1) \qquad (6A.2.2)$$

For $n = 2$, it can be shown that $\sigma_{12}(y/y_1)\sigma_{12}^*(x/x_1) = 1$ for equilibrium pairings of $(y/y_1, x/x_1)$. For $n = 3$, Hicks (1970) shows how $[\sigma_{ij}]$ and $[\sigma_{ij}^*]$ can be related.

Earlier, Allen (1938) related his $\sigma_{ij}(y/y_1)$ to the bordered matrices of $Q(x)$ for any n. Sato and Koizumi (1973a, equations 13) relate these coefficients by means of dual bordered determinants.

Here I shall present an alternative procedure, one that avoids bordered determinants and is capable of dealing directly with either the industry problem or with the $[\sigma_{ij}]$ and $[\sigma_{ij}^*]$ relationships for their own sake. My exposition goes as follows:

$$\sigma_{ij}(y/y_1) = [y_j P_{ij}/P_i]\,[y_j P_j/P]^{-1}$$

$$= \left[\frac{\partial \log P_i}{\partial \log y_j}\right] k_j^{-1}$$

$$= \frac{\partial[\log x_i + \log q]}{k_j\, \partial \log y_j} \tag{6A.2.3}$$

by the duality of (6A.1.4.3)

$$= [k_j^{-1} Ex_i/Ey_j] + [(Eq/Ep)(k_j/k_j)]$$

$$= k_j^{-1}(Ex_iEy_j) + (Eq/Ep) \tag{6A.2.4}$$

$$[Ex_i/Ey_j] = [\sigma_{ij} + (Eq/Ep)]k_j$$

Note that (6A.2.4) is precisely the Allen-Robinson relation of (6.17), derived here without explicit inversion of any matrix relations.

In duality's usual two-for-the-price-of-one way, we immediately write down the counterpart of (6A.2.3) and (6A.2.4) as applied to σ_{ij}^*, namely

$$[Ey_i/Ex_j] = [\sigma_{ij}^* + (Ep/Eq)]k_j \tag{6A.2.5}$$

Note that use has been made of the fact that (Ep/Eq) is dual to (Eq/Ep).

Since (6A.2.4) and (6A.2.5) are inverse matrices, our avoiding bordered determinants gives us the following infinity of relations between $[\sigma_{ij}]$ and $[\sigma_{ij}^*]$,

$$[\sigma_{ij}k_j + \lambda k_j]\,[\sigma_{ij}^* k_j + \lambda^{-1}k_j] \underset{\lambda}{\equiv} I \tag{6A.2.6}$$

Since (6A.2.6) holds for any negative λ, it must hold for the simplest case where industry has *unitary* elasticity of demand: $P[q] = a/q, Eq/Ep = -1, Ep/Eq$

$= 1/(-1) = -1$. This gives us $n \times n$ unbordered matrices convenient for relating the dual families of elasticities:

$$[(\sigma_{ij} - 1)k_j] [(\sigma_{ij}^* - 1)k_j] = I \qquad (6A.2.7)$$

We can check by considering the Cobb-Douglas case where $Q(\mathbf{x})$ and $P(\mathbf{y})$ are self-dual. For this case, (6A.2.6) becomes $(-I\lambda)(-I\lambda^{-1}) = I$.

6A-3. Polar Cases of Zero or Infinite Elasticity of Industry Demand

For completeness, one may analyze these limiting cases to relate the above analysis to the bordered matrices of Allen (1938) and Sato and Koizumi (1973a). First, note that we can write down by duality (6.18) and its dual counterpart, each respectively corresponding to $Eq/Ep = 0$ and $Ep/Eq = 0$.

$$(Ex_i/Ey_j)_{\bar{q}} = \sigma_{ij}(y/y_1)k_j \qquad (6A.3.1)$$

$$(Ey_i/Ex_j)_{\bar{p}} = \sigma_{ij}^*(x/x_1)k_j \qquad (6A.3.2)$$

Consider inverse systems relating $(p, x_1, \ldots, x_n)$ and $(q, p_1, \ldots, p_n)$, where I replace $\mathbf{y}$ by $\mathbf{p}$ to emphasize that this section deals only with polar cases. If we adopt the convenient convention of writing $x_0 = p$ and $p_0 = q$, we have:

$$Q(x_1, \ldots, x_n) = p_0$$
$$x_0 Q_i(x_1, \ldots, x_n) = p_i \qquad (i = 1, \ldots, n) \qquad (6A.3.3)$$

By duality, the inverse to (6A.3.3) takes the form

$$P(p_1, \ldots, p_n) = x_0$$
$$p_0 P_i(p_1, \ldots, p_n) = x_i \qquad (i = 1, \ldots, n) \qquad (6A.3.4)$$

These pairs of relations make no use of the industry's demand curve, $P[q]$ or $Q[p] = P^{-1}[p]$.

It is easy to verify that the following are line integrals (of *exact* differentials) that are independent of path.

$$\int \sum_0^n p_j dx_j = \int d\{x_0 Q(x_1, \ldots, x_n)\} \qquad (6A.3.5)$$

$$(\partial p_0/\partial x_{0+j}) \equiv Q_{0+j}(\mathbf{x}) \equiv (\partial P_{0+j}/\partial x_0) \qquad (j = 1, \ldots, n)$$
$$(6A.3.6)$$
$$(\partial p_{0+i}/\partial x_{0+j}) \equiv Q_{ij}(\mathbf{x}) \equiv (\partial p_{0+j}/\partial x_{0+i}) \qquad (i, j = 1, \ldots, n)$$

$$\int \sum_0^n x_j \, dp_j = \int d\{p_0 P(p_1, \ldots, p_n)\} \qquad (6A.3.7)$$

And so on, as in (6A.3.6).

So (6A.3.3) and (6A.3.4) are related dually by a Legendre transformation:

$$\mathrm{Min}_{x_0}\mathrm{Max}_{x_i}\left\{x_0 Q(x_1, \ldots, x_n) - p_0 x_0 - \sum_1^n p_j x_j\right\}$$

$$= p_0 P(p_1, \ldots, p_n) = qP(\mathbf{p})$$

$$(6A.3.8)$$

$$\mathrm{Min}_{p_0}\mathrm{Max}_{p_i}\left\{p_0 P(p_1, \ldots, p_n) - x_0 p_0 - \sum_1^n x_j p_j\right\}$$

$$= q_0 Q(x_1, \ldots, x_n) = pQ(\mathbf{x})$$

$$(6A.3.9)$$

$$[x_i] = [\partial\{p_0 P(p_1, \ldots, p_n)\}/\partial p_i] \qquad (i = 0, 1, \ldots, n)$$
$$= \mathrm{grad}\{p_0 P(\mathbf{p})\}$$
$$[p_i] = [\partial\{x_0 Q(x_1, \ldots, x_n)\}/\partial x_i] \qquad (i = 0, 1, \ldots, n)$$
$$(6A.3.10)$$
$$= \mathrm{grad}\{x_0 Q(\mathbf{x})\}$$

$$\begin{bmatrix} 0 & Q_j \\ Q_i & Q_{ij} \end{bmatrix} \begin{bmatrix} 0 & P_j \\ P_i & P_{ij} \end{bmatrix} \equiv I \qquad (6A.3.11)$$

From (6A.3.11) and the definitions of σ_{ij} and σ_{ij}^*, we can derive

$$\begin{bmatrix} 0 & 1 & \cdots & 1 \\ 1 & & & \\ \cdot & & & \\ \cdot & \sigma_{ij}^*(x/x_1) & \\ 1 & & & \end{bmatrix} \begin{bmatrix} 1 & 0 & \cdots & 0 \\ 0 & & & \\ \cdot & & & \\ \cdot & k_j \delta_{ij} & \\ 0 & & & \end{bmatrix} \begin{bmatrix} 0 & 1 & \cdots & 1 \\ 1 & & & \\ \cdot & & & \\ \cdot & \sigma_{ij}(p/p_1) & \\ 1 & & & \end{bmatrix} \begin{bmatrix} 1 & 0 & \cdots & 0 \\ 0 & & & \\ \cdot & & & \\ \cdot & k_j \delta_{ij} & \\ 0 & & & \end{bmatrix} = I$$

$$(6A.3.12)$$

These are essentially the bordered-matrix relations of Sato and Koizumi (1973a, equations 13).

Remark: Either of the polar cases, zero elasticity of industry demand or infinite elasticity, results in a degeneracy of determinateness. When $Eq/Ep = 0$, factor inputs x cannot all be independently inelastic in supply to the industry; even when $(x_1, \ldots, x_n, q)$ are compatibly given to the industry, p is not determinate and neither is the absolute level of $(y_1, \ldots, y_n)$; only price ratios, (y_j/y_1) or (y_j/p) are then determinate. Dually, when industry demand is infinitely elastic (as in a one-product Solow-Douglas economy), all factor prices cannot be in real terms *independently* prescribed to the industry: when $(y_1, \ldots, y_n)$ are prescribed consistent with the factor-price frontier relation, $1 = P(y/p)$, the scale of q and of $(x_1, \ldots, x_n)$ is indeterminate; only the ratios, (x_j/x_1) and (x_j/q) are then determinate. It is interesting to analyze "mixed" cases where some factor prices are given to the industry, $(y_1, \ldots, y_r)$, $1 \leqslant r < n$; and where the remaining set of factor quantities are given to the industry, $(x_{r+1}, \ldots, x_n)$, $1 \leqslant n - r < n$. Then the remaining variables $(x_1, \ldots, x_r;$ $y_{r+1}, \ldots, y_n : p, q)$ are determinate in all cases, even in the polar cases of zero or infinite industry elasticity. The next section analyzes the case of mixed variables.

6A-4. Factor-supply Responses and Le Chatelier Principle

It is customary to consider more and more inputs as fixed in the short run. As the run is made longer and longer, less and less such inputs are fixed, their prices instead being given as constants to a small industry.

Consider

$$x_i = X_i(y_1, \ldots, y_n) \qquad (i = 1, \ldots, n)$$

with partitioned Jacobian matrix

$$J_n = \begin{bmatrix} \alpha & \beta \\ \beta' & \gamma \end{bmatrix} \qquad (6A.4.1)$$

where α is a symmetric negative definite matrix, γ is a $(n - r) \times (n - r)$ negative definite matrix; and where J_n is itself a symmetric negative definite matrix.

Consider the alternative *mixed* set of relations

$$x_i = X^i(y_1, \ldots, y_r; x_{r+1}, \ldots, x_n) \qquad (i = 1, \ldots, r \geqslant 1)$$

$$\equiv X_i(y_1, \ldots, y_r; x_{r+1}, \ldots, x_n)$$

$$(6A.4.2)$$

$$y_i = X^i(y_1, \ldots, y_r; x_{r+1}, \ldots, x_n) \qquad (i = r+1, \ldots, n > r)$$

$$\equiv -X_i(y_1, \ldots, y_r; x_{r+1}, \ldots, x_n)$$

where $X(y_1, \ldots, y_r; x_{r+1}, \ldots, x_n)$ is an existent "potential" function, whose semicolon serves to distinguish it from $X(y_1, \ldots, y_n)$ of (6.9.2). The Jacobian matrix of the relation of (6A.4.2) can be shown to be expressible in terms of the submatrices of J_n, as in Samuelson (1960), namely as

$$J_r = \begin{bmatrix} \alpha - \beta'\gamma^{-1}\beta & -\gamma^{-1}\beta \\ \beta'\gamma^{-1} & \gamma^{-1} \end{bmatrix}$$

$$= \begin{bmatrix} I & 0 \\ \hline 0 & -I \end{bmatrix} [\partial^2 X(\mathbf{z})/\partial z_i \partial z_j]$$

(6A.4.3)

where $\mathbf{z} = (y_1, \ldots, y_r; x_{r+1}, \ldots, x_n)$.

Since γ is negative definite, so must be γ^{-1}. Therefore, the diagonal coefficients of J_r can be shown to be negative (this even though J_r is not itself a negative definite matrix!). We infer that $\alpha - \beta'\gamma^{-1}\beta$ is negative definite since it is dual to γ^{-1}, which is negative definite. We also infer the symmetry of the terms $+\partial x_i/\partial x_{r+j}$ and $-\partial y_{r+j}/\partial y_i$.

One way of expressing the generalized Le Chatelier principle is to note that a quadratic form made up of α is "more negative (if anything)" than one made up of $\alpha - \beta'\gamma^{-1}\beta$. Hence, as r drops from n to ever lower values in the shorter run, we have

$$(\partial x_i/\partial y_i)_n \leqslant (\partial x_i/\partial y_i)_{n-1} \leqslant \ldots \leqslant (\partial x_i/\partial y_i)_r \qquad (i < r < n)$$

(6A.4.4)

For $n = 2$, γ is a scalar and $\beta'\gamma^{-1} \equiv (\partial y_2/\partial x_1)_{\bar{x}_2}$ must agree in sign with $(\partial x_2/\partial y_1)_{\bar{y}_2} = \beta' \equiv \beta$, just as was already indicated in connection with the mention in note 6 of the Nelson (1957) unconscious rediscovery of the Robinson (1933) cross-elasticity sign criterion.

6A-5. Effects of Supply Elasticity of Factors

Marshall (1920, pp. 385-7, 853, Note XV) gave the classic analysis of the four conditions that make for elastic demand, Ex_i/Ey_i in our notation. Hicks (1932, 241-6) gave the definitive discussion of these four conditions, correcting

Marshall's erroneous belief that low k_i will always reduce $|Ex_i/Ey_i|$ (even when the elasticity of substitution exceeds $|Eq/Ep|$, which is false).

Our present discussion throws light on the third condition, which points out that $|Ex_i/Ep_i|$ will be greater when the elasticity of supply for x_i is positive and great. $X_1(p_1; x_2)$ in (6A.4.2) corresponds to zero-elastic supply of x_2, while $X_1(p_1, p_2)$ corresponds to infinite-elastic supply of x_2; the Le Chatelier principle thus guarantees the correctness of Marshall's third condition as applied to extreme polar cases. I can now indicate briefly how intermediate degrees of positive supply elasticity in (6.3) will accord with the Marshall-Hicks third rule. (Space does not permit full treatment of the general case where the supply relation for x_2 may have a negative slope, as with "backward-bending" and "forward-falling" supply; nor does the question of *proper* "stability conditions" receive in note 1 of the appendix the full treatment it needs.)

Equation (6.3) made the supply of x_2 to an industry depend only on y_2, and not on other y_j, which does seem rather special. However, this is usually done in the literature and that lends interest to such an assumption.

Let (6.3) be written as a *rising* supply relation

$$y_i = \pi_i + s_i'(x_i) \qquad s_i' > 0 \qquad (6A.5.1)$$

Here $(\pi_1, \ldots, \pi_n)$ are parameters of upward-vertical shifts of the respective supply schedules. The integrals of $s_i'(x_i)$ are defined by

$$s_i(x_i) = \int_{x_i^0}^{x_i} s_i'(t)\, dt \qquad (6A.5.2)$$

We again have a maximum formulation

$$\mathrm{Max}_{x_i}\left\{ Y(x_1, \ldots, x_n) - \sum_1^n \pi_j x_j - \sum_1^n s_j(x_j) \right\}$$

$$= Y(\mathbf{x}^*) - \sum_1^n \pi_j x_j^* - \sum_1^n s_j(x_j^*) \qquad (6A.5.3)$$

$$= -X(\pi_1, \ldots, \pi_n)$$

where the optimal amounts demanded satisfy the gradient relations

$$Y_i(x_1, \ldots, x_n) - s_i'(x_i) = \pi_i \qquad (i = 1, \ldots, n) \qquad (6A.5.4)$$

$$x_i = X_i(\pi_1, \ldots, \pi_n) \qquad (6A.5.5)$$

For brevity, write $(\partial x_i/\partial \pi_j) = (\dot{x}_{ij})$, a symmetric matrix by virtue of (6A.5.3) through (6A.5.5). Then the linear equations satisfied by $\dot{x}_{ij}$ are seen to be

$$[Y_{ij} - s_j''\delta_{ij}][\dot{x}_{ij}] = I \qquad (6A.5.6)$$

where $[\delta_{ij}] = I$.

It is now easy to verify the Marshall-Hicks rule that, "Increased supply elasticity of x_2, which means *lower* positive s_i'', will increase own-demand elasticity for factor 1, $|\partial x_1/\partial \pi_1|$ (or $|\partial x_1/\partial y_1|$ if $s_1'' \equiv 0$)."

Straightforward differentiation of $\dot{x}_{11}$ with respect to s_2'' in (6A.5.6) leads, as in Dorfman, Samuelson, and Solow (1958, p. 254) to

$$\partial(-\dot{x}_{11})/\partial s_2'' = -\dot{x}_{12}\dot{x}_{21} = -\dot{x}_{12}^2 \leqslant 0 \qquad (6A.5.7)$$

Here, a change in s_2'' is thought of as a change in the supply slope of the curve going through the same (unchanged) equilibrium point.

Thus, we verify for $n \geqslant 2$ the Marshall-Hicks third rule, in agreement with Sato and Koizumi (1970). Hicks (1932, p. 245) did not mention the fact brought out in (6A.5.7) that the effect can be *zero* in the case where $\dot{x}_{12} = 0$ (as in Mrs. Robinson's case where $\sigma = \eta$). Likewise in Sato and Koizumi (1970, pp. 111–12), $\partial\lambda/\partial e_j > 0$ would seem to be better if written as $\partial\lambda/\partial e_j \geqslant 0$. We may also note that, even when the supply curve is forward-falling[1] with $s_2''(x_2)$ < 0, the third rule may still apply. Indeed, even when we have a steeply backward-bending supply curve, with s_2'' near negative infinity and the maximizing formulation vitiated, we may still opportunistically predict that $\dot{x}_{11}$ will be near to that given by $(\partial x_1/\partial y_1)_{\bar{x}_2}$ and that Marshall's third rule is still operative.

6A-6. Machlup's 1935 Discussion

The present notation can clear up any questions left open in Machlup (1935). I follow his Roman numeral sectioning.

I. Here he considers exclusively a single output that, in effect, constitutes the whole (macro- *and* micro-) economy: $q = Q(x_1, x_2) \equiv m^{-1}Q(mx_1, mx_2)$, where x_1 and x_2 are labor and ("homogeneous") "capital," each *inelastic in supply.* Labor's share in total product is $k_1 = x_1 Q_1(x_1, x_2)/Q(x_1, x_2)$, with capital's share, $k_2 = 1 - k_1$.

To study how a change in x_1 alone, or in x_1/x_2, alters k_1, his diagram at the bottom of page 204 unfortunately implicitly defines an elasticity of substitution that is a variant of that of Hicks (1932) and of the equivalent definition of Robinson (1933): their coefficient measures the change in $k_1/(1 - k_1)$ whereas Machlup's measures the change in k_1 alone. Obviously, when k_1 is unchanged, all three coefficients are unity. Machlup's measure, call it σ_M to contrast it from $\sigma_H = \sigma_R$, has the virtue that sign $[\sigma_M - 1]$ = sign $[\sigma_H - 1]$. Thus, for the Cobb-Douglas case of $x_1^{3/4} x_2^{1/4}$, all three σs are unity; but for the CES family, $[a_1 x_1^\gamma + a_2 x_2^\gamma]^{1/\gamma}, 1 > \gamma \neq 0$, σ_H and σ_R are constants equal to $(1 - \gamma)^{-1}$, but $\sigma_M - 1$ varies with k_1 and x_2/x_1 although agreeing in sign with $(1 - \gamma)^{-1} - 1$. It can be verified that $\sigma_H - 1 = (\sigma_M - 1)[1 + (k_1/k_2)(\sigma_M - 1)]k_1$. Since Machlup never actually proposes using his diagram's σ_M except as a test of when $\sigma_H = 0$, 1, or ∞, I shall ignore its difference with σ_H and the complications thereby encountered in M. Friedman (1936).

II. Under Machlup's one-good economy, we can provide for him his desired relation between labor-demand-elasticity and the elasticity of substitution: when $x_2 = \bar{x}_2$ and $Eq/Ep = -\infty$,

$$(-Ex_1/Ep_1) = \sigma_{12}/(1 - k_1) > \sigma_{12} = \sigma_H = \sigma_R \qquad (6A.6.1)$$

This agrees with the general formula in Hicks (1932, p. 244), being a special case of it.

Machlup's concern lest σ_H and σ_R be different coefficients can be put completely to rest when $n = 2$ and Q is homogeneous-first-degree.

Robinson (1933, p. 260) was merely meaning to enunciate a correct conclusion:

$$\text{sign of } [(-Ex_1/Ey_1) - \sigma_{12}] = \text{sign of } [\sigma_{12} - (-Eq/Ep)]$$
$$= \text{sign of } [Ex_2/Ey_1] \qquad (6A.6.2)$$

Equation (6A.6.2) is clearly implied by Hicks (1963, p. 374, equation 4). It agrees with (6A.6.1) when $(-Eq/Ep) = \infty$. If elasticity of supply of x_2 is allowed to be positive, the equality in (6A.6.1) should be replaced by ">". Again, all this agrees with Hicks (1932, p. 244).

Machlup (1935, p. 205) rightly chides Douglas (1934, p. 133) for liking elasticity of labor demand while disliking elasticity of substitution: after all, (6A.6.1) does relate them.

III. Machlup (1935, p. 206) rightly points out that agreement in sign of $\partial[k_1 Q]/\partial(x_1/x_2)$ and $[(Ex_1/Ey_1) - 1]$ provides no "explanation," but is merely a reiteration. He nods, however, in thinking that a large value of σ_{12} in $\sigma_{12}/(1 - k_1)$ provides a *deeper* "explanation." Actually, one can invert (6A.6.1) and write $\sigma_{12} = (1 - k_1)(-Ex_1/Ey_1)$. It is no better—but, notice, *no worse!*—to "explain" large σ_{12} by large $(-Ex_1/Ey_1)$ than vice versa. Actually, in the relation $y_1/p = Q_1(x_1/x_2, 1) = f(x_1/x_2)$, there is but one *empirical* function involved:

its properties we can point to, but they are their own "explanation" or "description."

IV, V, VI. Here, Machlup relaxes his one-product assumption. He considers in a vague way many products and the *intercommodity* substitutions that an increase in total x_1 will generate when $\bar{x}_2$ is constant.

To illustrate Machlup's insistence on intercommodity substitution, consider the following special case of Samuelson (1968, Part II). Three goods, corn, cotton, and ballet, are produced by labor and land. (Avoid "capital" to avoid its extraneous complications.) Cobb-Douglas functions characterize each industry: one-third corn cost *always* goes to wages; two-thirds cotton cost goes to wages; one hundred per cent of ballet costs goes to wages. Now suppose everyone spends equal thirds of income on each of the three goods.

What will a Kuznets observe of this "macro" economy? *Always* two-thirds of national income goes to wages and one-third to land rent.[2] It is *precisely as if* a Solow-Douglas production function holds for the macroeconomy—
$\bar{q} = (\Sigma x_1)^{2/3}(\Sigma x_2)^{1/3}$.

Robinson (1936), Lerner (1936), and Hicks are correct to point out to Machlup that their *formal* σ measures—but now applied to some *aggregate* production function—still serve to show how aggregate wage share changes. But Machlup is right to insist, as Hicks (1963, p. 298) agreed, that the relevant coefficient of the aggregate function is a *complicated* function of both *intra*- and *inter*commodity substitutions.

We see this best when we leave Cobb-Douglas production functions behind. Suppose labor and land in *fixed proportions* produce the goods: 1 labor and 2 land for each 1 corn; 2 labor and 1 land for 1 cotton; 1 labor and 0 land for 1 ballet. Again, everyone spends one-third on each good. Then, for fixed totals of labor and land, $\Sigma x_1 = L$ and $\Sigma x_2 = T$, *everything* is determinate (relative shares, relative prices, quantities, etc.).

Thus, begin with 300 labor and 150 land. It can be shown that 50 labor and 100 land produce 50 corn; 100 labor and 50 land produce 50 cotton; 150 labor produce 150 ballets. Each corn and each cotton is three times as dear as each ballet. Again, what Kuznets *initially* observes is two-thirds to wages and one-third to rents.

But now increase the labor supply—say from 300 to 301 or to 400 or to 3 million. To get it all "absorbed," Machlup correctly insists that *only* intercommodity substitutions can do the trick when technical substitutability is zero. And here it can do the trick!

Higher L/T means lower Wage/Rent, W/R. It means cheapening of ballet most; but, also, some cheapening of cotton relative to corn. All the relatively labor-using goods have their physical demands expanded: when W/R falls enough, the new equilibrium is achieved. Note that Kuznets records a *drop* in the aggregate share of labor $\bar{\alpha}$. Evidently the *overall* $\bar{\sigma}$ is less than one.[3] (Why does $\bar{\alpha}$

drop? Why is $\bar{\sigma} < 1$? Because lowered W/R lowers α_j for corn, cotton, and all industries using both factors: hence $(\alpha_1 + \alpha_2 + \alpha_3)/3$ falls.)

The reader can verify that increasing T/L, from 150/300 to 0.51 or to 1 or to 3 will lower R/W and land-rent's share. Indeed, when land is more than twice labor (which is the maximum ratio used in *any* industry), land becomes redundant in supply and a free good with zero share in income. Again, $\bar{\sigma} < 1$.

My assumption of uniform-homothetic tastes is needed if I am to reduce Machlup's general equilibrium to the case of an aggregate production function for all of society. But, in general, my assumption is too strong a one for realistic economic theory. Machlup would be quite right to insist that general equilibrium is more complicated than in this model.

VII. This leads to, and justifies, Machlup's questioning the necessary symmetry, in qualitative sign or algebraic quantity, of the effect on factor shares of an increase in labor or an increase in land (the *other* factor in my exposition).

Lerner (1936) never met Machlup's valid point. Instead Lerner concentrated on a banality: any arc elasticity between A and B, call it $(\log a - \log b)/(\log \alpha - \log \beta)$ is of course the same as between B and A; we need only reverse signs consistently, or work with instantaneous derivatives $d \log t/d \log \theta$ and not care about the direction in which the slope is traversed. What Lerner never faced up to was the fact that, (1) once we leave the two-input first-degree-homogeneous case, or (2) increase the number of goods and number of people with different tastes, (3) we no longer end up with a *single* relation between factor-price and factor-quantity ratios and (4) we certainly can not any longer calculate the change in $\bar{\alpha}_1$ from a coefficient definable only along an (one!) isoquant.

Thus, suppose we find W/R is a function of total labor and total land and *not* of their ratio. The *single* curve relating W/R and L/T along which Lerner purports to measure Marshallian elasticity simply does not exist. So, Lerner ought to have agreed with Machlup's point that $\partial \bar{\alpha}/\partial L$ and $\partial(1 - \bar{\alpha})/\partial T$ need not even be of the same sign.

VIII. Let me add that when one comes to generalize σ to $(\sigma_1, \sigma_2, \ldots, \sigma_n)$ in the n-factor case, as in Samuelson (1968, Part I), one confirms Machlup's denial that $\sigma_1 = \sigma_2 = \ldots = \sigma_n$ necessarily.[4]

What Schumpeter would call the general "vision" of Machlup's 1935 article has been seen to be fully vindicated by the present investigation.

Notes

1. Strictly speaking, if the industry's demand price, $p = P[q]$, is measured in $/q$, then the $Y[q]$ of (6.8) will be measured in $. The "real" meaning of such $ will depend upon what Cournot-Marshall presuppose in their partial equilibrium

analysis. My own taste is for not defending partial equilibrium, but for reaching past it toward a more general equilibrium.

2. There is no single standard notation. Hicks (1932, 1963, 1970) uses $(a, b, \ldots; p_a, p_b, \ldots; x, p_x, \ldots)$ or $(a_1, a_2, \ldots; p_1, p_2, \ldots; x, p_x, \ldots)$ where I here use $(x_1, x_2, \ldots; y_1, y_2, \ldots; q, p)$. Using capital letters to denote a function, as in $q = Q(x_1, x_2, \ldots)$, I use subscripts in $Q_i(\ )$ and $Q_{ij}(\ )$ to represent $\partial Q(x_1, x_2, \ldots)/\partial x_i$ and $\partial^2 Q(x_1, x_2, \ldots)/\partial x_i \partial x_j$; for brevity, I sometimes write $Q(x_1, x_2, \ldots)$ as $Q(\mathbf{x})$, boldface representing vectors or matrices. The careful use of brackets, as against parentheses, rules out ambiguity in expressions such as $Y(x_1, x_2, \ldots) \equiv Y[Q(x_1, x_2, \ldots)]$ and $q = Q[p] \equiv Q[P(\mathbf{y})]$, or $Y_i(\mathbf{x}) \equiv Y'[Q(\mathbf{x})] Q_i(\mathbf{x})$. With good notation, one is able to write $y_i = Y_i(x_1, x_2, \ldots)$ and their inverse functions $x_i = X_i(y_1, y_2, \ldots)$ and, at equilibrium, $[X_{ij}(\mathbf{y})]^{-1} = [Y_{ij}(\mathbf{x})] \equiv [Y_{ji}(\mathbf{x})]$. Elasticities can be denoted by $Ep/Eq = d \log P/d \log q$, or $Ex_i/Ey_j = y_j X_{ij}(\mathbf{y})/X_i(\mathbf{y})$. Thus Ez is short for $dz/z = d \log z$ or for $\partial z/z$.

Warning: my (x_j) variables are *industry* input totals, not a firm's; my (y_j) variables are input prices, presumably in \$, and not real prices relative to the industry's p as numeraire. My demand relations do not hold industry q constant; nor do they assume infinite elasticity of industry demand such as would keep its price unchanged; these limiting poles can be approximated as I make the industry's elasticity of demand become almost 0 or almost infinite.

3. The attentive reader will realize that, if any firm were free to imitate the constant-returns $Q(\mathbf{x})$, entry would occur to deprive any one firm of its monopoly possession of the industry's demand curve: the only final industry equilibrium would be the competitive industry solution given by (6.4) rather than (6.5); the indeterminateness of interindustry allocation among zero-profit firms is of no importance, contrary to the apprehensions of Sraffa (1926), Kaldor (1934), and other post-Marshallian worriers. To make the present formal point, suppose entry is legally closed.

4. For $n = 2$, Hicks (1932, p. 244) had derived this result: in his notation, it would read, $-\lambda = \kappa(-\eta) + (1 - \kappa)(-\sigma) < 0$. To prove this for $n = 3$, Hicks (1963, 1970) uses the trick that inputs (2, 3) can be made into a composite single (Hicksian) input if their relative prices are frozen: and so $n = 2$ arguments suffice. Allen (1938, p. 508) gives formulas for this result for any n, utilizing symmetric bordered determinants and quasi-concavity conditions implied on them; and for cross-elasticities, Allen generalizes to $n \geq 2$ the Robinson-Nelson criteria about to come, namely replacing $\eta \gtrless \sigma$ by $\eta \gtrless \sigma_{ij}$.

5. Curiously, Hicks (1932, 1963, 1970) and later writers put no stress on these reciprocity conditions (which are *not* for any conscious firm decision maker). Perhaps the use of oversteemed Ex_1/Ey_j elasticities deflected attention from symmetry conditions. Allen (1938) gives formal results that point in the desired direction. And actually, if anyone had commented on the symmetry, $\partial\{P[\ ]Q(\ )\}/\partial x_i \equiv \partial\{P[\ ]Q(\ )\}/\partial x_j$, so that $\int \Sigma y_j dx_j$ is an exact line integral independent of the path that equilibrium moves along between endpoints,

the point would have been obvious without the industry maximand or any bordered matrices.

6. Here, in present notation, is a demonstration that Nelson's ratio of elasticities is precisely Hicks's elasticity of substitution,

$$AVC = \bar{y}_1 x_1 / Q(x_1, \bar{x}_2) \qquad MC = \bar{y}_1 \frac{\partial x_1}{\partial q} = \bar{y}_1 / Q_1(x_1, \bar{x}_2)$$

$$\frac{\text{Elas.}\, AVC}{\text{Elas.}\, MC} = \frac{[\partial \{\ln \bar{y}_1 + \ln x_1 - \ln Q(x_1, \bar{x}_2)\}/\partial \log x_1]}{[\partial \{\ln \bar{y}_1 - \ln Q_1(x_1, \bar{x}_2)\}/\partial \log x_1]} \frac{[\partial \log x_1 / \partial \log q]}{[\partial \log x_1 / \partial \log q]}$$

$$= \frac{1 - x_1 Q_1 Q^{-1}}{-x_1 Q_{11} Q^{-1}} = \frac{x_2 Q_2 Q^{-1}}{x_2 Q_{12} Q_1^{-1}}$$

using Euler's theorems

$$= \frac{Q_1 Q_2}{Q Q_{12}} = \sigma \text{ of 1932-3} \qquad\qquad Q.E.D.$$

It is easy to show that $(\partial x_2 / \partial y_1)$ with y_2 constant, Robinson's object of study, must for $n = 2$ have exactly the same algebraic sign as $(\partial y_2 / \partial y_1)$ with x_2 constant: one has only to apply the algebra of Samuelson (1960), or of (6A.4.3) in the appendix to this chapter.

7. The explanatory emptiness of taxonomic descriptions in terms of elasticity and elasticity-of-substitution coefficients was already forcefully argued in Marion E. Crawford's 1937 Radcliffe undergraduate honors thesis on the elasticity of substitution. A terse reprise of this truth reappears in Samuelson (1974).

8. Note that my quarrel with Hicks's language in no way demeans his accomplishment, but rather spotlights its true magnificence. For $n = 2$, the standard textbook case, the sole content of preference theory can be summed up by the two-variable demand function, $x_1 = D^1(P_1/M, P_2/M)$, which must be (a) nonnegative, (b) as also must be $1 - (p_1/M)D^1(p_1/M, p_2/M)$; then the *only* other requirement, stemming from $x_{11}(\ ) < 0$, is (c) that $[\partial \log x_1 / \partial \log p_1](1 - k_1) < k_1(\partial \log x_1 / \partial \log p_2)$. How many students know this? How many professors?

Notes

1. Some element of *monopoly* is probably present *outside* this industry if x_2 is supplied to it along a forward-falling supply curve. The case of a back-

ward-bending negatively sloped supply curve for x_2 could arise when owners of x_2 are choosing between it and leisure in a budget-constraint maximization problem offstage. If $0 > \partial x_2/\partial y_2 \gg -1$ along a steeply backward-bending supply curve, $s_2''(x_2)$ will be so greatly negative as to make $\partial^2 \{Y(x_1,x_2) -y_1x_1 -x_2 -s_2(x_2)\}/\partial x_2^2 > 0$, in violation of the industry's macimum achievement. Hence, $x_{22} = \partial x_2/\partial \pi_2$ would be "perversely" positive, "in violation" of some presumed (dynamic?) stability conditions. Yet Marshall's third rule would apply! When x_2's supply curve is negatively sloped, somewhere between the case of a gently forward-falling curve and the case of a steeply backward-bending one, we reach the critical point where $|Y_{ij} - s_j''\delta_{ij}|$ changes sign, making $[\partial x_i/\partial \pi_j]$ all go through infinity and change sign. (Remark: When a change in s_2'' is regarded as changing $\partial x_1/\partial y_1$, the exact meaning is murky; one useful interpretation is to imagine the supply curve of x_2 pivoting ever more steeply through the same previous equilibrium point (x_2, y_2), and then asking what this does to the slope of the demand curve for x_1 at the same old equilibrium point (x_1, y_1). The literature leaves all this in a hazy state.)

2. Explanation: $[(1/3) + (2/3) + (1)]/3 = 2/3$. The problem is only a bit more complicated if wages get spent in three fixed fractions different from rent's three fixed fractions. Thus, if wages are spent only on corn and land rents only on ballet, Kuznets will observe that three-fifths of national income always goes to wages (but now with no cotton produced). Let the wage shares in the industries be $(\alpha_1, \alpha_2, \alpha_3)$; the expenditure fractions of wage earners and retainers be $(\omega_1, \omega_2, \omega_3)$ and (ρ_1, ρ_2, ρ_3). Then the aggregate wage share, $\bar{\alpha}$, is given by $\Sigma_1^3 \rho_j \alpha_j/[1 - \Sigma_1^3 \omega_j \alpha_j + \Sigma_1^3 \rho_j \alpha_j] = [0 + 0 + 1]/[1 - 1/3 + 1] = 3/5$.

3. See Samuelson (1968, Equation 20) for the definitions of the *aggregate production function*, $\bar{q} = \bar{Q}(L, T)$ that Kuznets will find himself observing and for which Hicks could compute his $\bar{\sigma}$. Warning: Only if everyone has uniform homothetic tastes (albeit not necessarily of fixed-fractional-expenditure type) are we assured that such a nicely defined function exists. To prove it does, suppose as in Samuelson (1968, Part II), there are M industries, each with first-degree homogeneous, concave production functions: $q^m = Q^m(x_1^m, \ldots, x_n^m)$. Then subject to $\Sigma_1^M x_j^m \leqslant x_j$, maximize $u[q^1, \ldots, q^M] \equiv u[Q^1( ), \ldots, Q^M( )]$ and call the result $u(x_1, \ldots, x_n)$. If $u[ ]$ is first-degree homogeneous and concave, this aggregate $u(x_1, \ldots, x_n)$ has *all* the properties of a one-good neoclassical production function, being first-degree homogeneous and concave. (Moreover, it may be everywhere differentiable even when the constituent $Q^m( )$ functions are not.) See Akerlof and Burmeister (1970) for a needed correction of my slip in Samuelson (1968, p. 475) where I wrongly argued that differences in industry factor intensities will augment $u(x_1, x_2)$'s overall $\bar{\sigma}$: when $Q^m(x^m)$s have greater σs than does $u[q^1, q^2]$, factor-intensity differences lower $\bar{\sigma}$, as is shown in R. Jones (1965) and Dixit (1976, p. 129). My pen also slipped in claiming that $\bar{\sigma} \geqslant \text{Min} [\sigma^1, \sigma^2]$ and σ of $u[ ]$, as in note 2 of the chapter proper.

4. Robinson (1933, pp. 149–50) scolds Machlup for saying that, hoarding of money aside, "the elasticity of demand for all commodities together . . . is unity." One understands her dislike for such a Quantity-Theory hypothesis, and her defense of Hicks's infinite-elasticity of real demand for a one-good macro-economy. Still, as Marshall (1923, Appendix C) suggested, Machlup's case is a possible case. Thus, apply it and ask how, with land fixed and *money* wage rate prescribed, the demand for labor behaves. Then, as in my (6A.2.7) but with $n = 2$ and $x_2 = \bar{x}_2$, the Hicks-Robinson algebra could be validly applied by Machlup. (Example: with pq a constant and WL a constant fraction of it, the demand for labor has unitary elasticity; this is just what Robinson's own relation (6A.6.2) asserts when $\sigma = \eta = 1$, so that $(-Ex_1/y_1)$ also equals 1.) Robinson does not provide argument to deny this, and there is none; what she can argue is that the case is not of much actual interest in a depression decade.

In VIII, Machlup rightly indicates, as did Shove's 1933 *Economic Journal* review of Hicks (1932), reproduced in Hicks (1963, pp. 249–67), that "capital" is not just a second factor parallel to "labor."

References

Akerlof, G.A., and E. Burmeister. 1970. "Substitution in a General Equilibrium Framework," *Journal of Economic Theory* 2, pp. 411–422.

Allen, R.G.D. 1938. *Mathematical Analysis for Economists*. (London: Macmillan).

Champernowne, D.G. 1935. "A Mathematical Note on Substitution," *Economic Journal* 45, pp. 246–258.

Crawford, M.S. 1937. *A Mathematical Reconsideration of the Elasticity of Substitution*. Undergraduate Honors Thesis, Radcliffe College.

Diewert, E.W. 1971a. "An Application of the Shephard Duality Theorem: A Generalized Leontief Production Function," *Journal of Political Economy* 63, pp. 481–507.

——. 1971b. "A Note on the Elasticity of Derived Demand in the N-Factor Case," *Economica* 38, pp. 192–198.

Dixit, A.K. 1976. *The Theory of Equilibrium Growth*. (London: Oxford University Press).

Dorfman, R., P.A. Samuelson, and R.M. Solow. 1958. *Linear Programming and Economic Analysis*. (New York: McGraw-Hill).

Douglas, P.H. 1934. *Theory of Wages*. (New York: Macmillan; and Kelley & Millman).

Friedman, M. 1936. "Further Notes on Elasticity of Substitution. I. Note on Dr. Machlup's Article," *Review of Economic Studies* 3, pp. 147–148.

Hicks, J.R. 1932. *Theory of Wages* (1st edition). (London: Macmillan), 2nd edition, 1963.

——. 1933. "A Note on Mr. Kahn's Paper [Elasticity of Substitution]," *Review of Economic Studies* 1, pp. 78–80.

——. 1934. "A Note on the Elasticity of Supply," *Review of Economic Studies* 2, pp. 31–37.

——. 1936. "Distribution and Economic Progress, A Revised Version," *Review of Economic Studies* 4, pp. 1–12.

——. 1939. *Value and Capital.* (London: Oxford University Press).

——. 1963. *Theory of Wages* (2nd edition). (London: Macmillan), 1st edition, 1932.

——. 1970. "Elasticity of Substitution Again: Substitutes and Complements," *Oxford Economic Papers* 22, No. 3, pp. 289–296.

Jones, R. 1965. "The Structure of Simple General Equilibrium Models," *The Journal of Political Economy* LXXIII, December, pp. 557–572.

Kahn, R.F. 1933. "The Elasticity of Substitution and the Relative Share of a Factor," *Review of Economic Studies* 1, pp. 72–77.

——. 1935. "Two Applications of the Concept of Elasticity of Substitution," *Economic Journal* 45, pp. 242–245.

Kaldor, N. 1934. "Equilibrium of the Firm," *Economic Journal* 44, pp. 60–76.

Lerner, A.P. 1933. "Notes on Elasticity of Substitution. II. The Diagrammatical Representation," *Review of Economic Studies* 1, pp. 68–70.

——. 1934. "Notes on the Elasticity of Substitution. II [Reply to L. Tarshis]," *Review of Economic Studies* 1, pp. 147–148.

——. 1936. "Further Notes on Elasticity of Substitution," *Review of Economic Studies* 3, pp. 150–151.

McFadden, D. 1963. "Constant Elasticity of Substitution Production Functions," *Review of Economic Studies* 30, pp. 73–83.

Machlup, F. 1935. "The Commonsense of the Elasticity of Substitution," *Review of Economic Studies* 2, pp. 202–213. (Reproduced as chapter 6 in *Selected Economic Writings of Fritz Machlup,* 1976. (New York: New York University Press), pp. 119–130.)

——. 1936. "Further Notes on Elasticity of Substitution. IV. Reply," *Review of Economic Studies* 3, pp. 151–152.

——. 1976. *Selected Economic Writings of Fritz Machlup,* edited by George Bitros. (New York: New York University Press).

Marshall, A. 1920. *Principles of Economics* (8th edition). (London: Macmillan).

——. 1923. *Money Credit and Commerce.* (London: Macmillan).

Meade, J.E. 1934. "Elasticity of Substitution and the Elasticity of Demand for One Factor of Production," *Review of Economic Studies* 1, pp. 152–153.

Mosak, J.L. 1938. "Interrelations of Production, Price, and Derived Demand," *Journal of Political Economy* 46, pp. 761–787.

Mundlak, Y. 1968. "Elasticities of Substitution and the Theory of Derived Demand," *Review of Economic Studies* 35, pp. 225–236.

Muth, R. 1964. "The Derived Demand Curve for a Productive Factor and the Industry Supply Curve," *Oxford Economic Papers* 16, No. 2, pp. 221–234.

Nelson, R.R. 1957. "Increased Rents from Increased Costs: A Paradox of Value Theory," *Journal of Political Economy* 65, pp. 387-393.

Pigou, A.C. 1934. "The Elasticity of Substitution," *Economic Journal* 44, pp. 232-241.

Robinson, J. 1933. *Economics of Imperfect Competition.* (London: Macmillan), chapter 22.

——. 1936. "Dr. Machlup's Commonsense of the Elasticity of Substitution," *Review of Economic Studies* 3, pp. 148-150.

Sakai, Y. 1975. "Substitution and Expansion Effects in the Theory of the Firm: New Results in an Old Framework," *Seikei Ronso* 25, pp. 95-118.

Samuelson, P.A. 1947. *Foundations of Economic Analysis.* Cambridge, Mass.: Harvard University Press).

——. 1953. "Prices of Factors and Goods in General Equilibrium," *Review of Economic Studies* 21, pp. 1-20. (Reproduced as chapter 70 in *Collected Scientific Papers,* Vol. II., 1966.)

——. 1960. "Structure of a Minimum Equilibrium System," in Ralph W. Pfouts, ed., *Essays in Economics and Econometrics: A Volume in Honor of Harold Hotelling.* (Chapel Hill: University of North Carolina Press), pp. 1-33. (Reproduced as chapter 41 in *Collected Scientific Papers,* Vol. I, 1966.)

——. 1962. "Parable and Realism in Capital Theory: The Surrogate Production Function," *Review of Economic Studies* 29, pp. 193-206. (Reproduced as chapter 28 in *Collected Scientific Papers,* Vol. I, 1966.)

——. 1965. "Using Full Duality to Show That Simultaneously Additive Price and Indirect Utilities Implies Unitary Price Elasticity of Demand," *Econometrica* 33, pp. 781-796. (Reproduced as chapter 134 in *Collected Scientific Papers,* Vol. III, 1972.)

——. *Collected Scientific Papers of Paul A. Samuelson.* Vol. I and II, edited by Joseph E. Stiglitz, 1966; Vol. III, edited by Robert C. Merton, 1972; Vol. IV, edited by Hiroaki Nagatani and Kate Crowley, 1977. (Cambridge, Mass.: MIT Press).

——. 1968. "Two Generalizations of the Elasticity of Substitution," in J.N. Wolfe, ed., *Value, Capital and Growth: Papers in Honor of Sir John Hicks.* (Edinburgh: Edinburgh University Press), pp. 467-480. (Reproduced as chapter 133 in *Collected Scientific Papers,* Vol. III, 1972.)

——. 1971. "Maximum Principles in Analytical Economics," (Nobel Memorial Lecture, Stockholm, 1970) in *Les Prix Nobel en 1970.* (Stockholm: Nobel Foundation), pp. 273-288. (Reproduced in *American Economic Review* 62, 1972, pp. 249-262; also reproduced as chapter 130 in *Collected Scientific Papers,* Vol. III, 1972.)

——. 1972. "Unification Theorem for the Two Basic Dualities of Homothetic Theory," *Proceedings of the National Academy of Science* 69, pp. 2673-2674. (Reproduced as chapter 4 in *Collected Scientific Papers,* Vol. IV, 1977.)

——. 1973. "Relative Shares and Elasticities Simplified: Comment," *American*

Economic Review 63, pp. 770-771. (Reproduced as chapter 5 in *Collected Scientific Papers*, Vol. IV, 1977.)

——. 1974. "Complementarity, An Essay on the 40th Anniversary of the Hicks-Allen Revolution in Demand Theory," *Journal of Economic Literature* 12, pp. 1255-1289. (Reproduced as chapter 1 in *Collected Scientific Papers*, Vol. IV, 1977.)

Samuelson, P.A., and S. Swamy. 1974. "Invariant Economic Index Numbers and Canonical Duality: Survey and Synthesis," *American Economic Review* 64, pp. 566-593. (Reproduced as chapter 2 in *Collected Scientific Papers*, Vol. IV, 1977.)

Sato, R. and T. Koizumi. 1970. "Substitutability, Complementarity and the Theory of Derived Demand," *Review of Economic Studies* 37, pp. 107-118.

——. 1973a. "On the Elasticity of Substitution and Complementarity," *Oxford Economic Papers* No. 25.

——. 1973b. "Relative Shares and Elasticities Simplified: Reply," *American Economic Review* 63, p. 772.

Shephard, R.W. 1953, 1970. *Theory of Cost and Production Functions.* (Princeton, N.J.: Princeton University Press).

Shove, G.F. 1933. Book review of J.R. Hicks, *The Theory of Wages* in *Economic Journal* 43, pp. 460-472. (Reproduced in Hicks (1932), pp. 249-267.)

Silberberg, E. 1971. "The Le Chatelier Principle as a Corollary to a Generalized Envelope Theorem," *Journal of Economic Theory* 3, pp. 146-155.

Sraffa, P. 1926. "The Laws of Returns under Competitive Conditions," *Economic Journal* 37, pp. 535-550. (Reproduced as chapter 9 in G.J. Stigler and K.E. Boulding, eds., *Readings in Price Theory.* Chicago: Richard D. Irwin, 1952.)

Stigler, G.J. 1965. *Essays in the History of Economics.* (Chicago: University of Chicago Press).

Sweezy, P.M. 1933. "Notes on Elasticity of Substitution. I. A Note on Relative Shares," *Review of Economic Studies* 1, pp. 67-70.

Tarshis, L. 1933. "Notes on the Elasticity of Substitution. I," *Review of Economic Studies* 1, pp. 144-147.

Uzawa, H. 1962. "Production Functions with Constant Elasticities of Substitution," *Review of Economic Studies* 29, pp. 291-299.

Vázquez, A., and T. Puu. 1973. "Factor Demand Functions in Long-Run Equilibrium," *Revista Internazionale di Scienze Economiche e Commerciale* 20, pp. 1209-1228.

Part IV:
The Expert in International
Finance

7

Optimal Policy of Reserve Management: A Re-examination of Mrs. Machlup's Wardrobe Theory

Jacob S. Dreyer

The intensification of worries about the adequacy of supply of international liquidity in the 1960s was accompanied by an outburst of research activity by many economists who attempted first to determine the extent of need for international reserves and then to juxtapose that assessed need with the actual supply of reserves, thus hoping to confirm or refute the claims, repeatedly made, that the world is heading toward a liquidity shortage. Following Robert Triffin's [1960] pioneering effort, over the next several years the literature on the subject has become voluminous enough to justify at least five comprehensive surveys between 1968 and 1973.[1]

The conclusions arrived at by the authors of studies investigating the need or demand for reserves varied widely and so did their implicit or explicit recommendations. Perhaps even more disconcerting was the lack of agreement on the meaning of concepts and terms used both in economic literature of the early 1960s and everyday pronouncements by practitioners. The distinction between "liquidity" and "reserves" was often blurred, and "need," "demand," "adequacy," and "optimality" were used interchangeably, thus adding to the existing confusion.

1.

The situation was ripe for Fritz Machlup's *grande entrée*. As early as in 1962 he started dispersing the fog of ambiguity in which those concepts were enshrouded.[a] In 1964, in his well known book *International Payments, Debts, and Gold* he devoted a whole chapter in his continuing effort to discourage fuzzy thinking and silence loose talk about those issues. Two years later he published his famous article "The Need for Monetary Reserves." Remaining faithful to his habit of making unmistakably clear what the subject of his analysis is, Professor Machlup entitled the first two sections of his study "Liquidity Is More Than Reserves," and "Need Is Not the Same As Demand." It would

---

[a]"Liquidité, internationale et nationale," *Bulletin d'information et de documentation,* Banque Nationale de Belgique, February 1962.

be impossible to prove that subsequent improvement of semantic mores among the writers on the subject was due entirely to Professor Machlup's beneficial influence, but the fact is that by the early 1970s in most scholarly writings, if not official pronouncements, the "demand for monetary reserves" ceased to be equivalent to the "need for international liquidity."

In "The Need for Monetary Reserves," Professor Machlup examined the ratios between officially held reserves and six different variables for fourteen industrial countries. He found that "some countries hold *large* reserves no matter how the relative size is measured, and others hold *low* reserves on all counts. In some instances, however, the picture is confusing, showing high and low reserve ratios depending on the magnitudes with which the size of reserves is compared." His conclusion was that "reserves were not needed for any of the purposes emphasized by either theorists or practitioners . . . but it can be said convincingly that an *increase* in reserves will be needed or adequate to prevent restrictions on foreign trade and payments."

What are then the determinants of the stock of foreign reserves? Professor Machlup maintains that there are none that are universally valid. He compares the attitude of a typical central banker to Mrs. Machlup's *expressed need* for new clothes. Just as "the right amount of clothes owned by [Mrs. Machlup] is that which keeps her from fussing and fretting . . . the 'need' for reserves is determined by the ambitions of monetary authorities."

Professor Machlup notes that "This idea has become known as the 'Mrs. Machlup's Wardrobe Theory of Monetary Reserves.'" In presenting an amended, one may say "dynamized," version of this theory he is even more emphatic regarding the irrelevance of the size of reserves in a central bank's possession: a central banker feels content ". . . if only his reserves increase, however, modestly, and do not decrease."

While Professor Machlup's refutation of hypotheses explaining the size of reserves by the volume of imports, size of consecutive balance of payments deficits, money supply, and the like, is unchallengeable, his own description of central bankers' behavior does not appear very convincing even to some of his most avid readers.[b]

2

In the years following "The Need for Monetary Reserves," the literature on the demand for international reserves has become enriched by a number of contributions emphasizing a cost-benefit approach to the problem of *demand* for reserves by a central bank. In fact, this approach was pioneered by Professor Machlup himself in 1964.[c] Careful reading of his exposition of the problem,

---

[b]See, for example, the surveys by Grubel [1971] and Williamson [1973].

[c]*International Payments, Debts, and Gold,* chapter 18, pp. 266–268.

especially with the benefit of hindsight, reveals that all ingredients of this approach, developed rigorously by Robert Heller [1966], and refined by Peter Clark [1970a] and Michael Kelly [1970], are contained in the Machlup earlier contribution. Why didn't he pursue this avenue of inquiry which proved so fruitful in subsequent years? In Professor Machlup's own words, he ". . . tossed aside all these subtleties [of the cost-benefit approach] because [he] realized that no central banker in the world had the vaguest notion of the social costs and social benefits of their reserve holdings. None of them had the sophistication needed for using economic theory in their improvisations of monetary policy."[d] Moreover, Professor Machlup expresses doubt that the monetary officials' "actual behavior in the past has reflected the findings of an analysis which did not even exist at the time they had to act." "This does not mean," he adds, "that we should not develop cost-and-benefit analyses, or that we should not plead with the officials that they pay heed to such analyses."[e]

In the rest of this chapter, first I shall follow Professor Machlup's advice and develop such an analysis, and next, attempt to re-examine Mrs. Machlup's Wardrobe Theory in the light of that analysis.

3

At the heart of the cost-benefit approach to the problem of demand for international reserves lies the question: given the expected cost associated with a depletion of the stock of reserves, what is the size of that stock that would make the expected cost equal (at the margin) to the cost of holding reserves? Depletion in this context need not mean exhaustion; if one anticipates a speculative run on a country's reserves when they fall below some specified level, the task of monetary authorities would be to prevent a run-down of their reserves to this level.

The cost of holding reserves is relatively easy to define. Since one of the alternatives to holding a dollar in reserves is acquisition of one dollar's worth of investment goods abroad, the marginal cost of holding reserves is the difference between the return on such investment and yield on reserves. Clearly, it will vary from country to country, insofar as marginal productivities of capital are not equalized across nations. It will also vary with the level of reserves held, insofar as average yield on reserves increases with the increase in their stock on account of increments being held in less liquid high-yield assets.

The benefit from holding reserves is more difficult to specify. It may be equated to the avoidance of the cost of taking corrective actions so as to prevent the stock of reserves from being depleted. First, the evaluation of such cost will greatly depend on what kind of corrective action is envisaged: deflation, depre-

<hr>

[d]Private correspondence with the author.

[e]Ibid.

ciation, restrictions on imports, and the like, in the case of reserves depletion; and inflation, appreciation, capital controls, and the like, in the case of reserves build-up. Second, the cost of any given corrective measure may be taken to increase with the speed at which that measure is implemented.[2] Third, the benefit derived from holding reserves depends on the probability that the cost of adjustment entailed by a given corrective action would actually have to be incurred. Obviously, this probability declines as the stock of reserves held by a country increases. But this probability, and hence the expected benefit from holding reserves depends crucially on the choice of statistical representation of autonomous changes in the level of reserves held.

Given the above notions of the cost and benefit of holding reserves, is it possible to specify, in addition to the optimal stock of reserves, an optimal policy of reserve management, that is, the rate at which the reserves are optimally accumulated or decumulated under a given set of circumstances? The answer is positive, and in what follows I shall attempt to specify such policy.

4

Let the stock of reserves of a single country at the end of period n be

$$R_n = R_o + \sum_{t=1}^{n} \epsilon_t$$

We shall assume that the external account of the country is characterized by a structural equilibrium, that is, the process generating *autonomous* changes, ϵ_t, in the stock of reserves, R, is a white noise, or that

$$E(\epsilon_t) = 0 \qquad \text{for all } t$$

$$E(\epsilon_t \epsilon_j) = 0 \qquad \text{for all } t \neq j$$

The probability density function is defined as

$$f(s)\, ds = P[s < \epsilon < s + ds]$$

$$\int_{-\infty}^{+\infty} f(s)\, ds = 1 \qquad E(s) = \int_{-\infty}^{+\infty} (s)\, ds = 0$$

E stands for the expectation operator, and P for probability.

If at the end of the period t the policy maker decides to remain passive, he should expect the level of reserves by the end of the next period to be $R_t + \epsilon_{t+1}$. But by taking some policy measures he can bring the expected stock of reserves to the level Y_{t+1}.

Let u_t be the *policy-induced* change in the stock of reserves in period t, where $u_t > 0$ would stand for a gain in reserves, and $u_t < 0$ would stand for a loss, and $u_{t+1} = Y_{t+1} - R_t$.

The cost associated with inducing a change, u, in the level of reserves is $c = c(R, u, \epsilon, v)$, where v is a random variable describing the state of the economy.[3] Since $c(\cdot)$ is not explicitly dependent on time and v can be taken as independently distributed, the mathematical expectation of the cost function is identical for all time periods:

$$E[c(R_t, u_t, v_{t+1}, \epsilon_{t+1})|v_{t+1}, \epsilon_{t+1}] = C(R_t, u_t)$$

Let us denote the realized values of random changes in the stock of reserves by $s_t = -\epsilon_t$, that is, autonomous increments in reserves are denoted as negative, decrements as positive.

The cost of holding reserves is, as was mentioned in the previous section, the difference between the yield on real assets, ρ, and the yield on reserves, i. Without loss of generality we may assume ρ and i to be constant. Moreover, $\rho > i$; otherwise the optimal policy would call for investment of all nation's savings in reserve assets.

If $s_{t+j} \leq 0$, that is, the size of reserve holdings increases, the marginal cost of holding this increment per time period is given by

$$\int_{Y_t}^{Y_t + s_{t+1}} r \, dR$$

where $r = (\rho - i)$ is the marginal cost of holding reserves.

If $s_{t+1} \geq 0$ and $s_{t+1} \geq R_t$, the stock of reserves is depleted. The consequence of this depletion is the necessity to endure the cost of illiquidity, p, plus the cost associated with the necessity to return the stock of reserves to position zero. The latter can be interpreted as the cost of measures required to be taken to avoid default on external obligations by the central bank. In our notation its expected value is $C(0, Y_{t+1} - s_{t+1})$.

Since the process generating changes in the stock of reserves is mean-stationary over an infinite horizon, the problem to be solved by the decision maker is the same in every period. Let the stock at $t = 0$ be R and the social rate of discount be denoted by δ. If we simulate hands-off policy, the cost $\psi(R)$, associated with an autonomous evolution of the system will have the following functional form:

$$\psi(R) = \delta \int_{-\infty}^{R} \left\{ \psi(R+s) + \int_{R}^{R-s} r\, dR \right\} f(s)\, ds$$

$$+ \delta \int_{-\infty}^{R} \left\{ \psi(R-s) + \int_{R}^{R+s} r\, dR \right\} f(s)\, ds$$

$$+ \delta \int_{R}^{+\infty} \psi(0) + \left\{ \int_{R}^{0} r\, dR + p + C(0, s-R) \right\} f(s)\, ds \qquad (7.1)$$

The first component of the sum assumes nonzero values when $s \leqslant 0$, the second when $R > s > 0$, the third when $s \geqslant R$. In other words, when reserves autonomously increase the cost of holding them becomes higher but the *expected* cost of future adjustment becomes lower. When reserves autonomously decrease but still remain above zero (or, in a more general case, above some chosen critical level) the cost of holding them—the opportunity loss stemming from not using them—decreases but the *expected* cost of future adjustment increases. When reserves autonomously decrease below zero, the penalty cost of illiquidity, p, must be borne and an additional cost of returning to zero (e.g., repaying debts) must be incurred.

Unless autonomous changes in officially held reserves are neutralized by offsetting changes in reserves held by the private sector or are accompanied by changes in the exchange rate, passive behavior regarding autonomous changes in reserves held by the monetary authority cannot be said to constitute optimal policy. To behave optimally the policy maker should react to departures of the stock of reserves from the level at which marginal cost of holding them equals the expected benefit of avoidance of adjustment costs rendered necessary by their depletion. Each period when the observed level of reserves is R, the policy maker may adopt some corrective measures designed to bring the level of reserves in the next period to $Y(R)$. These corrective measures entail real cost to the society which is lower, however, than the cost that would have to be incurred if the reserves were depleted. The expected cost of these corrective measures is $C[R, Y(R)-R]$. Hence, we can express the total expected cost associated with a *managed* evolution of the system as:

$$\psi_1(R) = C[R, Y(R)-R]$$

$$+ \delta \int_{-\infty}^{Y} \left\{ \psi_1(Y+s) + \int_{Y}^{Y-s} r\, dY \right\} f(s)\, ds$$

$$+ \delta \int_{-\infty}^{Y} \left\{ \psi_1(Y-s) + \int_{Y}^{Y+s} r\, dY \right\} f(s)\, ds$$

$$+\delta \int_{Y}^{+\infty} \left\{ \psi_1(0) + \int_{Y}^{0} r\, dY + p + C(0, s-Y) \right\} f(s)\, ds \qquad (7.2)$$

The second component of the sum assumes nonzero values when $s \leqslant 0$, the third, when $Y > s > 0$; the fourth, when $s \geqslant Y$.

It can be shown that the general solution to a simplified version of equation (7.2) is

$$\gamma \left(\frac{1-\delta}{\delta} \right) = [p - r(Y+s)]\, f(Y) \qquad (7.3)$$

when $s > 0$, that is, when the stock of reserves autonomously decreases, and it is

$$\gamma \left(\frac{1-\delta}{\delta} \right) = [p - r(Y-s)] f(Y) \qquad (7.4)$$

when $s \leqslant 0$, that is, when the stock of reserves autonomously increases or remains unchanged.[4]

It can be easily seen that at the end of each time period the level of reserves that minimizes the total cost of reserve management will depend, in a rather complex manner, upon the probability of the stock of reserves attaining various levels, the prevailing level of reserves, and the parameters involved.

The implicit solution of (7.2), say, for the case of a decline in the stock of reserves, can be represented graphically. Let us rewrite (7.3) as

$$\gamma \left(\frac{1-\delta}{\delta} \right) / [p - r(Y+s)] = f(Y) \qquad (7.5)$$

and denote the left-hand side of the above equation by g.

The optimal stock of reserves, in the sense discussed above, is depicted in Figure 7-1. First, it is quite obvious that the solution is extremely sensitive with respect to the shape of the function $f(Y)$. In other words, the optimal size of reserves will vary considerably with the policy maker's assessment of the probability of future (cumulative) changes in the level of reserves. Next for a given $f(Y)$, the optimal stock of reserves increases as g decreases. Treating g as a function of the parameters of $\psi_1(R)$ in (7.2), and assuming that the cost of illiquidity, p, is sufficiently large, or more precisely that $p > r(Y+s)$, one can ascertain that

$$\frac{\partial g}{\partial \gamma} > 0 \qquad \frac{\partial g}{\partial \delta} > 0 \qquad \frac{\partial g}{\partial p} < 0 \qquad \frac{\partial g}{\partial r} > 0$$

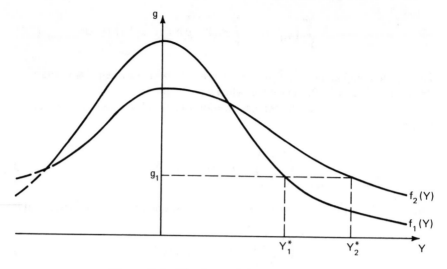

Figure 7-1. The Optimal Stock of Reserves

These results are unexceptional. The optimal size of reserves will be greater the larger the cost of being illiquid, and the lower the cost of holding them. Also, the higher the speed of adjustment between the actual and desired stocks of reserves, or stated alternatively, the greater the willingness and ability of the decision maker to take drastic actions in order to attain desired levels of reserves, the lower is the optimal stock of reserves. Finally, the optimal stock of reserves varies inversely with the "social" rate of discount.

From (7.5), it can be seen that the value of g varies positively with Y. For a given set of values for γ, δ, p, and r, when the stock of reserves is high relative to its mean, the response, $Y^*_{t+1} - Y_t$, will be less energetic than when the stock of reserves is low relative to its mean. The process of acquisition or disposal of reserves continues until $Y^*_{t+1} - Y_t = 0$, or $Y^* = R^*$; at this point the process becomes stationary.

For a given set of values for γ, δ, p, and r, the optimal policy of reserves management could be represented as a convergent process (see Figure 7-2).

For any level of reserves the optimal policy response, that is, the amount of reserves added to or disposed of from the existing stock is given on the vertical axis. The optimal policy of reserves management is thus fully specified.

5

In all fairness to Professor Machlup it should be noted that a definable policy of optimal reserves management does not by itself constitute a refutation of Mrs.

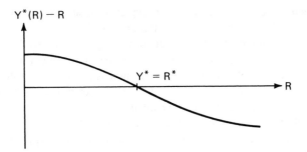

Figure 7-2. Optimal Policy of Reserves Management

Machlup's Wardrobe Theory. But neither, of course does the lack of a systematic relationship between reserve levels and other aggregates that he established constitute in itself a confirmation of this theory.

Empirical evidence on this score is mixed. Monetary reserves of most countries have been rising almost uninterruptedly. This accumulation of reserves would strongly support Professor Machlup's view of central bankers' behavior. But payments imbalances, not to mention prices and the volume of trade also have been increasing rather dramatically.

On the other hand, models incorporating the cost-benefit approach to reserves management were tested on several occasions in the early 1970s.[5] Although the overall results suggest that most central bankers' demand for monetary reserves is somewhat responsive to the determinants of the optimal stock emphasized by the cost-benefit approach, the evidence is not overwhelming. The reported results are extremely sensitive to the specifications of particular models; they vary considerably across countries; in the case of the industrial countries, their central bankers exhibit a consistent bias toward overaccumulation of monetary reserves relative to what the models specify to be their optimal size.

It appears that while the monetary authorities recognize that excessive accumulation of reserves is wasteful, they are unable to overcome their desire to overstock. Commenting on the reserves policy pursued by the Bank of England in the late 1960s, Peter Oppenheimer [1968] stated ". . . that in London Mrs. Machlup is delighted to wear an evening gown if someone presents her with it; otherwise she's happy in a miniskirt." Other central bankers are not so indifferent. They seem ready to pay a price for an evening gown even when the circumstances make the miniskirt entirely appropriate. Thus, while Mrs. Machlup's satisfaction obtained from acquiring more or longer dresses does not entail, in the analogy of Professor Machlup, any additional costs that she (as distinct from her husband) has to incur, the satisfaction derived by central bankers from having large stocks of reserves does entail an additional cost to the nations. To put it differently, while Mrs. Machlup's behavior is perfectly rational, the behavior of central bankers is not (quite apart from Professor Machlup's statement, which I find

unchallengeable, that ". . . comparing the typical central banker with my wife
. . . might be too flattering for most central bankers.")

Even if Professor Machlup's view of continuing additions to the stock of
monetary reserves as being the only goal of reserves management policy can be
contested on the basis of available evidence, there is no doubt that the Mrs.
Machlup type of behavior on central bankers' parts exerts a very strong influence
on their policies. How can this bias be explained?

On purely technical grounds, one could argue that the probability of
depletion of reserves is essentially a subjective measure and that central bankers,
being proverbially cautious, would tend to err on the side of overestimating this
probability. Similarly, they would tend to overstate the penalty cost of reserve
depletion. On both counts the optimal stock of reserves computed by a central
banker may be substantially higher than the size of an optimal stock computed
by a knowledgeable outsider.

I would submit, however, that the main reason for the disparity between
Professor Machlup's assessment of what an optimal stock of reserves should be
and that of a central banker resides in the treatment of the costs of holding reserves by the latter. This cost is essentially "invisible," not reflected in central
banks' balance sheets or income statements. It is an opportunity cost, borne by
the nation, of having the current or future consumption curtailed, a cost which,
in many cases, monetary authorities can afford to ignore. Moreover, if these
authorities have a much higher rate of discount than the social rate, and if the
nation's opportunity cost of holding reserves accrues in the future, it can be seen
from equation (7.5) and Figure 7-1 that the optimal size of reserves based on
such perceptions would tend to infinity.

If this is the case, then overaccumulation of monetary reserves by central
banks, deplored by Professor Machlup, reflects after all a case of perfectly
rational bureaucratic attitudes. The stocks of reserves, or additions to them, become determined by noneconomic arguments in the utility functions of central
bankers and the relative ease with which bureaucratic decisions are being made.
More precisely, the upper limit of the stock of reserves of a country in a permanent balance of payments surplus becomes determined by the ability of its
central bankers to get away with much too high a social cost incurred to achieve
their particular goals.[6] As constitutional constraints on the central bankers'
freedom of action vary across countries and over time, so does the extent of
overaccumulation of reserves. Needless to say, this variability of constitutional
constraints is likely to be completely unrelated to the variability of economic
determinants of the optimal stock of reserves. As a consequence of this, all
attempts to relate either the stock of reserves or changes thereof to a single magnitude or to a multitude of economic variables turned out to be less than
resounding successes. If economic constraints do not bind central bankers effectively, Professor Machlup may be right after all, at least as far as the traditional
surplus countries are concerned.

To pursue Professor Machlup's analogy, although in his opinion his wife's wardrobe is more than abundant, he has some good reasons for tolerating her continuing propensity to acquire more dresses. However, there appears to be much less justification for nations to extend similar generosity to their central bankers indulging in an unadulterated waste of resources by continuously expanding the size of their monetary reserves.

Notes

1. Robert Clower and Richard Lipsey [1968], Jürg Niehans [1970], Herbert Grubel [1971], John Williamson [1973], and Benjamin Cohen [1975].

2. This is the point emphasized by Peter Clark [1970a]. In his model high speed of adjustment causes greater variability of income and thus reduces the value of his quadratic utility function.

3. As a digression, it may be noticed that the presence of the argument R in the cost function allows for the integration of the possibility of a "capital flight." If the level of reserves is taken as an index of confidence in the stability of a currency's exchange value, and $C(R, u)$ is written in an explicit form as $C[u + \xi(R)]$ or $C[u + \xi(R), u]$ the first of these expressions can be interpreted as a capital outflow, $\xi(R)$, occuring at the level of reserves R, while the second expression would mean that some energetic policy measure leading to $u > 0$ limits the capital outflows to $\xi(R, u) < \xi(R)$ as a result of re-established confidence in the ability of the monetary authority to prevent the currency from depreciating.

4. Before proceeding with the solution of equation (7.2), several remarks about the function of $\psi_1(R)$ are in order.

The existence and convergence of the integrals require that

$$(a) \qquad \lim_{s \to \infty} f(s) = 0$$

and

$$(b) \qquad \int_{-\infty}^{+\infty} C[0, s]$$

be defined.

In addition, for the continuity and proper curvature of $\psi_1(R)$ we require that $C[R, Y(R)]$ be continuous and convex in both R and Y. We also note that since the mapping R onto $Y(R)$ is generally multivalued and uppersemicontinuous, it is continuous in the intervals where it is univalued;

$$(c) \qquad f'(s) < 0 \qquad \text{for } s > 0$$

$$(d) \qquad \int_{-\infty}^{+\infty} sf(s) \, ds = 0$$

Finally, we shall assume that $C[Y, Y(R)]$ is of linear form: $\gamma [Y(R) - R]$ where γ stands for the speed of adjustment measured as a fraction of the gap reduced over the same unit of time as that for which parameters r and δ are defined.

Under these assumptions and simplifications the solution of equation (7.2) is $\gamma(1 - \delta)/\delta = [p - r(Y \pm s)] f(Y)$.

Proof:

Consider (7.2) rewritten as

$$Z(R) = \min_{Y>0} \left\{ \gamma (Y-R) + \delta \int_{-\infty}^{Y} [b(0) + \gamma (Y+s) - rs] f(s) \, ds \right.$$

$$+ \delta \int_{-\infty}^{Y} [b(0) - \gamma (Y-s) + rs] f(s) \, ds$$

$$\left. + \delta \int_{Y}^{+\infty} [b(0) + \gamma (s-Y) - rY + p] f(s) \, ds \right\}$$

$$= \min_{Y>0} F(Y,R) \qquad\qquad (7.1')$$

Since the second component of the sum corresponds to an autonomous increase or no change in reserves ($s \leqslant 0$), while the third component to a decrease in reserves ($s > 0$), they are mutually exclusive. Let us take the case of $s > 0$, that is to investigate the optimal response to an autonomous decline in reserves.

For the function $F(Y, R)$ to be at the minimum, $\partial F/\partial Y = 0$, or

$$\gamma - \delta \int_{-\infty}^{Y} f(s) \, ds - \delta rsf(Y) - \delta \int_{Y}^{+\infty} f(s) \, ds - \delta (rs + p) f(Y) = 0 \qquad (7.2')$$

This simplifies to

$$\gamma \left(\frac{1 - \delta}{\delta} \right) = [p - r(Y+s)] f(Y) \qquad\qquad (7.3')$$

Similarly, for $s \leqslant 0$, the optimal response is found to be

$$\gamma \left(\frac{1-\delta}{\delta} \right) = [p - r(Y-s)] \, f(Y) \qquad (7.4')$$

5. Peter Clark [1970b], Mordechai Kreinin, and Robert Heller [1974], Jacob Frenkel [1973], Willy and Brigitta Sellakaerts [1973], among others.

6. A good description of the case of Japan in the late 1960s and early 1970s is given by Yasuba in this volume, pp. 221-237.

References

Clark, Peter B. "Optimum International Reserves and the Speed of Adjustment," *Journal of Political Economy*, March 1970 (a).

——. "The Demand for International Reserves: A Cross-Country Analysis," *Canadian Journal of Economics*, November 1970 (b).

Clower, Robert W., and Richard G. Lipsey. "The Present State of International Liquidity Theory," *American Economic Review*, May 1968.

Cohen, Benjamin J. "International Reserves and Liquidity," in *International Trade and Finance*, P.B. Kenen, ed., Cambridge University Press, New York, 1975.

Frenkel, Jacob A. "The Demand for International Reserves by Developed and Less-Developed Countries," *Report* No. 7334, Center for Mathematical Studies in Business and Economics of the University of Chicago, July 1973.

Grubel, Herbert G. "The Demand for International Reserves: A Critical Review of the Literature," *Journal of Economic Literature*, December 1971.

Heller, H. Robert. "Optimal International Reserves," *Economic Journal*, June 1966.

Kelly, Michael G. "The Demand for International Reserves," *American Economic Review*, September 1970.

Kreinin, Mordechai, E., and H. Robert Heller. "Adjustment Costs, Optimal Currency Areas and International Reserves," in *Essays in Honour of Jan Tinbergen*, W. Sellekaerts, ed., White Plains, N.Y.: International Arts and Science Press, 1974.

Machlup, Fritz. "Liquidité, internationale et nationale," *Bulletin d'information et de documentation*, Banque Nationale de Belgique, Brussels, February 1962.

——. *International Payments, Debts, and Gold*, Charles Scribner's Sons, New York, 1964.

——. "The Need for Monetary Reserves," *Banca Nazionale del Lavoro Quarterly Review*, September 1966.

Niehans, Jürg. "The Need for Reserves of a Single Country," in *International*

Reserves: Needs and Availability, p. 43, International Monetary Fund, Washington, D.C., 1970.

Oppenheimer, Peter M. "International Liquidity: The Case of the United Kingdom," *American Economic Review,* Supplement, May 1968.

Sellekaerts, Willy, and Brigitta Sellekaerts. "Balance of Payments Deficits, the Adjustment Cost and the Optimal Level of International Reserves," *Weltwirtschaftliches Archiv,* 1973, Vol. 103.

Triffin, Robert. *Gold and the Dollar Crisis,* Yale University Press, New Haven, Conn., 1960.

Williamson, John. "Surveys in Applied Economics; International Liquidity," *Economic Journal,* September 1973.

8

Trade Balances in Current and Constant Prices When the Terms of Trade Change: Questions About Some Eternal Truths

Walter S. Salant

In these days of large changes in prices and exchange rates the choice of units in which to measure some economic aggregates and net balances, and especially the changes in them over time, presents problems that cannot as easily be ignored as they were in more stable times. It is appropriate to draw attention to these problems in a volume honoring Fritz Machlup, who more often than anyone else forces his professional colleagues to face the question, "Exactly what do you mean when you say . . .?" and who then also addresses the question of what one should mean.

This chapter calls attention to one category of problems arising from changes in relative prices: the possible effects of changes in the terms of trade on the relation between changes in a country's international balance on goods and services measured in current and in constant prices. These effects are generally neglected and the neglect of them may lead to erroneous conclusions. It begins with a reminder that when the terms of trade change, the change in the trade balance measured in current prices may differ from its change measured in constant domestic prices, and then considers the question of which method of measurement is appropriate for what purpose. Consideration of this issue leads to a questioning of some identities that are regarded as eternal truths and this, in turn, to correction of what I believe to be an error in the income-absorption theory of adjustment.

It should be noted that while the chapter addresses the effects of only one kind of change in relative prices, a change in the terms of international trade, the same issues may also arise in connection with other net balances of open economic units, such as the budget deficits and surpluses of governments and the net balances of other sectors of the economy.

Changes in Current Prices versus Changes in Constant Prices

One effect of changes in the relative prices of broad categories of goods and services that commands little attention when those changes are moderate is that they may cause the nominal (current-price) and real (constant-price) values of

135

economic net balances to change not only in different proportions but in opposite directions. Changes in relative prices may also upset some relationships that
are commonly assumed to be identities in real as well as in nominal terms; that
is, some economic aggregates that in nominal values are identical may become
unequal when the prices appropriate to deflating them change in different proportions. Although these effects command little attention when relative price
changes are small, when they are substantial the possible differences between
effects on nominal and real values deserve attention because neglect of them
may lead to errors of analysis and policy.

Striking instances of the difference between nominal and real changes were
provided by the change in the terms of trade of large net importers and exporters
of oil associated with the rise in its price between 1973 and 1974. The trade balance of the United States, shown in Table 8-1, provides a good illustration. In
nominal values it was almost unchanged; exports and imports of goods and services rose almost equally. But the change in nominal exports reflected an increase in the average quantity as well as the average price, while the increase in
nominal imports consisted almost entirely of an increase in average price much
greater than for exports, with the average quantity increasing hardly at all. In
other words, the deterioration in the terms of trade offset what would have
been, in its absence and with the same quantities of trade, a very large increase
in the export surplus.

The net export balance is generally recognized to be identical to the difference between total national output (GNP) and total national absorption or
expenditure on goods and services (GNE), GNP being the sum of national expenditure on domestic output and exports while GNE is the sum of national expen-

Table 8-1
**United States Net Exports of Goods and Services in Current and 1972 Prices,
1973 and 1974** (money figures in billions of dollars)

	1973	1974	• Change
In current prices			
Exports	101.6	144.4	42.8
Imports[a]	94.4	136.9	42.5
Balance[a]	7.1	7.5	0.4
Price index (1972 = 100)			
Export Prices	116.2	148.6	27.9%
Import Prices	118.2	169.6	43.5%
In 1972 prices			
Exports	87.4	97.2	9.8
Imports[a]	79.9	80.7	0.8
Balance[a]	7.6	16.5	8.9

Source: U.S. Department of Commerce, *Survey of Current Business,* July 1976, pp. 24
and 58.

[a]Excludes payments of income on U.S. government liabilities.

diture on domestic output and imports. It is evident, therefore, that when the average prices of exports and imports change in different proportions the difference between GNP and GNE expressed in current prices can change in a different direction than when it is expressed in constant prices.[1]

Which Balance Is Relevant to Real Aggregate Demand?

The possibility of difference between changes in the nominal and the real trade balances raises the question of which balance is relevant to effects on real aggregate demand. Consider first the effect of an autonomous increase in nominal exports. From the point of view of effects on domestic economic activity, an increase that takes the form entirely of an increase in the quantity of exports clearly is a direct addition to the demand for domestic output; one that reflects only an increase in export prices is not. This difference may appear to imply that only a change in real values is relevant. Thus Williamson and Wood, in discussing the degree to which the foreign sector has acted as a built-in stabilizer of the British economy, say, " . . . it is not the change in trade balance in nominal terms, but rather its change in real terms that is relevant from the standpoint of providing a built-in stabilizer." Later in the same article they say about the British experience in 1973–74, "Although the current balance deteriorated in nominal terms, this was attributable to a deterioration in the terms of trade caused principally by the world commodity boom, while the current balance in real terms stabilized in 1973 and improved in 1974, *thus doing nothing to ease the pressure of demand.*"[2]

In fact, however, although the change in the real value of the trade balance is relevant, this does not imply that the change in its nominal value is not. If the nominal value of exports rises owing solely to a rise in export prices, the nominal income of at least one factor of production in the export sector of the economy increases. Given that the terms of trade have improved, total real income—defined as nominal income deflated by a price index appropriate to spending rather than to output—will increase. Consequently, if the recipients have a marginal propensity to spend out of real income exceeding zero, there will be some induced increase of real aggregate demand.[3] This fact is sufficient to establish that the change in the nominal balance is also relevant.

This conclusion is not confined to the case of a rise in export prices. Corresponding reasoning applies to an improvement in the terms of trade resulting from a fall of import prices. Consider the case in which such a fall is accompanied by a proportionate decrease in the nominal value of imports, there being no increase in the quantity of imports, and in which exports remain unchanged in both price and quantity. The real trade balance then remains unchanged but the nominal balance increases. Domestic residents have the same nominal income and produce the same real output as before, but their real incomes (defined as the purchasing power of their output) is increased. This increase will presumably induce an increase in aggregate real demand. Again, we see that the change in the nominal as well as the real balance must be taken into account in an analysis of the effects.

This conclusion, of course, applies as much to an adverse as to a favorable change in the terms of trade. The response of demand managers in the United States to the multiple rise in foreign oil prices in late 1973 may be interpreted as in part a result of failure to recognize the demand-decreasing effects of a deterioration in the terms of trade. Looking only at changes in the real trade balance, which increased by nearly 9 billion dollars in 1972 prices, one might have concluded that, since (as Table 8-1 shows) exports rose by nearly 10 billion dollars while imports rose by less than 1 billion, the international sector was exerting a stimulating influence on aggregate demand for output. Evidently, the stimulating effect of the rise in the quantity of exports was at least partially offset by (among other things) the real income effect of the 12 percent rise in import prices relative to export prices (as measured by the notoriously defective indexes of unit values), so that a billion dollars of *real* gross national product had a purchasing power over real gross national expenditures 1 percent less in 1974 than it had in 1973 [1.0 less (1974 GNP deflator on 1973 base ÷ 1974 GNE deflator on 1973 base)]. If the change is measured between the second quarter of 1973 and the first quarter of 1974, when gross national product in constant (1972) prices was the same (annual rates of 1231.1 billion and 1230.4 billion dollars), its purchasing power over the goods and services absorbed in the second quarter of 1973 had shrunk by an annual rate of about 1.3 percent.

The adverse change in the terms of trade reduced real income relative to real product (which, because the price elasticity of the demand for imports was low, showed up *ex post* as a difference between the changes in the real and the nominal trade balances) and this reduction may have accounted, at least in part, for the weakness of consumer expenditure. This suggestion is consistent with Arthur Okun's conclusion that consumer expenditure for the year 1974 as a whole bore its normal relation to real disposable income so that the basic question about it was what made real disposable income so weak. He notes that real disposable income fell about 2 1/2 percent below the level that its average postwar relation to real GNP would have suggested, and that the rise in the price of imported oil accounted for about half of that abnormal decline.[4] This decline in the relation of real disposable income to real GNP reduced the level of real GNP. The other element in the decline of real GNP was the fall in residential construction, which has been attributed by Okun (and others) to a tightening of monetary policy. This policy action apparently was at least in part an effort to counter the effects of the oil price rise (as well as other upward pressures on prices) by action that would restrain increases in the price level generally. If policy makers had been much influenced by the rise in the real trade balance (as they probably were not) that influence certainly would have strengthened their belief that real aggregate demand was being expanded by the rise in the quantity of exports, and might have led to neglect of the depressing effect on aggregate real income of the rise in the price of imports.

This discussion of the effects of changes in the terms of trade has shown the need to distinguish between changes in aggregate real product and in aggregate real income. The distinction has implications for the income-absorption approach to the adjustment of trade balances, which we now consider.

The Terms of Trade and the Income-Absorption Approach to Trade Adjustment

In discussions of policies for reducing trade deficits, the concern is invariably with nominal deficits. It is generally accepted that elimination or reduction of such a deficit requires an increase in the excess of total output over total domestic absorption, defined as expenditure by domestic residents (C + I + G in the conventional notation) or a reduction in the excess of absorption over output. It is generally assumed that this requires either an increase in real output, a reduction in real absorption, or some combination of the two. Enough has already been said to make clear that this assumption is incorrect. But it is also questionable whether such changes are needed to reduce a real deficit when the terms of trade change.

In Alexander's classic article expounding the income-absorption approach to analysis of changes in the "trade balance" the balance being analyzed and all the variables determining it were specified to be real variables.[5] The real balance was identified as the difference between "real income" and "real absorption." From the section of the article that considers the effect of changes in the terms of trade, it becomes clear that by "real income" Alexander does not mean real output. He speaks of the income from which absorption must be subtracted as being reduced by a deterioration of the terms of trade. Since such a deterioration can result from any rise of import prices relative to export prices, it is clear that "real income" in this context means the money value of output deflated by a price index appropriate to expenditure by domestic residents, not one appropriate to output. This definition underlies his statement that it is fallacious to argue "that a deterioration in the terms of trade . . . will improve the foreign balance since it reduces the real income of the country and hence the demand for imports. . . ." While the change in the terms of trade will induce a reduction of real absorption, Alexander argues that this reduction will normally (i.e., if the ratio of the induced cut in absorption to the cut in income that induces it is less than unity) be less than the initial cut in real income caused by the change in the terms of trade, so that a deterioration in the terms of trade implies a deterioration in the foreign balance.

This concept of real income, that is, nominal income deflated by a price index for expenditure, is what most people think of as the real income of individual households, firms, and larger sectors of a national economy—or, to put it more generally, any open subnational economies. For example, if the average price of what a firm or sector (e.g., the agricultural sector) buys has risen more than the average price of what it produces and its real product remains constant, we normally say its real income has fallen, not remained constant. In calculating real disposable income we deflate nominal disposable income by a price index relevant to consumers' purchases. In discussions of national aggregates, however, we have fallen into the habit of treating output and income as identical. But output is what the economic unit has produced, and income is only the claim it derives from its current production on what it or others have produced, while expenditure is "the exercise of those claims."[6] That the values of national product and national income expressed in non-current prices of goods and services included, respectively, in output and in expenditure may differ and so may change differently is illustrated by the difference between real product and real income (as defined above) in the hypothetical example shown in Table 8-2.

Table 8-2
National Aggregates in Current and Constant Prices

	Period 1	Period 2	Change
In current prices			
1. Product and income (GNP)	1,000	1,100	100
2. Absorption $(C + I + G)$	800	975	175
3. Difference (net export balance, $X - M$)	200	125	−75
Price indexes (period 1 = 1.0)			
4. For product	1.00	1.10	
5. For purchases	1.00	1.25	
6. Ratio purchase to product prices (5 ÷ 4)	1.00	1.136 . . .	
In period 1 prices			
7. Product (line 1 ÷ line 4)	1,000	1,000	0
8. Income (line 1 ÷ line 5)	1,000	880	−120
9. Absorption (line 2 ÷ line 5)	800	780	−20

This numerical example is consistent with some of the national product's being exported and some being sold at home while the national expenditure is partly on home-produced goods and partly on imports. It is also consistent with export of the entire national product and import of the entire national expenditure. Let us assume, for simplicity in dealing with the price indexes, that it represents the latter situation. In that case, real exports (equal to real product) are unchanged and real imports (equal to real expenditure or real absorption) have fallen by 20 units, so the real current-account balance, having risen from 200 to 220 units, has also improved by 20 units. The excess of real income over real absorption, however, has fallen from 200 to 100 units, or by 100 units. Thus, in Period 1 prices, we have:

	Period 1	Period 2	Change
Excess of real income over real absorption (line 8 less line 9)	200	100	–100
Real current-account balance (line 7 less line 9)	200	220	20

It is clear from this illustration that the real balance, expressed in prices of a period when the terms of trade were different than those of the current period, is not equal to the excess of real income over real absorption and, therefore, that the changes from that period in these two variables are also not equal. When both the income-absorption relationship and the current-account balance are measured in the prices of some third period, say Period 0, and the terms of trade in both Periods 1 and 2 differ from those of Period 0 as well as from each other, the excess of real income over real absorption will differ from the real current-account balance in both Periods 1 and 2, so their changes between these two periods must also differ.[7]

If it is recognized that income and product in noncurrent prices may differ, the question arises whether Alexander's article is correct in concluding that when the marginal ratio of real absorption to real income is less than unity an adverse change in the terms of trade will worsen the current balance. That conclusion is derived from three propositions. First, real absorption is a function of real income such that when real income changes, real absorption changes in the same direction but by a smaller amount. Second, an adverse change in the terms of trade constitutes a reduction of real income. Third, the real current-account balance is the excess of real income over absorption. These three propositions taken together imply that an adverse change in the terms of trade reduces real absorption, but by less than it reduces real income, so that it reduces the excess of real income over real absorption and thus the real current-account surplus (or increases any excess of real absorption over real income and thus the real current-account deficit).

The first proposition is a behavior equation that can be accepted as a plausible assumption. The second is a definition that is generally accepted, at least in other contexts (although the neglect of it in the analysis of the current account is the burden of my present argument). The third proposition, however, is incorrect. As was shown in the preceding tables, the real current-account balance is not the excess of real income over real absorption but of real product over real absorption. It follows, therefore, that while a deterioration in the terms of trade may reduce real absorption, it does not necessarily also reduce real product. It is not correct, therefore, to conclude that if the marginal ratio of real absorption to real income is less than unity a deterioration in the terms of trade necessarily decreases the real export balance.

Notes

1. The difference between GNP and GNE in current prices and in constant prices can also change in different directions even when the terms of trade remain unchanged if the prices of both imports and exports change by a different percentage than prices of domestic purchases of domestic goods and the trade balance was not zero in the initial period.

2. John Williamson and Geoffrey E. Wood, "The British Inflation: Indigenous or Imported?" in *American Economic Review,* Vol. 66, No. 4 (September 1976), pp. 524 and 528. I have added the emphasis in the second quotation.

3. It should be noted that this increase in real income will be matched by a reduction in the real income of foreigners, whose terms of trade have deteriorated by a corresponding absolute amount, and this reduction in their real income may reduce their demand for the output of the country in question. Effects on foreign real incomes and expenditures should be taken into account in all cases of changes in the terms of trade.

4. See Arthur M. Okun, "A Postmortem of the 1974 Recession," in *Brookings Papers on Economic Activity, 1:1975,* esp. pp. 210–11. Okun attributes the other half of the abnormal decline in real disposable income to the effect of increases of nominal income in pushing income taxpayers into higher tax brackets and to the increase in personal contributions for social insurance resulting from a rise in the maximum earnings base.

5. Sidney S. Alexander, "Effects of a Devaluation on a Trade Balance," originally published in *International Monetary Fund Staff Papers,* Vol. II (April 1952), pp. 263–78, and republished in R.E. Caves and H.G. Johnson (eds.) *A.E.A. Readings in International Economics* (Homewood, Ill. : Richard D. Irwin, 1968), pp. 359–73, and elsewhere.

6. Quoted from Thomas C. Schelling, *National Income Behavior* (McGraw-Hill Book Co., 1951), p. 10. Schelling's book begins by saying, "The national income has three interpretations. It represents a receipt total, it represents an expenditure total, and it represents a total value of production." (page 3) In its introductory pages, it refers to these as "three significant interpretations of the same total." The last section of the chapter entitled "Real Values versus Money Values, " explains why some accounting identities disappear when selective price indexes are used for deflations (pp. 143–49). See also Walter S. Salant, "International Transactions in National Income Accounts," *Review of Economics and Statistics,* Vol. 33, No. 4 (November 1951), pp. 304–06, especially the reference to Schelling in footnote 1a.

7. It might be thought that the changes between Periods 0 and 1 could differ and those between Periods 0 and 2 also could differ while those between Periods 1 and 2 need not, but this would be incorrect; they must differ if the terms of trade change between Periods 1 and 2.

Part V:
The Initiator of Reform

9

The Impact of the Bellagio Group on International Monetary Reform

Robert Triffin

Since 1963, the Bellagio Group has associated academic economists and official negotiators in a marathon, and still unfinished search for a more rational world monetary order. It should call for a weighty volume rather than for only the few and rather haphazard personal recollections and comments that I am able to present here. I very much hope that their very inadequacy will induce Professor Machlup himself to draw on his memory and voluminous files to provide future historians, economists, and policymakers with the fuller record needed to explain—and draw the lessons from—this unique enterprise which he initiated and led throughout with inimitable skill and unquestioned authority.

1.

I have been privileged to observe at first hand, over a period of about twenty-five years, the unusual blend of theoretical rigor and pragmatic realism which characterizes Professor Machlup's methodology and is the key to his unique achievements in this particular area as well as in the many others that have attracted his insatiable curiosity and indefatigable energy.

I had met him only rarely and briefly until we were both invited by Willard Thorp, in the summer of 1952, to join a brilliant galaxy of American and foreign academic and government economists, at the Merrill Center in Southampton, in a broad-ranging exploration of major international economic problems and policies. This gave us a marvelous opportunity to compare and debate at length in unhurried fashion, on the beach as well as around the conference table, our widely divergent approaches to these problems, and particularly to the reconstruction of a world monetary order left in utter shambles by the war and its immediate aftermath. We shared the conviction that the first order of priority was the dismantling of the pervasive bilateral shackles that were then strangling and distorting world trade and payments, but we advocated two very different solutions to this common objective.

My approach was inspired by my experience with the IMF (International Monetary Fund) on the one hand and, on the other, with the EPU (European

145

Payments Union), which I had just helped devise and negotiate in Paris. The EPU focused on the modest, but germinal, measures that could be realistically negotiated and enforced immediately, and then expanded step by step, rather than on an ideal blueprint—like the IMF Agreement—whose actual implementation could only be hoped for at the end of an indefinitely protracted "transition period." It recognized that the enormous balance of payments disequilibria inherited from the war could not be eliminated overnight, and tried to elicit from all member countries a gradual liberalization of bilateral trade and exchange restrictions, through multilateral commitments supported by mutual credits, conditional themselves upon agreed readjustment policies by surplus and deficit countries alike.[1]

Professor Machlup stressed instead the basic readjustment, rather than financing, of existing disequilibria. His devotion to individual freedom and mistrust of government interference in economic life inclined him to advocate, already then, flexible exchange rates in free markets as the most practical way to reach such basic adjustments through the reconciliation, rather than harmonization, of divergent national policies. Even though adopted in despair some twenty years later, this simple prescription was then scornfully dismissed or even ignored by most academic and virtually all government experts.

My reason for bringing this up is that our Merrill Center discussions anticipated by more than ten years the fundamental technique imparted by Professor Machlup to our Bellagio Group meetings. Rather than try to convince me and come to an agreement, he was interested only in bringing out—or "smoking out"—the reasons explaining why we could logically argue for such different means to reach our common objective.

To our happy surprise, we came to a mutual understanding that was to guide us ever since about the double task of economists. As day-to-day policy advisers, they should strive to disentangle from the existing state of imperfect knowledge and understanding the best agreements practically negotiable at any point of time. As academic economists they should try to enlarge and improve such knowledge and understanding by others as well as themselves through further research, writings, and debates on the problems at issue.

The simultaneous pursuit of both types of activities by Professor Machlup is only partly reflected in his abundant bibliography. As Director of the International Finance Section of Princeton University, he elicited and edited more than eighty *Essays and Studies in International Finance* and *Special Papers in International Economics,* many of which are among the most topical and stimulating in the field. I strongly suspect that an even much larger number of Ph.D. dissertations, books, and articles were directed or inspired by him.

His most direct and immediate impact on the shaping of policy debates and decisions, however, undoubtedly came from his close personal contacts with many of the central bankers and other officials, here and abroad, most continuously involved in the negotiation of international monetary reform. Particularly crucial in this respect were the meetings of the Bellagio Group.

2.

Former Secretary of the Treasury Douglas Dillon unwittingly triggered the formation of the Bellagio Group when he announced, in a press conference during the 1963 annual meeting of the IMF, that the International Monetary Fund and the Ministers of Finance and Governors of Central Banks of the Group of Ten would undertake a thorough review of the functioning of the international monetary system. Following this announcement, Edwin Dale, of *The New York Times,* asked whether the academic economists who had argued for years the need for a fundamental reform of the system would be invited to testify, as they had repeatedly been invited to do by various committees of the U.S. Congress. Secretary Dillon ruled out any such invitation; he claimed that economists could never agree, even among themselves, and could not therefore provide useful guidance on problems that should be discussed with the utmost discretion in closed meetings by responsible officials only.

As we filed out of the conference room, Professor Machlup suggested to William Fellner and myself that this statement should not go unchallenged. Academic economists should conduct parallel meetings of their own, clarify the reasons for their different recommendations, and interpret their disagreements in a form potentially useful to policymakers.

Four such meetings were convened during the following year, alternately in Princeton and Bellagio, with financial support from the Ford and Rockefeller Foundations. They produced a report[2] that attracted considerable attention and praise from the officials attending the 1964 annual meeting of the IMF. At the request of a few of them—particularly Otmar Emminger and Robert Roosa—we agreed also to organize in the future joint meetings of academics and negotiators and have held in fact nearly twenty such meetings since then. Seven to eighteen academic economists from eight to eleven countries met each time for one to three days and were then joined for another few days by six to twenty-three high officials from national Central Banks and Treasuries, the IMF, the European Community, the OECD, the BIS, and, on one occasion, from UNCTAD.

In order to ensure the fullest and frankest discussion, no record of these joint meetings was ever kept or will ever be published. Some of the papers contributed by the academic participants have, however, been published individually by them in various journals, and particularly in the Princeton *Essays in International Finance.* On only one occasion were such papers published in a joint volume: *Maintaining and Restoring Balance in International Payments* by

William Fellner, Fritz Machlup, Robert Triffin, and eleven others (Princeton University Press, 1966).

The very fact that such meetings continued to be held, usually several times a year, and attended each time by overburdened official negotiators, is the best demonstration of how useful they were deemed by them as well as by the academic participants. Innumerable topics were explored over those years, often well before they were, or could be, broached in the more formal official meetings of the IMF, the Group of Ten, the Committee of Twenty.

Let me mention, for instance, two key features of the international monetary system which officials were specifically barred by their instructions from discussing for a long time in their own meetings: fixed exchange rates and the price of gold, at $35 an ounce! Both were amply discussed at our first four academic meetings and later on at our joint meetings. These discussions undoubtedly initiated a slow but radical evolution in the thinking of our official colleagues, preparing them at least for the decisions that were finally forced upon them by events rather than as a deliberate choice many years later in 1971 and 1973.

3.

The most distinguishing feature of our debates reflected the overriding preoccupation of Professor Machlup with *explaining,* rather than with *resolving,* our disagreements about international monetary reform.

He saw himself—and we agreed with him—four possible sources for such disagreements among rational economists:

1. logical fallacies in reasoning;
2. semantic confusions flowing from different interpretations of ill-defined terms, such as "liquidity," balance of payments "deficits" or "surpluses," "adjustment," "flexible rates," and the like;
3. different "hunches" about essential, but unavailable information, particularly the unpredictable policy responses of central bankers and other decision-makers to future problems and developments;
4. different value judgments and priorities about conflicting social goals, such as full employment, price stability, an efficient allocation of resources, the reduction of income inequality, the preservation of individual freedom against government interference, and so on.

The first two should yield to rational debate, and Professor Machlup has long been tireless in his efforts to define precisely many of the key concepts too often used too loosely and ambiguously by us in our writings. He regarded, however, the latter two sources of conflicting economic advice as untractable and legitimate. All we could and should do to guide policy decisions was to make fully explicit the different assumptions and value judgments underlying our different recommendations.

Our painstaking "ferreting out" of the assumptions underlying our different recommendations confirmed, however, what I suspected from the beginning, that is Freud's old observation that man's logic is most often used to rationalize ex post instinctive, gut preferences linked to basic value judgments and priorities. The assumptions and "hunches about the future" brought out to explain and justify our recommendations were unsurprisingly predictable. Proposals other than our own would be unnegotiable. Proponents of a semiautomatic gold standard and of unmanaged floating rates both distrusted government interference in economic life, but the former felt confident that downward price and wage adjustments could be enforced by proper monetary policies "without undue hardship," while the latter stressed that downward price and wage adjustments would entail wasteful and intolerable levels of unemployment. National "monetary sovereignty" was a favorite argument of the opponents of radical reforms as well as of the proponents of managed flexible rates, the latter arguing that such flexibility was needed to protect the better managed countries—presumably their own—from imported inflation or deflation from badly managed foreign countries. Those favoring a centralization of reserves were more skeptical of the virtues of national sovereignty in an interdependent world, and more concerned about the ability of the reserve currency centers to export their own inflation to the rest of the world.

I often argued also that our role as *advisers* should not be unduly affected by our desire to *forecast* correctly which advice is most likely to be accepted. Our personal "hunches" about the probable policy responses of official decision makers might justify different forecasts, but *not* different recommendations, when asked by them what reforms or policies we deem most appropriate as economists. Politics "as the art of the possible" should be left to them, but we should be particularly anxious to help those statesmen who view it also as "the art of making possible tomorrow what may still be impossible today."

The most valuable aspect of the "cross-examination" procedures adopted in all our debates was to avoid the succession of monologues too often characteristic of such meetings. Each of us had to defend his proposals against the criticisms of other participants and to explain why he could not agree with their own proposals. Long speeches were ruled out and brief interruptions, not exceeding a minute or so, permitted by the Chairman—on a show of *two* hands—to comment quickly and immediately on a particular point of clarification or disagreement with the speaker.

4.

Most of the key questions and answers raised in later years of unending debates about international monetary reform were anticipated, from the very outset, in

our academic meetings in Princeton and Bellagio, and even earlier in Professor
Machlup's comprehensive and incisive study, "Plans for Reform of the International Monetary System."[3] Three closely interrelated problems (adjustment,
liquidity, and confidence) were identified as calling for reform of the system,
and four major approaches selected for analysis: the semiautomatic gold standard, centralization of international reserves, multiple currency reserves, and
flexible exchange rates.

The degree of agreement that soon began to emerge among all or most
of the participants was all the more surprising as several of them had been
selected chiefly because of their well-know opposite views, and as our chairman
strenuously discouraged most attempts to reach a consensus, which he deemed
less useful to decision makers than clearly stated and explained conflicting
opinions.

Most striking of all was the fact that the very first shortcoming of the
present system unanimously selected for criticism was the same, and was de-
nounced in identical terms:[4]

The present system, which relies [mainly] on the deficits of [one or two]
reserve-currency countries to supplement the growth of monetary gold reserves,
cannot continue indefinitely: since the system necessitates a progressive increase
in the ratio of the liquid liabilities of the reserve-currency countries to their
gold holdings, it creates a growing threat to the value of the reserve holdings of
other countries, with the result that confidence in the stability of the system is
undermined.

Other specific points of agreement are too numerous to be noted, and I
can only refer the reader to the full text of our *Report*[5] and particularly to
three policy statements jointly formulated by all, or most (ten to sixteen) of
those present at the end of three of our meetings.[6] The first of them resulted
from my suggestion that agreement on feasible solutions might be helped if each
of us were asked to express his *second-best* answer to the three problems under
debate, as well as his preference for any of the four "supposed panaceas" that
were being compared:

Many apparent divergencies between us reflect the fear that any attention given
to any two of these three problems might divert attention from the one to which
each of us, as an individual, attaches primary importance and has devoted most
thought and attention, and which he tends as a consequence to regard as more
important or urgent than the others.[7]

We could all agree on this basis on the urgency of a funding of official
dollar and sterling balances, as a first, conservatory, step needed to protect the
international monetary system against the most evident and immediate threat
to its survival and stability.

Our second statement stressed that "the price of gold or flexible exchange rates, which the Group of Ten has excluded from its agenda, deserve and will receive our full attention in our next meeting."[8]

The most comprehensive agreement, formulated on June 5, 1964, stressed among other points:

1. The need for *financing* reversible disequilibria, as well as for initiating promptly the *adjustment* of enduring ones, partly through more frequent changes in exchange rates than currently contemplated by major governments.
2. "The mechanism of reserve creation should be overhauled to adjust the expansion of reserves to needs," and "the rate of reserve creation should be sufficient to sustain the growth of world production without inducing price inflation."
3. "The protection of the large outstanding foreign exchange component of the world reserve pool against sudden or massive conversions into gold should receive a high order of priority."

The Group also commented that:

1. "The convergence of opinions and the degree of consensus actually achieved were in fact greater—in scope, depth, and number—than is indicated here. When this section of the Report was formulated on the last day of the last conference, the fourteen members still present were reluctant, without a confirming canvass of the entire Group, to state several points on which presumably most members would have agreed."
2. "Surveying this consensus, . . . members discovered a complementarity between proposals they had first thought to be rivals. Thus many advocates of limited exchange-rate flexibility would now combine it with centralization of international reserves."
3. "There was, in addition, an impressive convergence of opinions reflected by important changes in participants' views. Thus some previous advocates of unlimited, unmanaged flexibility in exchange rates tended, after consideration, to favor some form of limited flexibility. Such instances of convergence were gratifying consequences of the Group's deliberations."[9]

These comments are particularly noteworthy as they single out *"limited exchange-rate flexibility,"* and *"centralization of international reserves"* as complementary, rather than alternative, proposals for world monetary reform. Professor Machlup still had to point out, twelve years later, that "the absence of an adjustment mechanism and the failure to control international liquidity are so closely related that they can be seen as two aspects of the same problem."[10]

Of the four, or rather five, approaches proposed to solve these problems, three
had been politely dismissed in effect in the final Bellagio "Consensus" referred
to above. Neither the semiautomatic gold standard, nor the multiple currency
reserve system, nor the unlimited, unmanaged flexibility of exchange rates ever
gained any wide adherence from academic—and even less from official—participants of the Bellagio Group meetings. On the other hand, the role of limited,
managed flexibility of exchange rates in balance of payments adjustment and
the centralization of international reserves—including the funding of the outstanding "overhang" of reserve currency balances—stressed by most of us in
1964 were increasingly endorsed also, over a period of eleven years, by most
official as well as academic economists concerned with international monetary
reform. They were indeed advocated nearly unanimously, as late as June 1974,
in the final *Outline of Reform* of the Committee of Twenty,[11] before being
abruptly discarded or ignored, in effect, in the Jamaica Agreement and the proposed Second Amendment to the Articles of Agreement of the International
Monetary Fund.

5.

The participation of officials in the Bellagio Group certainly added a new, and
welcome, dimension to our discussions, without altering in the least their in-
formality and utter frankness. The same old issues had to be rehashed, of course,
again and again, in the light of new developments, but also with better awareness
of fast-changing official attitudes toward what might, or might not, be negotiable
in the short run. Many new issues were added such as the kind of "objective
indicators" of emerging disequilibria, the "guidelines" that might be used for
market interventions in a system of managed floating rates, the role of central
banks in the mushrooming of private as well as official Euro-dollar balances and
Xeno-currencies—to use Professor Machlup's term—in general, the allocation of
"lender of last resort" responsibilities in this respect between central banks and
other monetary authorities, the redefinition of the SDR and other units of
account, the definition of "optimum currency" areas, the progress—or lack of
progress—of hoped-for regional monetary integration, particularly in the
European Community, the proposed "link" between reserve creation and the
financing of development in the Third World, the two-tier arrangements for
gold and its "phasing out" from the reserve system, and so forth.

To determine how much the thinking of the officials influenced the thinking
of the academics, and vice versa, would be an impossible task. We rarely thought
in those terms, and the views of all participants were discussed by all on their
merits, with little or no attention being paid to the official or academic status of
the speaker. All that I can say is that many of the ideas later discussed by

academics in their writings and by officials in their negotiations were first broached and explored in our joint debates and deeply influenced by them.

A disabusing, and possibly even devastating, remark is also called for. Our impact on the actual course of events—rather than on each other—proved minimal indeed. Few, if any, of the conclusions most generally shared by us about the major needs for reform ever led to negotiated agreements, and the officials theoretically in charge increasingly lost control, or even relinquished it, under the new philosophy and economic policies initiated in the United States by Messrs. Nixon and Connally and their successors: "benign neglect" at first, soon followed by the unilateral repudiation of Bretton Woods convertibility commitments and the generalized adoption of nationally managed, mismanaged, or unmanaged flexible rates of exchange, the abandonment of any attempt to control overall reserve creation, and an increasing switch of actual responsibilities for balance of payments credit assistance from the official authorities to the private sector, particularly the mushrooming xeno-currency market.

All that we could claim for our discussions is that they helped us understand and explain the progressive collapse of the international monetary system and—at least for a time—of our hopes and plans for rational, concerted reforms.

6.

Let me conclude with a few observations on my personal reactions to Professor Machlup's role in our debates.

I hardly need point out how extensive and fundamental our agreement has been, throughout the years, on most of the basic issues of international monetary reform. I have learned far more from him in this field than from anybody else, even as to the exact meaning of my initial proposals.[12] He also strengthened and supplemented them indeed in several respects, particularly regarding the role of gold—about which his proposals were far more radical and devastating than mine—and the irrelevance of liquid reserves or other "backing" for SDR obligations. He noted himself that our views—and those of Professor Fellner—"on major issues are converging where they are not identical."[13]

Our disagreements, if any, are far less fundamental and have yielded more and more over the years, as far as I am concerned, to his impeccable logic and persuasiveness.

The first is merely a question of nuance, rather than disagreement. I would not even mention it if it were not raised also by Professor Williamson in another contribution to this volume.[14] I have always put relatively more stress than Professor Machlup on the appropriateness of *financing* some balance of payments disequilibria than on the prompt *adjustment* emphasized in most of his writings. I am sure, however, that Professor Machlup would also agree with Professor

Williamson, myself, and many others, that the prompt elimination of balance of
payments disequilibria—on current account, of course, but also sometimes on
overall account—is not the overriding goal of rational economic policies, for
surplus as well as well as for deficit countries. The financing of the disequilibria
triggered by postwar reconstruction needs, for instance, and more recently by
the sudden explosion of oil prices was certainly preferable to overnight adjustment policies. On the other hand, there is no doubt that officials need far more
preaching about the need for adjustment than about the need for financing.

Our slightly different emphasis on adjustment versus financing may have
influenced my reluctance to follow fully Professor Machlup's leadership on the
virtues of exchange rate flexibility. I confess to have been totally, if belatedly,
convinced by the highly pragmatic "consistency" argument lucidly and forcefully presented by him in several of his books and articles: "We must distinguish
those who *recommend* an autonomous monetary policy—a credit policy independent of the balance of payments—from those [including presumably Professor
Machlup] who do *not* recommend it but regard it as a given and unalterable
fact with which realistic observers should reckon. . . . Those who are prepared to
put the money-creating power of the banking system at the disposal of full
employment and growth policies regardless of the state of the balance of payments cannot in all consistency oppose exchange-rate flexibility."[15]

Following the same reasoning, he would endorse stable exchange rates and
even monetary union within a regional group of countries "linked . . . through
a common monetary ideology . . . [and agreeing] that their credit and fiscal
policies should be coordinated so that through central-bank action a high degree
of conformity can be achieved in the supply of money. . . . Fixed exchange rates
among countries with coordinated monetary policies, and flexible exchange rates
among countries pursuing autonomous policies—this appears the maxim consistent with the theorems of monetary economics."[16]

Professor Machlup noted, in his introduction to *Maintaining and Restoring
Balance in International Payments* (p. 6) that one of the few differences between
us was "the greater faith—or hopes—Triffin has in international coordination of
national policies, and . . . the leanings of Fellner and Machlup—as indeed of most
of the academic specialists today—toward greater exchange rate flexibility."
Events have obviously confirmed his skepticism about effective coordination,
even in the tightly knit European Community.

Yet, I remain unconvinced that *day-to-day floating* is the only realistic
alternative to *unalterably fixed* exchange rates. The Bretton Woods "adjustable
peg" system worked, after all, reasonably well for a considerable period of time
among the major countries of the industrialized world. For countries professing
their determination to avoid inflation as well as unemployment, the need to
alter exchange rates among themselves arises only from the occasional failure of
these preferred policies. The sad experience of the last few years should not be
extrapolated indefinitely into the future as a peremptory demonstration of the
inevitable, day-to-day failure of first-best policies.

I remain equally unconvinced by Professor Machlup's prescription of the practical implementation of a flexible rates system. His "favorite recipe is [or was] a general approval of a band widened to 5 percent, that is 2 1/2 percent up or down from a parity adjustable by no more than 2 or 3 percent over any twelve-month period, but never more, and preferably less, and 1 percent at a time."[17]

So-called "crawling pegs" or "bands" may be even more difficult to enforce and make credible to speculators than the adjustable peg. Crawling will do no good when wide disparities in monetary policies and in price and cost changes make "jumping" practically unavoidable. Recent shifts of far more than 3 percent *in a single week,* rather than over a twelve-month period, in Mexican, Australian, New Zealand, Italian, British, and even Canadian exchange rates, as well as the *rapid* crawl or jumps of many other currencies have reinforced this skepticism. I am even still tempted, in this matter, to accept the old wisdom that only exchange-rate changes well in excess of 3 percent are worth considering as unavoidable, or even preferable to other adjustment policies.

A final difference of emphasis may be noted. We both agree on the need to "phase out" both gold and reserve currencies from the international monetary system, but Professor Machlup's main—and earlier—insistence has been throughout on a rapid elimination of the former rather than the latter, more repeatedly emphasized in my writings. Again, this may be connected with his greater faith in flexible rates as effective dikes against the flooding of world reserves by reserve currencies. In fact, however, neither the inconvertibility of the dollar nor the generalization of "managed" exchange rates have decreased perceptibly the overwhelming role of the dollar in reserve creation, and Professor Machlup would agree, I think, that a better control of reserve creation is nearly as essential to the satisfactory functioning of a managed flexible rates system as of a pegged rates system.

7.

As a member of the group which recently drafted, under the chairmanship of Professor Jan Tinbergen, the RIO (*Reshaping the International Order*) report, I should add a brief comment on the attention paid by the Bellagio Group to the concerns of the less developed countries in the issues we were discussing.

These were certainly not entirely ignored. We mentioned—rather summarily, I admit—in our very first report that "some variants of the proposals to increase the supply of monetary reserves would put at the disposal of developing countries the real resources obtained in exchange for the additional reserves created. However, virtually any reform of the international payments system would, if successful, promote aid for development by facilitating the international transfer of funds."[18] Our second report included a full chapter by Robert L. West on the "Impact of the Adjustment Process on Developing Countries."[19] The "link" between reserve creation and development financing was repeatedly debated in our joint meetings—particularly in Taormina, in January 1971—as was also the impact of the energy problem on the less developed countries, and our discussions undoubtedly contributed to various individual publications on these topics,[20] testimonies to the Congressional Subcommittee on International Exchange and Payments chaired by one of our members, Congressman Henry Reuss, and to the recommendations issued by that Subcommittee and the Joint Economic Committee.[21]

Participation in the Bellagio Group, however, remained practically confined to representatives of the developed countries—particularly the Group of Ten— and of the IMF, the OECD, and the BIS. I remember only one occasion on which we were joined, in Taormina, by a delegate from UNCTAD.

As for Professor Machlup, his interests have centered throughout mostly on the role of the major industrial and financial countries in the world monetary and reserve system. His rare references to the problems of the less developed countries, however, have done a lot to clarify the main issues, and to dispel widespread prejudices and misunderstandings about the "link." His arguments in the "Cloakroom Rule of International Reserves: Reserve Creation and Resources Transfers" conclusively showed that the growth of international reserves could be used to finance long term loans and investments, or even grants, as well as short term "liquid" credits. He concluded this article by pointing out that "the acquisition of reserves under the gold standard involved the surrender of real resources. If additional reserves under the new system can be created at no cost, the saving will benefit someone and its distribution must be arbitrary. If developing countries were made the beneficiaries, the cost to reserve holders would be no greater than under the gold standard. This may be proposed as an argument in support of schemes linking the creation of international reserves with aid to developing countries. On the other hand, the industrial countries may object to clandestine aid schemes and claim that they, as the chief holders of reserves should be allowed to create additional reserves without having to 'earn' them through transfers of real resources to developing countries. Both arguments are persuasive and can be reasonably defended."[22]

8.

The most fitting conclusion of this article is the expression of deep gratitude that academic as well as official economists feel for Professor Machlup. He became, by general acclaim, the unquestioned intellectual leader and mentor of our vain efforts to reform the crumbling international monetary system of the postwar years. The Bellagio Group, which he created and led throughout, inspired most of the constructive research and mutual interchanges that have enabled us all to gain a better understanding of major problems and possible solutions.

As most recently noted by Professor Machlup, academics and officials had agreed that "adjustment and liquidity . . . were the key issues . . . [and] emphasized the importance of building into the reformed system an effective adjustment mechanism and international control and management of international liquidity. These objectives were still prominently displayed in the *Outline of Reform* released by the Committee of Twenty on June 14, 1974. They were conspicuously absent from the Jamaica Agreement of January 8, 1976 [and from the Amendment to the Articles of Agreement of the IMF], except for some empty phrases regarding further 'evolution' in future years."[23]

The Jamaica abdication, however, will not last forever. The problem of international monetary reform will not fade away. Whenever the negotiators resume the task abandoned in Jamaica, they will have to turn back for guidance to the agreements ironed out, over a period of more than ten years, by the Bellagio Group, at the initiative and under the unique leadership of one man: Professor Machlup.

Notes

1. See my book on *Europe and the Money Muddle: From Bilateralism to Near-Convertibility, 1947-1956* (New Haven, Conn.: Yale University Press, 1957).

2. *International Monetary Arrangements: The Problem of Choice. Report on the Deliberations of an International Study Group of Thirty-two Economists* (International Finance Section, Princeton University, 1964); referred to in later notes as the *"Report."*

3. First published in August 1962 as *Special Paper in International Economics,* No. 3 (International Finance Section, Princeton University), and expanded in Part Four of *International Payments, Debts and Gold* (New York: Charles Scribner's Sons, 1964), pp. 282-366.

4. Except for words in brackets, added respectively by the tenants of flexible rates, on the one hand, and the tenants of multiple currency reserves, on the other.

5. Referred to in note 2 above.

6. Only the last of these, released on June 5, 1964, is included in the *Report* (pp. 101-107) noted above. The first (January 1964) and the second (March 22) are reproduced on pp. 320-326 of my book, *The World Money Maze. National Currencies in International Payments* (New Haven, Conn.: Yale University Press, 1966).

7. *The World Money Maze,* p. 321.

8. Ibid., p. 323.

9. Pages 101-102, 105 and 106 of the *Report.*

10. "Between Outline and Outcome the Reform Was Lost," in *Reflections*

on Jamaica, by Edward M. Bernstein et al., *Essays in International Finance* No. 115 (Princeton University, April 1976), p. 30.

11. See *International Monetary Reform. Documents of the Committee of Twenty,* International Monetary Fund, 1974, pp. 7–48, and particularly the brief summary on p. 8.

12. Particularly on the major difference which he stressed, from the very beginning, between my proposals and the Keynes plan for a Clearing Union. See *International Payments, Debts and Gold,* p. 324.

13. *Maintaining and Restoring Balance in International Payments,* p. 4.

14. Chapter 10, particularly pp. 159–172.

15. *International Payments, Debts and Gold,* pp. 358 and 361.

16. Ibid., pp. 360–362.

17. *Changes in the International Monetary System and the Effects on Banks,* 24th International Banking Summer School (Chinciano, Italy, May 1971), p. 20.

18. *International Monetary Arrangements: The Problem of Choice,* p. 41. See also pp. 85 and 88.

19. *Maintaining and Restoring Balance in International Payments,* pp. 223–241.

20. See, for instance, R. Triffin, "The Use of Finance for Collectively Agreed Purposes," and G. Haberler, "The Case against the Link" in the *Banca Nazionale del Lavoro Quarterly Review,* March 1971.

21. See, among others, the Hearings of May 28, 1969, and May 13–19, 1970, and particularly the report entitled "A Proposal to Link Reserve Creation and Development Assistance."

22. *Quarterly Journal of Economics,* August 1965, p. 355. Needless to say, I regard the argument *for* the link—as one of several "agreed" uses of the lending potential derived from reserve creation—as far more persuasive than the argument against it. For further discussion of this issue, see Professor Machlup's remarks in *Remaking the International Monetary System. The Rio Agreement and Beyond* (Baltimore: Johns Hopkins Press, 1968), pp. 52–76, and my article "The Use of SDR Finance for Collectively Agreed Purposes," in the *Banca Nazionale del Lavoro Quarterly Review,* March 1971. Let me note also that under the present system, about 95 percent of reserve increases have been invested in recent years in the developed countries (overwhelmingly in the United States) and 5 percent only in the less developed countries; and that reported DAC official assistance to the latter totalled only about one half of the credits accruing to the former from the system, and only one fourth in the case of the United States.

23. "Between Outline and Outcome the Reform Was Lost," *Reflections on Jamaica,* p. 31.

10 Machlup and International Monetary Reform

John Williamson

It must be comparatively rare to find a scholar pioneering the development of a new field after his sixtieth birthday. If one is prepared to define the outburst of intellectual activity devoted to the task of designing a more rational world monetary order that followed publication of Robert Triffin's *Gold and the Dollar Crisis* as constituting a "new field"—a semantic question I leave to those better qualified to undertake the task!—this is precisely what Fritz Machlup accomplished. For, with the possible exceptions of Triffin himself and the late Marcus Fleming, there is no-one whose intellectual contributions played a more central or constructive role in the fascinating interaction between academic economics and diplomatic negotiation that characterized the quest for reform of the international monetary system.

Not that Fritz Machlup's interest in international monetary economics was a new one. His doctoral dissertation, completed in 1923, was on the gold-exchange standard,[1] and was followed in 1927 by a second book which described how one country after another had adopted this system.[2] He participated in the Keynes-Ohlin debate on the transfer problem.[3] In 1940 he discussed the future of gold at the AEA meetings, revealing what the gold lobby would regard as his prejudice against the precious metal.[4] And he was a major architect of what exponents of the monetary approach to the balance of payments like to label traditional theory: he was a codeveloper of the elasticities analysis,[5] he wrote the authoritative work on the foreign trade multiplier,[6] and he participated constructively, if critically, in the development of the absorption approach.[7] I suspect that my own inability to be fired by missionary zeal for the monetary approach owes a great deal to my recollection of the occasion when as a graduate student I heard this apparent arch apostle of despised traditional theory recall approvingly Viner's comment on his *International Trade and the National Income Multiplier,* to the effect that the best chapter was the last (where he emphasized the limited scope of the foreign trade multiplier analysis, and in particular its abstraction from the monetary repercussions of an imbalance as analyzed in the classic price-specie-flow mechanism).

Fritz Machlup therefore came to the debate on international monetary reform with a well-established reputation as a leading international monetary

159

economist. My purpose in this chapter is to provide an account and assessment of his published contributions to the debate, thus complementing Triffin's chapter on his role in the Bellagio Group.

Defining the Issues

Most of Machlup's early contributions to the debate—and some of his later ones as well—were based on the exploitation of his formidable pedagogical abilities. The exception was his very first contribution, which was an amusingly unorthodox proposal to reduce the price of gold.[8] While others were producing a variety of plans to augment international liquidity by creating new reserve assets or advocating an increase in the price of gold, Machlup reasoned that the latter proposal was counterproductive in that it decreased reserves by promoting gold speculation. He therefore proposed the opposite—a series of small *decreases* in the gold price, to be announced in advance, so as to provide an incentive to shift from gold to dollars. Had near-agreement been reached on the creation of a new reserve asset at the time, this might have been a very useful step as a holding operation, but without such an agreement on the horizon one must doubt whether it could have achieved market credibility even at that time. And even if it had, I suspect that many economists would nowadays be inclined to worry about the possible inflationary implications of attracting gold out of private hoards. Furthermore, in the light of the intervening development of the analysis of seigniorage and the empirical evidence that central banks are by no means indifferent to the yield on the assets they hold, there is a certain implausibility in the implicit assumption that the major central banks would unhesitatingly buy an asset being surrendered by the private sector on account of its unattractive prospective yield.

The first of his pedagogical contributions was "The Fuzzy Concepts of Liquidity, International and Domestic",[9] which contained a protest against the popular uncritical use of the term "international liquidity" and the light-hearted aggregation procedure used to measure global liquidity. He argued that the term "international liquidity" was best avoided unless one first defined its precise meaning in terms of the sources of funds one was defining as liquid, and the uses and users of those funds. While I agree completely with his strictures on the inadequacies of standard practice (which has not been modified with the passage of time), Machlup and I have long differed on what should be done about it. In my very first paper on international monetary economics I proposed (despite Machlup's gentle criticism) to define a country's international liquidity as ". . . the size of the total deficit . . . that the country could incur without being forced to take 'undesirable' corrective action,"[10] and it still seems to me that a concept very similar to this is both useful and in close accordance with what is generally meant when this term is used. Thus my own preference would be for trying to develop an operational measure close to this concept rather than for Machlup's taxonomic approach.

Machlup first entered the center of the reform debate with the publication of his Princeton paper *Plans for Reform of the International Monetary System* in 1962.[11] This still provides the best taxonomy of the early plans for augmenting the supply of international liquidity. After two introductory sections devoted to describing the Bretton Woods system and the charges against it, he presented a "selection" of nearly twenty plans for reform. These were classified as extension of the gold-exchange standard (e.g., the multiple currency proposal), mutual assistance among central banks (directly through swaps or indirectly through the IMF, e.g., via the General Arrangements to Borrow), centralization of monetary reserves (the Keynes and Triffin Plans and a number of other proposals for the creation of a fiduciary reserve asset), an increase in the price of gold, and the adoption of flexible exchange rates. As well as expounding these proposals, often with the aid of T-accounts, he offered a number of criticisms, several of which will be referred to in subsequent sections of this chapter.

Perhaps Machlup's biggest contribution to the reform debate was his organization of the Bellagio Group. His motivation, methods, and accomplishments are discussed at length by Robert Triffin in this volume. Suffice it to note here that at the conclusion of the first sessions of the group (which were confined to academics) a report was issued,[12] of which he was the senior editor and whose style bears his unmistakable imprint, which was largely successful not merely in its avowed objectives of isolating the differences in factual assumptions and normative judgments that underlay the differing policy prescriptions espoused by the participants, but also in providing a taxonomy of the problems of the system that rapidly became standard. The problems identified were those of adjustment, liquidity, and confidence. I propose to discuss Machlup's substantive contributions to the reform debate under these headings.

Adjustment

The Bellagio conferees defined payments "adjustment" as "the process whereby deficits and surpluses are eliminated." I have for some time believed that this definition was unfortunate,[13] insofar as it suggests that a state of balanced international payments (on whatever concept) is necessarily to be desired. This is clearly not the case: if, for example, the concept of payments balance is the balance on official settlements, a country with a shortage or excess of reserves *should* pursue an objective other than flow balance. The implications of the Bellagio definition are that payments objectives can be confined to flow balance without regard for stocks, and hence that problem of selecting payments objectives do not exist. Thus a range of problems that were at the heart of the negotiations in the Committee of Twenty (C-20), and that have subsequently emerged as of major practical concern in terms of the distribution of the "oil deficit," were denied recognition. The cost of academic neglect of these problems has in my judgment been considerable: for example, the Committee of Twenty was hampered by the lack of any academic analysis of the question as to what constitutes appropriate payments objectives, which resulted in discussion of the U.S. reserve indicator proposal being conducted at an undesirably low intellectual level and leading to unnecessary international antagonism.[14]

A more appropriate definition of payments adjustment would in my view be "the process by which payments flows are altered so as to realize payments objectives." This gives scope for recognition of the important but neglected range of problems concerned with determining payments objectives, while changing nothing so far as the analysis of adjustment *techniques* is concerned. This latter problem received a great deal of attention from the academic economists, including the Bellagio conferees and certainly including Fritz Machlup. He repeatedly emphasized the fundamental importance of the system containing a viable adjustment mechanism, and was critical of the obsession of the officials with the liquidity problem at the expense of the adjustment problem during the 1960s. History proved only too quickly that he was right.

Machlup's first major contribution to the literature on the adjustment problem was his paper in *Maintaining and Restoring Balance in International Payments*.[15] This was a collection of papers initially written by academic members of the Bellagio Group for the benefit of the official members who were then working on the OECD Report on adjustment,[16] and subsequently published. Machlup's paper was one of three general surveys of the subject; it was not a pioneering contribution, but a competent presentation of what was then (and to a large extent still is) the consensus view of academic economists on the choice of desirable policies to effect adjustment. The monetary mechanism of adjustment was described, as was its near impotence in dealing with cases where cost levels had got out of alignment in an era of downward wage rigidity and commitments to full employment policies. The principal conclusion indicated, though not underlined out of (mistaken?) deference to the fact that the study was commissioned for the official world which at that time had a theological aversion to exchange rate flexibility, was that such flexibility was essential if faster adjustment were desired than that which could be produced by a deficit country holding its wage level constant in an inflationary world. (Many economists believed at the time that even this overstated the potency of adjustment through monetary restraint in "dilemma" cases, insofar as the Phillips curve would imply a high cost to achieving wage stability in terms of lost output. Those of us who doubt whether the long run Phillips curve is vertical at very low rates of inflation would still maintain this criticism.)

The reasoning was subsequently amplified and stated more forcefully. A mainly taxonomic paper[17] distinguished between "real adjustment" (income and/or price inflation/deflation and/or exchange rate changes), "compensatory corrections" (actions, such as import or capital account controls, that do not constitute real adjustment but nevertheless remove the need for financing an imbalance), and "financing," as the three possible responses to a payments imbalance. He argued that compensatory corrections, although often seemingly an easy way out, were not likely to be effective in the long run due to the offsetting reactions they usually brought into play, and that they were in any event prejudicial to economic efficiency. Hence he concluded that "our task . . . remains to find how our political idiosyncrasies can be made compatible with the unpleasant necessities of real adjustment". The chief political idiosyncrasy he had in mind was the aversion to exchange rate flexibility, and in due course he concluded that the most hopeful way around this aversion was the promotion of limited flexibility in the form of a wider band and a crawling peg.

Fritz Machlup's main contribution to the promotion of limited flexibility took the form of convening (in association with Fred Bergsten, George Halm, and Robert Roosa) a second mixed group of academics and practitioners. In this case, the "Bürgenstock group," the practitioners came from the banking rather than the official world. The proceedings of the resulting two conferences were in due course published,[18] and provide the most comprehensive investigation of the analytics of limited flexibility. Machlup's own two substantive contributions both exploited his semantic proclivities: the first was a useful clarification of the semantics of limited flexibility, the second a dissection of the differences in the language used to describe operations in the forward market by practitioners on the one hand and the academics on the other. He demonstrated that the terms used by the dealers tended to lead to unduly pessimistic conclusions about the capacity of the market to satisfy an increased demand for forward cover, and about the social cost of providing such cover.

Machlup argued forcefully for the adoption of limited flexibility in numerous spoken addresses, though he remained more qualified in print.[19] His central argument remained the necessity of incorporating an adequate adjustment mechanism in the system while respecting such political realities as the widespread commitment to full employment and the apparent aversion to floating exchange rates. The one idiosyncrasy in his exposition was the suggestion that par values should be changed regularly (though always by very small amounts) even when there was no evident need for a change, so as to ensure that authorities remained used to changing them and did not come to attach prestige to the maintenance of a particular rate. Surprisingly, for one who regarded floating as the first-best solution and limited flexibility as a second-best dictated by the need to accommodate political reality, he continued to advocate limited flexibility even after the demise of the adjustable peg and the widespread resort to managed floating in March 1973. Perhaps he took too literally the official avowals that a return to the par value system was intended as soon as circumstances permitted: it is understandable if one who is so careful in using language to clarify should overlook the fact that others are less scrupulous, though one might have expected him to have been warned by his own eulogy on the "linguistic pragmatism" that the official world had utilized on a previous occasion.[20] Only after the Jamaica agreement in early 1976 had convinced him that the C–20's *Outline of Reform* was not a program of action did he reflect that

Floating is now the only system that can work without continuously recurrent crisis in the exchange markets, and all talk about an early return to a system of fixed par values is just for the birds—for the consolation of traditionalists sick with nostalgia and for the reassurance of exporters weak in the art of multiplication.[21]

Liquidity

Although Fritz Machlup was foremost among the academic economists who were critical of the priority given to solving the liquidity problem, at the expense of near neglect of the problems of adjustment and confidence during the 1960s, he did not on that account deny the importance of the liquidity problem or contract out of the debate on it. On the contrary, he contributed a series of distinguished papers on the issues that arose as the debate progressed. His ability to sustain contributions of such quality and topicality no doubt depended heavily on his participation in the Bellagio conferences, where the issues that were arising in the official negotiations were being discussed with the academics. But no one can grudge Machlup this advantage, for whereas most of those who gain entrance to these groups do so through a process that involves a substantial element of luck,[22] Machlup in large measure created the groups that provided these opportunities.

In 1962 Machlup criticized the multiple reserve currency proposal, which at that time appeared to be the preferred U.S. solution to the liquidity problem, on the ground that it would inevitably intensify the confidence problem.[23] In that year he also produced the first version of *Plans for Reform of the International Monetary System,* which voiced similar criticism of the multiple currency approach and was also strongly critical of the then-popular proposal to increase the price of gold. The dangers and disadvantages he outlined included intensification of the confidence problem, the creation of inflationary potential, rewarding those who had speculated against the word of the United States at the expense of those who had trusted it, and arbitrary income redistribution. In addition to thus dismissing the alternatives, this monograph launched his discussion of the issues involved in the design of a fiduciary reserve asset that constituted his seminal published contribution to the reform debate.

The three issues that attracted Machlup's major attention were (a) whether a scheme provided for credit creation, or merely for credit transfer; (b) whether it made provision for steady growth in the stock of reserves; and (c) the type of asset to be acquired by the credit-creating (or credit-transferring) institution. In his first monograph he argued that schemes that merely provided for easier access to credit would have been less expansionary than those that would have involved bestowing additional reserves on countries. On the second issue, he contrasted the failure of the Keynes Plan to provide for steady growth of reserves with the potential for such expansion in the Triffin Plan and argued that this implied that although the Keynes Plan might have been more expansionary in the short run it would have been less so in the long run. The third issue involved the question of "backing" for newly created reserves. At that time Machlup regarded this as an important issue, and criticized the Stamp Plan on account of the unsuitability of the assets that the IMF would have acquired in the process of reserve creation, which would have made it difficult to reverse expansionary operations should this have proved desirable. He asked rhetorically whether central banks would not be regarded as financially irresponsible if they created money by giving it to poor widows and orphans.

On the first two of these questions Machlup turned from analyst to advocate in subsequent contributions. He likened those opposing the extension of the IMF from its past credit-transferring role to a new credit-creating role to those who would have stopped monetary innovation at the stage where the goldsmiths issued warehouse receipts for gold but had not got round to loaning out a prudent part of the sums deposited with them.[24] He also developed more analytically his reasons for preferring a scheme that involved credit creation (or "reserve allotments") to one that merely eased borrowing rights.[25] He retained the previous argument that reserve allotments would have a more expansionary impact on government policy, but this in itself would hardly have been decisive for a monetary conservative such as Machlup. The essential additional argument was that the major effects of perceived reserve shortages were to be found in the imposition of additional payments restrictions rather than the resolve to strengthen anti-inflationary monetary policies. When the SDR agreement was finally announced in September 1967 Machlup was quick to recognize that behind the semantic veil cunningly drawn to obscure where victory lay the SDR was in fact to be a true reserve asset. This was one reason that he was an enthusiastic supporter of the agreement.

Similarly, Machlup emerged as a strong champion of insuring the ability to provide for regular growth in the stock of reserves. His central paper in this context was "The Need for Monetary Reserves,"[26] in which he expounded what had already been christened "the Mrs. Machlup's Wardrobe Theory of Monetary Reserves." The "demand"[27] of central bankers for reserves, like that of women for clothes, is, he argued, a simple desire for a little more than last year.[28] The implication is that prevention of the defensive restrictions that Machlup believed to be induced by dissatisfaction with payments outcomes required not a high *level* of reserves, but secular *growth* in the reserve stock. Once again, Machlup could take comfort from the form of the SDR system as ultimately agreed.

Initially Machlup had joined a number of other writers in attaching great significance to the assets acquired by the IMF in the course of credit creation being "sound" and therefore salable—although he was careful to note the economic rationale of this requirement, which is to allow a reversal of the process of credit creation should this appear desirable. On this third issue, however, his views were rapidly and significantly revised. In "The Cloakroom Rule . . ."[29] he argued forcefully that the question of backing was irrelevant. For payments among customers of the same bank, the assets held by that bank are irrelevant; for payments within the same country, the assets held by its central bank are irrelevant; and, similarly, for payments within the same world (provided the system is essentially closed), the assets held by the international central bank are irrelevant. What matters is therefore not the preservation of the liquidity of the international reserve-creating institution, but rather the effects of its reserve creation on such macroeconomic variables as price inflation or the intensity of payments restrictions, and also the effects of its selection of assets on the international distribution of income. (He ignored the possible need for credit contraction to which he had previously drawn attention, perhaps because he may by then have formulated the "Mrs. Machlup's Wardrobe Theory.") Since the international reserve-creating institution would not have a brake on its credit-creating potential imposed by any possible threat of illiquidity one would have to rely on it being responsibly managed to avoid the danger of it indulging in irresponsibly expansionary policies likely to promote global inflation.[30]

The remainder of "The Cloakroom Rule . . ." was devoted to the first systematic exploration of what has since become known as the "seigniorage problem." If new reserves were to be created, they necessarily had to be injected into the system through some country acquiring additional international purchasing power, which would give that country the opportunity of acquiring a transfer of resources. He outlined alternative possible ways in which new reserve assets might be distributed, and argued that only if they were given as repayable loans to deficit countries could one ensure that no significant resource transfers would occur as a result of reserve creation. But this would risk nullifying the objective of insuring continuous growth in the stock of reserves. Hence the possibility of resource transfer had to be accepted. There were no objective criteria that would indicate who *should* get the benefits of potential resource transfer, and hence could be invoked in support of or opposition to the "aid link." If the developed countries wanted to get together to increase the stock of tokens they used as reserves between themselves, why should they not be allowed to? Equally, why shouldn't the developing countries be the beneficiaries of the technical progress in money production that was represented by replacing gold by fiat money? The following year he repeated that there was no "just" way of distributing the newly created reserves (although distribution in proportion to gold holdings would be "intolerably unfair") but argued that the exact share a country received was "relatively unimportant."[31]

Machlup's enthusiastic endorsement of the SDR scheme[32] was in part on account of its rejection of "the fiction of a central debtor." The SDR Account involves the creation of reserves by crediting countries with SDRs (in proportion to their IMF quotas) without requiring them to deposit any liabilities in exchange. There is thus no formal backing. The logic of Machlup's argument was accepted and indeed carried beyond the point that he had dared to advocate, for instead of the IMF's assets being "dormant," as he had urged,[33] they were nonexistent. He proposed that the "experts of the Fund and the negotiating governments" be "granted honorary doctor's degrees by the great universities" for their role in fathering this breakthrough in monetary practice.[34]

One may in fact feel that Machlup exaggerated. To the extent that interest is paid on SDR holdings in excess of cumulative allocations, there is a need for interest to be charged on net use of SDRs. Hence in a very real economic sense the SDR is "backed" by all participating countries in proportion to their cumulative allocations. The accounting conventions are indeed unimportant, but the assurance that interest will continue to be paid is surely essential to preservation of confidence in the SDR. In my judgment the principal criticism that can be made of Machlup's distinguished contributions to the debate that led to the creation of the world's first fiduciary reserve asset is that he overlooked the significance of paying a competitive interest rate on the SDR, which he indeed argued was unimportant so long as the system contained adequate rules governing settlement obligations.[35] If the SDR is ever to emerge as the basic reserve asset, it is surely essential that countries be content to hold the bulk of their reserves in the form of SDRs, and this is hardly conceivable while the yield on the SDR is dominated by that on alternative assets. Settlement rules can restrain short term switching, but they cannot be expected to produce a willingness to tolerate permanent deviations from a country's preferred reserve composition.

Confidence

The confidence problem was described by the Bellagio conferees in the following terms.[36]

If major holders of reserves sought suddenly to substitute one international reserve asset for another, they could drain reserves from a reserve center and put unbearable strains on the adjustment mechanism. They could even cause a drastic contraction in the global total of reserve assets, subjecting the world economy to deflationary pressures.

Fritz Machlup always took the confidence problem very seriously, which is perhaps hardly surprising when one recalls that his doctoral dissertation (1923) was on the gold-exchange standard, which is a system that collapsed because of the confidence problem during the Great Depression (1931) with calamitous results. The importance he attached to this problem was evident in many of the contributions that have already been cited. Thus his proposal to reduce the price of gold was motivated in part by the (hardly controvertible) conviction that mere discussion of the opposite proposal provoked destabilizing shifts from dollars to gold. Even more clearly, his criticism of the multiple currency proposal[37] was based on the historical analogy with bimetallism and Gresham's Law, and his solution was always to move toward one international money (following the route previously taken within individual countries) issued by an international central bank.

In common with other economists, Machlup recognized that the SDR scheme, while containing adequate settlement rules in the form of the designation mechanism to prevent introduction of the SDR leading to an intensification of the confidence problem, did not provide a solution for it. Hence he was among the economists who in 1968 proposed the creation of a Reserve Settlement Account in the IMF.[38] This would have been an account that accepted as assets all forms of reserves—gold, currencies, and SDRs—and issued deposit claims in return, which would then have circulated as the sole reserve asset between the participants. This would have achieved a single international money and would thus have banished the confidence problem, at least so far as the official sector was concerned.

A Scoresheet

The foregoing review has indicated five major causes with which Fritz Machlup identified himself in the course of the debate on international monetary reform: the demonetization of gold, opposition to a multiple reserve currency system, the promotion of a fiduciary reserve asset, the introduction of a Reserve Settlement Account, and exchange rate flexibility. In concluding this chapter I shall provide a brief appraisal of the progress of the causes that he has espoused.

For a long time it looked as though gold was indeed in the process of being phased out as a reserve asset, as Machlup wished. The introduction of the two-tier gold market in 1968, the closing of the gold window in 1971, and the emergence of a significant premium of the market price over the official price coupled with the prohibition on central banks buying above the official price, served to eliminate gold transactions between central banks. This process was, however, reversed by the agreement on gold ratified at Jamaica in January 1976. Machlup condemned this agreement as a blatant backsliding on the commitment to reduce the monetary role of gold that was contained in the *Outline of Reform* published by the Committee of Twenty at the conclusion of its deliberations.[39] Whether the Jamaica provisions will in fact be effective in reinstating gold as a serious reserve asset remains to be seen: my own view is that they probably will not be, since gold lacks most of the characteristics of a desirable reserve asset, but one would be foolish to be dogmatic.

The multiple reserve currency system never became the subject of serious official international discussion. This fact might possibly owe something to Machlup's prompt action in exposing the vulnerability of this system (in conjunction with adjustably pegged exchange rates) to confidence crises. On the other hand, the proposal has never been definitively renounced either: the U.S. position in the Committee of Twenty at times echoed the idea, and there has been a significant growth in "new" reserve currencies in the 1970s. Machlup would probably (and rightly) regard this failure to suppress reserve diversification with greater equanimity in the present floating regime than he did in the previous par value system.

The world did get a fiduciary reserve asset, in the form of the SDR. Its design followed the principles that Machlup espoused, in certain respects beyond the point that he had regarded as prudent to advocate. When Dr. Emminger publishes his memoirs we may get some clues as to whether the similarity between the design of the SDR and the principles recommended by Machlup was entirely coincidental. But, as with gold, Machlup's high hopes were ultimately disappointed. The C-20 agreed on nothing to promote the role of the SDR, other than a change in the basis of its valuation (to the basket method) which was essential in a floating world—and which is mainly relevant to making the SDR a useful unit of account rather than promoting its role as the basic reserve asset. But the Committee at least hid its failure to agree behind a figleaf of aspirations about making the SDR the principal reserve asset. When Jamaica removed the figleaf and revealed that the *Outline of Reform* was not "linguistic pragmatism but failure to agree on anything substantive, and that in consequence the prospects for the future of the SDR were bleak, Machlup wondered "whether the parties to such an agreement are trying to deceive themselves or the public".[40] (The answer is, probably, both.)

The proposal made by Machlup and others in 1968 for a Reserve Settlement Account never came to anything. One might in fact feel that it was already redundant at the time it was made, despite the importance of the problem to which it was addressed, since it was easy to devise alternative ways of achieving the same objectives through substitution of SDRs for gold or currencies. Such proposals were generally regarded as an important part of the mandate given to the C-20, but once again no agreement was reached. Possibilities, but not agreed proposals, were listed in the *Outline of Reform,* and when no action on them was taken at Jamaica Machlup again voiced his dismay.

The world has indeed adopted flexible exchange rates in the 1970s, even though the process perhaps owed more to the force of events than to the advocatory writing of the academics. Machlup's economic logic has been vindicated in the process, but his political judgment about the depth of the official attachment to a par value system proved mistaken. I find it surprising that Machlup chose to criticize the Jamaica Agreement for saying nothing explicit about the adjustment mechanism[41] when a major feature of the Agreement was the legalization of floating, which has at least provided the system with an adjustment mechanism that is both legal and viable, and for which he had been calling for so long.

Despite my general sympathy for the positions that Machlup had adopted, I have not attempted to conceal my criticisms of his work. It would be an insult to his dedication to clear and honest analysis to impute to him an omniscience that none of us can claim. His work contained seminal contributions that no student of the history of international monetary reform can afford to ignore. It is in my view much to be regretted that the official world did not take greater note of some of those contributions while there was still time to organize an orderly evolution from the Bretton Woods system, but if his work did anything to prepare the officials for graceful acquiescence in the acceptance of floating, it at least helped insure that the long-feared breakdown of world monetary order did not bring disaster in its wake.

Notes

1. Published as *Die Goldkernwährung*, Meyer, Halberstadt, 1925.

2. *Die neuen Währungen in Europa*, Enke, Stuttgart, 1927.

3. "Währung und Auslandsverschuldung: Bemerkungen zur Diskussion zwischen Schacht und seinen Kritikern," *Mitteilungen des Verbandes österreichischer Banken und Bankiers*, 1928, and "Transfer und Preisbewegung," *Zeitschrift für Nationalökonomie*, 1930. English translations appear as chapters 16 and 17 in his *International Payments, Debts, and Gold*, Charles Scribner's Sons, New York, 1964.

4. "Eight Questions on Gold," *American Economic Review*, February 1941, reprinted as chapter 10 in *International Payments, Debts, and Gold*.

5. "The Theory of Foreign Exchanges," *Economica*, November, 1939, reprinted as chapter 1 in *International Payments, Debts, and Gold*.

6. *International Trade and the National Income Multiplier*, Blakiston, Philadelphia, 1943.

7. "Relative Prices and Aggregate Spending in the Analysis of Devaluation," *American Economic Review*, June 1955, reprinted as chapter 8 in *International Payments, Debts, and Gold*.

8. "Comments on the 'Balance of Payments' and a Proposal to Reduce the Price of Gold," *Journal of Finance*, May 1961; the relevant portion is reproduced as chapter 11 in *International Payments, Debts, and Gold*.

9. "Liquidité, internationale et nationale," *Bulletin d'Information et de Documentation, Banque Nationale de Belgique*, February 1962, reprinted as chapter 12 in *International Payments, Debts, and Gold*.

10. J. Williamson, "Liquidity and the Multiple Key Currency Proposal," *American Economic Review*, June 1963, p. 428.

11. *Special Papers in International Economics* No. 3, Princeton 1962, revised edition 1964, reprinted as chapter 14 in *International Payments, Debts, and Gold.*

12. *International Monetary Arrangements: The Problem of Choice,* International Finance Section, Princeton, N.J., 1964.

13. See, for example, J. Williamson, "Payments Objectives and Economic Welfare," *IMF Staff Papers,* November 1973, p. 573. Machlup himself subsequently criticized this definition in "Real Adjustments, Compensatory Corrections, and Foreign Financing of Imbalances in International Payments," R.E. Caves, H.G. Johnson, and P.B. Kenen, eds., *Trade, Growth, and the Balance of Payments,* Rand McNally, Chicago, 1965, pp. 188–89, but on the quite different ground that it precludes adjustment occurring in a system of freely floating exchange rates where deficits and surpluses can never exist to require elimination.

14. See J. Williamson, *The Failure of World Monetary Reform, 1971–1974,* Nelson, London, 1977, chapter 5.

15. Edited by W. Fellner, F. Machlup, R. Triffin, *Maintaining and Restoring Balance in International Payments,* Princeton University Press, Princeton, N.J., 1966.

16. OECD, *The Balance of Payments Adjustment Process* (a report of Working Party No. 3), Paris, 1966.

17. "Real Adjustments, Compensatory Corrections . . ."

18. C.F. Bergsten, G.N. Halm, F. Machlup, R.V. Roosa, eds., *Approaches to Greater Flexibility of Exchange Rates,* Princeton University Press, Princeton, N.J., 1970.

19. *The Alignment of Foreign Exchange Rates,* Praeger, New York, 1972, and "Exchange-Rate Flexibility," *Banca Nazionale del Lavoro Quarterly Review,* September 1973.

20. *Remaking the International Monetary System: The Rio Agreement and Beyond,* Johns Hopkins, Baltimore, 1968, chapter 2.

21. "Between Outline and Outcome the Reform Was Lost," in *Reflections on Jamaica,* Princeton Essays in International Finance No. 115, 1976, p. 33.

22. I recall that my own ultimate entrance to the Bellagio Group occurred because the organizers forecast (wrongly) that the other British academic invitee would decline his invitation!

23. *Outlook for U.S. Balance of Payments,* Hearings, Sub-Committee on International Exchange and Payments, Joint Economic Committee, U.S. Congress, Washington, D.C., December 1962, reprinted in H.G. Grubel, ed., *World Monetary Reform,* Stanford University Press, Stanford, Conn., 1963.

24. "From Dormant Liabilities to Dormant Assets," *The Banker,* September 1967.

25. "Credit Facilities or Reserve Allotments?" *Banca Nazionale del Lavoro Quarterly Review,* June 1967.

26. Published in the *Banca Nazionale del Lavoro Quarterly Review,* September 1966.

27. The word appears in quotes out of deference to Machlup's criticism of its use in this context, but it still appears because that particular criticism was a little too puritanical for my taste!

28. In my survey article ("International Liquidity—A Survey," *Economic Journal,* September 1973, p. 694) I commented on the paradox that it should have been the economist who so vigorously resisted the suggestion that businessmen are satisfiers who should have so readily assumed that central bankers are. Machlup commented that it *was* rather amusing, but he actually thought it was true: central bankers, unlike businessmen (?), do not risk their own shirts.

29. "The Cloakroom Rule of International Reserves: Reserve Creation and Resources Transfer," *Quarterly Journal of Economics,* August 1965.

30. Incidentally, the "international quantity theory"—the theory that reserve creation will not increase the level of real reserves except in the short run, because of the inflationary policies induced by reserve ease—was noted by Machlup as a possibility as early as 1961–62. See "Further Reflections on the Demand for Foreign Reserves," chapter 13 in *International Payments, Debts, and Gold,* p. 275.

31. "World Monetary Debate—Bases for Agreement," *The Banker,* September 1966.

32. *Remaking the International Monetary System.*

33. "From Dormant Liabilities to Dormant Assets."

34. *Remaking the International Monetary System,* p. 65.

35. "World Monetary Debate," final page.

36. *International Monetary Arrangements: The Problem of Choice,* p. 34.

37. See, for example, *Plans for Reform of the International Monetary System,* revised edition, p. 28.

38. *Next Steps in International Monetary Reform,* Hearings before the Subcommittee on International Exchange and Payments of the Joint Economic Committee, U.S. Congress, Washington, D.C., 1968.

39. "Between Outline and Outcome the Reform was Lost,"

40. Ibid., p. 38

41. Ibid., p. 33

11

International Monetary Reform— Design and Reality

Otmar Emminger

How the Reform Discussion Started

Over the last fifteen years the reform of the international monetary system has been one of the most fascinating subjects of international discussions and negotiations. Scores of academic economists as well as experts from governments and central banks, organized in all kinds of groups, committees, and international institutions, took part in these discussions and negotiations.

The official reform discussion had been preceded by reform proposals from academic quarters. Already in the fifties, some economists were criticizing one or the other feature of the Bretton Woods system, such as the rigidity of the par value system, the inadequate price of gold, the alleged insufficiency of international liquidity, and some dangerous features of the "gold-dollar standard." The official discussion on reform was initiated in early summer 1963 when a number of American and European officials from governments and central banks agreed, at informal meetings in Frankfurt and Paris, to propose the setting up of a high level group of "Deputies" from the Group of Ten countries.[1] In September 1963, on the occasion of the Annual Meeting of the IMF in Washington, the Ministers of the Group of Ten gave their Deputies a mandate to study "the outlook for the functioning of the international monetary system." The IMF followed suit. In the following years the Group of Ten was the focal point of international monetary negotiations. These studies and negotiations of the Deputies of the Group of Ten led, in close collaboration with the Executive Directors of the IMF, to the first major amendment of the Bretton Woods Agreement, introducing Special Drawing Rights (SDRs) into the world's monetary system in 1968.

The Grand Design

A new and much more ambitious effort at reform followed upon the suspension of the gold convertibility of the dollar in August 1971 and the currency realignment of the Group of Ten countries ("Smithsonian Agreement") of December

173

1971. In the Communiqué of the Group of Ten of December 18, 1971, it was "agreed that discussions should be promptly undertaken, particularly in the framework of the IMF, to consider reform of the international monetary system over the longer term." Subsequently, the Fund set up for this purpose the "Committee of Twenty" composed of twenty delegations representing every member country of the Fund. For two years, from September 1972 to June 1974, this Committtee of Twenty, meeting both at ministerial and deputy levels, tried hard to lay the foundations for a new world monetary system, a "grand design" which would solve all the major international monetary problems that had arisen over the last two decades. This period from 1972 to 1974 represented the climax of the reform effort. Its outcome was an "Outline of Reform," a report of June 1974 to the Board of Governors of the IMF. In the introduction to this "Outline" the main components of the envisaged new system were enumerated. They give a flavor of the ambitions and high hopes that permeated the work of the Committee of Twenty, and are worth recalling. According to paragraph two of the Outline, "the main features of the international monetary reform will include":

(a) an effective and symmetrical adjustment process, including better functioning of the exchange rate mechanism, with the exchange rate regime based on stable but adjustable par values and with floating rates recognized as providing a useful technique in particular situations;
(b) cooperation in dealing with disequilibrating capital flows;
(c) the introduction of an appropriate form of convertibility for the settlement of imbalances, with symmetrical obligations on all countries;
(d) better international management of global liquidity, with the SDR becoming the principal reserve asset and the role of gold and of reserve currencies being reduced;
(e) consistency between arrangements for adjustment, convertibility and global liquidity; and
(f) the promotion of the net flow of real resources to developing countries.

How were these high-sounding goals to be achieved? It was here that the major gap between design and reality arose. A number of interesting proposals had been discussed in the Committee of Twenty and its various working groups. But none had met with full acceptance, and some had already been definitely found to be impracticable. These proposals and the state of discussion reached upon them were set out in ten Annexes to the "Outline of Reform," where they make interesting reading. This was the terminal station of the great reform movement. For practical purposes, the Committee of Twenty resigned itself to proposing a minimal program of "immediate steps," comprising mainly the setting up of a Ministerial Council, the legalization of floating rates during the interim period, the "trade pledge" (i.e., the promise to refrain from restrictive import measures for balance of payments reasons), and some amendments on gold and SDRs. After having submitted its Report of June 1974, the Committee of Twenty was dissolved and the "Outline of Reform" was shelved.

The final anticlimax to the effort at a "grand design" of reform came with the meeting of the IMF Ministerial Committee ("Interim Committee") in Jamaica in Janaury 1976. There a number of amendments to the Articles of Agreement of the IMF were agreed upon. They were subsequently approved by the Board of Governors of the IMF and submitted to the parliaments of member countries for ratification. The most important of these amendments refer to the exchange rate system on the one hand, and the role of gold and SDRs on the other. By incorporating floating rates in due form into the international monetary system they accept and legalize practices that have evolved over the last few years under the pressure of events. The one point where there is an advance on what had already developed in practice is the provision that gives the Fund the power to exercise some surveillance over exchange rate policies, whatever the exchange rate system chosen by the member countries.

Essentially, the evolution of the international monetary system has been determined by events, and especially by the monetary crises of the early seventies. These events have not only caught up with, but have overtaken the reformers. Their theoretical blueprints had to yield to harsh realities, and particularly to the inevitable advent of widespread floating.

From Design to Reality: The Reserve System

It is worthwhile examining why so many of the reform efforts have aborted and why the world's monetary system has developed "in reality" so differently from the ambitious design.

A useful guide for this purpose are the many writings of Fritz Machlup on the problems of international monetary reform. He has contributed more than any other economist, in his articles and speeches dealing with these questions, to elucidate the issues and possible remedies. When in the fall of 1963 the first general reform mandate was given to the Deputies of the Group of Ten, he assembled thirty-two renowned academic economists in what was later to become the Bellagio Group, in order to conduct a parallel study. The outcome— a booklet entitled "The Problem of Choice"—formed a useful starting point, also for official experts, to rethink the problems involved.

Machlup belonged to the group of economists who simplified the discussion on reform by clearly isolating three problems: "adjustment," "liquidity," and "confidence," that is, (1) what to do in order to improve, and facilitate, the adjustment of persistent payments imbalances, (2) what to do in order to provide for an orderly increase in needed monetary reserves for the world, and (3) what to do to prevent currency crises and massive destruction of international liquidity due to a loss of confidence in the reserve currencies.

Machlup, like many other academic economists, thought that solutions to the problems of confidence and adjustment were more urgent than the problem of liquidity. Nevertheless, a new reserve asset in the form of the SDR was the first item of reform put into effect, and this was the only objective of reform that was achieved without the pressure of events. It was Machlup who in his appraisal of the SDR scheme outlined a likely scenario (in 1968!) of unilateral action by the United States to sever the link between the dollar and gold in order to avert the threat of confidence crises while at the same time calling it "the most disconcerting thought . . . that unilateral action by the United States may so seriously offend the spirit of international cooperation that the pretty solution that was formed for the liquidity problem might be ruined, or at least tabled for an indefinite period."[2]

During the discussions on reform in the Group of Ten, several participants, in particular the German delegates, stressed the paramount importance of improving the adjustment process. In 1966 the Ministers of the Group of Ten asked Working Party Three (the balance of payments committee) of the OECD to examine this question, and a report on the adjustment process was duly submitted to them. It contained useful proposals on the respective responsibilities of surplus and deficit countries, and on the various instruments of adjustment, but only cautious hints at exchange rate changes as methods of adjustment. The discussion in the committee of Deputies of the Group of Ten had from the beginning been under an injunction from the Americans that flexible exchange rates and a change in the official price of gold were "off limits." However, it was precisely these two problems that came back with a vengeance during the currency crises from 1971 to 1973.

Special Drawing Rights were primarily considered as a supplement to gold reserves, as it was evident that gold would no longer make any significant contribution to the world's reserves on the basis of the then obtaining official price of gold. But SDRs were also intended to be a supplement, or even a substitute, for dollar reserves, which were thought to have risen to the limit of tolerance, and which were expected to be less abundant in future through a reversal in the U.S. balance of payments.[3] The transition to SDRs looked like diminishing the privileged position of the dollar and the (alleged) unequal burden of payments adjustment. It was expected that in the future SDR allocations would be the major source of new monetary reserves; and thus collective control of international liquidity and a rational distribution of the newly created liquidity was hoped for.

In reality, the world's holdings of *dollar reserves* increased more than five-fold after 1969 and are still increasing every year by double-digit billions, in spite of the suspension of the dollar's convertibility into gold and the introduction of floating. Thus the SDR has no real chance to soon "become the principal reserve asset"—the declared goal in the Jamaica decision of January 1976. It has, however, replaced gold as the unit of account for all the Fund's transactions, and may become an international unit of account elsewhere. This would, however, require a strengthening of its value in terms of currencies, as the present definition of the value of the SDR is likely to make it weaker than the dollar.

Gold had disappeared as the numeraire of the system. It has catapulted itself out of the system by the great fluctuations in its price in the free markets. Thus, every central bank is left to deal with its own monetary gold as it wishes— except for a voluntary commitment by a group of central banks connected with the BIS to refrain from adding to the total of monetary gold held within this group and the IMF. The only provisions on gold left to be agreed upon in Jamaica concerned the disposal of the Fund's gold holdings.

Hence the practical evolution of the international reserve system has led to gold being pushed into the background, SDR's leading a wallflower existence, and currency reserves, in particular the U.S. dollar, still being in the center of the reserve system. This has run counter to one of the main original goals of reform, that is, to reduce the role of the reserve currencies. Have we moved from a gold-dollar standard to a pure dollar standard? It is true that the new system has in practice become even more *dollar-centered* than the previous one. But it is a very different dollar standard. In the former system of fixed par values, a country was obliged by the rules of the system to purchase all dollars offered in the market at the official support point if it did not want to take the formal step of changing the par value of its own currency in the Fund. Nowadays countries may again accumulate dollar reserves, but they do so on an entirely voluntary basis.

Widespread Floating—Turning Point in the World's Monetary System

The most important reason why such a huge discrepancy has developed between the former design of monetary reform and reality is the introduction of *floating exchange rates* in a number of major countries.

The reform discussion in the Committee of Twenty from 1972 to 1974 was centered on an *"exchange rate regime based on stable but adjustable par values,"* with "floating rates providing a useful technique in particular situations." It has always been questionable what "stable but adjustable" would mean in practice. But it is quite obvious that only in a system of "stable" exchange rates—with formally declared parities—did "symmetrical" rules of adjustment, based on reserve indicators or other objective criteria, as well as convertibility "with symmetrical obligations"—meaning asset convertibility also for reserve currencies—make sense.

The amended Articles of Agreement of the IMF, which are based on the decisions made in Jamaica in 1976, leave no trace of declared parities, even though it is possible that such a system could be reintroduced by an 85 percent majority of the total voting power in the IMF at a later date. In a speech in January 1972 in Stuttgart, Fritz Machlup had envisaged such a system without par values as one possible scenario, but added that it was so far away he would not live to see it accepted by monetary authorities. However, fifteen months later, in March 1973, it was introduced through the joint floating of several EEC currencies in relation to the dollar and other currencies; and it seems to be here for good.

What had happened to bring about such a fundamental change? The proximate cause was the enormous destabilizing money flows out of the dollar and into the Deutsche mark and a number of other European currencies. Were these flows due to lack of adequate payments adjustment on the part of the United States? Only very partially. For there had been attempts at adjustment, for example, the currency realignment of December 1971 ("Smithsonian") and several important exchange rate moves in February 1973—a 10 percent devaluation of the dollar and an agreed upward floating of the yen. The major cause of the breakdown of the fixed rate system was the size of speculative money flows that threatened to completely upset the domestic monetary systems of Germany, Switzerland, and other countries. No amount of recycling the inflows by the monetary authorities would have undone the inflationary impact in the recipient countries. So was it, in the final analysis, the "confidence" factor that took its revenge? Yes—but it was now in a somewhat different framework from the one envisaged by Triffin and others at the beginning of the sixties.

It took the Committee of Twenty quite some time to realize what implications the transition to widespread floating in March 1973 were bound to have for the reform effort.[4] It took some further experiences to convince the reformers that floating was going to stay for a long time to come. In January 1974, immediately after the quadrupling of oil prices, Mr. Witteveen, the Managing Director of the IMF, said in a speech in London "In the present situation, a large measure of floating is unavoidable and indeed desirable." Indeed, if floating had not come about in the currency crisis of February/March 1973, it would quite certainly have become inevitable around the turn of the year 1973/74. But even then it was difficult for some people to grasp fully the implications of the transition to floating for the reform.

In the preface to the "Outline of Reform" of June 1974, the Committee of Twenty noted "that, in view of present uncertainties related to *inflation*, the *energy situation* and other *unsettled conditions*, it is not appropriate to attempt to determine the full details of all aspects of the future international monetary system, many of which can better be decided in the light of future developments." If "unsettled conditions" are interpreted to mean the huge potential of volatile money in the world and a lack of confidence in exchange rate relations, then the main factors are adduced which have made the advent of flexible exchange rates inevitable.

I mentioned already that in a system of widespread floating—and in particular of a floating dollar—major aspects of the intended reform have lost their significance or would at least look very different. But it must also be conceded that important parts of the envisaged reform were overambitious and could not have been achieved even under more "normal" circumstances. As examples I would mention the envisaged strict rules for a symmetrical adjustment process on the basis of reserve indicators, a symmetrical intervention system (e.g., by means of a worldwide system of multicurrency intervention), a comprehensive system of asset settlement, and a consolidation of the dollar overhang through a substitution account in the IMF. We have also seen how difficult it is to achieve collective control of international liquidity and to deal effectively with disequilibrating capital flows—except by recourse to more flexible exchange rates.

Some people doubt whether the Jamaica adaptations of the international monetary system to practical evolution really constitute a "reform" at all. I would, however, agree with Paul Volcker that it would be erroneous to conclude that the job of monetary reform "has been done in, as it were, a fit of absent-mindedness." I would prefer to label it the recognition of the realities of our time—the disparities in rates of inflation and in economic performance in general, the huge potential amounts of money that can easily be shifted from one currency to another, the erratic fluctuations in the gold price, and so on. We have learned a fundamental truth the hard way, that there can be no stability in the international monetary system except on the basis of domestic stability in all the major countries. In taking account of this fact, the new monetary system is more realistic that the old one and less crisis-prone.

I think it unlikely that future efforts at reforming the international monetary system will start from the unfinished business laid down in the "Outline of Reform" of 1974. It is more likely that such efforts will concentrate on improvements in the system of floating and better practical rules for the international adjustment process.

Notes

1. The Group of Ten itself had come into being in early 1962 with the establishment of the "General Arrangements to Borrow," which were designed to provide the IMF with additional resources to cope with unusually large capital movements.

2. "Remaking the International Monetary System," p. 121.

3. "For a variety of reasons, further substantial increases of dollar reserves are unlikely to occur and in our view it would indeed be undesirable that the increase in the external short-term indebtedness of the U.S. should continue as in the recent past." (Group of Ten, Report of Deputies, July 1966, para. 6).

4. When I reported to the Committee at the end of March 1973 on the transition to a floating Deutsche mark and the background to this decision I added that there seemed to be no prospect of going back to a parity system soon.

Part VI:
The Voice for Rational
Economic Policy

12 The Problem of Adjustment and Liquidity under a Regime of Widespread Floating

Gottfried Haberler

Introduction

The Bretton Woods par value system which had served the world so well during the first twenty years of its existence got into increasingly severe troubles when the dollar weakened after 1965. It received a staggering blow when the gold convertibility of the dollar was suspended on August 15, 1971, and it was finally replaced by widespread floating early in 1973.

The disintegration of the Bretton Woods system was accompanied by a continuing effort of the leading industrial countries in the International Monetary Fund, the OECD, and the Group of Ten, to reform the international monetary system. The reform effort culminated in the adoption of the Second Amendment to the Articles of Agreement of the IMF by the Interim Committee of the Board of Governors of the IMF at the Jamaica conference, January 7–8, 1976.

The official reform effort was prodded and stimulated by intensive discussion and criticism of academic economists. Professor Machlup has strongly influenced this process, both by his writings and by organizing a continuing creative dialogue between the official and academic world.[1] Machlup's influence on the evolution of the international monetary system through his writings is analyzed in the chapter by John Williamson in this volume, and the history and impact of the Bellagio Group through which Machlup, in collaboration with William Fellner and Robert Triffin, organized a continuing intensive dialogue between officials and academics, is described in Robert Triffin's contribution to this volume.[2]

In the present chapter I discuss some problems of balance of payments adjustment and of international liquidity as they present themselves under the present system of widespread floating. But first I must say a few words on why Bretton Woods broke down.

Why the Par Value System Broke Down

The main reason for the breakdown of the Bretton Woods par value system was a basic defect in the IMF charter which made the system unfit to cope with the

This chapter draws on two earlier papers of the author: "How Important Is Control over International Reserves?" presented at the *Marcus Fleming Memorial Conference,* November 11–12, 1976, published in *The New International Monetary System* (Robert A. Mundell and Jacques J. Polak, editors), Columbia University Press, New York, 1977 (available as Reprint No. 82, American Enterprise Institute, Washington, D.C., 1977) and "The International Monetary System after Jamaica and Manila," *Contemporary Economic Problems* (William Fellner, editor), American Enterprise Institute, Washington, D.C., 1977.

exceptional strains and stresses that developed in the late 1960s and early 1970s. This defect was that the method of occasional, discontinuous, and therefore large changes in exchange rates, the adjustable or jumping peg, opened the flood-gate for disruptive speculation.[3]

But why did this basic defect not show up earlier? In retrospect the explanation is not difficult. During the early years after the war when the economies of Europe and Japan were prostrate from war destruction and exhaustion, U.S. industries enjoyed a quasi-monopoly position and later foreign countries eagerly accumulated dollar balances to rebuild their international reserves. Generous U.S. foreign aid financed large deficits, and tight controls in many countries sup-pressed remaining imbalances.

In the 1960s the dollar got into trouble, for several reasons. Due to the rapid recovery of Europe and Japan, U.S. industries lost their quasi-monopoly position. Numerous currency depreciations strengthened the competitive position of rival industrial countries. The strength of the dollar was finally under-mined by the inflation in the United States that followed the period of price stability from 1958–1964.

There is an alternative, though not necessarily contradictory, explanation of the decline of the dollar. For years Jacques Rueff and Robert Triffin had pre-dicted that, for reasons so well known that they need not be repeated, the gold-dollar exchange standard could not have lasted even if the United States had succeeded to keep its inflation to a tolerable level. It is a moot question what would have happened if the United States had kept the price level substantially stable after 1965. The fact that there has been no flight from the dollar in recent years of *comparative* price stability in the United States suggests that the alleged inherent instability of the dollar standard may have been exaggerated.[4]

Be that as it may, the worldwide wave of inflation after 1965 culminating in the price explosion of 1973–74 made widespread floating inevitable. It is in-conceivable that the industrial countries could agree on a common inflation rate, if the average rate of inflation were in the neighborhood of ten percent, because tolerance for inflation and unemployment differs greatly from country to coun-try. Differential inflation, the differential impact of the oil price rise, and differ-ential recession experience finally convinced most advocates of fixed exchange rates that floating is here to stay for the foreseeable future. In Machlup's words "it should be clear to anybody in his senses that under present conditions the world has no other choice. Floating is now the only system that can work with-out continuously recurrent crises in the exchange market."[5]

The framers of the second amendment to the Fund charter recognized the inevitability of floating. The amended charter legalized the status quo, floating is now permitted—"so that the Fund members need not go on living in sin."[6]

Some Problems of Adjustment under Widespread Floating

Recent Criticism and Doubts about Floating

Although it is almost generally agreed that floating is here to stay, floating is still being blamed for many ills besetting the world economy, even though most critics realize that there is no chance to return to the par value system. Much criticism of floating was voiced at the annual meeting of the Fund in Manila (October 4-8, 1976).

A frequent charge was that floating has had inflationary effects. The governor for Italy said: "The high rate of inflation [in Italy] is due in no small part to the sharp depreciation of the lira in the first months of the year. The high degree of indexation of the Italian economy has blunted the usefulness of exchange rate depreciation since it leads rapidly to higher domestic inflation."[7] Similarly the governor of the Banque de France: "Speculative anticipations by economic agents amplify the size of exchange rate movements. . . . A fall in the exchange rate in the market is reflected, even before the slightest impact is felt on export volume, in an immediate rise in the cost of imports. Thus, in the first phase, the external depreciation of the currency aggravates the internal inflation rate, . . . setting in motion a cumulative process at the end of which the currency's exchange value continues to fall." Such remarks have been amplified and sensationalized by financial journalists. There has been talk of vicious and virtuous circles: weak currency countries with high inflation rates such as Britain and Italy are said to be "trapped in a vicious circle," while strong currency countries with little or no inflation such as Germany, Switzerland, and the United States (but also the Netherlands despite an almost ten percent inflation rate) are said to enjoy a "virtuous circle." Thus floating is said to "drive a wedge between industrial nations".[8]

What is true is that under floating an inflationary country will feel the consequences of inflation more quickly than under fixed exchange rates because under the latter regime countries can alleviate their inflation by running a deficit—provided they have an ample reserve or credit line to finance their deficit; in other words, under fixed exchanges a country can export some of its inflation, while under floating it has to swallow the inflation it generates.[9] In that sense it can be said that floating has an inflationary effect on deficit countries. But by the same token it protects surplus countries from imported inflation. This is sometimes denied or played down on the ground that in the modern world prices and wages are rigid downward. It is true that wage rigidity gives rise to the well-known Hayek-Schultze ratchet effect: Every shift in demand raises the price where demand has increased and these price increases are not offset by price declines where demand has decreased.[10] (Needless to add that this kind of *ratchet* inflation, too, requires a permissive monetary policy to occur.) It follows that wage rigidity *reduces* the anti-inflationary effect of an appreciation of the currency, but it does not *eliminate* it for two reasons: First, wage or price rigidity obviously will not prevent the decline of prices of noncompetitive imports (i.e., of commodities that are not produced domestically)in terms of the *appreciated currency*. Second, as far as competitive imports (i.e., imports of commodities that are produced in the appreciating country) are concerned, additional supplies from abroad will at least slow down the ongoing inflation, although under a regime of rigid wages to a lesser extent and at a higher cost of unemployment than would be the case if wages and prices were more flexible. Germany and Switzerland provide dramatic proof, if proof is needed.

It is true that every long drawn-out inflation develops vicious circle properties and is apt to set "in motion a cumulative process" as the governor of the Banque de France said in Manila.[11] Inflation "feeds on itself," because people will try to reduce their cash balances by spending money faster on commodities and on foreign money, and it cannot be excluded that on some occasions the exchange rate in the market may overshoot its long run equilibrium. But the "cumulative" process could not go on without a permissive monetary policy and the vicious circle can be broken by tight money, although not without causing temporary unemployment.

It should be observed that import restrictions, whether in the form of tariffs, quotas, import deposit schemes, or a tax on the purchase of foreign exchange, do *not* alleviate the inflation. Financing a deficit by drawing down reserves or by borrowing abroad does reduce inflationary pressure because this policy permits an increase of the supply of goods in the home market. Import restrictions, in contrast, do not reduce inflationary pressures. On the contrary, they are counterproductive because of their protectionist effects, which imply a misallocation of resources and thus a reduction in aggregate supply.[12] While devaluation and downward floating stimulate exports and discourage imports, import restrictions operate only on imports.

It could be argued that an import deposit scheme, unlike tariffs and quotas, may have a slight deflationary (anti-inflationary) side effect if the deposits are effectively sterilized for some time. But the same anti-inflationary effect can be achieved by monetary policy without the distortions caused by import restrictions. In summary, import restrictions cannot do anything that devaluation or floating plus an appropriate monetary policy can do more cheaply and efficiently.

The main advantage that has been claimed for flexible exchange rates since Keynes is that it enables each country to pursue independently the demand management policy it prefers; expressed differently, floating can protect a country from inflation or deflation which under fixed exchanges is imposed on it by a balance of payments surplus or deficit. Keynes stressed the threat of having to submit to deflationary pressures from abroad; today inflationary pressures from abroad is the danger uppermost in one's mind. Doubts have been raised again recently about these claims for floating; it has not prevented a worldwide inflationary explosion, nor an equally worldwide stagflation and recession in 1973 and 1974, succeeded by an almost worldwide rapid recovery in 1975 which in turn was followed by a "pause" in 1976. A fairly large literature has sprung up under the heading "international transmission of economic disturbances" which investigates whether under floating there really was a greater divergence between different countries than there was under the par value system, with respect to business cycles, price stability, monetary growth, and the like.[13]

As it often happens, intensive econometric-statistical investigations have tended to obscure or lose sight of broad, basic facts and insights. One such fact is that, broadly speaking, in the intermediate and long run exchange rate changes reflect divergent inflation trends.[14] But in the era of stagflation *divergent* inflation rates between countries do not necessarily preclude *convergence* of real business cycles, that is, of cyclical fluctuations in output and employment, and it is not surprising that floating did not immediately change the worldwide nature of inflation, although some countries managed to reduce their inflation rate drastically (Germany, Switzerland). The inflation explosion of 1973 had after all originated during the fixed rate system and was intensified in all countries by the oil price rise and the policy reactions to the oil price boost. Nor is it surprising that attempts in all industrial countries to curb inflation produced, despite floating, a worldwide recession. Floating shields a country from *monetary* influences from abroad, in the sense that under floating countries cannot be forced (as they are under fixed rates) by inflationary neighbors to expand their money supply, or by deflationary neighbors to contract their money supply. But floating does not protect against *real* influences from abroad. Among such real influences, including those caused by monetary factors (by inflation or deflation), are changes in the terms of trade, the oil price rise, protectionist measures taken by foreign countries, recession abroad, which reduces real demand for imports, which implies a deterioration of the terms of trade and foreign competition for particular industries.[15] All this follows from generally accepted economic principles which do not require any further econometric confirmation.

The upshot of this discussion is to confirm our earlier conclusion that floating is here to stay for the foreseeable future. As Edward Bernstein put it, "the system of fluctuating exchange rates has worked reasonably well, much better than would have been possible if attempts had been made to perpetuate the Bretton Woods system of fixed parities by patchwork here and there."[16] We can take it for granted, however, that in most countries the float will be a managed one,[17] although much can be said in favor of free, unmanaged floating. The question remains how floating should be managed.

Managed Floating

The amended Articles of Agreement permit each country to adopt the exchange rate system it prefers but enjoins them to "avoid manipulating exchange rates or the international monetary system in order to prevent effective balance of payments adjustment or to gain an unfair competitive advantage over other members." (Article IV SectionI) The Fund is directed to "oversee the compliance of each member with its obligations," to "exercise firm surveillance of the exchange rate policies of members," and to "adopt specific principles for the guidance of all members with respect to these policies." (Article IV. Section 3)

The Fund has already tried its hand at surveillance of floating. Based on the work of the Committee of Twenty, the Executive Directors adopted in June 1974 "Guidelines for the Management of Floating Exchange Rates."[18] These guidelines are supposed to form the basis of the Fund's annual "consultations with members with floating currencies," and observance of the guidelines will presumably be required when such countries borrow from the Fund.

The guidelines deal with the mode of interventions in the exchange market, so as to prevent "competitive alterations of exchange rates." The difference between "competitive alteration" and what formerly used to be called "competitive depreciation" presumably is that alteration is the wider concept which covers also the case of "competitive appreciation," as it is sometimes called—a policy of keeping the exchange rate at a higher than the market-clearing level and financing the resulting deficit by running down reserves or by official borrowing abroad.[19] Such a policy can also be described as deliberate exportation of inflation so as to keep down the country's own rate of inflation.

The new article IV in the amended charter uses an even more comprehensive term than competitive alteration of exchange rates: It speaks of "manipulating exchange rates or the international monetary system" and enjoins countries to avoid such manipulations for the purpose of gaining "an unfair competitive advantage over other members." The concept, "manipulation of the international monetary system," covers abuses of managed floating as well as those of par value changes. The 1974 guidelines deal only with manipulations by interventions in the exchange market under floating. Actually there seems to have been very little competitive keeping down of floating exchange rates by interventions in the exchange market. True, Japan has been accused of depressing the yen by buying dollars and managing capital flows. But the case is not at all clear.

Probably more important than interventions for the purpose of gaining "an unfair competitive advantage" is "dirty floating." It is important in my opinion to distinguish between dirty floating and merely managed floating. By dirty floating I mean such policies as split exchange markets, multiple exchange rates, import deposit schemes, "taxes" on the purchase of foreign currencies differentiated according to the prospective use of the foreign currencies, and the like. These policies shade off into a policy of comprehensive exchange control and thus violate one of the basic objectives of the Fund, namely to avoid "restrictions for balance of payments purposes on current account transactions," to use the language of the Guidelines for floating.[20] It can be shown that the policy of having a separate exchange market for capital transactions unavoidably leads to restrictions and distortions of current transactions.

By merely managed floating I mean a policy that confines itself to influencing the exchange rates by buying and selling of foreign exchange in a free exchange in order to "prevent or moderate sharp and disruptive fluctuations from day to day and from week to week,"[21] as well as to moderate, though not suppress or reverse, longer run movements.

The 1974 guidelines, although they reiterate the basic objective of unrestricted current transactions, do not rule out dirty floating. On the contrary, the system of "separate capital exchange markets," in other words, the system of dual exchange rates, one for current the other for capital transactions, is expressly mentioned in the official commentary on the guidelines, along with exchange market interventions and other policies, as an acceptable "action to influence and exchange rate."[22] This is unfortunate because the system of split exchange market and dual exchange rates is the most widely used form of dirty floating.

There have been in recent years many cases of dirty floating of varying degrees of "dirtyness." Furthermore there have been last year two conspicuous cases of grossly mismanaged alterations (depreciations) of exchange rates—the case of the Mexican peso and the Australian dollar.

Now a few words on rules of exchange market interventions under managed but not dirty floating.[23] There is fairly general agreement that there are no objections to interventions to iron out short term fluctuations.[24] As far as fluctuations in the intermediate run, say from one to twelve months[25] are concerned, the situation is not so clear, although many experts who in principle are in favor of floating (as for example, E.M. Bernstein and Fritz Machlup[26]) feel strongly that since 1973 in many important cases the fluctuations have been much larger than can be justified and that such excessive fluctuations should be moderated, though not suppressed, by official interventions in the exchange market. What the advocates of intervention have primarily in mind is fluctuations of the dollar exchange rate, in particular the dollar Deutsche mark rate.

In the first two years of the float the dollar-Deutsche mark rate has indeed fluctuated sharply. Later the fluctuations became much milder and it should be pointed out that the fluctuations of the trade-weighted effective exchange rate of the dollar were much smaller than those of the dollar-Deutsche mark rate.

It should be kept in mind, that the years of 1973 to 1975 were a period of extreme turbulence and uncertainty in the world economy as well as in the U.S. economy. It was the period of two-digit inflation followed by worldwide recession and stagflation, the period of the oil shock. Inflation rates in different countries diverged sharply and so did the impact of the oil shock and of the recession. There were special disturbing factors shaking the confidence in the dollar: the Watergate affair and the forced resignation of President Nixon had a debilitating effect on the U.S. administration's ability to pursue a consistently vigorous anti-inflation policy. There were erratic shifts in the U.S. policies with respect to price and wage control and at times strong congressional pressure for a freeze or even a rollback of prices, wages, profits, rents. All that undermined the confi-

dence in the dollar at home and abroad. Still another factor causing large fluctuations was that the private operators in the market place had to adjust to the
floating system. Speculators had become used to the easy task of speculating
against the central banks whose hands were tied under the par value system (stable but adjustable exchange rates). Private firms—and public agencies—had to
learn how to live with the much greater risks of speculating against the market
under flexible exchange rates. The failure of the Herstatt Bank in Germany and
of the Franklin National Bank in the United States, and large losses of other
banks from foreign exchange dealings taught their lessons, but not without considerable cost.

Keeping all this in mind it is not at all surprising that there were sharp fluctuations in exchange rates. *Ex post* it is deceptively easy to conclude that some
of the fluctuations may have been unnecessary and that a lot of money could
have been made by private or official counterspeculation. However, *ex ante* most
of the exchange movements looked quite reasonable. Given the high degree of
turmoil and uncertainty of the period there is no reason whatever to assume
that the ex ante judgment of public officials (national or international) about
the "appropriate exchange rate" (to use a phrase favored by the advocates of
interventions) would have been better than that of the market. The record of
official judgments about exchange rates and balances of payments prospects
during the Bretton Woods period was anything but encouraging.[27] Time and
again exchange rates were defended stubbornly and hundreds of millions of dollars were lost by central banks in what turned out to be wrong speculations.[28]
The record of official interventions in the post-Bretton Woods period has not
been better in a number of cases. In Britain, Italy, Australia, and Mexico interventions have been highly destabilizing; overvalued currencies have been propped
up for a while and the subsequent inevitable plunge was then all the more abrupt
and disrupting.

Since there is no evidence that the fluctuations of the dollar-Deutsche mark
rate that have occurred did significant damage and since the fluctuations have
become milder as the turbulence in the world economy and in the American economy subsided, the case for extensive official interventions in the market, except
to iron out erratic very short run fluctuations, is not very strong.

Reference Rates and Target Zones

Ethier and Bloomfield have argued that the working of the floating system would
be greatly improved if countries could be persuaded to set what they call "reference rates" or "reference zones" for their currencies. This proposal has been
endorsed by John Williamson and is widely regarded as an imaginative, novel
idea. In the 1974 Fund guidelines, too, it is mentioned that countries may set
medium term norms or target rates (or zones) and the official commentary to

the Guidelines explains that the "medium-term" might be considered to refer to a period of about four years."[29]

The difference between a par value and a reference rate (or reference zone) is that, unlike the par value, the reference rate need not be defended by interventions. Interventions are permitted, but they are not mandatory and the interventions are subject to only one rule: If the exchange rate in the market is *below* the reference rate the central bank is allowed (not obligated) to intervene by selling foreign currencies in order to push the currency up to the reference rate; if the exchange rate is *above* the reference rate the central bank is allowed (not obligated) to intervene by buying foreign currencies in order to push the currency down to the reference rate. In other words, interventions must never push the exchange rate *away* from the reference rate, but interventions are permitted to move the exchange rate *towards* the reference rates. The reference rates should be "revised at periodic prespecified intervals, by some defined international procedure."[30]

The main advantage that is claimed for the reference rate proposal is that it would deal effectively with the problem of destabilizing speculation. Since there is no obligation for the central bank to intervene in order to keep the exchange rate at (or near) the reference rate, speculators would face greater risks than they face under the par value system. I agree with this argument. The reference rate system would be less prone to engender destabilizing speculation than the par value system.

But I am not convinced by the claim that, as compared with a floating system without reference rates, the reference rate system would have the advantage of eliminating or sharply reducing the alleged danger of destabilizing speculation. Williamson says that the reference rates would provide "a focus for stabilizing speculation." If "the rate moved away from the reference rate, the market would know that future interventions could only be in the direction of pushing the rate back towards the official reference rate, thus adding to the risk" of "further destabilizing behavior."[31]

I find this unconvincing. If destabilizing speculation is not discouraged under the par value system by the obligation of the central bank to defend the par value, why should it be discouraged under the reference rate system by the mere *permission* to defend the reference rate? All depends on whether the market finds the reference rate credible or not. Why should reference rates be more credible than par values? Reference rates that give the impression of being out of line and therefore liable to be changed at the next "prespecified" revision are very likely to cause heavy speculation, unless the revisions are small and are made at short intervals. But changing the reference rates at short intervals would be tantamount to replacing the reference rate system by a crawling peg system or a trotting peg system à la Brazil. The fear that changes in the reference rate may trigger speculative capital flows may well induce central banks increasingly to treat reference rates as par values.

John Williamson says that reference rates would be useful in "providing a focus for stabilizing speculation. The value of having such a focus is best demonstrated by the Canadian experience, where the $US1 = $CAN1 parity has long played this role" of inducing stabilizing speculation (see "The Future Exchange Rate Regime," p. 135–36). Some defenders of fixed rates, for example Robert Mundell, have tried to explain away the undeniable success and stability of the Canadian float by the fact that the Canadian monetary unit is called a dollar and has historically been on a par (or nearly so) with the U.S. dollar, thus serving as "a focus for stabilizing speculation." I find that explanation of the stability of the Canadian dollar unconvincing. The stability of the Canadian dollar (until now) and the absence of volatile capital flows is due to the long tradition of political stability and responsible financial and monetary policies (which probably were, in part, motivated by the wish to preserve the near-parity of the Canadian and the U.S. dollar).[32] Destroy this tradition, and the picture will change over night. Should we assume that Mexico—not to mention Argentina or Chile—could give its currency the stability of the Canadian dollar by renaming the peso as a Mexican dollar? Could the stability of the lira be promoted by calling it the "Italian mark"? A reputation of political stability and responsible economic policies once lost may take a very long time to regain.[33]

The assumption made in the IMF "Guideline 3 (b)" that "reasonable estimates of the medium-term norm" for a country's exchange rate can be made for "a period of about four years" ahead, as the "Official Commentary" to the IMF Guidelines assumes, seems to me unrealistic to the point of suggesting a typographical error.Should it be four months or four quarters?[34]

Ethier and Bloomfield stress repeatedly that their "rule is defined in terms of explicit, central-bank *behavior* rather than in terms of presumed central-bank motivations."[35] The difficulty of implementing that prescription is highlighted by the following remarks of the authors: "[The] Rule should be applied only to official interventions [of] the central bank. . . . [It] would [not] apply to purchases of foreign exchange by a central bank directly from state enterprises that had been encouraged [by the government or the central bank] to borrow abroad as has happened in Great Britain and Italy."[36] Since it is generally agreed that the huge British and Italian borrowings were made largely for balance of payments reasons, ignoring such transactions and restricting the rule to formal interventions by the central bank in the foreign exchange market would deprive the reference scheme of much of its relevance in the present day world.

Concluding Remarks

Our discussion of some problems concerning international surveillance of exchange rate policies has shown that it is not at all easy to formulate meaningful guidelines for floating. It would probably be best to forget about reference rates, not to mention medium-term norms or target-zones for exchange rates for several years ahead. The simpler rule contained in the IMF "Guideline (2)" that no country should "normally act aggressively with respect to the exchange value of its currency (i.e., should not so act [intervene in the market] as to depress that value when it is falling, or to enhance that value when it is rising)," is probably all that is needed and can reasonably be justified.

Of course, the questions remain what "normally" means, what the exceptions might be, and how one can tell whether a country has in fact observed the rule not to intervene "aggressively." Obviously it is not sufficient to look merely at the formal interventions of the central bank in the exchange market and to ignore completely borrowing by other public agencies abroad. It is hardly possible to spell out beforehand all possible exceptions to the rule. One has to rely on continuing multilateral surveillance among major countries and on the good judgment of the Fund. It is perhaps not unreasonable to hope the Fund will be able, in its regular annual consultation with members and in negotiations about member borrowing, to reach agreement on responsible policies without condoning every violation of the letter or the spirit of the Articles of Agreement.

This is after all not a new problem. It will be recalled that the original Articles of Agreement enjoined the Fund "not [to] object to a proposed change [in an exchange rate] because of the domestic social or political policies of the member proposing the change."[37] This injunction has not prevented the Fund from exercising, more or less discreetly strong influence on members' economic and financial policies in annual consultations or from attaching strings to borrowing agreements.

Finally, let me repeat that probably more important and conceptually though not politically easier than guiding interventions under a managed float would be trying to dissuade countries from engaging in dirty floating in the sense defined above, that is, in the sense of split exchange market, dual exchange rates, import-deposit schemes, and the like.

International Liquidity in a World of Floating Exchange Rates

Adjustment, Confidence, Liquidity

In the 1950s and 1960s it became customary to discuss the problems of international monetary reform under the three headings of adjustment, liquidity, and confidence.[38]

Confidence and liquidity problems arise primarily under fixed or stable but adjustable exchange rates. The confidence problem as defined in the report of the thirty-two economists relates to reserve currencies, primarily the most important one, the dollar. The possibility that lack of confidence could lead to large, sudden switches between different reserve media, concretely from dollars into gold, was regarded as a major weakness of the international monetary system in the 1950s and 1960s. The theory of Rueff and Triffin that the dollar-gold standard or the pure dollar standard are inherently unstable because they would sooner or later lead to violent and disruptive confidence crises has already been mentioned.

Since the suspension of gold convertibility and the advent of widespread floating little has been said or heard of the confidence problem. Does that mean that under floating there is no confidence problem? If the confidence problem is defined as it usually was in the 1950s and the 1960s (for example by the Machlup study group mentioned above) as the possibility of "sudden switches between different reserve media" there is no confidence problem any more under the present system of floating because the convertibility of currencies including the dollar into a "primary" reserve asset such as gold has been abolished.[39] In a wider sense confidence in a currency, a reserve currency or any other currency, is still and always will be a problem. Confidence in the dollar could conceivably be impaired. For example if the United States experienced again high inflation, the very large foreign dollar holdings—largely a legacy of the fixed rate system but now held voluntarily—could become a problem, threatening a depreciation of the dollar in terms of some other currencies.

I shall not, however, pursue that subject any further. Let me simply say that the conventional confidence problem as it was discussed in the 1950s and 1960s does not exist any more. But confidence in the stability of individual currencies is still important, and if the currency in question is a widely held reserve currency as the dollar, confidence in it becomes a matter of world concern. In Britain the problem of foreign sterling balances has become acute since confidence in the future of the pound waned.

International Liquidity

The problem of international liquidity, or better of the adequacy or inadequacy of international monetary reserves, has received a lot of attention in the discussions on international monetary reform before the advent of widespread floating—in fact too much attention compared with the adjustment problem in the opinion of many observers, including Fritz Machlup and the present writer. Innumerable plans for monetary reform, aimed at assuring an adequate but not excessive supply of reserves have been put forward.[40] In the whole postwar period until the late 1960s the emphasis was on the alleged dangers of a *shortage* of international liquidity. British economists especially almost unanimously (with the notable exception of Sir Ralph Hawtrey) predicted dire consequences, deflation and depression, unless the perceived growing inadequacy of international reserves was counteracted by the adoption of one of the numerous plans for reserve creation ranging from doubling the gold price to setting up the IMF as a real world central bank, a lender of last resort, with broad money creating powers. When the predicted deflation failed to materialize and it became clear in the later 1960s and early 1970s that inflation and not deflation was the threat, the emphasis shifted from the danger of inadequacy of reserves to that of excessive reserve growth. In the closing years of the Bretton Woods era international reserves grew indeed by leaps and bounds from SDR 93 billion in 1970 to SDR 180 billion in 1974, according to IMF statistics.[41] Through the mechanism of fixed exchanges the U.S. inflation that got underway in 1965 spread swiftly through the whole world.[42] After the advent of widespread floating the growth of reserves slowed sharply, and the largest part accrued to the oil exporting countries. The OPEC countries are, however, a very special case because, as is fairly generally agreed, additional reserves of the oil countries should be regarded as part of their long term foreign investments and not as the basis of increased money supply.

In view of all this it is not surprising that the excitement and worry about international liquidity that had dominated the discussions about monetary reform has greatly abated. Does that mean that international liquidity is no problem any more? Almost but not quite. Indeed, under a free, unmanaged float there would be no liquidity problem. Under managed floating, on the other hand, countries need reserves to intervene in the market. But there are several reasons why the need for reserves is much less urgent under floating, even if it is managed, than under the adjustable peg.

The liquidity problem is intertwined with the adjustment and confidence problems. If the adjustment mechanism does not work well and stubborn balance of payments disequilibria occur frequently, large reserves are required; and if there is a confidence problem in the sense that large sudden switches between different reserve media cannot be ruled out, countries, especially reserve currency countries, need large reserves. On both grounds reserve need is sharply reduced under managed floating. On the one hand the adjustment mechanism becomes much more efficient when exchange rates are allowed to float and, on the other hand, the confidence problem *has all but vanished* when currencies are no longer convertible at a fixed rate into some ultimate reserve medium such as gold.[43] As we have seen, disruptive speculation is greatly encouraged and facilitated by the adjustable peg ("stable but adjustable rates") and is discouraged and made hazardous by floating.

The present international monetary system of widespread floating as legalized by the amended charter of the Fund—or "non-system" as those whose blueprints were not followed like to call it—has been criticized on the ground that it failed to put any limit or control on global monetary reserves or liquidity. To come to grips with this criticism let us consider how under floating global reserves should be defined and measured and how important the control of global reserves, however defined, still is.

Under fixed and even semi-fixed exchange rates these questions permit of a fairly unambiguous and straightforward answer. Under the gold standard global reserves were defined as the world stock of monetary gold; to which later under the gold exchange standard, balances of reserve currencies held by central banks of nonreserve countries should be added. Under the Bretton Woods system reserve positions in the Fund and SDRs were further additions. Large changes in these world aggregates surely had something to do with fluctuations in the world price level, with waves of world inflation and deflation—I say "large changes," because one would certainly not expect a close parallelism between minor fluctuations in these two very broad and even then (under the gold standard) somewhat hazy aggregates.[44]

Under widespread floating the two aggregates, global reserves on the one hand and the world price level and its changes on the other hand, have become highly fragmented magnitudes. Moreover, close substitutes for monetary reserves, namely official and semi-official borrowing, have grown by leaps and bounds in many countries. To be sure the Fund dutifully publishes every month the percentage change in consumer prices for the whole world. This is some sort of an average of changes of consumer prices in all member countries. For example in August 1976 the change in consumer prices for the world as a whole over the last twelve months was 10.5 percent. This figure is a weighted average of 5.6 percent for the United States, 1.5 percent for Switzerland, 396 percent for Argentina, 200 percent for Chile (down from 400 percent a year ago), and so forth. The Fund also publishes global reserves, of which foreign exchange is by far the largest component. (These figures do not make allowance for the growth of reserve substitutes, i.e., official and semi-official borrowing.) It is possible to correlate the two series or rather jumbles of figures. But who would be bold enough to attribute any causal significance to such an operation and derive policy conclusions concerning the adequacy of world reserves?

How would the Fund exercise control over global reserves? SDR creation and utilization of Fund quotas are under international control. But as mentioned, by far the largest component of world reserves consists of foreign exchange, mostly dollar balances. One can, of course, dream of a monetary reform that would concentrate all reserves including gold and foreign exchange in the Fund in exchange for SDRs.[45] That such a reform would be politically utterly impossible is perhaps not the main objection. It may not even be a nice dream. Given the present day drift in international politics and power struggle, such a concentration of power in the hands of an international organization could become very dangerous. It would be bound to become an issue in the international class struggle that is now going on under the slogan of a New International Economic Order.

My conclusion is that in the present world of widespread floating it is impossible to give a meaningful definition of global reserves, let alone to define an optimal or desirable level of global reserves or of reserve growth. It is the adjustment and not the liquidity problem that is of paramount importance, now more than ever. The Fund's main task should be "surveillance" of exchange rate policies, especially prevention of dirty floating and dirty fixing of exchange rates.

However, to say that control of global reserves is not an important or meaningful task for the Fund any more does not mean that for individual countries the size of their reserves and their external borrowing potential are unimportant, nor that the use countries make of their reserves and borrowing power cannot become a matter of international concern. It is possible that in the last few years there has been much international over-borrowing and excessive lending by banks to shore up shaky balance of payments positions. Another development that may cause legitimate worry is the rapidly growing volume of lending by Western banks to communist countries. All this may, indeed, cause serious trouble in the future. But if so, it has nothing to do with a lack of international control over the volume of *global* reserves in the conventional sense, and it could not have been prevented by such controls, unless Fund control over global reserves were unconventionally interpreted to include control over money supply as well as over monetary policy in at least the major countries and perhaps Fund supervision over the lending policies of large banks.

Furthermore, discounting the importance of global reserves and their control does not mean that inflation is no problem. On the contrary, inflation is a major world problem. But it has no longer anything to do with a lack of control over global reserves. It has it roots in *national* monetary, fiscal, and exchange rate policies of the major countries. The primary responsibility for curbing world inflation obviously falls on the leading industrial countries, especially the United States. This is so because, as noted above, the majority of smaller countries peg their currencies either to the currency of one of the leading industrial countries, most of them to the dollar, or to a basket of important currencies or SDRs. It is true that national monetary policies, inflation or deflation, in the many countries that peg their currencies to the dollar are profoundly influenced if not fully determined by the inflation or absence of inflation in the United States. If there is inflation in the United States, dollar balances are likely to pile up in countries that peg the dollar and inflation will spread. It follows that if the Fund could control inflation in the United States and in a few other key countries it would substantially control world inflation. If control of *global* monetary reserves is unconventionally interpreted to include control of money supply, monetary policy, and inflation in the major countries then, and only then, could it be said that control of global reserves is necessary to prevent world inflation.

Actually the Fund can do nothing about inflation in the United States and only in exceptional cases about inflation in other major countries. (The British and Italian borrowing from the Fund may be such exceptional cases.) If the United States again lapsed into high inflation, the only effective measure to prevent the piling up of dollar reserves in countries that peg to the dollar and the spread of the U.S. inflation, would be to stop pegging to the dollar. In other words, if there is inflation in the United States, floating is the only effective policy to avoid both an excessive growth of international liquidity in the form of dollar balances and the spread of inflation.

The upshot is that the Fund can do very little about world inflation. It is easier, in fact, to think of Fund policies that would add, though marginally under realistic assumptions, to world inflation than to identify measures that would help to curb inflation. Steps that would add to inflationary pressures are a general increase in the Fund's quotas and additional distribution of SDRs, especially if linked to foreign aid. Similarly adding to inflation would be a further proliferation and expansion of special lending facilities—such as the Oil Facility, the Buffer Stock Facility, the Extended Fund Facility, the Compensatory Financing of Export Fluctuations.

But this does by no means imply that such measures should not be taken under any circumstances. On the contrary, emergencies must be expected to occur from time to time which justify even large scale credit operations by the Fund to forestall some major or minor disturbances of the world economy, including inflationary and protectionist reactions in some countries. What it does mean is that the inflationary implications of such lending should not be overlooked, just as a fire brigade when throwing water on an attic fire should not be oblivious of the damage that flooding can do to the rest of the house. The two dangers, the threatening disturbance and the inflationary side effect of the monetary measures taken, should be weighed against each other, overreactions should be avoided, and the rescue operations should be properly dosed and pinpointed[46] so as to minimize the danger of intensifying inflation.

To pursue this highly important problem any further would burst the frame of the present study. However, one more observation may be permitted: *Conditional* lending by the Fund—"provision of conditional liquidity" to use official language—can be used as an inducement for countries to put their financial house in order and to curb inflation. *Unconditional* lending is likely to be counterproductive because it is likely to tempt countries to delay needed structural reform and anti-inflationary measures and to postpone changes in exchange rates or floating that may be required.

Notes

1. It should, however, not be forgotten that the Fund had a strong inclination, from its inception, unique among international agencies, to pay attention to the theoretical foundations of its work, and to cultivate its relations with academic economists. This was due to the forceful leadership of Edward M. Bernstein and his able successors, Marcus Fleming, Jacques Polak, and others too numerous to mention.

2. "In general the [first] report of the Bellagio Group holds up well in the

light of subsequent developments." Robert Solomon, *The International Monetary System 1945-1976. An Insider's View,* New York, 1977, p. 71.

3. Probably the first who recognized this defect of a fixed rate system once the confidence in the fixity of the peg was gone, was Frank D. Graham. In his "Achilles Heels in Monetary Standards" (*American Economic Review,* March 1940, pp. 16-32,) Thomas D. Willett has pointed out that Graham's important paper was completely ignored at the time in academic as well as in official policy discussions. (See Thomas D. Willett, *Floating Exchange Rates and International Monetary Reform,* American Enterprise Institute, Washington, D.C., 1977.) Ten years later the one-way-bet criticism of the adjustable peg system was frequently made in the academic literature. See for example Milton Friedman's famous paper, "The Case for Flexible Exchange Rates," written in 1950 and first published in Milton Friedman, *Essays in Positive Economics,* Chicago, 1953; and James Meade's standard work, *The Balance of Payments,* London, 1951, chapter 17, "The Role of Speculation," pp. 218-231. It took two more decades for this insight to gain official recognition.

4. Lawrence Officer and Thomas D. Willett in "Reserve Assets Preference and the Confidence Problem in the Crisis Zone," (*Quarterly Journal of Economics,* Cambridge, Mass., 1969) and in "The Interaction of Adjustment and Gold Conversion Policies in a Reserve Currency System," (*Western Economic Journal,* March 1970) have argued that the case for the inherent instability of the reserve currency system has been greatly overdone. I find the Officer-Willet theory convincing if the reserve currency country keeps inflation sufficiently in check.

5. F. Machlup, "Between Outline and Outcome the Reform was Lost," in *Reflections on Jamaica: Essays in International Finance,* No. 115, April 1976, International Finance Section, Princeton University, Princeton, N.J., p. 33.

6. Ibid.

7. It is true, a high degree of indexation of wages and other incomes is a major roadblock for a stabilization policy whenever real wages have gotten out of line. For example, when an external deficit has to be eliminated because reserves are running out, the level of real wages ("absorption") has to be reduced if unemployment is to be avoided. In such a situation indexation becomes a serious hurdle for adjustment, irrespective of whether the adjustment is attempted by internal deflation, depreciation, or downward float. If real wage rates cannot be reduced, unemployment becomes the only method to bring about the unavoidable reduction of absorption and adjustment of the balance of payments.

8. Paul Lewis, *New York Times,* October 10, 1976.

9. In modern economic jargon this simple proposition has been expressed by saying that there is a feedback from a depreciating currency on domestic prices and costs which in turn worsens the short run trade-off between inflation and unemployment, that is, it steepens the short run Phillips curve. See, for example, Rudiger Dornbusch and Paul Krugman, "Flexible Exchange Rates in the

Short Run." As D.H. Robertson once said: "Well, that is just fine. We all have our funny little ways of putting things." D.H. Robertson, *Utility and All That and Other Essays,* London, 1952.

10. It has been objected that the ratchet mechanism does not operate in an inflationary environment for the following reason: In such an environment industries where demand has decreased can make their contributions to keeping down the overall rate of inflation by reducing the rate of price and money wage rise without making the change negative. (See for example W.M. Corden, *Inflation Exchange Rates, and the World Economy. Lectures on International Monetary Economics,* Oxford, Clarendon Press 1977, p. 70.) This would be true if it were not for the fact that in an inflationary environment *real* wages, too, tend to become rigid downward. Why do workers and their unions resist money wage restrictions in a stable price environment? Because they wish to protect their living standard. It follows that in an inflationary environment they resist a reduction in their real wage.

11. To demonstrate that polarization and vicious or virtuous circles have their deepest roots in the underlying conditions, in the presence and absence of inflation, and not in the exchange rate regime, consider the following mental experiment: Suppose there are two groups of countries which have little or no trade. The one group pursues prudent financial policies and enjoys price stability; the other group suffers from chronic and accelerating inflation. In that case polarization will develop; the inflationary group would be engulfed in a vicious circle and retarded growth while the other group would enjoy stability and rapid growth. Since trade is assumed to be insignificant, the particular international monetary arrangements, like floating, adjustable peg, or exchange controls have nothing to do with polarization.

12. Here the usual marginal qualifications to the proposition that import restrictions reduce GNP should be mentioned: The terms of trade could conceivably be improved and, with a lot of unemployment in particular industries, a tariff can increase aggregate employment and production.

13. This literature has been well reviewed by Marina v.N. Whitman in her contribution "International Interdependence and the U.S. Economy," to *Contemporary Economic Problems 1976,* William Fellner, editor, American Enterprise Institute, 1976. See especially pages 194-208.

14. See for example the IMF *Annual Reports,* especially the one for 1975. There are, of course, short run deviations between inflation rates and exchange rate changes. It is, furthermore, well known from the theory of the purchasing parity that occasionally fairly large, long run deviations of exchange rates from the purchasing power parity occur, if the latter is defined in terms of consumer price levels. These deviations are mainly due to differences in productivity growth between countries. For details and references to the literature see G. Haberler, "International Aspects of U.S. Inflation," in *A New Look at Inflation,* American Enterprise Institute, Washington, D.C., 1973, especially pp. 91-93; and "Infla-

tion As A Worldwide Phenomenon—An Overview," in *The Phenomenon of World Wide Inflation,* edited by D. Meiselman and A. Laffer, American Enterprise Institute, Washington, D.C., 1975, pp. 24–25.

15. The literature on the problem of transmission of and insulation from different types of external disturbances under a regime of floating exchange rates has been well reviewed by Edward Tower and Thomas D. Willett in *The Theory of Optimum Currency Areas and Exchange-Rate Flexibility, Special Paper in International Economics* No. 11, 1976, Princeton University, Princeton, N.J.

16. Edward M. Bernstein, "The Monetary Authorities and the Free Exchange Market," speech at Foreign Exchange Conference of American Bankers Association, New York, November 4, 1976. (mimeographed).

17. ". . . [M]anaged flexibility is preferred and, even to the purist, quite acceptable, provided the managers do not resist movements dictated by market forces that push in a definite direction for more than a few weeks." Machlup, "Between Outline and Outcome. . . ."

18. See IMF *Annual Report* for 1974, pages 112–116.

19. Official foreign borrowing surely should include part of the foreign borrowing by state enterprises and in some cases even officially induced borrowing by large private firms. It stands to reason that the line between genuinely private and official borrowing (and lending) tends to become more and more blurred in modern highly planned and manipulated economies, such as the British and Italian ones.

20. "Guideline (5), " IMF *Annual Report* for 1974, p. 114.

21. The quote comes from "Guideline (1)."

22. IMF *Annual Report* for 1974, p. 115.

23. In the literature the dividing line between clean and dirty floating is often drawn differently. Many authors use the word "clean floating" synonymously with free unmanaged floating. Others deny that there is such a thing as clean floating on the ground that "the authorities affect the exchange rate through their macropolicies whether they want it or not." (June Flanders, "Some Problems of Stabilization Policy under Floating Exchange Rates," in *Trade, Stability and Macroeconomics: Essays in Honor of Lloyd Metzler,* George Horwich and Paul A. Samuelson, eds., New York, 1974, p. 123. Of course, everything depends on everything else and everybody is free to define his terms as he wants. But it would be rather awkward and misleading to speak of a managed, "unclean" float, if the monetary authorities of a country, to stop a decline in external value of the currency, instead of intervening in the exchange market, took steps to slow down an ongoing inflation by reducing the rate of monetary growth.

24. For a thorough discussion of the problems of official interventions that raises some doubts about the wisdom of trying to smooth short run fluctuations in exchange rates, see Leland B. Yeager *International Monetary Relations:*

Theory, History, and Policy, New York, 1966, chapter 13, "Stabilizing Official Interventions," pp. 232–247.

25. The IMF guidelines define "medium-term" as a period of about four years. See below.

26. "To be sure, wildly roller-coasting exchange rates are so disconcerting for all but the bravest souls; hence managed flexibility is preferred. . . ." Machlup, "Between Outline and Outcome. . . ."

27. It may be recalled that the Smithsonian realignment of exchange rates was based on what was supposed to be the best expert advice available anywhere in the world, viz., an IMF econometric world model. Actually, the new pattern of exchange rates was proved to be hopelessly wrong within a few months. But the Smithsonian agreement was hailed at the time as a tremendous achievement (not only by politicians) and is even now, hindsight notwithstanding, mentioned as an example that it is not utopian to assume that countries will be "able to agree regularly on a consistent structure of spot reference rates." Consistent perhaps, but totally wrong nonetheless. (See John Williamson, "The Future Exchange Rate Regime," *Quarterly Review, Banca Nazionale del Lavoro,* Rome, June 1975, p. 140.)

28. It should, however, not be overlooked that under the adjustable peg central bankers and ministers of finance who contemplate a change in the exchange rate—up or down—have to pretend solemnly to the last moment that they would never, never do such a thing—an obnoxious feature of the par value system. Many examples of that painful behavior could be cited, even from the very recent experience in the European snake when the German mark was appreciated by a few percent.

29. See Ethier and Bloomfield, *Managing the Managed Float,* Essays in International Finance, No. 112, October 1975, Princeton University, Princeton, New Jersey. Passim, and John Williamson "The Future Exchange Rate Regime," in the *Banca Nazionale del Lavoro, Quarterly Review,* Rome, June 1975, pp. 127–144, also IMF "Guideline 3 (b)" and commentary thereto in IMF *Annual Report* for 1974, p. 115. See also the interesting pamphlet, *Rules for a Floating Rate Regime,* by Raymond F. Mikesell and Henry N. Goldstein, *Essays in International Finance* No. 109, April 1975, Princeton University, Princeton, New Jersey.

30. Ethier and Bloomfield, *Managing the Managed Float,* Essays in International Finance, No. 112, October 1975, Princeton University, Princeton, New Jersey, p. 10.

31. Williamson, "The Future Exchange Rate Regime," p. 134–136.

32. If this is the case it confirms the opinion of Machlup and other advocates of floating that under floating worries about the exchange rate provide an anti-inflationary incentive.

33. The French franc was not saved by the fact that for many years (1865 to 1914) it was rigidly joined in a one-to-one relationship with the Swiss franc

in the so-called "Latin Union," which was organized in 1865 between France, Belgium, Italy, and Switzerland and joined by Greece in 1868.

34. Balance of payments and exchange rate projections, even for only a year ahead, have been notoriously unreliable. For example, see Thomas D. Willett, *Floating Exchange Rates and International Monetary Reforms,* American Enterprise Institute, Washington, D.C., 1977.

35. Ethier and Bloomfield, *Managing the Managed Float,* Essays in International Finance, No. 112, October 1975, Princeton University, Princeton, New Jersey, p. 11. Italics in original.

36. Ethier and Bloomfield, *Managing the Managed Float,* Essays in International Finance, No. 112, October 1975, Princeton University, Princeton, New Jersey, p. 101.

37. Article IV Section 3 (f). The amended charter substantially repeats this injunction: "These principles [of surveillance over exchange arrangements] shall respect the domestic social and political policies of members," Article IV Section 3 (b).

38. The problems were set out in these terms in *International Monetary Arrangements: The Problem of Choice. Report on the Deliberations of an International Study Group of Thirty-Two Economists,* International Finance Section, Princeton University, Princeton, N.J., 1964. This was the first report of what has become known as the Bellagio Group. See Robert Triffin's contribution to the present volume.

39. It should be recalled that convertibility has two distinct meanings— asset convertibility (convertibility into some "primary" reserve asset) and market convertibility (convertibility into other currencies in a free, unrestricted foreign exchange market). The dollar still is and always was fully convertible in the important market sense except that for Americans (not foreigners) capital transfers were restricted for several years. But these restrictions were lifted in 1974.

40. Most of these plans were well described and analyzed by Fritz Machlup in *Plans for Reform of the International Monetary System, Special Papers in International Economics* No. 3, International Finance Section, Princeton University, Princeton, N.J., second revised edition, 1964; reprinted as chapter 14 in *International Payments, Debts and Gold,* Collected Essays by Fritz Machlup, New York, 1964, 2nd ed., 1976.

41. Total reserves of all IMF members end of period in SDRs. See *International Financial Statistics,* any recent issue.

42. This does, however, not mean that the United States was the only culprit. Many countries inflated even faster than the United States and the majority of countries followed the U.S. lead without resistance if not with pleasure, in some cases with the added satisfaction of being able to put all the blame on Uncle Sam.

43. Let me repeat that the much more important market convertibility of

currencies is fully preserved under floating, unless convertibility is restricted or abolished by exchange control. The danger of controls being imposed is much greater under the adjustable peg than under floating.

44. On the so-called "international quantity theory," which postulates a *close* relationship between international liquidity and the world price level, and on the criticism that the international quantity theory has received from Marcus Fleming, Jacques Polak, Egon Sohmen, and Thomas Willet, see my paper, "How Important is Control Over International Liquidity?" The criticism of the authors mentioned largely antedated the period of widespread floating. Floating has all but obliterated any correlation that may have still existed between the two magnitudes.

45. Before the advent of widespread floating, plans for the concentration and consolidation of world monetary reserves in the Fund have in fact been put forward by the dozen (see F. Machlup *Plans for Reform of the International Monetary System,* revised edition, 1964, for an early selection), and the Committee of Twenty wrestled with this problem for years.

46. To illustrate: An across the board distribution of additional SDRs or a general increase of country quotas in the Fund would clearly be an inflationary move. But the use of international liquidity, even of ad hoc created additional liquidity, for a loan to an inflationary country as part of a comprehensive agreement on a change in policy that enables the country to get out of the inflationary rut can be defended as an anti-inflationary one.

13

Floating and Flexibility

George N. Halm

The Compromise of Bretton Woods

The creation of the International Monetary Fund was a compromise according
to which stable parities were to be maintained by Fund members, who were
free to follow domestic policies of their own choosing. It was a marriage of
nascent Keynesianism with the discipline of the old gold standard. Of course
it was understood that a conflict between divergent national employment
policies could create fundamental disequilibria, but in such an event the members were to be permitted to adjust their parities. The Bretton Woods system
was characterized by "stable but adjustable" exchange rates, a formula that
seemed to include two adjustment mechanisms: pressures from changes in
international reserves on domestic monetary policies, and changes in exchange
rates. The dividing line between the application of the two mechanisms was
the existence of an undefined "fundamental disequilibrium" that was obviously
meant to be a rare event. Whether the rare parity changes that were to be permitted could be called a "mechanism" must have been doubtful from the start.
But the question was not asked. The concept of fundamental disequilibrium
was not defined, according to Fritz Machlup's law that political agreement can
only be achieved when excessively clear language is avoided.[1]

I shall try to show that this basic shortcoming of Bretton Woods is still
with us. Even after the Jamaica Amendment of January 1976 we do not know
which adjustment process is to be used under given circumstances, because
managed floating of exchange rates need not be different from a system with
stable but adjustable exchange values.

Had the members of the IMF been limited to the use of their drawing
rights in the Fund while trying to "correct maladjustments in their balance
of payments without resorting to measures destructive of national or international prosperity,"[2] they would not have been able to pursue full employment
policies and simultaneously to maintain stable exchange rates. Fundamental
disequilibria would have developed instantly, and relatively frequent adjustments
of parities would then have become a necessity. That is the way Keynes envisaged
it. However, at the time of Bretton Woods most experts would have considered

205

frequent adjustments of parities as "destructive of national or international prosperity."[3]

A choice between unemployment and depreciation was often avoided through large (but haphazard) liquidity creation via the emergence of the gold-dollar standard. Being able to rely on a rapid growth of international reserves outside the IMF, the members of the Fund were able to maintain stable parities for lengthy periods, often at unrealistic levels, while carrying on independent domestic policies. The discipline of the old gold standard did not prevail.

Without orderly and exclusive liquidity creation by the Fund (which would have permitted it to exert pressure on the members) the old (gold-standard type) adjustment mechanism was largely inoperative, yet was not replaced by a system of really flexible exchange rates. The parity changes that did occur were rare and "traumatic" events rather than normal adjustment procedures. They did not constitute a "mechanism." Excess liquidity ruined a system in which, supposedly, controlled liquidity maintained an orderly adjustment process either via prompt parity changes or via adequate changes in aggregate demand.

The Keynesian Clearing Union

The many attempts to correct the weaknesses of the Bretton Woods system can be brought into better focus when we compare them with the *Keynes Plan* of 1943,[4] a work of genius that contained all the elements of an international monetary system that could have functioned properly even if its members had refused to follow gold-standard rules in the pursuit of their monetary policies. Though not perfect, the Keynes Plan is still the most consistent proposal to date and can be used as a focal point whenever we try to sort out the many conflicting suggestions that face us today.

Instead of contributing gold and national currencies to an international pool (as in the IMF), the members of Keynes's proposed *International Clearing Union* would have been asked to accept payments by other members by having international bankmoney, called *bancor,* credited to their accounts in the books of the Union. In other words, deficit countries could have bought needed foreign currencies with bancor up to a certain figure called "quota." Debits and credits in the Union would have balanced automatically. However, while the right of a deficit country to draw bancor checks would have been limited by its quota, the obligations of a surplus country to accept bancor would have been unlimited, or limited only by the aggregate of quotas of all potential deficit countries.

Keynes emphasized that "the plan should not wander from the international *terrain.*"[5] The members would have been left free to follow policies which we are now accustomed to call Keynesian.

While Keynes did not want to make fixed par values the mainstay of his system, he admitted the need "for an orderly and agreed method to determine the relative exchange values of national currencies, so that unilateral action and competitive depreciation are prevented."[6] However, he stressed that "instead of maintaining the principle that the internal value of a national currency should conform to a prescribed *de jure* external value" we should provide "that its external value should be altered if necessary so as to conform to whatever *de facto* internal value results from domestic policies."[7]

Keynes's preferred adjustment mechanism did not consist of pressure by the Union on members to change their domestic monetary policies, but of frequent and almost automatic use of changes of parities. The latter did not have to wait until fundamental disequilibrium became manifest. He suggested "a stated reduction in the value of a member's currency" when the deficit of the country in the Union was rising. Similarly, a surplus country would have to upvalue its currency continuously as its balance in the Union kept rising above one-half of its quota.

Keynes was very conscious of the fact that an adjustment process is likely to work asymmetrically if the deficit countries are forced to depreciate when their reserves run out, while the surplus countries are not under equal pressure to upvalue. Therefore the request for unlimited acceptance of bancor by surplus countries, their obligation to upvalue on the basis of growing credit balances, and the suggestion that interest charges should be paid on both the debit and the credit balances in the Union "as a significant indication that the system looks on excessive credit balances with as critical an eye as on excessive debit balances."[8]

We see that Keynes's adjustment mechanism rested mainly on parity flexibility and was tightly connected with the financial operations of the Union. This connection would have been lost if the members could have circumvented the Union by using national currencies (as they did later as members of the Fund). Keynes requested, therefore, that the members of the Union "keep their reserve balances with the Clearing Union and not with one another." To make sure that he was understood, he added that "in order that sterling and dollar might not appear to compete with bancor for the purpose of reserve balances, the United Kingdom and the United States might agree together that they would not accept the reserve balances of other countries in excess of normal working balances except in the case of banks definitely belonging to a Sterling area or a Dollar area group."[9]

Keynes connected bancor with gold by fixing its value in terms of gold (but not unalterably), and by permitting a member "to obtain a credit balance in terms of bancor by paying in gold to the Clearing Union"[10] but not entitling it to demand gold against a balance of bancor. In other words, gold was permitted to expand but not to contract the quantity of international money. However, since upward revisions of quotas would have been possible, nothing was achieved in letting gold distort the elegant structure of the scheme. Keynes felt it "advisable to retain a provision for gold since no scheme which did not make such a provision would have the smallest chance of acceptance. . . ."[11] I have often wondered whether his support of the par-value system, that is, of stable but adjustable exchange rates, was, similarly, only due to the fact that otherwise his proposal would not have had the smallest chance of acceptance.

On the basis of its consistency (and with the benefit of hindsight) we must come to the conclusion that the Keynes Plan was far better than Harry D. White's more conservative proposal for an *International Stabilization Fund,* which, with minor changes, became the IMF. To summarize, the merits of Keynes's Clearing Union were:

1. Establishment of a powerful international institution in practical control of international liquidity.
2. Creation of a true adjustment mechanism based on frequent parity changes and giving members of the system nearly complete freedom in their internal economic affairs.
3. Prevention of the development of an international gold-exchange standard and a corresponding confidence problem by making a growing divergence between rising foreign-held dollar balances and falling U.S. gold reserves impossible.
4. Emphasis on the special responsibility of surplus countries.

The Keynes Plan was considered unacceptable in 1944 and it is extremely unlikely that it could be resurrected. But the Keynes Plan can still be used to put the many reform proposals that have been made since 1944 into their proper place. New proposals in the direction of greater flexibility of exchange rates and consolidation of international liquidity reserves are encouraging, assuming that we succeed in achieving Keynes's aim of getting away from our preoccupation with stable par values.

From Bellagio to Bürgenstock

After the creation of the IMF in 1944, the international payments system seemed at first quite satisfactory. Convertibility was gradually reestablished and world trade expanded. However, it was not the Fund but the gold-dollar standard that supported this expansion. When around 1958 the dollar shortage changed into a dollar glut, Robert Triffin's challenging book *Gold and the Dollar Crisis*[12] suggested grave dangers. The continuous growth of foreign-held, gold-convertible dollar balances, together with a deteriorating gold-reserve position of the United States, pointed to a potential collapse of the convertibility of the dollar. Reform seemed urgent.

While the IMF and the monetary authorities of its members remained unshaken in their trust in the par-value system of Bretton Woods, economists (under the leadership of Fritz Machlup and others) began to probe into the intricate relationships between adjustment, liquidity, and confidence.[13]

Of the approaches chosen by the Bellagio Group in 1963–64, two were concerned with the supply of international liquidity, that is, with attempts to replace the haphazard reserve creation under the existing gold-dollar standard by either a centralization of international reserves in the IMF or by a multiple currency reserve system in which major countries would hold a mixture of currencies and gold, would avoid making abrupt changes in the composition of their portfolios, and would coordinate their policies concerning the growth rates of gross reserves.

The connection of these proposals with the adjustment problem is to be found in the fact that, without elimination of the haphazard growth of reserves, adjustments will tend to be delayed and that the mechanism of adjustment needs either an international institution that controls reserves and can exert pressures, or else a close cooperation of the monetary authorities of the major countries. This is the very problem Keynes tried to avoid from the start by making his Clearing Union the exclusive supplier of international reserves.

The adjustment mechanism was not discussed in connection with these proposals aiming at improving the international liquidity situation. No specific adjustment mechanism was implied. However, adjustment was the core of two other proposals examined by the Bellagio Group: the semiautomatic gold standard and flexible exchange rates. These two mechanisms constituted the extreme positions that the compromise of Bretton Woods had tried to straddle. Of the two, Keynes favored the flexibility of exchange rates.

The semiautomatic gold standard maintains fixed parities and connects the international flow of gold reserves directly with the domestic monetary circulation of the member countries. Two conditions for the working of the semiautomatic gold standard must be fulfilled: (1) the maintenance of permanently fixed parities is to be considered more important that the pursuit of high employment policies; and (2) key-currency balances must be removed from international reserves by permitting the key-currency countries to rid themselves of their obligations out of profits from a one-time gold upvaluation.

The first condition can no longer be fulfilled. As Fritz Machlup says, "the world will not return to any scheme that includes automatic or semiautomatic controls of the supply of domestic money and credit, and the hope that the convertibility into gold would restore 'discipline' in national monetary management is in vain, at least for large industrialized countries."[14]

The elimination of key currencies through a radical upvaluation of gold would show that such upvaluations can happen and can be repeated, and that gold can be as much subject to manipulation as other reserve assets. This would refute the argument that only gold can be trusted.

However, when we reject the gold mechanism as politically unacceptable, we simultaneously reject all other mechanisms in which flows of reserves (no matter what the reserves happen to be) determine automatically the aggregate demand policies of the participating countries. Indeed, such a system would contain an adjustment mechanism in the full sense of the word and would be attractive in its consistency and simplicity. But it would be incompatible with modern "Keynesian" policies—which is the very reason why it was excluded from the Keynes Plan in favor of an exchange rate mechanism.

The Bellagio Group also discussed several forms of flexible exchange rates.

While the group did not aim at unanimous agreement, "substantial consensus" developed that in the case of *enduring* disturbances the adjustment process would be induced "either by changes in aggregate demand or by changes in the exchange rate." It was emphasized, however, that the prompt identification of the type of disturbance, whether only temporary or enduring, may be very difficult and sometimes impossible.[15] There was consensus that exchange rate adjustments in the past had often been unduly delayed. But no answer was forthcoming as to when precisely these changes should occur or where the dividing line between the two adjustment mechanisms (exchange rate changes or changes in aggregate demand) was to be drawn.

Five years later a new effort to discuss the adjustment mechanism was undertaken, this time, however, devoted entirely to greater flexibility of exchange rates. In other words, the discussion shifted more and more to Keynes's original position. While the Bellagio Group was composed of economists alone, the so-called Bürgenstock Group included both practitioners and economists. Articles written in connection with these discussions were published under the title *Approaches to Greater Flexibility of Exchange Rates. The Bürgenstock Papers.*[16]

Machlup's contribution, "Terms, Concepts, Theories, and Strategies in the Discussion of Greater Flexibility of Exchange Rates,"[17] provides an overview of exemplary clarity of the many existing possibilities.

Proposals for managed flexibility of exchange rates under a par-value system fall into two main categories which, fortunately, can be combined to the advantage of both. In the so-called "band" proposals, the margins for fluctuations around the parity are widened. Inside the band, exchange rates are permitted to fluctuate freely or with government intervention. Variations of this proposal could distinguish between an inner band without intervention and outer fringes in which intervention is permitted. Furthermore, the margins could be asymmetrical, permitting a correction for the superior position that surplus countries enjoy and that Keynes tried to remedy. The Keynes Plan did not try to make use of the band proposal, but Keynes was the original modern advocate of this attractive device.[18]

A widened band has the function of letting market forces determine the price of foreign currencies within a broader range. If par values were to be changed occasionally, this price movement inside intervention points would be one of the indicators for par-value adjustments.

The second proposal concerning greater flexibility of exchange rates concerns frequent but small parity changes which are to replace the rare but large devaluations and upvaluations characteristic of the Bretton Woods system. With respect to the size of these changes it is interesting that the Keynes Plan of 1943 considered changes of an order of magnitude that come close to the modern proposals. The important difference is that the changes envisaged by Keynes were still much less frequent. It is doubtful whether or not the Clearing Union could have avoided disequilibrating speculation. Keynes would then probably have argued for controls, since the frequent changes now under consideration (e.g., weekly changes of 1/26 of 1 per cent) would have been considered just as unacceptable as the demonetization of gold.

There is now a strong tendency to go back to the idea of connecting changes in par values with changes in a country's international reserves. The difficulty lies in the fact that we must now deal with the aftermath of having "solved" the international payments problem with massive and haphazard liquidity creation outside the Fund. It will not be possible to reach a clear-cut connection between the adjustment of par values and changes in liquidity reserves as under the Keynes Plan. But target reserves and limits to variations in reserves may provide a tolerable substitute, particularly when we consider that greater flexibility inside a wider band can help us decide in which direction and how far these small parity changes should go.

The *Bürgenstock Communiqué*[19] reported that "a majority favored both widening the range (or 'band') within which exchange rates may respond to market forces, and permitting a more continuous and gradual adjustment of parities."

The Fund's Position

The authorities of the IMF were slow in reacting to the proposals favoring a system of greater flexibility of exchange rates. Even today, despite the legalization of floating, the Fund's attitude does not seem to have changed very much. The official position can be gleaned from several publications of the IMF.[20]

In their report, *The Role of Exchange Rates in the Adjustment of International Payments* (1970), the Executive Directors expressed the opinion that "the par value system based on stable, but adjustable par values at realistic levels, remains the most appropriate general regime to govern exchange rates in a world of managed national economies." Similarly, the "Guidelines for Floating" of the *Outline of Reform* (1974) begin with the statement that "countries authorized to adopt floating rates would be guided by the same principles

governing adjustment action as countries maintaining par values." Finally, in
the *Jamaica Communiqué* (1976), the Interim Committee carries the principle
of avoiding excessively clear language to the extreme by saying that, concerning
the important problem of exchange rates, "the new system recognizes an
objective of stability and relates it to achievement of greater underlying stability
in economic and financial factors."

The report of 1970 made the attempt to explain the elusive concept of
"fundamental disequilibrium" and suggested that such a state exists when
internal and external considerations are pulling in opposite directions as regards
domestic stabilization measures, "for instance in a high employment country
with an international surplus." The report on *Reform of the International
Monetary System* (1972) emphasized "that par value changes would have to be
made before the evidence becomes overwhelming that adjustment was necessary."
This statement admitted that an adjustment mechanism based on fundamental
disequilibria is far too rough to serve as a guide for changes in parities. Mere
reference to fundamental disequilibrium certainly does not elucidate the
"specific principles of guidance" on which the Fund's surveillance or the international cooperation of its members is to be based.

But while both reports admitted that par-value changes have been far too
infrequent and too large, the members were also urged to avoid "premature"
changes in par values. In other words, the members face the difficult task of
changing parities before they become "unrealistic," while leaving them unchanged in all situations in which imbalances are not "basic" but only "cyclical."
Obviously the parity (or exchange rate) is seen as a price that is to remain stable
for years to express underlying long-run developments.

In the old gold standard days it made sense to speak of the par value as
"fixed point of reference," because the adjustment process automatically
induced changes in aggregate demand and, through these changes, supposedly
achieved a new equilibrium at the old par value. In other words, the economic
policies of the members of the system were integrated in the long run. However,
once such adjustments of national policies can no longer be counted upon, it
makes no sense to wait for cyclical reversals as results of policies that are now
rejected, and it becomes virtually impossible to know what the "underlying"
long run development will be. In all probability it will be the result of *diverging*
national economic policies.

To justify the "norm of fixity" the Fund authorities even argue that
eventual exchange rate adjustment is an aid to equilibrium because it promotes
"political willingness to impose unpopular domestic restraints." The Executive
Directors go even further when they argue that "where the attempt to defend
the parity is ultimately unsuccessful the psychological shock of a devaluation
may promote broad support for the adoption of the necessary associated measures to curtail domestic demand." A more continuous adjustment of parities
"without the trauma implicit in the act of exchange adjustment as a last resort,

would exert less pressure for domestic corrective measures."[21] This statement describes the very antithesis of a system with more flexible rates that is designed to spare the participating countries the disturbing effects of unrealistic rates and their belated adjustment.

It seems to be the attitude of the Executive Directors that premature (compared with delayed) adjustments are the greater evil because they undermine discipline, open the door to beggar-thy-neighbor policies, make international transactions insecure, shift factors of production during a merely temporary state of imbalance, and are difficult to supervise. Accordingly, the Executive Directors tend to reject various proposals to effect par-value changes automatically and frequently on the basis of objective indicators "such as movements in a member's official reserves or in the spot rate of a member's currency in the foreign exchange market." The reason is that "objective indicators based on exchange rate or reserve movements may reflect short-term features of the balance of payments rather than the development of an underlying situation or its causes."[22]

Nevertheless, in 1970 the Executive Directors considered not only a modest widening of the band but an amendment to the Articles of Agreement "to allow members to make changes in their parities without the concurrence of the Fund as long as such changes did not exceed, say, 3 per cent in any twelve-month period nor a cumulative amount of, say, 10 per cent in any five-year period."[23] This suggestion was omitted in their second report and did not reappear in either the *Outline* or the *Jamaica Agreement.*

The *Outline of Reform of the Committee of Twenty,* while still favoring "stable but adjustable" exchange rates, contained some interesting suggestions. Unfortunately, they are "conspicuously absent from the Jamaica Agreement."[24] The proposals of the *Outline* concern an adjustment mechanism based on objective indicators which have to do with the definition of reserves and liabilities, target reserve levels, and a point system for the activation of the mechanism.[25] The basic idea is that the official reserves of the members should neither rise too high above nor fall too far below a proper reserve level. As the reserves moves too far away from the target, they would pass, first, a "consultation point," then a point at which a country would become subject to "examination" and, finally, points at which it would be exposed to increasing "pressures." In the case of a surplus country such pressures could consist of (1) "a charge on reserve accumulations above a reserve norm . . . graduated with respect to the size of the reserve accumulation and the duration of the imbalance"; (2) depositing "of reserves above a specified level with an Excess Reserve Account to be established in the Fund at zero interest"; (3) withholding of future SDR allocations; (4) a report on the external position and policies of the country; and, finally, (5) the suggestion that "countries could be authorized to apply discriminatory trade and other current account restrictions against countries in persistent large surplus."

These proposals combine valuable suggestions from Keynes's negative rate of interest to Donald Marsh's fixed reserve standard.[26] But it is essential to remember that, when the Committee of Twenty refers to adjustment, it is not predominantly thinking of adjustment via parity changes. Quite to the contrary. Having in mind periods as long as four years, the Committee of Twenty considers it desirable "to the extent that it is possible to form a reasonable estimate of the medium-term norm of a country's exchange rate, to resist movements in market rates that appear to be deviating substantially from that norm.[27]

However, we are not told which market forces will or will not reverse themselves or why there should be cyclical changes once we decide to do without a gold-standard type integration of the national policies of the members of the system. In fact, the Committee of Twenty itself expressed doubts that a medium term norm of a country's exchange rate can be established, for such a rate would have to take into account "that national policies, including those relating to domestic stabilization, should not be subjected to greater constraints than are clearly necessary in the international interest; . . . that a degree of uncertainty necessarily attaches to any estimate of a medium-term normal exchange rate, that this uncertainty is particularly great in present circumstances, and that on occasion the market view may be more realistic than any official view whether of the country primarily concerned or of an international body"; and that it may, therefore, at times be unavoidable "to forego or curtail official intervention that would be desirable from the standpoint of exchange stability, if such intervention should involve an excessive drain on reserves or an impact on the money supply which it is difficult to neutralize."[28]

These are the very reasons that lead to the demand for greater flexibility of exchange rates. But it is obvious that the Committee of Twenty had rather long periods of stability in mind when it suggested "that countries, whether in surplus or in deficit, make appropriate par value changes promptly."[29] Of course, the terms "appropriate" and "prompt" were left vague, just as when Keynes and White disagreed thirty-four years ago.

Nevertheless, the positive proposals of the *Outline* could be used to great advantage if we connected them directly with the adjustment of parities or exchange rates rather than with adjustment in general (i.e., including changes in domestic monetary policies).

Another important suggestion in the *Outline* concerns "better international management of global liquidity, with the SDR becoming the principal reserve asset and the role of gold and of reserve currencies being reduced."[30] Paragraph 22 of the *Outline* says that "the Fund will, as necessary, make provision for the consolidation of reserve currency balances" with the help of a Substitution Account. Reserve consolidation is a must if haphazard liquidity creation is to be stopped, SDRs are to become the principal reserve asset, the aggregate volume of official currency holdings is to be kept under international surveillance, gold is to be demonetized, and, most importantly, a system of official indicators is to be used.

The suggestions of the *Outline* were steps in the right direction. But the adjustment mechanism should have been pointed clearly toward frequent exchange rate changes rather than toward long run stability of exchange rates. Also, it would have been better if the original suggestion of the report of 1970, concerning a sliding band, could have been retained.

Jamaica and After

The *Jamaica Amendment* is disappointing. "Only empty phrases from the *Outline* were preserved in the final accord; the important principles were lost in the shuffle, or deliberately dropped."[31] However, Jamaica has legalized managed floating which is, technically speaking, very similar to a system with a sliding band. "In principle, writes Fritz Machlup, "it would be possible to operate a system of managed floating that is *de facto* equivalent to a system of gliding parities. This may sound paradoxical in as much as floating currencies have no par values. However, central values or central intervention rates may take over the role that parities have under a crawling-peg system. Instead of altering the official parities with strict limits regarding the size of each single change and the size of the cumulative change over each twelve-month period, one may manage the floating in precisely the same way, observing the same limits for alterations of intervention rates. From a strictly economic point of view there need not be any difference between the two systems."[32]

As already reported above, the *Jamaica Communiqué* says that the new Article IV establishes a system of exchange arrangements that recognizes "an objective of stability and relates it to the achievement of greater underlying stability in economic and financial factors."[33] The statement is so vague that we do not know what is stabilized and by what means. Are both the underlying factors and the exchange rates to be kept as stable as possible or, if not, which is to be adjusted to give greater stability to the other? In any case, it is interesting that stability is being stressed and not flexibility. Floating has been legalized, but what is meant is certainly *managed* floating and nothing in the amendment suggests that this management is to aim at greater flexibility than contemplated in the *Outline of Reform* or the earlier reports by the Executive Directors.

As far as the adjustment mechanisms is concerned, Jamaica has not been a breakthrough. Floating was permitted because it could not be suppressed. An unavoidable infraction of the rules of the Fund had to be legalized, but the philosophy behind the new Article IV is still basically the old philosophy of stability, even if the statement of Bretton Woods that "each member undertakes to collaborate with the Fund to maintain exchange stability" has been transformed into a collaboration "to assure orderly exchange arrangements and to promote a stable system of exchange rates."[34] The idea still prevails that the members' financial policies are to be influenced and that competitive exchange depreciation is to be avoided. The Interim Committee connects the latter with managed or "manipulated" rates but does not condemn the maintenance of unrealistic par values.

The *Outline,* while leaning too heavily toward exchange rate stability, had made progress in the direction of suggesting ways by which an undue delay of parity adjustments could be avoided. The *Jamaica Amendment* barely mentions these constructive proposals. Section 3 of the new Article IV declares that "the Fund shall exercise firm surveillance over the exchange rate policies of members, and shall adopt specific principles of guidance of all members with respect to those policies." What these specific principles are we are not told. It is difficult to see what the Fund can do, unless floating is to be managed with the help of presumptive criteria. In this context, changes of international reserves of members come first to mind. But the Outline's attempt to create a basis for Fund surveillance by consolidating reserve assets, by demonetizing gold, and by making the SDR the principal reserve asset has gained only lip service in the new amendment. The SDR is decidedly not the principal reserve asset, gold has not been demonetized as preferred reserve asset (with a fall-back value as commodity),[35] and the Fund is decidedly not in command of international liquidity creation, nor can it exert the different degrees of pressure envisaged by the *Outline.* In short, we are still far from a system in which adjustment is tightly connected with variations in a country's liquidity reserves.

Perhaps even more important is a second point. Suppose that we have succeeded in using reserve movements as objective adjustment criterion. We should then still be exposed to the danger of repeating the mistake that plagued the Bretton Woods system, that is, we might still aim at adjustment predominantly through changes in domestic monetary policies that are no longer operative.

If we take it for granted that the domestic economic policies of the members can no longer be decisively influenced through the discipline of stable exchange rates, we must then also assume that we can no longer return, more or less automatically, to international payments equilibrium at stable rates of exchange. Then it makes no sense to wait for a change in "underlying conditions" that would adjust the internal value of a country's money to its external value. Maintenance of exchange rates over longish periods (such as four years) means under such conditions the maintenance of undervaluations and overvaluations, misallocations of productive resources, and, finally, delayed and "traumatic" adjustments of the exchange rates. In short, it means repeating the mistakes of the Bretton Woods system.

The danger is great that the Fund's "surveillance" and "specific principles of guidance" will err in the direction of delaying adjustment of exchange rates in favor of a vague principle of stability which dominates Section 1 of the new Article IV, while no equivalent emphasis on flexibility can be found in all of the *Jamaica Amendment.*

The urge to maintain stable exchange rates rests on the following points:

(1) the wish to maintain discipline in the members' monetary policies and to coordinate these policies through reserve flows; (2) the belief that certain trends will reverse themselves and that it often would be counterproductive to adjust exchange rates under such conditions; (3) the difficulty of changing exchange rates against the wishes of the parties engaged in international transactions; (4) the reluctance to admit that previous stabilization policies had been wrong; and, finally, (5) the need to coordinate intervention in the exchange markets by different central banks.

(*re* 1) The advocates of stable exchange rates who claim that flexibility would lead to inflationary domestic policies forget that, once par values are no longer *unalterably* fixed, their argument loses its cogency. Inflationary policies can be compensated by exchange depreciations. And if they are not, the disease will spread to the surplus countries in the form of "imported" inflation. On the other hand, under a system with floating rates, "when the balance of payments is kept continuously in equilibrium, a country has to swallow the inflation or deflation it generates and cannot get relief by unloading part of the burden on others."[36]

(*re* 2) In trying to maintain exchange rates over years because of hoped-for cyclical reversals, the monetary authorities of the member countries and the Fund undertake an impossible task, since no reversal need be forthcoming after the demise of the gold mechanism. Even in the more closely knit European Monetary Union these hopes have been in vein.

(*re* 3) Central bankers are under the influence of strong pressure groups which argue against changes of a given exchange rate. Since undervaluation can be maintained indefinitely through the purchase of foreign currencies and devaluation can be delayed by massive reserve flows, the chances are that adjustments will tend to be delayed unless a special effort is made toward greater flexibility of exchange rates.

(*re* 4) There always exists the psychological danger that it will be irresistibly tempting for monetary authorities to maintain wrong exchange rates simply because they do not want to admit to having been mistaken. "Having made a mistake, there will be a strong resistance to recognizing it, a strong tendency to hang on and hope that circumstances will change and show that it was not a mistake, a strong tendency to convert what might have been a minor exchange rate movement into a major disequilibrium and crisis."[37]

(*re* 5) Since freely fluctuating exchange rates are overwhelmingly rejected by international bankers, that is, since market intervention is to be taken for granted, the interventions by different Fund members must be coordinated to avoid inconsistent cross rates. We can only hope that these continuous discussions between central bankers "will not be misused for the purpose of keeping misaligned rates from getting adjusted."[38] Managed floating implies the danger that rates should perhaps be kept stable for days or weeks will, in fact, be kept stable for months and years.

Conclusion

Jamaica was disappointing, but it does not preclude further efforts in the right direction. What is urgently needed is a new trend away from a vague preference for "stability" even though it concerns a market price.

Properly managed floating does not have to wait for the day when the SDR will "play a pivotal role in a system of international liquidity control."[39] Exchange-rate variations inside a reasonably broad "band" might suffice as indicator, provided we trust the market more than our ability to foretell what the leading governments' actions will be over the next few years.

It is high time that ardent advocates of the market mechanism (the central bankers) should stop manipulating the most strategic price in the world economy. Long ago, the fixing of gold parities made sense because it did integrate the national economic policies of the members of the system. Since there is no longer the slightest chance that this mechanism can be revived, only well-managed flexibility (and not a search for some vague "stability") will enable us to improve the international payments system in a community of market economies.[40]

Notes

1. Fritz Machlup, *Remaking the International Monetary System. The Rio Agreement and Beyond* (Baltimore: The Johns Hopkins Press, 1968), p. 1.

2. *Articles of Agreement of the International Monetary Fund* (July 22, 1944). Reprinted in *The International Monetary Fund 1945-1965*, Vol. III *Documents* (Washington, D.C.: International Monetary Fund, 1969), Article I.

3. Ibid.

4. *The Keynes Plan: Proposals for an International Clearing Union* (April 1943). Reprinted in *The International Monetary Fund 1945-1965*, Vol. III *Documents*.

5. *Keynes Plan*, Preface.

6. *Keynes Plan*, Section I.

7. Speech before the House of Lords, May 23, 1944. Reprinted in Seymour E. Harris, ed., *The New Economics: Keynes' Influence on Theory and Public Policy* (New York: Alfred A. Knopf, 1948).

8. *Keynes Plan*, Section II.

9. *Keynes Plan*, Section V.

10. *Keynes Plan*, Section VI.

11. Letter to George N. Halm, quoted in Don D. Humphrey, "The Case for Gold," in C. Fred Bergsten and William G. Tyler, eds., *Leading Issues in International Economic Policy* (Lexington, Mass.: Lexington Books, D.C. Heath and Company, 1973), p. 97.

12. Robert Triffin, *Gold and the Dollar Crisis. The Future of Convertibility* (New Haven: Yale University Press, 1960).

13. See *International Monetary Arrangements: The Problem of Choice. Report on the Deliberations of an International Study Group of Thirty-Two Economists* [referred to below as Bellagio Group], Fritz Machlup and Burton G. Malkiel, eds. (International Finance Section, Princeton University, 1964); William Fellner, Fritz Machlup, and Eleven Others, *Maintaining and Restoring Balance in International Payments* (Princeton, N.J.: Princeton University Press, 1966); *Approaches to Greater Flexibility of Exchange Rates. The Bürgenstock Papers,* arranged by C. Fred Bergsten, George N. Halm, Fritz Machlup, and Robert V. Roosa (Princeton, N.J.: Princeton University Press, 1970).

14. Fritz Machlup, "The Role of Gold in the International Monetary System," in *Economic Notes,* Vol. I (Monte dei Paschi di Siena, 1972).

15. *International Monetary Arrangements,* p. 103.

16. See note 13.

17. *The Bürgenstock Papers,* pp. 31-47.

18. George N. Halm, *The "Band" Proposal: The Limits of Permissible Exchange Rate Variations, Special Papers in International Economics,* No. 6, International Finance Section, Princeton University, 1965, pp. 26-32.

19. *The Bürgenstock Papers,* pp. vii-viii.

20. *The Role of Exchange Rates in the Adjustment of International Payments.* A Report by the Executive Directors, International Monetary Fund, Washington, D.C., 1970; *Reform of the International Monetary System.* A Report by the Executive Directors to the Board of Governors, International Monetary Fund, Washington, D.C., 1972; Committee of Twenty, *Outline of Reform, IMF Survey, June 17, 1974; Jamaica Meetings,* January 7-8, 1976, *IMF Survey,* January 19, 1976. Reference to the Rio Amendment and the SDR has been omitted because the SDR scheme does not support an adjustment mechanism. Indeed, the main (and to some the most attractive) feature of the SDR arrangement is the replacement of conditional by unconditional reserve assets.

21. *The Role of Exchange Rates,* p. 32.

22. *Reform of the International Monetary System,* pp. 14-15.

23. *The Role of Exchange Rates,* p. 73.

24. See Fritz Machlup, "Between Outline and Outcome the Reform was Lost," In Edward M. Bernstein et al., *Reflections on Jamaica, Essays in International Finance,* No. 115, April 1976, International Finance Section, Princeton University.

25. *Outline of Reform,* Annexes 1 and 2.

26. *The Bürgenstock Papers,* pp. 261-274.

27. "Guidelines for Management of Floating," *IMF Survey,* June 17, 1974, pp. 181-183.

28. Ibid.

29. *Outline of Reform,* paragraph 11.

30. Ibid., paragraph 2.

31. Fritz Machlup in *Reflections on Jamaica,* p. 30.

32. Fritz Machlup, "Exchange-Rate Flexibility," in *Banca Nazionale del Lavoro Quarterly Review,* No. 106, September, 1973.

33. *IMF Survey,* January 19, 1976, p. 18.

34. *IMF Articles on Agreement,* Article IV, Section 4 (a); *Jamaica Amendment,* Article IV, Section 1.

35. See Don D. Humphrey in *Leading Issues in International Economic Policy,* p. 89.

36. Gottfried Haberler, in *The Bürgenstock Papers,* p. 120.

37. Milton Friedman, Statement before the Subcommittee on International Exchange and Payments of the Joint Committee of the Congress, U.S. Congress, Washington, D.C., June 21, 1973.

38. Fritz Machlup, in *Reflections on Jamaica,* p. 33.

39. H. Johannes Witteveen, "The Emerging International System," in *IMF Survey,* June 21, 1976.

40. See Fritz Machlup, "International Monetary Systems and the Free Market Economy," *Reprints in International Finance* No. 3, International Finance Section, Princeton, N.J.: Princeton University, 1966.

14

Imported Inflation and the Upward Revaluation of the Yen, 1965-1974

Yasukichi Yasuba

The German mark and the Japanese yen have proved to be the strongest major currencies in the world, experiencing in the last twenty years several upward revaluations relative to the dollar. Of the two, the German mark has been studied rather extensively and the story of its changing dollar value is well-known to the readers of the English language literature.

In contrast, relatively little has been written in English on imported inflation in Japan and the upward revaluation of the yen. In Japan these questions, understandably, were a subject of heated controversy. One of the non-Japanese economists whose writings were not only extensively invoked in the debate on the subject, but who was also personally involved in this debate in the early 1970s was Fritz Machlup.

Prolog: The First Phase of Inflation, 1960 and 1965

Fritz Machlup once compared the demand for international reserves to the size of Mrs. Machlup's wardrobe, which is presumably determined more or less by her ambitions.[1] To him, it is of course better to make the wardrobe as small as possible, or to make the skirt as short as possible. Perhaps in Britain of the 1960s, as P.M. Oppenheimer put it, "Mrs. Machlup . . . [was] happy in a mini-skirt,"[2] but, Professor Machlup would have been happier if the mini-skirt got shorter and shorter, until "Mrs. Machlup found herself in a nudist camp."[3]

The macromanagement of the Japanese economy between 1960 and 1965 should have pleased Professor Machlup, since this was basically what the Japanese Government tried to do. Real GNP grew at a rapid annual rate of 9.9 percent in this period, and GNP expressed in dollars increased at the still faster rate of 12.0 percent. In the meantime international reserves stayed almost constant at the relatively low level of $2 billion, with the result that the ratio of international reserves to GNP declined from 5.0 percent in 1960 to 3.1 percent in 1965. Since trade expanded as rapidly as GNP, the ratio of international reserves to the value of imports also decreased drastically from 43.2 to 26.4 percent (see Table 14-1).

Table 14-1

Some Indicators of the Japanese Economy, 1960-1965

	1960	1965	Annual rate of change (%)
GNP in constant (1970) prices (billion yen)	26,184	41,592	9.9
GNP in U.S. dollars (millions)	39,255	69,183	12.0
Imports in U.S. dollars (millions)	4,512	8,149	–
International reserves in U.S. dollars (millions)	1,949	2,152	–
Ratio of reserves to GNP	5.0%	3.1%	–
Ratio of reserves to imports	43.2%	26.4%	–
Wholesale prices (1958 = 100)	102	104	0.4
Consumers' prices (1958 = 100)	105	142	6.2
Export prices (1958 = 100)	105	100	-1.0
Import prices (1958 = 100)	96	95	-0.2

Source: *International Financial Statistics,* July 1966.

One can complain about the frequent use of the accelerator and the brake by the government. However, the Japanese economy grew so rapidly that the intervention had a "walk and run" effect rather than the "stop and go" effect experienced in other industrialized countries. This was the period in which the government's growth targets, often challenged by Marxist critics as being too optimistic, were exceeded year after year. Rapid growth was accompanied by an equalization in the distribution of income. Hence, people were generally disposed to support economic growth even if they did not care for some of the other aspects of economic changes.

One issue that irritated a number of people was the rise in consumers' prices at a rate exceeding 5 percent per annum. This rise may seem strange, since in the same period wholesale prices remained almost stable and the prices of traded goods were declining slightly as shown in Table 14-1. However, the diveregent movements can be readily explained. Wholesale prices and the prices of exports in Japan at this period were largely those of the products of relatively large-scale businesses in manufacturing industries, whereas consumers' prices repre-sented a smaller proportion of these products and a larger proportion of the products of small-scale manufacturing businesses and services such as personal services, housing, and retailing.[4] Since productivity rose more rapidly in large-scale manufacturing than in other sectors, the process of factor price equaliza-tion, if effective, would have brought about divergent movements in these prices.

In reality, factor prices were not equal in the 1950s. In the latter half of the 1950s wages paid by small-scale businesses in manufacturing industries were

25 percent lower than those paid by large firms even when the composition of the labor force was standardized.[5] Rapid economic growth and the relatively moderate union demands at large firms in the 1960s caused a tightening of the labor market and the narrowing of wage differentials between large and small firms. By 1965, differentials in wages, standardized with respect to the composition of labor, were no larger than 10 percent. This narrowing of wage differentials was another factor behind the divergence between consumers' prices, wholesale prices, and the prices of traded goods.[6] While there was general agreement among economists on the causes of the divergence in price movements, opinions were divided as to whether to call the rise in consumers' prices inflation and, if so, as to whether that inflation should be diagnosed as being of a demand-pull or cost-push variety.

Osamu Shimomura, a somewhat maverick but influential banker-turned economist, was against calling the rise in consumers' prices inflation, since consumers' prices, according to him, represent not only the prices of commodities but also the price of labor, or the value of human beings. Hence, he argued, it was only natural that consumers' prices should rise in a growing economy with the rising value of human beings. Of course, if wholesale prices, that is, mainly the prices of basic commodities, could be continually reduced, it should be possible to have stable consumers' prices even in a growing economy. However, Shimomura was not so much interested in price stability itself as in equilibrium in the balance of payments. As a result, he proposed that, as long as the payments position permitted it, the government should try to inject into the economy sufficient effective demand in order to fully utilize its growth potential. Shimomura argued that, given fixed exchange rates and stability of prices abroad, his suggestion would lead to the stabilization of prices of traded goods, or wholesale prices as their proxy.[7]

Shimomura's semantics and policy proposals suited Premiers Ikeda and Sato, whose governments pursued an aggressive policy of expansion of effective demand, conveniently neglecting the price issue. In 1961 they went so far as to reduce the government-determined interest rate payable on time deposits at banks and post offices (from 6.0 percent to 5.5 percent in the case of a one-year bank deposit) in the face of an accelerated rise in consumers' prices (from less than 2 percent per annum between 1953 and 1960 to an annual rate of 6.2 percent between 1960 and 1965).

Most other economists rejected Shimomura's semantics, but they could have benefited from more careful consideration of some parts of his argument. In particular, it was unfortunate that they neglected Shimomura's concern with the international aspect of the price problem and the "elasticity optimism" implicitly included in his argument.[8] The critics of Shimomura were divided into the proponents of the then fashionable cost-push thesis and the advocates of the old-fashioned demand-pull thesis.

Predictably, the most ardent supporters of the cost-push thesis were

Marxist-oriented economists, who simply took for granted the downward rigidities of the prices of commodities produced by large firms. Non-Marxists were more cautious, but some of them found the existence of cartels, government "guidance," and the domination of half a dozen markets by a few large firms to be indirect evidence supporting the hypothesis of the downward rigidity of prices.[9]

It was quite true that monopolistic factors could be detected in certain sectors of the economy but the link between them and inflation did not seem to be strong enough to jusitfy the diagnosis of cost-push inflation. A number of empirical studies found that most of the oligopolistic prices moved quite flexibly in both directions.[10] If the cost-push thesis had any validity, it was the Phillips's curve version proposed by Watanabe, Ono, and others.[11] Since unemployment statistics showed a rather peculiar movement in Japan, most of the Phillips's curve proponents had to use proxy variables. But in any case, they managed to show the existence of a trade-off relationship between inflation and employment.

The demand-pull thesis was advocated by some Marxists as well as by bankers. The best argument presented in its support seems to be that of the economists at the Bank of Japan[12] who demonstrated that changes in the money supply could explain business cycles quite well. Consequently, the demand-pull advocates suggested that the long term rate of increase in money supply should be curbed to control inflation.

As their critics pointed out, they should have read Fritz Machlup's "Another View of Cost-push and Demand-pull Inflation."[13] He demonstrated in this article that when the monetary authority is ready to "accommodate" inflation caused by cost-push factors, a close correlation between the rate of increase in money supply and the rate of inflation is bound to appear. Therefore, it becomes impossible, or extremely difficult, to identify the basic nature of inflation.

What really separated the advocates of the demand-pull thesis from the advocates of other theses was not the conviction of the former group concerning the possibility of reducing the rate of inflation by a more stringent monetary policy, but their evaluation of the cost entailed by such a policy. As long as the advocates of the demand-pull thesis neglected to evaluate the importance of the real issue, and simply continued to preach the truism that inflation would not be slowed down unless a more stringent monetary policy was adopted, their plea was not persuasive.

Imported Inflation and the Upward Revaluation of the Yen, 1965–1971

Prices of traded goods in different countries do not necessarily move in parallel because of such factors as changes in tariff rates an in quatitative restrictions.

Also, it is usually difficult to get a proper index of the prices of traded goods. Nevertheless, in the case of Japan and its most important trading partner, the United States, wholesale price indexes (proxies for prices of traded goods) showed surprisingly similar movements between 1959 and 1970. Moreover, when there was a significant divergence from parallel movement, as in 1959, 1961, 1965, 1967, and the period after 1968, its effect showed up readily in the balance of payments of Japan, the smaller of the two nations. As shown in Figure 14-1, wholesale prices in the United States remained virtually stable from 1960 to 1965 and so did wholesale prices in Japan. It appears clear that wholesale prices in Japan in this period were kept stable basically by a combination of fixed exchange rates, the stability of prices abroad, and the Japanese effort for equilibrium in the balance of payments.

As noted before, consumers' prices in Japan were rising in the same period at an annual rate of more than 6 percent. If monetary retrenchment and the continuous revaluation of the yen had taken place, it may have been possible to reduce the rate of inflation by one percentage point or two without causing noticeable real damage. However, it is doubtful whether the government could have gone further and achieved a zero increase in consumers' prices without causing unemployment and a significant slowing down of growth, since this would have meant continuous reduction of wholesale prices, at an annual rate of 5 to 6 percent.

The situation was different in 1965 and thereafter, when wholesale prices

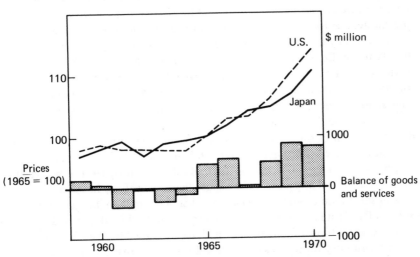

Source: Toyokeizai, '75 Keizai Tokei Nenkan (Tokyo: Toyokeizai Shimposha, 1975). p. 375; Bank of Japan, Economic Statistics Annual, 1971, pp. 249 and 286.

Figure 14-1. Wholesale Prices, Japan and the United States, and Balance of Goods and Services for Japan, 1959-70

both in the United States and Japan were rising more or less continuously. Most economists were still diagnosing inflation in terms of the old-fashioned cost-push and demand-pull theories.[14] The 1968 report of the Commission for the Study of Incomes Policy overlooked rising prices in the United States and Europe and suggested that increased downward rigidity of wholesale prices in recent years was caused by the increased price-controlling power of large enterprises.[15] Other economists were talking about the second round of inflation in which wage cost-push was an important factor. Proponents of the demand-pull thesis were doing even worse. In April 1969, the Committee for Price Stabilization, an advisory committee to the Japanese Government, recommended that greater use should be made of aggregate demand policy, in particular, monetary policy, to combat inflation.

Inflation in the United States showed signs of acceleration in the summer of 1969 when wholesale prices were nearly 5 percent higher than one year earlier. The Japanese economy at full employment could not but be adversely affected by such a large change in the price level of its major trading partner. Wholesale prices in July 1969 were 2.4 percent higher than in the same month in the previous year, and international reserves were accumulating at an annual rate of $800 million. It seemed clear that upward revaluation of the yen was the only sensible policy open to Japan.[16]

At that time only a few people were ready to accept such an unconventional measure. In fact, in September 1969, the Bank of Japan adopted monetary retrenchment as proposed by the Committee for Price Stabilization. The policy, of course, proved to be disasterous. In the first place, it did not work as quickly as previously, due to price pressures from abroad, the pressure on aggregate demand caused by the export surplus, and the inability of the monetary authority to sterilize fully the increment in international reserves. As a result, the rate of increase in the supply of high-powered money continued to rise until the second quarter of 1970. Only then was the rate of increase of total money supply reduced sufficiently to cause a slowing down in inflation.

Secondly, the tight money policy increased the export surplus and also induced an inflow of short term capital. The balance on current account, which was already as large as $1,048 million in 1968, increased to $2,119 million in 1969, and stood at $1,970 million in 1970. By the middle of 1971, it was clear that the balance in that year would be larger than ever before. In 1970 the inflow of short term capital had been more than $700 million, but just in the first half of 1971 it had already exceeded this amount. Thus, despite a drastic increase in the outflow of long term capital, partly caused by the effort of the monetary authority for reasons of window dressing, international reserves increased from $3,126 million in August 1969 (before monetary retrenchment) to $4,399 million in December 1970 and to $7,599 million in June 1971. To Japan, "involuntary foreign lending"[17] of such a magnitude meant a ridiculous waste of resources.

It was the United States that was borrowing these resources. Yet, instead of enjoying the unexpected bonus, it was complaining bitterly about unemployment caused by the excess of imports over exports. The U.S. government was criticizing Japanese policy, and protectionist sentiment was voiced by various domestic interests. Japan's exports of steel to the United States were already under "voluntary control," and the pressure was on for the control of textiles.

Faced with such an unhappy situation, more and more non-Marxist economists in Japan came to support the upward revaluation of the yen. Much of the theoretical elaboration was done by Yoichi Shinkai[18] and a careful econometric evaluation of the effect of the revaluation was conducted by Masahiro Tatemoto and Mitsuho Uchida.[19] Fritz Machlup, who came to Japan for three months in 1970 to teach at Osaka University, played an important role in this debate by lecturing energetically to academics and wider audiences in various places in Japan.[20] He also appeared on television to recommend the upward revaluation of the yen. Finally, thirty-six economists got together in July 1971 to propose "a gradual upward readjustment of the yen rate."[21]

Although their view reflected the opinion of most non-Marxist economists, they enjoyed no public support and no major political party subscribed to their view. In the opinion poll of "leaders" conducted by the Japan Economic Research Center as late as June 1971, 72 percent were found to be against revaluation.[22]

It was only after the announcement by the Nixon Administration, in August 1971, of a series of rather drastic measures including the imposition of an import surcharge, that the Japanese Government yielded to the pressure for revaluation. Even at this stage, the Bank of Japan tried to keep the old parity for eleven days, buying some $4 billion dollars in a futile fight against speculators.[23] Another $2.7 billion was accumulated in the period of the ensuing "dirty" float. By the time of the Smithsonian agreement in December 1971, the Japanese Mrs. Machlup was wearing a maxi-skirt: international reserves of the Bank of Japan were more than $15 billion—nearly equal to the value of imports in that year (see Table 14-2).

The upward revaluation of a currency tends to be unpopular in most countries, since vested interests such as export industries, industries competing with imports, and central bankers are more vocal than unorganized consumers.[24] Japan certainly had its share of vested interests, but the central bankers were opposed to revaluation for a special reason. In other countries, central bankers may be opposed to the upward revaluation of their currency for fear of the accounting loss caused by the depreciation of foreign reserves they own. In Japan, they did not have to be concerned with such a loss because they were to be compensated automatically by the Ministry of Finance.[25] In Japan, central bankers and officials at the Ministry of Finance were presumably opposed to the revaluation, because of the position of their friends in business.

It is not surprising that revaluation was resisted. But were there any reasons

Table 14-2
Some Indicators of the Japanese Economy, 1965-71

	1965	1971	Annual rate of change (%)
Imports (million U.S. dollars)	8,145	20,218	16.4
International reserves (million U.S. dollars)	2,152	15,360	38.8
Ratio of reserves to imports (%)	26.4	76.0	—
Wholesale prices (1970 = 100)	89.9	99.2	1.7
Consumers' prices (1970 = 100)	76.7	106.3	5.6

Source: *International Financial Statistics*, December 1971 and February 1977.

for the Japanese monetary authority to be opposed to revaluation well after monetary authorities in other countries had reacted? I believe there were several special reasons.

First, the Japanese public probably saw relatively little value in the slow-down of inflation that could be achieved by the elimination of its imported portion. After all, the country lived with a rise in consumers' prices exceeding 5 percent per annum for more than ten years. Between 1960 and 1970, consumers' prices rose 76 percent of which only 14 percent was accounted for by a rise in wholesale prices. If the rate of inflation could be lowered only by the margin of the rise in wholesale prices without causing unemployment, the relief resulting from the upward revaluation of the yen would be rather small compared with the present rate of inflation. As seen in Table 14-2, the relief (namely the rise in wholesale prices) as a proportion of the rise in consumers' prices was larger in the period after 1965. Yet, the annual rate of increase in consumers' prices was no larger than before, presumably because the narrowing of the wage gap between large and small firms came to an end.

Besides, most people gained from inflationary growth of the 1960s. There certainly was a lag in wages behind the rise in prices in the early phases of inflation, but this lag was gradually eliminated by the end of the decade. In fact, in the last two years of the decade, real wages increased at an unprecedented annual rate of 10.4 percent. A similar catching up was taking place in most other areas. Thus, for example, the public old-age pension increased at an annual rate of 15 percent and the public welfare stipend at the rate of 14 percent in the same period. The only important group of people who lost out permanently were savers who had deposits at banks and post offices. In view of the relatively early retirement age—55 at most firms in this period— and the fact that the general public kept most of their financial assets in the form of bank and postal savings accounts, the plight of depositors could hardly be overlooked. But even so, gains in other areas tended to overshadow depositors' losses.

In fact, the concern over inflation was so limited at the time of policy-induced recession in 1970–71 that a number of people insisted that the government should return to an aggressive expansionary demand policy even at the expense of price stability. Of course, their demand to facilitate recovery from a mini-recession was quite justified, but the fairly wide support for the argument for "adjustment inflation," that is, inflation intentionally caused by the government to adjust domestic prices for inflation abroad,[26] may be somewhat surprising to foreign observers.

The second reason for the officials' resistance to a revaluation of the yen was the existence of a number of factors that made it difficult to diagnose definitively that the fundamental disequilibrium in the Japanese balance of payments in 1970 was genuine. A number of economists, including government economists, pointed out that the Japanese economy, unlike others, was heavily protected by such artificial measures as quantitiative restrictions on imports and high import duties as well as by tax credits and subsidies to promote exports. They proposed that all these protective devices be removed before the revaluation of the yen was considered.[27]

Some of these people may have been using this argument just as an excuse for not revaluing immediately but others apparently wanted to take advantage of the occasion to accomplish reform. In any case, in June 1971 the government was eventually forced to adopt the so-called "Eight-point Program to Cope with the Yen Issue" including (1) the reduction of the number of imported goods subject to quantitiative restriction, (2) an early granting of preferential duties to developing countries, (3) the reduction of certain tariff rates, (4) the liberalization of controls on capital movements, (5) lowering of nontariff barriers to trade, (6) the expansion and untying of foreign aid, (7) the termination of the preferred treatment of export industries in financing and taxation, and (8) expansionary fiscal and monetary policy.

It was ironical that under foreign pressure reforms, many of which would have been impossible under normal conditions, were put into practice with unprecedented expediency. Subsidies on export loans were virtually abolished and the system of tax credits for exports was terminated. The number of import quotas was reduced from 120 in September 1969 to 40 in September 1971. The Kennedy Round tariff cuts were completed ahead of schedule and further unilateral tariff cuts were being considered. Preferential duties were extended also ahead of schedule. Yet these reforms proved to be insufficient to wipe out the huge surplus in the balance of payments.

The third reason for resistance was the close relationship between the government and business.[28] Such a relationship exists in many countries. It was suggested, however, that the collusion was closer in Japan than in other countries, with the result of vocal business interests being more influential. In particular, when the demands of the vested interests had some element of rationality, as in the case of the demands of the ship-building industry and other holders of dollar assets,[29] the collusion proved to be extremely effective. When Japanese ship builders exported ships, they typically received 20 percent of their dollar proceeds in cash and the remaining 80 percent over an eight-year period. At the same time, they were financed by yen loans from the Export-Import Bank of Japan and domestic commercial banks. Thus, ship builders had assets expressed in dollars and debts expressed in yen. The revaluation of the yen was bound to reduce the value of their assets in terms of the yen and yet would not change the value of their debts, whereas imported inflation would simply reduce the real value of the yen they were to receive and pay back to banks. Hence, ship builders would prefer imported inflation to revaluation.

Bankers, on the other hand, would prefer revaluation, if they had to choose between the two alternatives. Thus, it may appear that the interests of ship builders and bankers were diametrically opposed. However, there was another possible course that would leave both ship builders and bankers happy, that is, the policy of keeping the yen undervalued as long as possible.

Since in 1971, ship builders' dollar assets were substantial, they warned that the loss resulting from the revaluation would create serious social confusion. Furthermore, most of the new export contracts were now expressed in yen, and it was expected that within a few years the bulk of the loans outstanding would be hedged against revaluation. Hence, the strategy of postponing revaluation as long as possible must have appeared to be an eminently sensible one for the government which wanted to protect both interests. Of course, it would have been possible and more advantageous for the government to offer some compensation to the ship-building industry so that it could revalue the yen right away, as suggested, among other people, by Machlup,[30] but the industry would have driven a hard bargain in that case, since the dollar-asset issue was not the only reason for its opposition to revaluation.

The final and perhaps the most important reason for the delay in revaluing the yen was the economic illiteracy of the opposition parties and the Marxist economists who supported these parties. In Japan, in 1970 and 1971, not only the Communist Party but also the Socialist Party were dominated by Marxism of a very unrealistic variety. Both parties tended to be highly ideological, putting political issues before bread-and-butter ones. Thus, as late as in June 1971, the head of the Socialist Party issued a statement opposing revaluation, saying that it would mean yielding to the demands of the United States, which was pursuing the Vietnam War and a policy of inflation.[31] This attitude of the Japanese Socialist Party was in striking contrast, for example, to that of the German Social Democrats.

Most of the Marxist economists in Japan were insisting that the nations mismanaging their economies, mainly the United States, should make the adjustment,[32] forgetting that a key-currency country was not in a position to devalue its currency unilaterally *vis-a-vis* other currencies. They were also agitating for a return to the gold standard. In so doing they were in effect offering an alibi to the conservative government, which wanted to postpone revaluation for other reasons.

The Second Revaluation and Hyper-Inflation, 1972–74

The debate in 1970 and 1971 considerably enlightened the thinking of Japanese economists. In 1972, almost all non-Marxist academic economists were prepared to propose a more flexible management of the exchange rate. Because of constraints faced by government economists, it is difficult to judge what their real position was, but the *Economic White Paper* for 1972 at least mentioned "the exchange rate policy" as one of the policy tools to combat inflation, even though it did not fail to add that "in the international monetary order of the future fixity of exchange rates should remain the governing principle."[33]

Probably more important was the changed attitude of some of the Marxist economists who supported the opposition parties. *Kokumin no Keizaihakusho* [People's Economic White Paper], which used to present anachronistic analyses in the 1960s, became more realistic by 1970 when Kimihiro Masamura took over as the keynote writer. By 1972, its analysis became thoroughly modern and more objective than that of the government *White Paper.* Criticizing the traditional unholy alliance of the government, business, and labor unions in resisting revaluation, the 1972 *People's White Paper* called for "a flexibility of the exchange rate" and stressed "the importance of asserting the positive value of the adjustment of the [yen] rate at a time when the argument for adjustment inflation was gaining force."[34]

Unfortunately, their plea for enlightenment could not persuade other Marxists at this stage. Most Marxists still opposed the adjustment of the exchange rate, and some of them explicitly supported "adjustment inflation for the sake of welfare." They insisted, rightly, that the government should use accumulated reserves for expanding welfare expenditure rather than hoarding them. For this the transfer mechanism would have to be activated somehow. However, it was not at all necessary to "adjust the domestic equilibrium to the international equilibrium under a given exchange rate" and to avoid "becoming a sole exception in the environment of a world inflation."[35]

Major opposition parties were still highly politicized and ready to resist any pressure applied by the United States. In economic matters, while they were opposed to inflation, they demanded the utilization of the accumulated reserves for the benefit of the people, making their position suspiciously similar to that of the proponents of adjustment inflation. Moreover, they were extremely sensitive to the possible distress of small-scale firms.

At the other end of the spectrum, there were established vested interests, namely, export and import-competing industries and the conservative

Table 14-3

Prices, the Exchange Rate and International Reserves, 1972-1974

	1972 IV	1973 II	1974 IV	1974 II	1974 IV
Wholesale prices (1970 = 100)	102.7	111.3	127.3	150.8	157.0
The rate of change over the past year	4.1	12.4	24.0	35.5	23.3
Consumers' prices (1970 = 100)	113.7	123.0	130.8	150.2	162.0
The rate of change over the past year	4.8	10.9	15.0	22.1	23.9
Exchange rate (yen per one dollar)	302	265	280	284	301
International reserves (million U.S. dollars)	18,365	15,199	12,246	13,428	13,519

Source: *International Financial Statistics,* November 1974 and February 1977.

forces associated with them. Some of the old arguments had been demolished, but they could still rely on the lingering belief in the fixed exchange rate and the dollar asset thesis (promoted by the ship-building industry). Besides, the seeming failure of the first revaluation promptly to restore international equilibrium made it possible for them to propose "elasticity pessimism."[36] Socialist opposition to the United States foreign policy and Marxist demand for "adjustment inflation" helped their position.

Thus, when pressure for another yen revaluation mounted in 1972 as inflation in the United States and price stability in Japan aggravated the balance of payments problems between the two countries, it was not just vested interests and conservative politicians who insisted on the continuation of the policy of undervaluing the yen. Major opposition parties also demanded that the government not give in to the American request for yen revaluation. Premier Tanaka pledged in the Diet that he would feel grave responsibility if the government again were forced to revalue the yen by a large amount.

The second and third packages of "measures to cope with the yen issue" were adopted in 1972. The second package, adopted in May, included measures to expand domestic demand by fiscal and monetary tools and to promote imports and the outflow of capital. The third package, adopted in October, further liberalized the control on imports by an across-the-board tariff cut, an increase in the quotas for items under quantitative restriction and lowering of nontariff barriers to imports. It also put an end to the preferential treatment of export industries in taxation and finance. Terms of economic assistance were improved and a highly expansionary budget for 1973 was proposed.

By the end of 1972, wholesale prices were rising at an annual rate exceeding 10 percent per annum, but, despite protests by a number of economists,[37] yen revaluation was still resisted and an effort to overheat the economy continued. The floating of the yen (de facto revaluation by 16 percent) in March 1973 came too late to calm the already rampant inflation.

Given the rapid rise in commodity prices and the significant deterioration in the terms of trade since the summer of 1972 (12% deterioration by October 1973), complete suppression of inflation in 1973 and 1974 might have been impracticable. But it is difficult to defend the policy of "adjustment inflation" that resulted in an annual rate of increase of 20 percent in wholesale prices even before the oil crisis. High rates of increase in the money supply and in government expenditure, which lasted at least until the third quarter of 1973, set the stage for the price explosion following the oil crisis. By the second quarter of 1974, wholesale prices were up 35.5 percent compared with the same quarter in the previous year, and consumers' prices were not far behind. By the end of 1974, the yen rate had fallen to a level not much different from that of 1972 (See Table 14-3).[38]

Epilog

Perhaps I should not be so masochistic. Mrs. Machlup's wardrobe may still have been too large when Japan's international reserves stood at $13.5 billion at the end of 1974, but at least she had great success in dieting (liberalization) partly because of the strange thinking of the revaluation.

I have already referred to measures toward trade liberalization, but it may help at this point to summarize them. As Table 14-4 indicates, liberalization was rather sweeping. Particularly noteworthy were the several rounds of tariff cuts which reduced the average rate of duty on all imports from 6.9 percent in 1970 to 2.7 percent in 1974. In the same period, the average rate of duty on taxable imports declined from 17.0 to 5.3 percent. The number of items under quantitative restriction was also greatly reduced. Lowering of nontariff barriers to imports, such as red tape, discriminatory excise taxes, and monopolistic trade practices, was another significant achievement.

The benefit to the national economy must have been considerable, but it may be argued that some of the measures, such as the termination of the favorable treatment of export industries, would have been realized without the pressure on the yen. The extent of damage to big business through import liberalization was probably minimal, since most of the big businesses were exporters by this time.

General public understanding of the mechanisms of international finance is still far from satisfactory as is evident from the policy of undervaluing the yen in an effort to promote exports in 1976 not having been criticized vigorously enough. It is true that this time the domestic implication was different, because of the existence of unemployment, but the international implications of undervaluation were similar to those of the early 1970s, since the relative size of Japan's exports was even larger than before.

Criticism from foreign countries heightened as Japan maintained a large trade balance. It was at this point that Yomiuri Shimbun and the Tokyo

Table 14-4
Liberalization of Controls on Trade and Capital Movement

	Before June 1971	1974
Number of imports under quantitative restriction	80	31
Expansion of imports under such restriction (maximum proportion of domestic consumption)	2%	7%
Average tariff rates on imports (overall average rates)	6.9%	2.7%
(average on taxable imports)	17.0%	5.3%
Preferential duties for imports from developing countries	Adopted in August 1971 for 96 countries. Ten more countries included in 1972.	
Nontariff barriers	Automatic import quota (red tape) abolished in 1972. Reduction of discriminatory excise taxes (on larger cars) in 1973. Termination of the sole agency system for imports in 1972.	
Export promotion	Termination of accelerated depreciation in 1972. Termination of preferential rediscount rates at the Bank of Japan in 1972. Raising the interest rate on export credits of the Export-Import Bank in 1972.	
Capital movements	Several rounds of liberalization on investment in Japan. 100% liberalization by 1973 except for 5 industries. General liberalization of direct investment abroad in 1972.	

Source: *Zaisei Kinyu Tokei Geppo,* June 1973, pp. 6–7, June 1974, p. 69 and September 1976, p. 36.

Colloquium invited Fritz Machlup to Japan to give a series of lectures.[39] His criticism of the undervaluation of the yen was certainly timely, but the impact of his criticism is difficult to evaluate. Again, it appears that it was pressure by foreign governments rather than persuasion by Machlup and other scholars that pushed the yen rate upward. Besides, the adjustment was too slow and too small in magnitude to wipe out the imbalance.

I personally feel that the role of economic advisors in Japan will be limited until opposition parties become sufficiently free from ideologies to face economic realities and benefit from the findings of modern economic theory. There is some indication that a change in that direction is taking place, but it appears that at least one or two more elections will be needed for a significant improvement to be observed.

Notes

1. Fritz Machlup, "International Monetary System and the Free Market Economy," in *International Payments Problems: A Symposium* (Washington, D.C.: American Enterprise Institute for Public Policy Research, 1966).

2. "International Liquidity: the Case of the United Kingdom," *American Economic Review,* Vol. 58, No. 2 (May 1968), p. 606.

3. "Tekisei Gaika Jumbi," [Optimum reserves of foreign currency] in the collected lectures of Fritz Machlup published in Japanese, *Gendai Keizaigaku no Tembo* [Views on selected topics in modern economics], edited and translated by Yasukichi Yasuba (Tokyo: Nihonkeizai Shimbunsha, 1971), p. 55.

4. In 1965, 60 percent of the total weight of the wholesale price index was assigned to manufactured products made mainly by relatively large firms (capitalized at ¥50 million or more). In the same year, services other than retailing accounted for 31 percent of the total weight for consumers' prices. According to the input-output table, trade contributed 16 percent to private consumption expenditure. (Bank of Japan, *Economic Statistics Annual, 1969.* Tokyo: Bank of Japan, 1970, pp. 250, 260, and 292).

5. Here, wage differentials are defined as differentials of wages between small-scale firms employing 30–99 workers and large-scale firms employing 500 workers or more. Wages include bonuses and all other forms of monetary remuneration. The composition of labor is standardized with respect to sex, age, industry and white collar-blue collar status. Without the standardization, differentials in this period would be much larger. Akira Ono, *Sengo Nihon no Chingin Kettei* [Wage determination in postwar Japan] (Tokyo: Toyokeizai Simposha, 1973), p. 173.

6. A summary of these interpretations can be found in Yasuba, "Keizai Seicho to Infure," [Economic growth and inflation] *Keizai Hyoron,* Vol. 20, No. 1 (January 1971).

7. Shimomura wrote extensively, but his thesis on prices is conveniently summarized in chapters 4 and 10 in Osamu Shimomura, *Nihon Keizai Seichoron* [Essays in economic growth in Japan] (Tokyo: Kinyu Kaisei Jijo Kenkyukai, 1962).

8. Neither Machlup criticisms of the "elasticity pessimism" nor more technical reappraisal by Orcutt and Harberger affected the Japanese intellectual community at this stage. Even in the 1970s "pessimism" was used as an alibi for not revaluing the yen. I shall come back to this issue later. It was in 1973 that *International Payments, Debts, and Gold* (New York: Charles Scribner's Sons, 1964) was translated into Japanese.

9. Ryuichiro Tachi, Ryutaro Komiya, and Hiroshi Niida, *Nihon no Bukka Mondai* [Price problems of Japan] (Tokyo: Toyo Keizai Shimposha, 1964), Book I, chapter 1.

10. Masaichi Mizuno, *Nihon no Bukka Hendo* [Price changes in Japan] (Tokyo: Toyo Keizaishimposha, 1962), chapter 5, and Yoshihiro Kobayashi, "Wagakuni Kasen Shi jo ni okeru Kyoso to Kyocho," [Competition and cooperation in Japanese oligopoly], *Economic Studies Quarterly,* Vol. 18, No. 2 (September 1967).

11. Akira Ono, "Sengo Nihon no Chingin Dotai," [Changes of money earnings in postwar Japan] *Economic Studies Quarterly,* Vol. 16, No. 1 (November 1965); and Tsunehiko Watanabe, "Price Changes and the Rate of Changes of Money Wage Earnings in Japan," *Quarterly Journal of Economics,* Vol. 80, No. 1 (February 1966).

12. See for example, Toshihiko Yoshino, ed., *Keizai-Seicho to Bukka Mondai* [Economic growth and price problems] (Tokyo: Shunjusha, 1962).

13. *Review of Economics and Statistics,* Vol. 42, No. 2 (May 1960).

14. Shimomura was aware of the change and considered the upward revaluation of the yen as a possible course. Unfortunately, however, he rejected it, doubting its effectiveness and considering the probable opposition by business circles. "Nihon-Keizai no Atarashii Hakken," [New Discovery of the Japanese Economy] *Shukan Toyo Keizai,* August 31, 1968.

15. Hisao Kumagai et al., *Bukka Antei to Shotoku Seisaku—Bukka, Chingin, Shotoku, Seisansei Kenkyu-Iinkai Hokokusho* [Price stabilization and incomes policy: Report of the study committee of prices, wages, income, and productivity] (Tokyo: Keizai Kikaku Kyokai, 1968), pp. 20–25.

16. For my position, see the issues of *Nihon Keizai Shimbun,* of July 5, 1969 and August 25, 1969, reprinted, with modification, as "Inflation no Shinkyokumen," [A new phase of inflation] in Masahiro Tatemoto and Tsunehiko Watanabe, eds., *Gendai no Keizaigaku* [Modern economics] (Tokyo: Nihon Keizai Shimbunsha, 1970). See also "Yen Kiriage to Bukka," [Revaluation of the yen and prices] in *Boeki to Kanzei,* Vol. 19, No. 6, (June 1970) later reprinted in Hiroshi Niida and Yoichi Shinkai, eds., *Inflation* (Tokyo: Nihonkeizai Shimbunsha, 1974).

17. Fritz Machlup, *Involuntary Foreign Lending,* (Uppsala: Wicksell Lecture Society, 1965).

18. "Infure no Kokusaiteki Hakyu to Heika Choseisaku," [International propagation of inflation and the adjustment of exchange rates] in *Kikan Gendai Keizai,* Vol. 2, September 1971, reprinted in *Inflation.* See also "A Model of Imported Inflation," *Journal of Political Economy,* Vol, 81, No. 4 (July/August, 1973).

19. *En Kiriage* [The revaluation of the yen] (Tokyo: N.H.K., 1971).

20. Machlup, *Gendai Keizai no Tembo,* chapter 1.

21. *Shukan Toyokeizai,* Special Issue on the Yen Revaluation, pp. 129 ff.

22. *Nihon Keizai Shimbun,* July 1, 1971.

23. According to an unconfirmed report, the Bank of Japan took this action partly to save certain commercial firms and foreign exchange banks caught off balance. See *Asahi Shimbun,* August 28, 1971.

24. Machlup, *Gendai Keizaigaku no Tembo*, chapter 1.

25. Of course, the Bank of Japan should have been responsible for the loss to taxpayers, but it has escaped criticism because of the opposition parties attacking the act of revaluation itself.

26. See, for example, Eiji Ozaki, "Tsuka Fuan-jidai no Zaisei Kinyu Seisaku," [Fiscal and monetary policy at the time of currency crisis] *Nihon Keizai Shimbun*, May 31, 1971. Also Osamu Shimomura, "Infure no Honshitsu o Misugosuna," [Do not overlook the basic characteristics of the inflation] *Shukan Toyo Keizai*, Special Issue on Contemporary Inflation, May 20, 1971.

27. See, for example, the discussion by two anonymous government economists at the Symposium on the Revaluation of the Yen, *Shukan Toyo Keizai*, Special Issue on the Yen Revaluation, August 30, 1971.

28. Yoichi Shinkai, recently maintained that this was in fact the major factor. "Wagakuni de Anteiseisaku wa Kano ka?" [Was a stabilization policy possible?] in Saburo Okita and Tadao Uchida, eds., *Atarashii Hanei o Motomete* [In search of a new prosperity] (Tokyo: Nihonkeizai Shimbunsha, 1977).

29. Nippon Choki Shinyo Ginko, *En Kiriage to Nippon Sangyo no Jitsuryoku* [The revaluation of the yen and the strength of the Japanese economy] (Tokyo:Toyokeizai Shimposha, 1971).

30. "Kokusaishushi no Kinko to Kawasereito no Chosei," [Equilibrium in the Balance of Payments and the Adjustment of Exchange Rates] in *Gendai Keizaigaku no Tembo*, p. 26.

31. *Asahi Shimbun*, June 14, 1971.

32. See for example. Shoichi Kase, "Beikoku wa Doru o Kirisageru Bekida," [The United States would devalue the dollar] *Ekonomisuto*, May 25, 1971.

33. Economic Planning Agency, *Keizaihakusho Showa-45-nenban* (Tokyo: Ministry of Finance, 1972), p. 216.

34. Heiwa Keizai Kenkyu Kaigi, *Kokumin no Keizaihakusho, Showa 47-nendo* (Tokyo: Nippon Hyoronsha, 1972), pp. 88–90.

35. Yoshihiro Takasuga, "Chosei Infure o Minaose," [Reconsider adjustment inflation] *Ekonomisuto*, September 19, 1972. p. 23.

36. It was conveniently forgotten that once the industrial structure was adapted to an unrealistic exchange rate, it would take considerable time to readjust.

37. See for example, statements by Buntaro, Tomizuka and Akihiro Amano in *Ekonomisuto*, October 31, 1972, pp. 40–42. Also Tadao Uchida, "Saikiriage to Koteibuai Hikiage o," [Revalue the yen again and raise the discount rate] *Ekonomisuto*, January 23, 1973.

38. For an analysis of inflation in this period, with special emphasis on money supply, readers are referred to Ryutaro Komiya, "Showa 48-9-nen Inflation no Genin," [Causes of inflation in 1973–74] *Keizaigaku Ronshu*, Vol. 42, No. 1, April 1976.

39. *Yomiuri Shimbun*, October 4 and 11, 1976.

Part VII:
The Student of Technical Progress

15

Optimal Lags in a Schumpeterian Innovation Process

*William J. Baumol and
Dietrich Fischer*

The economics of patent protection is one of the many areas of our discipline whose analysis takes its roots from the work of Fritz Machlup. Many significant writings on the subject have since appeared, work by such eminent writers as Griliches, Mansfield, Nordhaus, Stiglitz, and Das Gupta. But all of them must acknowledge their descent from Machlup's work. The piece that follows is clearly no exception.

Costs and Benefits of Increased Schumpeterian Lag

The very nature of the Schumpeterian mechanism for the inducement of innovation precludes the attainment of what might be considered a platonic ideal in the utilization of resources. For the instrument that serves as the heart of the mechanism, by its very nature, introduces an imperfection into the resource allocation process. That instrument is the temporary monopoly that falls into the hands of the entrepreneur the moment he establishes a successful innovation, and which remains his, albeit in diminishing degree, until the accumulation of imitators or of other innovations finally removes from him any advantages that his innovation had initially conferred. The problem is that monopoly is itself a source of imperfection in the process of resource utilization. That is, it prevents the attainment of the maximum of any social welfare function that encompasses Pareto optimality as a necessary part of its welfare goal.

This, then, is the problem: if no such temporary monopoly is conferred upon the successful innovator, he will be deprived of most, if not all, returns to his innovation and so the process will be inhibited if not halted altogether.[1] On the other hand, the longer the monopoly remains in effect, the longer will be the period in which output will be restricted and consumers' surplus con-

The preparation of this chapter was supported by a grant from the National Science Foundation, which we gratefully acknowledge. It was earlier part of a report to the Office of National Research and Development Assessment, National Science Foundation, entitled "Towards Empirical Estimation of the Externalities of Innovation" by Robert J. Anderson, Jr., William J. Baumol, Ralph C. d'Arge, and Dietrich Fischer, MATHEMATICA, Inc., November 1975.

241

sequently lost. Thus the problem becomes a matter of compromise—of optimal balancing of the two undesirable consequences. Presumably neither a zero nor an indefinitely long lag before the monopoly is eliminated will best serve the interests of the community. For the former will produce stagnation and the latter will amount to the institution of permanent monopolies.[2] That is, there should be some intermediate lags which are more desirable than either extreme. Since the amount of innovative activity and the value of any plausible welfare function are both surely bounded, it follows that there must be one or more intermediate values of the lag that are optimal.[3] The task then is to find such a value. We will presently construct a formal model designed to deal with this problem.[4]

Unfortunately, the model is expressed in such general terms that an explicit solution cannot be obtained. Instead, we are forced to offer a simplified version of the control problem described by the model and provide solutions to it by computer simulation. The simulation analysis compares the social benefits of the privately financed innovation that can be induced by a patent period of optimal duration with those of an idealized process of innovation that is completely financed by government investment and in which the technology made possible by the information is made freely available to everyone.

The following conclusions are suggested by the simulation:

The optimal length of the patent period is a function of the discount rate and the rate of return on investments in innovation. If the discount rate is held fixed, then the optimal patent life is shorter the larger the rate of return on investment in innovation, presumably because a shorter duration of the monopoly is then sufficient to call forth a given level of investment in innovation. If the discount rate is proportionate to the rate of return on investment in innovation, then the optimal patent life is inversely proportional to either of these two variables.

Nevertheless, even with a patent period of optimal length, the results of the private investment model are found to be inferior from the viewpoint of society to the results of the idealized governmental investment program that is formulated as an abstract standard of comparison. The amount of investment in innovation by a profit-maximizing private entrepreneur induced by the patent arrangement is found to be lower than the optimal amount in the public investment model. This results in a lower economic growth rate than the one that maximizes social welfare. It may be interesting to note that the loss to society from reliance on the patent system to stimulate innovative activity is larger than the resulting gain to the entrepreneur, and that the bulk of the loss to society does not result from the monopoly profit earned by the innovator but from the misallocation of resources that his decision must produce in providing those monopoly profits to him.[5]

It will be seen that the approach toward the analysis of patent periods undertaken by this study has yielded a model that is rather rich in its implications. Obviously, it constitutes only a first step and needs to take account of many other important considerations. Yet it does indicate the directions in which further analysis can profitably proceed.

The Problem Restated in Terms of Possibility Loci

The production frontier diagram can help to bring out the nature of trade-off involved in the choice of an optimal Schumpeterian lag. In Figure 15–1 the vertical axis indicates the quantity of some output for which we are considering the effects of variation in the lag period. The other axis shows the quantities of the Hicksian market basket that includes all other goods. The curve AB then represents an initial production possibility locus, and AC and AD are the loci describing the expanded output possibilities permitted by innovation, the latter

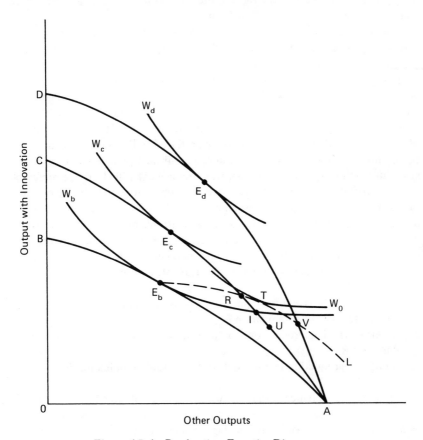

Figure 15–1. Production Frontier Diagram

curve obviously corresponding to the more radical change in technology. The curves labelled W_b, W_c, W_d, and W_0 are iso-welfare loci of a welfare function assumed to remain stationary throughout the analysis. Points E_b, E_c, and E_d, the points of tangency between the welfare loci and the production frontiers, then are the static optima corresponding to these various frontiers.

Suppose now that with the production frontier given by AC, the innovating industry (Industry 2) is run by a monopoly, while the rest of the economy is perfectly competitive. By the standard analysis it follows that output 2 will be less than its optimal amount and the quantity of output I will therefore be correspondingly excessive. However, in the absence of monopsony or externalities, both the competitive and the monopoly industries will as usual find it in their interests to produce their outputs efficiently, that is, for whatever bundle of inputs they do utilize they will produce as large an output as possible. It follows that the market equilibrium point will then fall *on* the possibility frontier, but somewhere to the right of the optimal point, E_c. That is, it will be represented by a point such as R or U on AC.

Next, suppose that society is faced with the choice between a strictly competitive regime without innovation[6] and a monopoly which does induce technological change. In that case the pertinent options are not E_c and, say, R but E_b and R. That is, one can have either the competitive output combination E_b on the more restrictive possibility frontier AB, or a nonoptimal combination on the superior frontier AC. Then the monopoly will be the preferable choice so long as R lies to the left of I, the point of intersection of the welfare locus W_b with AC, for then R will obviously be preferred to the stagnant competitive equilibrium E_b. However, if the monopoly equilibrium point is like U, and so lies to the right of I, then the competitive arrangement will clearly be preferable.

To carry the argument one step further, suppose now that the lag can be varied, and that with increased assurance of freedom from competition (i.e., increased lag), the innovator sets a higher price for his product and so restricts its output further relative to the competitive level, but invests more effort and resources in innovation. Then consider the following menu of choices representing three of the candidate solutions in the available continuum of possibilities:

1. Zero lag, no deviation from pure competition, production frontier stationary at AB, output combination E_b.
2. Intermediate lag, production frontier shifted outward to AC, output combination R.
3. Long lag, production frontier out to AD, output combination V.

As the diagram happens to be drawn, R is preferable to either E_b or V, and E_b is superior to V. Thus, the intermediate lag represents a clear improvement over the zero lag while the long lag is much too much of what started off as a good thing.

Now, let broken line E_bL be the lag-possibility locus, that is, the locus of the different equilibrium points such as E_b, R, and V corresponding to different magnitudes of the Schumpeterian lag. If T is the tangency point between E_bL and an iso-welfare locus W_o, then this will be the point that corresponds to the optimal lag.

This, apart from the usual complications caused by inappropriate concavity-convexity relationships, discontinuous derivatives or corner maxima, is an outline of the structure of the issue—the nature of the quasi-optimum that represents the best choice open to the community.

However, before we go on to formalize the decision problem we must deal with two issues, one peripheral, but nevertheless potentially interesting, and another that goes to the heart of the analysis.

Effects of Externalities in the Innovation Process

If the use of inputs in the process of innovation generates externalities either directly or indirectly it is no longer true that production will be carried out efficiently. On the contrary, it is easily demonstrated that in these circumstances the efficiency conditions are likely to be violated, and so the market equilibrium point will fall inside the pertinent production frontier.

It is to be noted that this is not inherently a problem of monopoly versus competition. On the contrary, in the presence of externalities both the competitive and monopoly production processes can be expected to be conducted inefficiently. The menu of choices now becomes like that represented in Figure 15-2. The lag possibility locus then will no longer go through points R and V as in Figure 15-1 but will instead be E_bL', which goes through equilibrium points R' and V' inside the corresponding production frontiers.

Though one cannot be certain of this, it is plausible that E_bL' will draw further apart from E_bL as one moves along it toward the right. For as the lag grows longer within the relevant range we expect an increase in the quantity of resources dedicated to innovation. The inefficiency associated with this use of resources and its creation of externalities may then be expected to grow commensurately.

In this case our trade-off grows more complex: since the externalities associated with innovation are usually presumed to be beneficial, we may take it that the optimal quantity of output 2 is greater than its competitive level, while the monopoly granted to the producers of that good leads to an output below the competitive amount. As a result, the resource misallocation resulting from the temporary monopoly may well be more serious than it would be in the absence of externalities. Second, the resources are now used inefficiently in addition to their being misallocated among the different outputs. Thus the benefits from the innovation stimulated by the lag must now outweigh a number

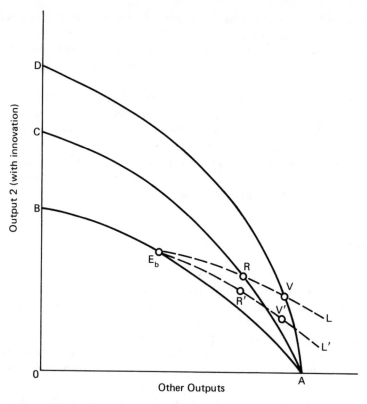

Figure 15-2. Production Frontiers in the Presence of Externalities

of costs in addition to those against which it was balanced off in the zero externalities case. It is therefore plausible that the optimal lag in this case will be reduced by the presence of externalities though we cannot be certain that this will be so. This pattern is suggested in Figure 15-3 where $E_b L$ and $E_b L'$ are the lag-possibility loci respectively corresponding to the cases with and without externalities. The tangency point with an iso-welfare locus, point T', is closer to the zero lag point, E_b in the externalities case than it is in the other (point T). It is easy to see, however, that this need not inevitably be so, if the iso-welfare loci become steeper below and to the right of T, at a point like T'' in Figure 15-3. This case will occur only if the relative marginal utility of output 2 decreases when its quantity goes down, holding output 1 constant. This may seem a peculiar case but it is by no means impossible to imagine.

The Role of the Time Path of Events

The significant shortcoming of the analysis up to this point (though it seems nevertheless to describe many of the relevant issues for cost saving inventions

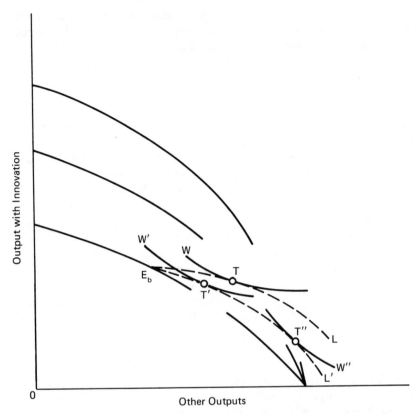

Figure 15-3. Lag-Possibility Loci with and without Externalities

appropriately) lies in its failure to take account of the temporal sequence of events inherent in the Schumpeterian process. An essential feature of this process is the *temporary* character of the innovator's monopoly. At the end of the lag period he is once again subject to the full forces of competition. Thus, at that point the outputs of our two industries can once again be expected to correspond to an optimal point on the prevailing production frontier. However, that possibility locus will lie further away from the origin than the one that would have represented the state of the world had no innovation ever taken place.

To keep matters still at a simple level, we can deal with the role of time by considering a single act of innovation, which may be more or less radical depending on the length of the Schumpeterian lag, that is, on the amount of time the entrepreneur can expect to derive his monopoly profit. In terms of Figure 15-1 this implies that with a zero lag the community will remain forever at point E_b. However, with a relatively long lag, it will move to point V for the duration of the lag period, and then to point E_d, the optimal point on the higher possibility locus AD permitted by innovation. Now, point V is inferior to E_b but

E_d is superior to it. The criterion of choice between the competitive (zero lag) solution and the long lag solution then essentially asks whether the discounted present value of the welfare level corresponding to V up to the end of the lag period, plus the welfare level of point E_d forever thereafter, is superior or inferior to the present value of welfare with permanent location at E_b. We now see that the long lag may well be superior to the zero lag solution even if the former yields a welfare return during the period of the temporary monopoly that is inferior to the return to the zero lag arrangement (point V beneath the iso-welfare locus through E_b in Figure 15-1).

The same sort of logic also applies to the appropriate optimality calculation. The choice now involves the calculation of the discounted present value of the stream of welfare returns corresponding to each relevant choice of Schumpeterian lag period. In each case one must consider the welfare that accrues both before the end of the period, and the returns obtained thereafter, once competition has been restored. The value of the lag that maximizes the discounted stream of welfare flows is then the optimal lag period.

Two more observations are required before we attempt to translate this loose description into a more rigorous analysis. We may note first that the transition from monopoly to competition at the end of the lag period can be gradual and continuous, and perhaps even subject to stochastic influences. This is likely to be the case if the monopoly is brought to an end by automatic market forces which, as Schumpeter described them, gradually produce a host of imitators, whose number and the rapidity of whose appearance depends upon the profitability of the initial innovation and the ease with which it can be copied, as well as upon fortuitous circumstances. However, if the lag period is imposed by policy through a patent law or some similar device, the dating of the appearance of competitors involves a minimum of chance, and the transition can indeed be rather sudden, just as we have been describing it.

The other preliminary point that needs to be considered is the fact that future history will not encompass only a single innovation. Our model treats the future as though the magnitude of that innovation (however measured) is all that there is to decide upon. However, in a Schumpeterian model, no sooner is one innovation brought into the world and absorbed by the economy than the entrepreneur begins to look for another innovation that may earn net returns which are positive.

Thus, in reality, the problem is to decide on a policy for the stream of potential innovations that the future offers, not on the terms that are best for a single innovative act. The presence of a stream of prospective innovations means that the future competitive state at the end of the lag period (point E_d) can be no more than a convenient analytic assumption. The industry may never really return to a competitive state, because a new innovation is likely to renew the entrepreneur's monopoly power even before the expiration of the monopoly derived from the previous innovation.

We will not really face up to the consequent analytic difficulties here. Rather, we will only offer a few remarks about their implications. First, suppose that the profitability and welfare yield of any one such future innovation is independent of the character of any of its predecessors or any of its successors. In that case nothing significant seems to be lost by decomposing the decision problem and treating each innovation decision in isolation, as though it were a unique phenomenon. For, then, whatever lag period maximizes the return to that one innovation will constitute neither an advantage nor a disadvantage for any other innovation. It does not follow that the optimal lag will assume the same value for all future time. As the nature of the innovation opportunities evolves with the course of consumer tastes and other influences, the optimal lag may well change. However, at each historical period one can proceed to calculate an optimal lag disregarding the value of that lag in the past or in the future.

Even in this case matters are complicated by the fact that innovations in different industries and lines of activity generally are under way simultaneously, though typically at different stages in their gestation process. The lag period that is best for one is unlikely to be best for another. Yet it is impractical to vary patent life from product to product. Some variation will occur where the lag period is determined by the timing of imitations but it is difficult to see why such variations should follow any particularly desirable patterns.

Toward a Formal Model

Continuing to work with our macro analysis, we can now construct a more formal model, taking the economy to have four activities whose levels are represented by:

$$x_1 = \text{market basket of all other goods}$$

$$x_2 = \text{output of the innovator}$$

$$x_3 = \text{current rate of investment in innovation}$$

$$x_4 = \text{unemployed labor} = \text{leisure}$$

$$u = \text{output competitive with that of the innovator}$$

$$R(t) = \text{quantity of resources available in period } t$$

The x_i are the state variables in the system and we treat u as the control variable whose time profile is to be selected by the policy maker. That is, the model takes the policy maker to encourage current investment in innovation by some degree of discouragement or suppression of the outputs of directly competing products, for a period of time that is to be selected by patent policy or other programs.

We have the following relationships:

$$\dot{x}_i = f^i(x_1, x_2, x_3, u) \qquad (i = 1, 2, 3) \qquad (15.1)$$

$$g(x_1, x_2, x_3, u) + x_4 = R(t) \qquad (15.2)$$

$$w^t = w^t(x_1, x_2, x_3, x_4, u, t) \qquad (15.3)$$

where the relationships (15.1) are the equations of motion of the system, the function g in (15.2) is the resources (labor) requirement relationship, and w^t is the value of the social welfare function at time t. We may well want to exclude x_3 from w^t on the grounds that it is an intermediate product rather than a consumers' good.

Here the f^i, which determine the growth rates, $\dot{x}_i$, of the corresponding outputs, presumably are related to the profit functions for those industries and are affected by other outputs in the economy in the usual way this occurs in a general equilibrium system.

$f^1(.)$ should presumably also exclude x_3, that is, the growth of output of other industries may not be affected directly by innovation designed for industry 2. In f^2, the function for the growth of output in the innovating industry, at any moment the cumulative effect of past innovation is introduced through two variables: x_{3t}, the current level of innovative expenditure, and x_{2t}, the current output of the innovating entrepreneur that is partly determined by the trajectory of innovation expenditure up to that point.

If we select the horizon date h, the objective of society may then be taken to be to maximize

$$J = \int_0^h w^t(x_1, x_2, x_3, x_4, u, t) e^{-rt} \, dt \qquad (15.4)$$

where r is the discount rate.

This is an optimal control problem which we can put in slightly more standard form by substituting for x_4 in (15.4) the expression $x_4 = R(t) - g(.)$ from (15.2). Then the objective function becomes

$$J = \int_0^h w^t(x_1, x_2, x_3, u, t) e^{-rt} \, dt \qquad (15.5)$$

which is to be maximized subject to the equations of motion (15.1). The Pontryagin maximum principle then calls for the addition to the problem of three costate variables $y_i(t)$ corresponding to the three equations of motion. We obtain the Lagrangian expression:

$$J = \int_0^h \left\{ w^t(x_1, x_2, x_3, u, t) e^{-rt} + \sum_{i=1}^3 y_i(t) [f^i(x_1, x_2, x_3, u, t) - \dot{x}_i] \right\} dt$$

(15.6)

with its associated Hamiltonian function

$$H = w^t(.) e^{-rt} + \Sigma y_i f^i(.)$$ (15.7)

Necessary conditions for our solution then require maximization of H with respect to u at each point of time over the range of u, which in turn requires

$$\frac{\partial H}{\partial u} = w_u^t e^{-rt} + \Sigma y_i f_u^i = 0 \qquad 0 \leqslant t \leqslant h$$ (15.8)

and satisfaction of the equations of motion (15.1) and

$$y^j = -\frac{\partial H}{\partial x_j} = -w_j^t e^{-rt} - \Sigma y_i f_j^i \qquad j = 1, 2, 3; \qquad 0 \leqslant t \leqslant h$$ (15.9)

as well as the initial boundary conditions for the state variables,

$$x_i(t_0) = x_{i0}; \qquad i = 1, 2, 3.$$ (15.10)

The objective then is to determine optimal trajectories $u^*(t), x_i^*(t)$, and $y_i^*(t)$ for the control variable, the state variables, and the costate variables, respectively. In particular, one may want to restrict the domain of the control variables to the class of functions

$$u(t) = \begin{cases} 0 \text{ for } t \leqslant s \\ \text{unrestricted for } t > s \end{cases}$$

which represents the working of a patent system in which competitive output is prevented totally for the patent period, s. In that case the solution yields an optimal period $s = s^*$ for which to keep $u(t) = 0$.

The necessary maximum conditions (15.8) describe directly the conflicting consequences of an increase in competitive output, u:

1. The output increase has a direct welfare contribution of its own given by $w_u^t e^{-rt}$ for any t, $0 \leqslant t \leqslant h$.

2. The competitive output increase affects the growth of the other three outputs including innovative output. These effects are given by the $f_u^i = \partial \dot{x}_i / \partial u$.

3. Those consequences for the $\dot{x}_i$ of an increase in u are each weighted by their respective shadow prices (marginal welfare yields) as given by the values of the corresponding costate variables y_i^*.

Thus, the conditions (15.8) constitute the intertemporal counterparts of the usual marginal conditions for optimization. They tell us that a policy measure (in this case the introduction of competition) is, optimally, carried to the point, at each moment, where its direct and indirect marginal welfare yield is exactly offset by the losses of benefits through the consequent discouragement of innovation output, those losses also being evaluated at their shadow prices.

Calculation of Optimal Lags in a Single-Good Economy and a Comparison of Privately and Publicly Supported Innovation

In the following sections a highly simplified version of the optimal control problem specified in the preceding section is considered, and explicitly solved. We will also calculate the cost of a Schumpeterian innovation process (where the innovator enjoys some degree of monopoly power in return for his entrepreneurship) as compared to an arrangement where society as a whole invests some portion of the output produced in expenditures on innovation, and where the latest technology is freely available to everybody. We begin with a description of the latter model (called Model 1), which is simpler, and then introduce an entrepreneur into the picture (Model 2). In Model 1 we will calculate the optimal rate σ_1 of investment in innovation which maximizes the discounted stream of society's welfare. In Model 2 we will calculate what rate σ_2 of investment in innovation is optimal for the entrepreneur, for any given lag s of patent protection he is granted by society. Then, given the entrepreneur's reaction to any lag s, we will calculate the optimal lag from society's viewpoint.

It may be surprising that even in this extremely simple model of a single-good economy and one-parametric policy choices a solution in closed form does not exist and we have to resort to numerical calculations on a computer to gain more insight into the behavior of optimal time lags and optimal rates of investment in innovation.

An Idealized Model of Publicly Supported Innovation (Model 1)

We consider an economy with a single good, which can be either consumed or invested in innovation. Investment in innovation has some similarity to investment in capital goods, which increase the productivity of labor. But there are two important differences. Firstly, innovations do not depreciate over time, like a stock of capital. Secondly, unlike a machine, an innovation has some characteristics of a public good insofar as it may be used by an arbitrary number of people simultaneously without additional cost.

At each moment in time, there is a given technology or production function which indicates how much of the good x_1[7] can be produced as a function of the labor input, L. We assume here a very simple production function which is linear in the amount of labor:[8]

$$x_1(t) = A(t)L(t) \qquad \text{with} \qquad L(t) \leqslant R(t).$$

Here $R(t)$ denotes the total amount of labor (or leisure) available at time t. To simplify the model as much as possible and keep only the most essential features of it, we assume that the amount of labor available over time is constant and set

$$R(t) \equiv 1.$$

In this model we will use a welfare function that is monotonically increasing in the amount of the good x_1 consumed, but does not contain any term for leisure. This will imply that an optimal policy always requires full employment (zero leisure).

There is a group of inventors (scientists and engineers) who have the ability to come forth with a constant stream of labor-saving devices and methods of production, in return for a portion of the good produced. We assume that if the inventors are given a fraction σ_1 of the output during a time interval dt, then they can improve the state of technology to such an extent that the amount of the good it is possible to produce with a given labor input is increased by the factor $(1 + g\sigma_1 \, dt)$ forever thereafter, g has the dimension of an interest rate, and we shall call it the rate of return on investment in innovation.

We assume that society can choose the single parameter σ_1, the rate of investment in innovation, and that σ_1 is constant over time. The objective of society is to maximize its discounted stream of future utility from consumption. We will use a logarithmic utility or welfare function,[9]

$$w(t) = \log[(1 - \sigma_1)x_1(t)]$$

Society's goal then is to

$$\underset{0 \leqslant \sigma_1 \leqslant 1}{\text{maximize } W(\sigma_1)} = \int_0^\infty w(t)e^{-rt} \, dt$$

where r is the discount rate.

To summarize, we are using the following notation:

r = the discount rate

g = the rate of return on investment in innovation

$x_1(t)$ = output rate (of the single good) at time t

σ_1 = fraction of the output invested in innovation

$w(t) = \log[(1 - \sigma_1)x_1(t)]$ = utility derived from consumption at time t

$$W(\sigma_1) = \int_0^\infty w(t)e^{-rt}\, dt = \text{objective function}$$

In order to calculate the optimal value of σ_1 we have to determine how $x_1(t)$ grows over time as a function of σ_1. We have seen that at the optimum we always have

$$L(t) = R(t) = 1$$

so that we obtain

$$x_1(t) = A(t).$$

The innovation process was defined in such a way that if society invests the amount

$$\sigma_1 x_1(t)\, dt$$

during a time interval dt, the output produced at time $t + dt$ is equal to

$$x_1(t + dt) = x_1(t)(1 + g\sigma_1\, dt)$$

or

$$\dot{x}_1(t) = g\sigma_1 x_1(t).$$

Assuming that the initial output rate is $x_1(0) = 1$, we obtain

$$x_1(t) = e^{g\sigma_1 t}.$$

The problem is then to maximize

$$W(\sigma_1) = \int_0^\infty w(t)e^{-rt}\, dt$$

$$= \int_0^\infty \log[(1 - \sigma_1)e^{g\sigma_1 t}] \, e^{-rt} \, dt$$

$$= \int_0^\infty [\log(1 - \sigma_1) + g\sigma_1 t] \, e^{-rt} \, dt$$

$$= \frac{1}{r}\log(1 - \sigma_1) + \frac{1}{r^2}g\sigma_1 .$$

Taking the derivative with respect to σ_1, we find

$$\frac{d}{d\sigma_1} W(\sigma_1) = \frac{1}{r} \cdot \frac{1}{1 - \sigma_1} \, (-1) + \frac{1}{r^2}g = 0.$$

Assuming that both r and g are positive[10] we find for the optimal value of σ_1

$$\sigma_1 = \begin{cases} 0, \text{if } 1 - r/g \leqslant 0 \\[2mm] 1 - r/g, \text{ otherwise} \end{cases}$$

If $g < r$, then it never pays to invest anything in innovation. In this case, the discount rate is so high that society maximizes its welfare by enjoying life to the fullest extent now and worrying later.

If $g > r$, the higher the rate of return g is, the higher is the optimal amount that should be spent on investment, as one would expect. When g tends to infinity or the discount rate r tends to zero, then σ_1 asymptotically approaches 1.

Privately Supported Innovation (Model 2)

In our second model we assume that all innovation is contracted for by an entrepreneur, who has sole access to the inventors. The inventors render the same services in exchange for the same amount of the good, regardless of whether they are hired by society as a whole, or by a single entrepreneur.

Society has the power to grant a patent to the entrepreneur, if it wishes to do so, in order to encourage him to invest in innovation. While the patent is in effect, the entrepreneur has a monopoly on the new technology. He can offer a certain wage,[11] and depending on the wage offered, the other members of society will choose to work for the entrepreneur, or to work independently, using a more obsolete technology. After the lapse of the patent, the new technology becomes available to everyone at no cost. Given a certain duration for a patent, the entrepreneur will choose the fraction of total output invested in innovation, σ_2, and the wage rate, $v(t)$, so as to maximize his profit.

In analogy to the first model, we will assume that the entrepreneur has a logarithmic utility in consumption, and that he tries to maximize the discounted stream of future utility from consumption, where the entrepreneur's consumption is equal to his output, minus wages paid, minus investments in innovation. Society's consumption is the sum of wages paid plus society's own production, if any. Given the entrepreneur's reaction to a given length s of the patent, society will choose s so as to maximize its discounted stream of logarithmic utility from consumption.

As before, we assume that the total amount of labor available is constant over time and equal to 1.

The notation is the same as in Model 1, except for the following new symbols:

σ_2 = fraction of the entrepreneur's output he invests in innovation

s = length of the patent

$\ell(t)$ = fraction of the labor force working for the entrepreneur

$v(t)$ = wage rate offered by the entrepreneur

This problem has some outward similarity to a two-person game, where one player is the entrepreneur (with the choice of σ_2 and $v(t)$ as his strategies) and the other player is society (with the choice of s and $\ell(t)$ as its strategies). Both are trying to maximize their utility, or payoff, as defined earlier. But there is a fundamental difference between this problem and a game which makes it much easier to solve than a game. The difference is that in a game the players do not know in advance what strategy their opponent is going to choose. Here on the contrary, the entrepreneur will announce a wage rate, and then society decides what fraction of the labor force will work for the entrepreneur at that wage rate. Similarly, society announces the length of the patent, s, and then the entrepreneur chooses σ_2 and $v(t)$, knowing that once s is announced, his reaction to it will not change it.[12]

Even for this simple model, there exists no explicit solution that expresses the optimal lag, s, and the optimal rate of investment in innovation, σ_2, by a closed formula in terms of g, the rate of return on investments in innovation. Therefore, the properties of the model were examined by a process of computer simulation and numerical calculations. How this was done is outlined briefly in the appendix to this chapter.

In the diagrammatic argument given in the earlier sections, it was stated that with an increased lag the innovator sets a higher price for his product (or, in this model, pays a lower real wage), but invests more effort and resources in innovation. Calculations for this model do indeed show that the longer the lag s is, the more the entrepreneur will invest in innovation, which results in a faster growing total output, but the smaller is the share society obtains from this output. Figure 15-4 shows the entrepreneur's and society's discounted streams of utility as functions of σ_2, the fraction the entrepreneur invests in innovation, for three different values of the lag, s. As the figure is drawn, the intermediate value of s is optimal from society's standpoint, since in each case the entrepreneur will choose the value of σ_2 indicated, which is optimal for him.

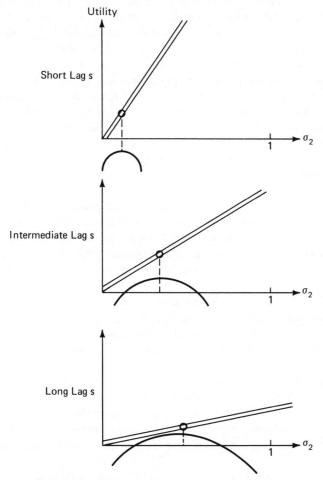

Figure 15-4. Discounted Streams of Utility of Society (double line) and the Entrepreneur (single line) as Functions of the Entrepreneur's Investment Rate, σ_2, for Three Different Lags s

Comparison of Results for the Two Models

In the following, a few computer generated tables and graphs are presented which should give some insight into the behavior of optimal lags and rates of investment in innovation, as well as a number of other variables.[13]

A simple dimensional consideration shows that the results are invariant under a compression or dilatation of time. That is, if both r and g are multiplied by the same factor λ, then the optimal lag s in model 2 is multiplied by $1/\lambda$, and the optimal values of σ_1 and σ_2 remain unchanged. Therefore, we need be concerned only with variations in a single parameter, the ratio g/r. In order to simplify the notation, we have, through the remainder of this section, used $1/r$ as the time unit, so that the discount rate r expressed on the basis of this time unit is equal to 1.[14] In that case, only values of $g > 1$ are of interest, for if $g \leqslant r = 1$, no innovation takes place, as was noted earlier.

Figure 15-5 shows plots of the optimal values of σ_1, σ_2, and s as function of g, for g ranging from 1 to 4. We see that both σ_1 and σ_2 increase monotonically with g, but σ_2 is always less than σ_1. This means that in model 2, where an entrepreneur makes investment decisions, there is an underinvestment in innovation, as compared to the social optimum calculated in model 1. We see further that the larger g is, the shorter is the optimal lag s. This indicates that the more profitable investment in innovation is, the shorter is the optimal time of protection from competition that an innovator should be granted.

For a selected value of $g = 1.5$ we have calculated, in both models, the time paths of total output, investment in innovation, and total consumption. For model 2, total consumption has further been divided into consumption by (the remainder of) society (or wages) and consumption by the entrepreneur (or profits).[15] The results are given in Table 15-1 and Figure 15-6. Consumption by society is initially higher in model 2, because of the lower rate of investment in innovation. But model 1 yields a higher rate of growth, and very soon consumption in model 1 exceeds consumption in model 2.

The entrepreneur's consumption is surprisingly low. His consumption reaches only 0.04 after three time units. But in order to realize this modest profit, he has reduced total output from 4.48 units in model 1 to 2.32 units in model 2, and society's consumption has been reduced from 2.99 to 1.85 units. This seems a rather high price for the modest gain made by the entrepreneur.

We can draw the following conclusions for this model:

1. The level of innovation by the entrepreneur stimulated by the patent arrangement tends to be lower than that in the idealized public investment model.

2. The optimal length of the patent period is smaller the greater the rate of return on investment in innovation.

3. If the rate of return on investment in innovation is proportionate to the interest rate, then the optimal life of the patent will vary precisely in inverse proportion to either of these two variables.

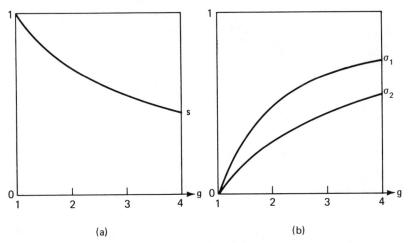

Figure 15-5. Plots of Optimal Values. (a) optimal time lag s and (b) optimal rates of investment in innovation σ_1 (for publicly supported innovation) and σ_2 (for privately supported innovation), as functions of g, the rate of return on investment in innovation. The time unit is chosen so that the discount rate is equal to 1.

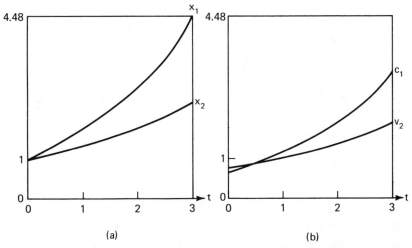

Figure 15-6. Sample Results for a Value of $g = 1.5$. The corresponding optimal rates of investment in innovation are $\sigma_1 = 0.333$ and $\sigma_2 = 0.187$. The optimal lag is $s = 0.816$ time units. (The discount rate is $r = 1$.)

(a) Total production as function of time, x_1 (for publicly supported innovation) and x_2 (for privately supported innovation).

(b) Consumption by society (exclusive of entrepreneur's consumption), c_1 (for publicly supported innovation) and v_2 (for privately supported innovation).

Table 15-1
Results of Calculations for Model 1 and Model 2

Total Output (X), Investment in Innovation (I), Total Consumption (C), Consumption by Society (V) and Consumption by Entrepreneur (P) as Functions of Time, for the Following Parameter Values

G = 1.5	Rate of Return on Investment in Innovation
Sigma1 = .333	Optimal Rate of Investment in Innovation (Model 1)
Sigma2 = .187	Optimal Rate of Investment in Innovation (Model 2)
S = .816	Optimal Time Lag for Patents (Model 2)

The Time Unit is Chosen Such That the Discount Rate R is Equal to 1

Model 1   Publicly Supported Innovation
Model 2   Privately Supported Innovation

Time	Total Output		Investment in Innovation		Total Consumption		Consumption by Society Entrepr.	
	X1	X2	I1	I2	C1	C2	V2	P2
.0	1.00	1.00	.33	.19	.67	.81	.80	.02
.1	1.05	1.03	.35	.19	.70	.84	.82	.02
.2	1.11	1.06	.37	.20	.74	.86	.84	.02
.3	1.16	1.09	.39	.20	.77	.88	.87	.02
.4	1.22	1.12	.41	.21	.81	.91	.89	.02
.5	1.28	1.15	.43	.22	.86	.94	.92	.02
.6	1.35	1.18	.45	.22	.90	.96	.94	.02
.7	1.42	1.22	.47	.23	.95	.99	.97	.02
.8	1.49	1.25	.50	.23	.99	1.02	1.00	.02
.9	1.57	1.29	.52	.24	1.05	1.05	1.02	.02
1.0	1.65	1.32	.55	.25	1.10	1.08	1.05	.02
1.1	1.73	1.36	.58	.25	1.16	1.11	1.08	.02
1.2	1.82	1.40	.61	.26	1.21	1.14	1.11	.02
1.3	1.92	1.44	.64	.27	1.28	1.17	1.15	.03
1.4	2.01	1.48	.67	.28	1.34	1.20	1.18	.03
1.5	2.12	1.52	.71	.29	1.41	1.24	1.21	.03

1.6	2.23	1.57	.74	.29	1.48	1.27	1.25	.03
1.7	2.34	1.61	.78	.30	1.56	1.31	1.28	.03
1.8	2.46	1.66	.82	.31	1.64	1.35	1.32	.03
1.9	2.59	1.71	.86	.32	1.72	1.39	1.36	.03
2.0	2.72	1.75	.91	.33	1.81	1.43	1.39	.03
2.1	2.86	1.80	.95	.34	1.91	1.47	1.43	.03
2.2	3.00	1.85	1.00	.35	2.00	1.51	1.47	.03
2.3	3.16	1.91	1.05	.36	2.11	1.55	1.52	.03
2.4	3.32	1.96	1.11	.37	2.21	1.59	1.56	.03
2.5	3.49	2.02	1.16	.38	2.33	1.64	1.60	.04
2.6	3.67	2.08	1.22	.39	2.45	1.69	1.65	.04
2.7	3.86	2.13	1.29	.40	2.57	1.73	1.70	.04
2.8	4.06	2.20	1.35	.41	2.70	1.78	1.75	.04
2.9	4.26	2.26	1.42	.42	2.84	1.84	1.80	.04
3.0	4.48	2.32	1.49	.43	2.99	1.89	1.85	.04

4. The loss to society from the institution of privately supported innovation is considerably larger than the gain to the entrepreneur. There is no doubt that in the second model society's welfare will be less than in the first model, since in model 1 the maximum possible welfare for society was attained, by definition. But one might have expected that the main reason for this reduction in society's welfare would come from society's loss of the profits the entrepreneur has extracted. However, this is not the main reason. In fact, the profits are quite modest compared to society's consumption. The main reason for the considerable reduction in society's welfare lies in the fact that the entrepreneur, in order to make a small profit, has to misallocate society's funds according to his own optimal program of production and investment, which differs substantially from society's optimal program. This then yields the paradoxical result that society could afford to pay to the entrepreneur an amount considerably larger than the profits he could ever earn, and still be better off, provided only the entrepreneur agrees not to interfere in society's affairs.

The conclusion is then that, at least in this model, research funded by the idealized government from general tax revenue and made freely available to everybody results in a much higher level of social welfare than innovation undertaken by a private entrepreneur.

Of course our comparison between an idealized government entrepreneur and a somewhat-less-idealized private activity is misleading if taken to represent the choice between the two types of agency in practice, for issues such as the motivations for efficiency have deliberately been abstracted from.

Concluding Comment

Our discussion has treated Schumpeterian lag as an instrument of policy which can stimulate the flow of innovation but which does so at a cost. It has a direct cost that takes the form of the use of resources in the innovation process, and an indirect cost in the misallocation of resources introduced through the implied grant of monopoly and the inefficiencies induced by any externalities generated by the innovation process. Optimality then requires the choice of a lag period that balances off these costs and benefits at the margin.

The Schumpeterian process implicit in this version of the problem is a very crude characterization of the matter, in which competition is entirely precluded within the lag interval, and then suddenly bursts forth in all its force just at the termination of the period.

This simple view of the matter has two justifications. First, it permits the entire range of policy choice to be expressed in terms of the selection of the value of a single variable—the length of the lag period. Moreover, it may not be too bad a representation of the workings of a patent system in which competition, at least of a certain type, is precluded completely until the date of expiration of the patent, with competitors entirely prepared to leap into the profitable field the moment the patent has expired. This is, indeed, a one-parameter policy problem in which only the period of the optimal patent life needs to be selected.

A more complex but flexible policy can also be envisioned in terms of our model in which competition is permitted to enter the field gradually. This can perhaps be carried out through a system of compulsory licensing whose fees are required to decline gradually with the passage of time. In that case the optimality requirements must be satisfied at every moment from the initial time to the horizon date, with the marginal yields of competitive outputs constantly equated to their marginal costs, direct and indirect. The solution to this control problem then yields no single solution value, that is, no single Schumpeterian lag period, but an optimal competitive output trajectory defined over the relevant time interval.

Notes

1. Presumably, it would not be stopped entirely. If adjustment were instantaneous, the competitive entrepreneur would still be left with a "normal" return on his investment in research and development, broadly defined, plus a premium just sufficient to reimburse him for the risk inherent in the introduction of novelty into his activities. Perhaps this is the *optimum optimorum,* with all activities including entrepreneurial activity producing equal returns at the margin (unless they happen to be zero or to take some other corner value). In such a world innovation would go on because its returns would be no worse (and no better) than those to any other activity available to the entrepreneur. In such a world of perfect dynamic equilibrium no Schumpeterian process would be needed to produce the desirable amount of innovative activity. Indeed, the Schumpeterian lag and the consequent profits would induce an excessive amount of innovation. This argument would appear to break down for the usual reason—the presence of externalities in the innovation process.

2. It can even be argued that the permanent monopoly will also have little motivation to innovate because it can count on a stream of monopoly profits forever. It is true that once such an arrangement is instituted the wealth of the (now vestigial) entrepreneur becomes fixed at the capitalized value of his stream of prospective monopoly profits. Thus, as Schumpeter reminds us, if he wishes to grow wealthier still he must return to his innovative activities. Consequently his motivation for innovation does not disappear altogether; but if continued entrepreneurship does ultimately become increasingly irksome or taxing with the passage of time as well as with intensity and if wealth has diminishing marginal utility, then it follows that innovation is unlikely to increase monotonically with the length of the Schumpeterian lag. Near the origin we would,

of course, expect innovation to increase with increased lag in imitation, but ultimately the curve might level off and even turn downward.

3. If we let s be the length of the Schumpeterian lag, and h represent the horizon (which can, if we wish, be long enough to encompass the likely period of survival of humanity) then the interval $0 \leqslant s \leqslant h$ is closed. If the welfare function is bounded it then follows that it must attain at least one maximal value somewhere in this interval.

4. Nordhaus (1969) has constructed a microeconomic model for the special case of linear demand curves and where cost savings are directly related to the "input" of "inventive activity."

5. Many of these results agree with what Nordhaus (1969) has found under a somewhat different set of assumption (see especially his chapter 5, "The Economics of Patents"). He considers a specific good, for which there is a linear demand curve, and an innovation which occurs at a given point in time and which reduces the cost of producing the given good. The longer the period of patent protection, the more the innovator will invest in research and development activities, and the larger is the corresponding cost reduction. This tends to increase welfare. On the other hand, the longer the period of time during which the innovator keeps selling his good at the higher price corresponding to the old production technique, the larger is the loss in welfare from monopoly pricing. Nordhaus derives the optimal period of patent protection at which those two effects balance at the margin. He also found that the inducement of innovation by a patent system incurs some loss in welfare when compared with the socially optimal amount of investment in innovation, that "patents for industries having more progressive (or easier) invention should have shorter lives," and that the optimal length of a patent varies inversely with the discount rate. The main difference between his approach and ours is that in his model Nordhaus looks at the effect of an invention on the cost reduction in the production of a good, while we consider an entire closed economic system with a given resource endowment, production possibility set, and general welfare function. In the simulation model we consider a continuous stream of innovations and examine primarily their effect on the rate of economic growth.

6. For simplicity, we will assume throughout the remainder of this section that the competitive case yields zero innovation, though, as was noted earlier, that is in fact not necessarily true.

7. The subscript of x_1 indicates that we deal with Model 1.

8. It is assumed throughout the following that labor is the only scarce factor in production.

9. A welfare function that is linear in the amount consumed yields the unrealistic result that it is optimal to invest either everything or nothing in innovation, depending on whether the rate of return on investments is higher or lower than the discount rate. If innovations were profitable, society would abstain completely from consumption and save everything for an ultimate

period of bliss. By assuming that the utility function is concave (e.g., logarithmic) we avoid this paradox. Alternatively, we could have assumed diminishing returns on investments in innovation, as Nordhaus did, instead of the constant returns assumed here.

10. g should always be positive, except in the unlikely case where the inventors produce a device that makes life more difficult.

11. We assume that the wage paid is a certain fraction of the output of the single good produced, that is, a real wage, so that the entrepreneur's pricing of his product is immaterial.

12. This asymmetry typically occurs between a lawmaker and his subject, where the lawmaker has to announce his laws (his strategy) first, and the subject can react to it. For example, Congress may try to pass legislation to close tax loopholes, but it has to announce the law first, and then corporations can try to find new loopholes. This gives the corporations a strategic advantage. If they had to submit their income statements first, and then Congress could pass tax laws, this would give a similar strategic advantage to Congress. But we follow the principle that laws should not be made retroactive. The same strategic asymmetry exists between a regulator and a regulated firm.

13. Additional results are given in Anderson et al. [1975], pp. 78–96. They confirm the findings reported here.

14. For example, if r = 5 percent per year, the time unit used will be twenty years.

15. We have tabulated actual consumption, rather than utilities, since there is no meaning to the addition of logarithmic utilities.

References

Anderson, Robert J., William J. Baumol, Ralph C. d'Arge, and Dietrich Fischer, "Towards Empirical Estimation of the Externalities of Innovation," Princeton, N.J.: Mathematica, Inc., November 1974.

Griliches, Zvi, "Hybrid Corn: An Exploration in the Economics of Technical Change," *Econometrica,* Vol. 25 (October 1957), pp. 501–522.

——, "Research Costs and Social Returns: Hybrid Corn and Related Innovations," *The Journal of Political Economy,* Vol. 66 (October 1958), pp. 419–431.

——, "Research Expenditures, Education and the Aggregate Agricultural Production Function," *The American Economic Review,* Vol. 54 (December 1964), pp. 961–974.

Machlup, Fritz, *An Economic Review of the Patent System* (Study of the Subcommittee on the Patents, Trademarks and Copyrights of the Committee on the Judiciary, United States Senate, Eighty-fifth Congress,

Second Session, Study No. 15), Washington, D.C.: U.S. Government
Printing Office, 1958.
——, *The Production and Distribution of Knowledge in the United States,*
Princeton, N.J.: Princeton University Press, 1962.
——, "The Supply of Inventors and Inventions," *Weltwirtschaftliches Archiv,*
Vol. 85 (1960), pp. 210–254.
Mansfield, Edwin, *Industrial Research and Technological Innovation,* New York:
Norton, 1968.
Nordhaus, William D., *Invention, Growth and Welfare,* Boston: M.I.T. Press,
1969.
Stiglitz, Joseph, and Pratha Das Gupta, "Market Structure and Research and
Development" (unpublished).

The model which was described in the section, "Privately Supported Innovation," was solved in the following four steps:

1. Given the length of the patent s, the fraction of the entrepreneur's
output invested in innovation σ_2, and the wage rate $v(t)$, *society* will choose
$\ell(t)$, the fraction of the labor force working for the entrepreneur, so as to
maximize its utility from consumption.[1]

2. Let s and σ_2 be given. From Step 1 we know how $\ell(t)$ reacts to any
wage rate $v(t)$ offered. The *entrepreneur* will choose $v(t)$ so as to maximize
his profit.

3. Let s be given. For any σ_2 the entrepreneur knows the corresponding
optimal wage rate $v(t)$, and the amount of labor $\ell(t)$ available to him. He chooses
σ_2 so as to maximize his discounted stream of utility from his consumption.

4. Given the entrepreneur's reaction to any time span s for a patent, society
chooses s so as to maximize its discounted stream of future utility from consumption.

Beginning with the first step, we know that the most advanced technology
society has available to it is the technology of time $t - s$, which enables society
to produce the amount

$$\left(1 - \ell(t)\right) \, e^{g\sigma_2(t-s)}$$

independently of the entrepreneur, given that a fraction $\ell(t)$ of the labor force
works for the entrepreneur and the fraction $1 - \ell(t)$ works independently.

Since society tries, at any point in time, to maximize

$$\ell(t)v(t) + \left(1 - \ell(t)\right) e^{g\sigma_2(t-s)}$$

it is immediately obvious that if

$$v(t) < e^{g\sigma_2(t-s)}$$

then all members of society will work on their own, using the more obsolete
technology invented at time $t - s$ which has just lost its patent protection.[2]
If

$$v(t) > e^{g\sigma_2(t-s)}$$

then all members of society will choose to work for the entrepreneur. If

$$v(t) = e^{g\sigma_2(t-s)}$$

then the members of society will be indifferent to working for the entrepreneur or working independently.

In Step 2, we have to maximize the entrepreneur's profit, given the reaction of the labor force to any wage rate $v(t)$ offered. As long as

$$v(t) > e^{g\sigma_2(t-s)}$$

the entire work force will choose to work for the entrepreneur. On the other hand, the smaller $v(t)$ is, the more will be left over in profits. Thus, the optimal wage rate is[3]

$$v(t) = e^{g\sigma_2(t-s)} + \delta$$

where δ is positive but arbitrarily small. For convenience, we will consider δ as negligible.

In Step 3, we have to determine the optimal value of σ_2, the fraction of the entrepreneur's output he invests in innovation, given a specified lag s of patent protection.

The entrepreneur's profit, at each point in time, is equal to

$$\pi(t) = x_2(t)[1 - \sigma_2] - v(t) = e^{g\sigma_2 t}\left[1 - \sigma_2 - e^{-g\sigma_2 s}\right].$$

His objective is to maximize his discounted stream of logarithmic utility from the consumption of his profit, over all possible values of σ_2:

$$\underset{0 \leqslant \sigma_2 \leqslant 1}{\text{maximize}} \quad \int_0^\infty \log\pi(t)\, e^{-rt}\, dt$$

$$= \int_0^\infty \left\{ g\sigma_2 t + \log\left[1 - \sigma_2 - e^{-g\sigma_2 s}\right] \right\} e^{-rt}\, dt$$

$$= g\sigma_2 \cdot \frac{1}{r^2} + \log\left[1 - \sigma_2 - e^{-g\sigma_2 s}\right] \cdot \frac{1}{r}.$$

Taking the first derivative with respect to σ_2 we obtain

$$\frac{g}{r^2} + \frac{1}{r}\frac{-1 + gse^{-g\sigma_2 s}}{1 - \sigma_2 - e^{-g\sigma_2 s}} = 0.$$

This is an expression that contains both linear and exponential terms in σ_2 and therefore has no analytical solution. A computer program using binary search was used to calculate the optimal value of σ_2, for any given s.

In Step 4, finally, we have to determine the optimal value of s, knowing how the other variables react to s. This was also done numerically using binary search.

Notes

1. If s, σ_2, and $v(t)$ are kept fixed, then society maximizes its discounted stream of future utility by simply maximizing its utility at each point in time.

2. In this particular model, a gradually declining license fee, instead of complete protection for a given time period as assumed here, would not introduce any essentially new analytic considerations. Instead of choosing between working for the monopolist at the given wage rate $v(t)$ and working independently with the latest technology that is freely available, members of society would then choose between the wage rate $v(t)$ and the most advantageous alternate technology available to them. The best alternate technology would be the one for which the difference between the possible output and the license fee to be paid is a maximum. In any case, all members of the society will either work independently, or for the entrepreneur.

3. The case

$$v(t) \leqslant e^{g\sigma_2(t-s)}$$

is clearly not optimal, because if nobody works for the entrepreneur, he will not be able to make any profit whatsoever.

16

Socially Optimal Patent Protection—Another Exercise in Utopian Economics?

Gerhard Prosi

In 1958 Fritz Machlup published an article entitled "The Optimum Lag of Imitation behind Innovation."[1] He determined the "adequacy" of the imitation lag[2] and, after some observations on fixed and variable patent terms, came to the conclusion that "no reliable clue has turned up as to the length of the 'optimum lag.'"[3] Fritz Machlup concentrated his analysis on the optimal length of a patent grant, one of the main two dimensions of patent protection, the second being the scope or breadth of protection. In the meantime, H.G. Johnson contributed some remarks on the nonoptimality of patent protection, and W.D. Nordhaus and F.M. Scherer discussed the problem of the optimum life of a patent.[4] Before taking up their findings, we want to concentrate on the question whether the traditional patent systems as used with only minor differences in most western countries can be designed in such a way that they yield socially optimum protection or whether their logic prohibits any such design.

With this goal in mind we define the social optimum as a situation in which marginal social costs of patent protection are equal to its marginal social benefits. In order to determine the optimum of patent protection one needs to know what additional costs and what additional benefits are created by marginal changes of the breadth or duration of patent protection. These changes in costs and benefits have to be made comparable or must be quantified.

H. Demsetz once stated that "a primary function of property rights is that of guiding incentives to achieve a greater internalization of externalities."[5] Since patents create property rights in the use of new technologies this is also true for the patent system. The internalization of externalities is necessary if a society predominantly relies on private, individual decision making in its economic system. If one assumes that one of the goals of this society is to achieve social optimality in the allocation of its resources, it is necessary to equalize the sum of private and social costs and the sum of private and social benefits. Only then can individuals make rational decisions that fulfill the criteria of social optimality. Since the main purpose of patent protection is to create incentives to invest in research and development, and to innovate,[6] and since it relies on decentralized, private decision making, socially optimal patent protection requires total internalization of the positive and negative externalities of

271

patentable new technologies. Otherwise, society's objective of socially optimal allocation of resources for research, development, and innovation cannot be achieved by using patents. The presently used patent systems obviously do not fulfill this condition. H.G. Johnson stated "that the private return from the creation of new knowledge will be less than the social return—a further reason for this is the temporal limitation of the monopoly privilege—and that there will therefore be a tendency toward underinvestment in the creation of new knowledge, from the standpoint of social optimality."[7]

K.J. Arrow took a similar position: "Clearly the potential social benefit always exceeds the realized social benefit. . . . The realized social benefit, in turn, always equals or exceeds the competitive incentive to invent and, *a fortiori,* the monopolist's incentive."[8]

These conclusions are derived from analyses based on market supply and demand functions, which are assumed to include all beneficial social effects of the production and use of new knowledge. However, as shown elsewhere,[9] these conclusions are not necessarily correct. If the use of new technology creates negative externalities it is possible that these more than compensate the social benefits, resulting in a net social loss. If the private returns from investment in this type of new technology are positive because of patent protection, then patents induce overinvestment in socially undesirable innovations. The public discussions on problems of environmental protection and technology in recent years may suffice as proof that these particular technologies exist.[10]

Nevertheless, it is correct that the results of the patent system as it is designed now are not optimal from society's point of view. Again, the reason for this is the lack of total internalization of external effects caused by new technologies and, therefore, the use of incorrect information in the decision making of the investor in research, development, and innovation. If the objective of patent protection is the socially optimal allocation of resources in research, development, and innovation, and if social optimality of patent protection is defined as that kind of protection that equalizes its social marginal costs and social marginal benefits, then the logical thing for economists and polticians to do would be to develop a patent system that totally internalizes all external effects of new technologies to the patent holder. After having achieved this objective, the duration of patent protection that equalizes the marginal social welfare gains of the last time unit of patent protection with its marginal social welfare loss would have to be determined.

Presently, a patent grants its owner the exclusive right to use the protected invention *commercially* for a limited period of time—seventeen years in the United States, for example, and eighteen years in the Federal Republic of Germany. Total internalization would imply that the exclusive right is not restricted to commercial applications but is extended to all uses of the patented new knowledge, since socially beneficial effects of new knowledge also exists, for example, when used as an input for new research projects. To demand and enforce such an extension of the patent grant would be unrealistic, since it seems to be impossible for the patent owner to monitor the use of "his" knowledge, for example, in usually secret research programs of other industrial enterprises. Apart from this practical argument, society would be badly served if the use of available knowledge could be generally prohibited by an individual even for a limited time period, making new research and development projects more difficult and more costly. The welfare losses to society would be tremendous.

The difficulties of internalization of negative externalities of an economic activity are well known from the environmental discussion. Total identification and quantification of the sources of externalities of patent protection seem to be an unsolvable problem, too. Even if practical or technical solutions for total internalization did exist, there is one basic problem making the demand for socially optimal patent protection scheme utopian or even nonsensical: To induce the socially optimum investment in research, development, and innovation the incentives to invest must exist *before* the decision to invest can be made, that is, before the new technology exists, in the case of research and development, and before all internal and external costs and benefits of a new production process or a new product are known, in the case of an innovation. The utopian element in the demand for social optimality in patent protection results from the fact that it requires perfect foresight or exact quantification of unknown effects of an unknown technology in a more or less distant future. Only this kind of ex ante knowledge enables the investor to make the socially desirable investment decision. But if he already knows the unknown, he does not have to invest in research and development to master new technologies, he bears no special risks from innovation. Consequently, there exists no justification for patent protection. This conclusion makes the demand for social optimality in patent protection nonsensical.[11]

The argument for the impossibility of socially optimal patent protection is strengthened by the fact that the protected good—"new technology"—is extremely heterogeneous. It is unreasonable to assume that there exists a typical production function for the production of new knowledge, which can be standardized and used for investment decisions in research and development for all kinds of projects. This implies that even the private costs of a research and development project are uncertain ex ante.

Considering that the present value of private returns on a patented new technology is extremely uncertain, too, there is no doubt that, considering only the private benefits and costs of inventive activities, it is impossible even to define an operational standardized patent grant for all inventions (fixed patent term) that is optimal. To solve this problem, some authors have recommended variable patent terms to take account of the uniqueness of each invention.[12]

Again, the problem with these concepts is that the necessary information for the determination of the optimal patent term for an invention is available only ex post, if at all. To induce the optimal investment in research and development, information is needed ex ante because the investor needs to know what kind of patent protection he can count on at the time of his investment decision.[13] As a conclusion of the Nordhaus-Scherer analysis of the optimal patent life Scherer, for example, recommends to "tailor the life of each patent to the economic characteristics of its underlying invention. This might be achieved through a flexible system of compulsory licensing, under which the patent recipient bears the burden of showing why his patent should not expire or be licensed at modest royalties to all applicants three or five years after its issue."[14]

Should this recommendation be accepted and implemented in shaping actual patent policy, it can be easily predicted that the investors in research and development would make their decisions on the basis of certain returns during the three or five years of patent protection and would consider returns from extended protection periods or royalties as windfall profits. In this system, any approximation to the socially optimal patent life is as accidental as in the present systems with patent terms of seventeen or eighteen years.

Despite these basic deficiencies of Scherer's policy recommendations, it is necessary to comment on the Nordhaus-Scherer model because it contains some mistakes typical of theoretical analyses of the patent system.[15] The major objections to the model are its static assumptions, that is, the given invention possibility function, the given market demand and competitive supply conditions,[16] and the lack of competing cost reducing innovations or other cost reductions during the lifetime of the patent.[17]

No further comment is needed on the assumption of given market and production conditions for any longer period of time. Furthermore, it is heroic to assume that the cost reduction caused by a process innovation can be used as an indicator for the applied new technology's social benefits, as Nordhaus realizes,[18] or that the lost welfare triangle[19] caused by maintaining the pre-innovation equilibrium output measures in combination with the resource costs of research the social costs of a patented new technology. The preceding discussion on the external effects of new technologies shows that it is insufficient to assume that all socially positive and negative effects of a new technology are represented by the supply and demand functions of a single market.

A few words need also to be said on the stability of the invention possibility function and implicitly the cost function of research and development during the time it takes to complete a research project. The production function for new knowledge is rather unique and not just an analogy to the production function of commodities. The reason for this is that the output of "new knowledge" becomes at the moment of its production an input for the production of more new knowledge. In terms of production theory, existing knowledge is the "fixed" factor of production for the invention possibilities function. By producing new knowledge, the "fixed" factor changes in quantity and quality shifting the invention possibilities function, that is, changing the

relationship between research outlay and the output of new knowledge.[20]
In this sense, the quantity and quality of the output is not only dependent on
the quantity and quality of the "fixed" inputs (existing knowledge), but it also
influences the quality and quantity of these "fixed" inputs. The "fixed" inputs
are a dependent variable of the output. How the invention possibility function
changes in the process of a research and development project is uncertain. Therefore, this function as well as the computed present value of the expected quasi-
rents of the potential innovation seem to have the quality of a reasonable guess
of a research and development planner. They may be helpful to demonstrate
the principle of decision making of an individual investor, but they cannot serve
as instruments to determine ex ante the optimal life of a patent. If, for example,
an official of the patent office had to determine the socially optimal duration
of the patent to be granted for the results of a proposed research and development project, he would have to know the results of this not yet started project
in detail. If this is the case, the resources allocated to this project are wasted
from the standpoint of social optimality, since the new knowledge to be produced already exists.[21]

A different approach to achieve more flexibility of the patent system, to
adjust to the heterogeneity of new knowledge and to the necessity of ex ante
information for the investor in research, development, and innovation, is to
form different classes of inventions according to their novelty level or their
degree of difficulty and, related to these, the predictability of costs required by
research and development projects. The German system of patents and *Geb-
rauchsmuster* can serve as example of a first step in that direction. Different
patent terms could be designed for each class of inventions. Research and development planners probably could roughly determine ex ante which class of
patent protection can be secured for the expected results of their program.
Whether such a differentiated system can be successful or not, depends heavily
on the competence of the experts and bureaucrats in the patent offices. As an
alternative to the system of fixed patent terms it certainly deserves more
attention that it has received so far by economists. However, it should be re-
membered that the basic problem of social optimality of patent protection,
the total ex ante internalization of externalities, cannot be solved by manipulating the patent terms, as long as perfect information about the future does not
exist.

In conclusion I maintain that it is utopian to demand and search for social
optimality of patent protection, defined as equalization of marginal social costs
and marginal social benefits.[22] This is not to declare that a social optimum of
patent protection for each invention does not exist, but only to point out the
impossibility of determining this optimum ex ante, that is, before the invention
is made. However, precisely such a determination would have to be made if the
objective of patent protection were to induce the socially optimal investment
in research, development, and innovation.

These negative conclusions should not discourage us from developing improvements in the design of the patent system. Particularly with respect to negative externalities, the patent system should be amended in such a way as to provide inducement for development of technologies that are less damaging to the social and natural environment of modern societies.[23] In order to create incentives to invest in research, development, and innovation the patent system relies on private returns from these activities. Patent induced technological development, therefore, is biased in favor of privately profitable technologies without taking account of potential social disadvantages. New technologies that reduce the internal costs of production, new products that increase the margin between unit cost and price fall into this class of profitable new knowledge whether or not they cause external costs far outweighing the internal cost reduction or the increase in profitability. Technical progress profitable for the firm or a utility increasing technical progress for the individual consumer, may be a costly technical regress for the economy or society as a whole.[24]

One can even state without exaggeration that the patent system is indifferent to social costs, that its prime effect is to create incentives to reduce private costs, and that it does not matter whether a cost reduction for the firm is just an externalization of previously private costs or whether it is even more than compensated for by increases in external costs. The same, however, holds true for the relationship of private and social returns. There should be no doubt that industrial research and development, and innovations by private enterprises must, in general, be profitable or they will be discouraged and eventually cease to exist. The objective of a reform of the patent system, therefore, should be at least a reduction, if not elimination, of the discrepancy between private and social returns of patentable new technologies, without reducing the incentives to invest in research, development, and innovation.

There are ways to accomplish this goal, as can be shown in the case of environmental effects of new technologies. First, one can impose certain upper limits on pollution that have to be met to secure a patent. The avoidance of negative environmental effects then has to become part of any research project that aims at patentable technology. The advantage of this method is that the environmental problems of new technologies have to be considered from the start of the program. A major disadvantage of this method lies in the fact that new technologies that are relatively harmless to the environment are patented, that is, their commercial use is restricted. Harmful technologies are not patented and can freely be imitated. Furthermore, research and development projects that include the solution of environmental problems generally will be more expensive than those that neglect these problems. Since this affects the rate of return and the incentives to invest in research and development negatively, it is necessary to impose pollution charges on the users of harmful technologies, which at least compensate for the higher costs of development in the costs of later application of patented new technologies.

Secondly, one can reduce the social disadvantages of the bias in favor of private profitability in technological development by internalizing external effects of production and consumption as completely as possible when they occur. As soon as external costs are transformed into internal costs of firms and consumers, they become the target of cost reducing efforts and will be integrated into the research and development programs. The dynamic forces of the private enterprise system will then be utilized to reduce previously external and, for the decision making of the firm, irrelevant costs.[25] The possibility of externalizing internal costs by developing patentable new technologies will be eliminated. The second proposal is a general approach to internalize as many external effects as possible, while the first proposal incorporates some internalization procedures in the patent system. Both methods will not yield a solution to the problem of socially optimal patent protection. They may help to achieve an optimal allocation of resources in the production and consumption of goods and services. But they will not solve the problems of socially optimal allocation of resources in research, development, and innovation because patent protection is restricted to the commercial use of new knowledge and because the argument still holds that for socially optimal patent protection all the unknown externalities of the future of a still unknown new technology need to be internalized ex ante. The proposed methods, however, internalize externalities *as they occur,* that is, ex post. The search for social optimality in patent protection seems to be futile, an utopian dream. Instead of designing inoperational static concepts of social optimality for dynamic processes, economists should try to develop incentive systems that are adequate to move these processes in directions that better serve the economy's needs.

Notes

1. F. Machlup, "The Optimum Lag of Imitation behind Innovation," in *Festskrift til Frederik Zeuthen,* Kopenhagen, 1958, pp. 239-256.

2. Ibid., pp. 243-246.

3. Ibid., p. 256.

4. H.G. Johnson, "The Efficiency and Welfare Implications of the International Corporation," in *The International Corporation—A Symposium,* ed. by Ch. P. Kindleberger (MIT Press), Cambridge, Mass., 1970, p. 38; W.D. Nordhaus, *Invention, Growth and Welfare* (MIT Press), Cambridge, Mass., 1969, pp. 76-86; W.D. Nordhaus, "The Optimal Life of a Patent: Reply," *American Economic Review,* Vol. 62, pp. 428-431; F.M. Scherer, *Industrial Market Structure and Economic Performance* (Rand McNally), New York, 1970, pp. 382-384, 388; and F.M. Scherer, "Nordhaus' Theory of Optimal Patent Life: A Geometric Reinterpretation," *American Economic Review,* Vol. 62, pp. 422-427.

5. H. Demsetz, "Toward a Theory of Property Rights," *American Economic Review* 57 (1967), Papers and Proceedings, p. 348.

6. For the various theories to justify patent protection see F. Machlup, *An Economic Review of the Patent System,* Study No. 15 of the Subcommittee on Patents, Trademarks and Copyright of the Committee on the Judiciary, U.S. Senate, 85th Congress, 2nd Session, Washington, D.C., 1958.

7. H.G. Johnson, "Efficiency and Welfare Implications," p. 38. He repeats this position in "Aspects of Patents and Licenses as Stimuli to Innovation," in *Weltwirtschaftliches Archiv,* Vol. 112, 1976, pp. 423, 424, and p. 427: "To summarize the analysis so far, the patents and licenses system does not encourage socially undesirable innovations; its defect is rather the opposite one of providing insufficient incentives for some socially desirable innovations. . . ."

8. K.J. Arrow, "Economic Welfare and the Allocation of Resources for Invention," in *The Rate and Direction of Inventive Activity,* NBER-Conference Report (Princeton University Press), Princeton, N.J., 1962, p. 622. See also pp. 616-619.

9. See G. Prosi, "Patents and Externalities," in *Zeitschrift für National-ökonomie* 31 (1971), pp. 68-80, and idem, "Wettbewerbspolitische Aspekte des technischen Fortschritts," in *25 Jahre Marktwirtschaft in der Bundesrepublik Deutschland* (Gustav Fischer), Stuttgart, 1972, pp. 93-103.

10. As an example of far reaching political conclusions derived from this experience, see E. Küng, *Steuerung und Bremsung des technischen Fortschritts* (J.C.B. Mohr), Tübingen, 1976, who demands some kind of social review board to evaluate research and development projects. It should have the power to terminate projects that it finds to be socially damaging even if they are funded privately.

11. The same problems arise in connection with the proposed technology review board (see note 10). Administrators or government officials or "experts" do not have ex officio perfect foresight, nor even adequate hindsight, as the occasional lack of learning processes in this area of social life convincingly demonstrates.

12. See for example F.M. Scherer, "Nordhaus' Theory," pp. 422-427; and W.D. Nordhaus, "The Optimal Life," pp. 428-431; and idem, *Invention, Growth, and Welfare,* pp. 76-78; also F.D. Arditti and R.L. Sandor, "A Note on Variable Patent Life," in *The Journal of Industrial Economics,* Vol. 21, pp. 177-183. These papers concentrate on the variability of the duration of patent protection, but there exists no fundamental reason not to include all dimensions of patent protection in the debate on variable patent terms.

13. Arditti and Sandor propose a system, in which "the patent life, *T,* is not calculated until all costs are in. thus insuring the complete recoupment of all development costs." In a footnote, they mention "that empirically it may be difficult to obtain all these costs." F.D. Arditti and R.L. Sandor, "Note on Variable Patent Life," p. 182. Since they take into account only the private costs of the firm, social optimality is not considered. On the contrary, the

guaranteed recovery of all costs may induce wasteful overinvestment in research
and development.

14. F.M. Scherer, "Nordhaus' Theory," p. 427.

15. For a short description of the model see F.M. Scherer, "Nordhaus'
Theory," pp. 422-427, and W.D. Nordhaus, "The Optimum Life," p. 428-431.

16. See F.M. Scherer, "Nordhaus' Theory," p. 423.

17. See W.D. Nordhaus, "The Optimum Life," p. 428.

18. See W.D. Nordhaus, "The Optimum Life," p. 428.

19. For the welfare triangle arithmetic, see A.C. Harberger, "Monopoly
and Resource Allocation," in *American Economic Review,* Papers and Proceedings, Vol. 44, 1954, pp. 77-78. For a survey of the discussion of this problem see F.M. Scherer, *Industrial Market Structure,* pp. 400-411.

20. For some general observations on macroeconomic production functions
for inventions see F. Machlup, "The Supply of Inventors and Inventions," in *The
Rate and Direction of Inventive Activity,* NBER-Conference Report, Princeton,
N.J., 1962, pp. 152-161, and idem, "Erfindung und technische Forschung,"
in *Handwörterbuch der Sozialwissenschaften,* Vol. 3, Stuttgart-Tübingen-
Göttingen, 1961, pp. 288 and 289. For some critical remarks see G. Prosi,
Technischer Fortschritt als mikroökonomisches Problem (Haupt), Bern, 1966,
pp. 139-142.

21. A different approach to show the absurdity of a variable patent term
"to fit each case" was developed in F. Machlup, "The Optimum Lag," pp.
246-249.

22. A methodological remark is in order at this point. The concept of
social optimality as defined is basically a static concept. Since patent protection
is meant to deal with a dynamic problem, namely the process of technological
development, static concepts are inadequate to analyze its effectiveness. To
postulate static optimality for dynamic processes is simply illogical.

23. The higher priority for efforts to internalize negative externalities has
political reasons. From the standpoint of sound economics the positive externalities are equally important.

24. Many of the progressive "throw away" articles may serve as examples.

25. See G. Prosi, "Wettbewerbspolitische Aspekte," pp. 98-100, and idem,
"Patents and Externalities," pp. 76-78.

Part VIII:
The Economic Historian

17

The Economics of the Stock Market and the Great Depression

Basil Moore

Introduction

The German edition of *The Stock Market, Credit and Capital Formation* (*SMCCF*) was written in 1929 and 1930, and published early in 1931. The English edition, published in 1940, is a revised version of the original text.[1] Professor Machlup seems to have agonized over whether to leave the original text unchanged, and his decision as revealed in the Preface was to adhere, somewhat patriotically, to the original structure, with the exception of the insertion of three new chapters in response to recent works by Keynes and Moulton.

What is one to make of this book today? After a short summary of the central thesis, I propose to consider the book from three perspectives. First, how does it relate to and anticipate developments in the neoclassical and Keynesian literature of its day? Second, what are the empirical implications of the questions it raises? Third, what contributions does it offer to our present understanding of the relationship between the stock market and the economy?

1.

The goal of *SMCCF* is to examine critically the assertion, common at the time of the bull market of the twenties, that the stock exchange absorbs capital. The argument in question is that industry is outbid for credit by the stock exchange at times when the "effortless" gains of speculators exceed profits from productive real investment.

Professor Machlup proceeds by distinguishing two meanings of capital: real capital—the produced means of production, and money capital—the funds made available for the construction of such goods. Since security speculation does not involve absorption of real capital, it is money capital, which comes from current loanable funds—savings, current replacement allowances, currently liquidated working capital, new bank credit, and disbursements of surplus cash balances—which may conceivably be tied up or absorbed by security speculation, so that other borrowers, especially industrial borrowers, may be deprived.

283

Machlup, like Keynes, emphasizes that the essential function of securities markets is to facilitate change in ownership of titles to real capital. What is a long term loan for the borrower is short term for the lender, and the increased liquidity provided by securities markets encourages investment of temporary savings. Machlup states explicitly that savings alone is not sufficient for capital formation, it also requires investment—"A process of capital formation is set in motion only if the income which is not consumed is used for production."[2] Nevertheless, the implication is clear that investment is limited in the long run by the amount of voluntary saving undertaken.

Consumption of share capital appreciation (capital gains) is recognized as an "absorption" at the expense of capital formation, but Machlup argues this is similar to consumption of profits from whatever source. Withdrawals by "temporary savers" are financed by new saving. Machlup argues that the proceeds from selling old securities may be used for investment as well as for consumption, but in any case the original real capital will remain fixed.

It is recognized that higher securities prices call forth new issues, "in normal times, . . . there can be no doubt that the demand for long-term capital is not too inelastic,"[3] but the empirical analysis is exceedingly rudimentary. "An attempt to demonstrate the speed of reaction of the stock market by statistical time series is made in the Appendix. There the time series for stock prices and new issues are set forth side by side. The results seem to bear out the theory that the issue of new shares follows immediately the rise in share prices."[4]

The consumption of savings induced by stock exchange gains has a counterpart in the formation of savings induced by stock exchange losses, since speculators consider their losses as a diminution of income and reduce consumption. Gains and losses affect saving only when wealth changes are regarded as changes in income. Surprisingly Machlup does not pursue defining a concept of comprehensive income to include capital gains and losses.

Machlup next tackles the question whether increased demand for money for stock exchange transactions takes circulating media away from other markets, so that security prices rise at the expense of commodity prices. After considering the arbitrary nature of *a priori* assumptions regarding transactions velocity, Machlup notes that a lasting boom in the securities markets presupposes additional inflationary credit from the banking system, which as new issues are floated will quickly spill over into production. Figures on increased brokers' loans tell nothing about the absorption of credit by the stock market, since they must be matched by increased brokers' payments to customers.

Keynes's argument that funds could be absorbed through the hoarding of sales proceeds by bearish sellers is conceded to have a potentially deflationary effect, as idle savings deposits increase at the expense of active business deposits. While savings deposits indeed grew rapidly from 1926 to 1929 (15%), demand deposits also grew (by 5%), and the velocity of circulation rose, rather than fell as implied by Keynes's hypothesis. Machlup takes the classical position that bearish sellers preferring liquidity will not hold cash or deposits, since call loans are as good as cash for satisfying the demand for liquidity. When bears lend their funds out to bulls on call, no hoarding of idle cash is involved. On these grounds Keynes's argument that the rise in brokers' loans was attributable to the piling up of idle deposits by bearish sellers is rejected. Similarly Moulton's argument that when capital gains are included in income, then savings will exceed investment, is shown to rest on an accounting error, since to be consistent, appreciation of capital assets must be included as capital formation or investment.

Following Hayek, Machlup argues that expansion of bank credit directs productive resources into roundabout processes of production which later turn out to have been misdirected. This inflated rate of investment can be sustained only by a continual expansion of bank credit. Since all inflations must sometime come to an end, cessation of credit inflation will lead to a contraction of production in the producer goods industries. The roundabout production process can in the long run only be maintained at that level allowed by a permanent and steady flow of money capital supplied by voluntary saving.

It is excessive credit expansion that leads to cyclical expansions in the production structure, and it makes no difference what kind of credit is given. It is also possible that the funds used to finance the boom initially need not come from bank credit expansions, but from increased lending of temporary surplus cash balances, with only slight support from bank credit. Qualitative controls confining credit to "legitimate productive activity" cannot prevent credit from flowing to a booming stock exchange if call money rates are high. Discrimination in lending is bound to fail so long as it does not imply quantitative restriction as well.

If the supply of bank credit is elastic, increased demand by stock speculators will, it is true, cause inflationary credit expansion. Expectations of further rises in security prices will cause money market interest rates to be driven up by increased demand for credit. Nevertheless Machlup argues that increased demand for stock exchange credit is not the ultimate cause of higher interest rates, but rather the fact that bank credit had originally been too easy. "Since the perfect, or practically perfect, elasticity of the credit supply is the result of political measures, I think there is little justification in the accusation that the blame for the credit inflation lies with stock exchange speculation."[5] Higher security prices involve a cheapening of industrial credit by the issue of common stock, even though short term rates rise. The explanation of the fact that bank credit can become so much dearer has to go back to the fact that bank credit had originally been too easy.

Machlup closes the book with a "docket" of thirty-seven theses. The central theme is that while the start of a business upswing can be financed out of dishoarding of surplus cash balances without an expansion of bank credit, a continual rise of stock prices presupposes an inflationary credit supply: the setback occurs when the credit expansion eventually stops. However, if bank reserves are controlled by the monetary authorities, the credit inflation should not be attributed to the stock-exchange boom. Since higher security prices mean cheaper capital for industry, it is not the stock market that competes with industry for funds, but rather industrial long term credit which competes with industrial short term credit.

Central bankers must first decide on their policy goals: whether it is more important to avoid cyclical fluctuations in industry or to strive towards industrial full employment. Machlup acknowledges still holding to the position, "not as dogma but as a statement of high probability value," that one can avoid the downswing only by avoiding the upswing. But he does not conclude that an upswing ought to be avoided at all costs, since he sees no other way, no feasible deflationary route, toward re-employment and improved economic conditions.

Since it is not possible to devise a system that excludes every expansion of credit, monetary control must devise sensitive indexes as guides to monetary management, what would today be called indicators. Machlup argues that security prices and the volume of stock exchange credit should be closely watched as indicators of the degree of inflationary use of credit, even though, if sellers lend to buyers, the volume of stock exchange credit may rise without any funds flowing to the stock exchange. The volume of all bank credits would have to be watched together with the movement of security prices and the volume of security issues. Even though none of these indexes individually is fully reliable as evidence for or against the presence of inflation, yet if all show an upward movement the presumption is very strong that (credit) inflation is taking place, even if the level of commodity prices does not show the least upward tendency. In addition to serving as a guide to credit control, the stock market is a good mechanism for control, providing it is used in conjunction with other guides and other mechanisms. Machlup concludes on the guardedly optimistic note that margin regulations plus control over the issuing of new securities "ought to be capable of preventing inflationary financing of private industry as long as the monetary authorities care to do so."[6]

2.

With regard to its relation to the neoclassical literature of the time, *SMCCF* appears to follow closely Friedrich Hayek's monetary theory of the investment cycle. The United States in the twenties experienced an expansion of its monetary base, its credit superstructure, and its general business activity, without an increase in its general price level. Hayek argued early in 1929 that the stability of the price level was covering up a large inflation of credit and overexpansion of investment, and that a crisis and downturn were imminent. Hayek followed Wicksell's argument that monetary causes necessarily lead to structural disturbances. By lowering the market rate of interest below the natural rate—the rate that would hold the rate of real investment down to the rate of voluntary saving—

the banking system was able to initiate a cumulative movement away from equilibrium. However, the credit expansion need not be initiated by the banks lowering the money rate of interest, but rather by a rise in opportunities for profitable investment which raise the natural rate. Hayek insisted that the rate of interest that stablizes the price level, because in a growing economy it permits credit expansion, must be below the rate that keeps the supply of money capital at the level of voluntary saving.

The essential feature of Hayek's theory of the investment cycle is the "scarcity of capital." The induced increase in investment financed by new bank credit causes a deepening of the capital structure (lengthening of the production process.) This can be maintained only if the new proportion between consumer and investment demand can be maintained, which requires that bank credit be supplied at a continually increasing rate. This cannot happen, either because banks find it impossible or too risky to continue expanding credit, or because investors find it too risky to go on borrowing and investing. As soon as the proportion of consumption to investment demand increases, productive factors will be shifted away from longer production processes, capital invested there will fall in value, and some will have to be abandoned.

The inevitability of the crisis after consumer demand reasserts itself is central to Hayek's theory of the trade cycle, and as mentioned, was accepted by Machlup "not as dogma but as a statement of high probability value." Machlup similarly shares Hayek's strictures against the "elastic system" that the monetary authorities try to manage with a view to keeping interest rates stable.

In what Sir John Hicks has referred to as the "drama" of the early thirties,[7] the leading characters were Hayek and Keynes. Who was right? With the appearance of the *General Theory* the drama ended. By then, after several years of the Great Depression, it had become clear that Hayek's prescription of waiting it out was inopportune. In those years a model for which full employment was the starting assumption could not compete with one that was based on underemployment equilibrium, and from which a prescription of vigorous government action for more employment was devised.

The victory of Keynes's new theory of underinvestment and underconsumption over Hayek's theory of overinvestment and overconsumption did not extend throughout all the halls of academe. Professor Machlup was in 1939 and remains today in 1977 an enthusiastic supporter of Hayek's views of the maladjusted time structure of production. In a recent testimonial to Hayek, Professor Machlup has stated, "It is however, my sincere conviction that this work (*The Pure Theory of Capital*) contains some of the most penetrating thoughts on the subject that have ever been published."[8]

3.

It is clearly unfair to judge Professor Machlup's modest empirical efforts by today's standards. National income accounting was virtually unknown in 1929, to say nothing of national flow of funds and national balance sheet accounting. It is to his credit that he was able to pose the questions to the absorption problem in such a meaningful way. I propose to pursue empirically two of the central issues raised by Professor Machlup's analysis.

The first concerns the effect of changes in the value of corporate stock owned by households on total consumption expenditures. Were the enormous increases in security values generated by the bull market of the late twenties predominately saved, or were they reflected in increased consumption spending? Conversely did the collapse of the stock market in 1929 depress the propensity to consume out of household wealth? Recent theoretical and empirical analysis suggests that wealth should be in the consumption function with a coefficient of about 0.05, but due to the severe statistical problems introduced by the presence of strong serial correlation in all of the time series data, it has been difficult to demonstrate its superiority to specifications that omit a wealth variable.[9]

Based on Goldsmith's data, Robert Lampman has derived estimates of the total value of corporate stock held by households for the years 1922, 1929, 1933, and 1939.[10] Annual values of household corporate stock holdings were estimated by the author using these years as benchmarks and interpolating from the Standard and Poor index of stock prices. Using data on personal consumption expenditures, personal saving, and disposable personal income based on National Bureau of Economic Research and Office of Business Economics series in *Long Term Economic Trends, 1860–1965,* the following regressions were estimated for the period 1920–1939 and the subperiods 1920–29 and 1930–39.

$$PCE = \alpha_0 + \alpha_1(DPI)_t + \alpha_2(CSH)_t + \alpha_3(PCE)_{t-1} \tag{17.1}$$

$$PCE = \beta_0 + \beta_1(PS)_t + \beta_2(CSH)_t + \beta_3(PCE)_{t-1} \tag{17.2}$$

$$PS = \delta_0 + \delta_1(DPI)_t + \delta_2(CSH)_t + \delta_3(PS)_{t-1} \tag{17.3}$$

where

PCE = Personal Consumption Expenditures, current dollars

DPI = Disposable Personal Income, current dollars

CSH = Corporate Stock of Households, estimated current market value

PS = Personal Saving, current dollars.

Due to the problem of serial correlation a first order autoregressive transformation was performed, and the regressions were run using levels, first differences, and log transformations of all the variables. The results are presented in Table 17-1.

Table 17-1
Wealth Formulations of Consumption Demand Equities, 1920-39 (Annual Rates in Billions of Current Dollars[a])

Period	Transformation	Dependent Variable	Explanatory Variables						$\bar{R}^2$	D.W.	Rho
			Constant	DPI	PS	CSH	PCE(-1)	PS(-1)			
1920-39	Levels	PCE	6.22 (1.5)	0.68 (12.2)		0.02 (1.0)	0.18 (3.0)		0.966	2.35	0.61
1920-39	Logs	PCE	0.44 (1.8)	0.70 (13.1)		0.02 (0.9)	0.17 (3.0)		0.997	2.16	0.56
1920-39	First Differences	PCE	0.29 (1.9)	0.71 (19.4)		0.02 (1.9)	0.14 (3.8)		0.982	2.25	-0.64
1920-39	Levels	PCE	31.79 (5.7)		0.99 (5.5)	0.07 (2.3)	0.35 (3.5)		0.868	1.98	0.19
1920-39	Levels	PS	-28.76 (8.1)	0.57 (8.7)		-0.035 (1.8)		0.34 (3.0)	0.842	1.75	0.46
1920-29	Levels	PCE	2.19 (0.5)	0.69 (12.9)		0.03 (1.6)	0.20 (2.3)		0.999	1.89	-0.79
1920-29	Logs	PCE	0.28 (0.7)	0.71 (11.7)		0.04 (1.4)	0.17 (1.7)		0.999	2.1	-0.80
1930-39	Levels	PCE	7.35 (2.7)	0.84 (13.0)		-0.01 (0.5)	-0.01 (0.9)		0.989	1.38	0.20
1930-39	Logs	PCE	0.51 (3.0)	0.82 (14.0)		-0.01 (0.2)	0.05 (1.0)		0.998	1.38	0.28

[a]The numbers in parenthesis are t-statistics.

While the addition of the household corporate stock variable does not significantly improve the exploratory power of the consumption demand equation, the coefficient on the wealth variable for the entire period is weakly significant in the first difference transformation, and of plausible magnitude throughout. Interestingly the parameter estimates are not stable when fitted to the two subperiods 1920-29 and 1930-39. For the decade of the twenties the coefficient on the wealth variable is significant in all transformations, with a value between 0.04 and 0.03. For the decade of the thirties the coefficient on the wealth variable is clearly insignificant in all transformations. When consumption is run against personal saving rather than disposable personal income the coefficient on the wealth variable is higher and significant, especially for the 1920s. Similarly when personal saving is the dependent variable the wealth coefficient is significantly negative and of plausible magnitude. Again these results are more significant for the 1920s, and do not hold for the 1930s.

In 1930 the number of stockholders has been estimated at ten million, or roughly one out of every eight adults.[11] Lampman estimated in his study from estate tax data that in 1929, 52 percent of all household equities were owned by his top-wealth-holder category, which formed 0.44 percent of the total adult population.[12] This very high degree of concentration of stock ownership clearly must have diluted the impact of changes in stock values on aggregate household consumption, and suggests a plausible explanation for the lower value of the coefficient on stockholding than for recent periods. However, the widespread purchase of stock on margin in the 1920s and subsequent margin calls of the 1930s may be expected to have sharpened the negative impact of a falling stock market on consumption.

The results of Table 17-1 suggest that during the bull market of the 1920s wealthholders were content to save 96 to 98 percent of their capital gains from stock ownership, realizing only from 2 to 4 percent for additional consumption. The stock market crash in 1929 was due primarily to speculative forces in the investment markets, and not to a wholesale attempt to transform wealth accumulations into consumption goods. Conversely, throughout the great depression the data provide no supporting evidence that the value of household stock portfolios significantly affected consumption expenditures. One possible interpretation is that the fall in wealth values raised desired saving propensities by roughly enough to offset the normal positive effect of wealth portfolios on consumption expenditure.

The second empirical issue concerns the responsiveness of new issues of securities and of corporate investment expenditures to the level of security prices. As mentioned above, Professor Machlup contented himself with merely listing time series of stock prices and new issues side by side in his appendix. From these monthly time series I ran the following regression to test the elasticity of the supply of new issues to the level of stock prices. An autoregressive transformation was performed to reduce serial correlation.

$$\ln \text{(issues)} = 9.686 + 0.467 \ln \text{(stock prices index)} - 0.155 \text{(trend)} \quad (17.4)$$
$$\phantom{\ln \text{(issues)} = } (11.02) \quad (2.60) \phantom{\ln \text{(stock prices index)}} (5.955)$$

RSQ adj. = 0.25 N = 200

D.W   = 1.58   1923.1 – 1938.8

Rho   = 0.665   (t-statistics in parenthesis)

Equation (17.4) suggests an elasticity of new issues to the contemporary level of stock prices of approximately 0.5. Since the lag relationship is certainly distributed rather than discrete, an Almon lag computation was then undertaken, imposing a third degree polynomial, a twelve-month lag, and no end point restrictions.

$$\ln \text{(issues)} = 1.474 + \sum_{i=1}^{12} b_i \ln \text{(stock price index)} - 0.0157 \text{(trend)} \quad (17.5)$$
$$\phantom{\ln \text{(issues)} = } (2.60) \phantom{\sum_{i=1}^{12} b_i \ln \text{(stock price index)} } (4.23)$$

RSQ adj. = 0.285 N = 200

D.W   = 2.02   1923:1 to 1938:8

Rho   = 0.765

$$\Sigma b_i = 2.29 \; (4.12)$$

The values of the b_i coefficients and their corresponding t-statistics are listed in Table 17–2.

These results permit a clarification of Professor Machlup's conclusions that "the issue of new shares follows immediately the rise in share prices." The Almon lag formulation reveals that the lag response of new issues to a change in share prices is distributed over nine months, with the bulk of the response occurring within six months. The coefficient on the sum indicates that the distributed response of new issues to a change in share prices is substantial, with an elasticity approximately equal to two.

The larger question concerns the responsiveness of corporate investment expenditures to the level of security prices. The stock market and investment behavior are intimately bound together, since firms invest to earn profits, and the level of stock prices represents an attempt by investors to evaluate the present value of that expected future stream of profits. Nevertheless, attempts to go beyond this obvious statement to determine a causal relationship involve many difficult issues that remain controversial.

Table 17-2
Almon Lag Coefficients

Lag	b_i Value	t-Statistic
$t-0$	0.238	1.24
$t-1$	0.299	2.12
$t-2$	0.332	2.29
$t-3$	0.340	2.32
$t-4$	0.327	2.46
$t-5$	0.296	2.67
$t-6$	0.251	2.53
$t-7$	0.195	1.77
$t-8$	0.132	1.00
$t-9$	0.065	0.45
$t-10$	-0.001	-0.01
$t-11$	-0.064	-0.46
$t-12$	-0.119	-0.62

The neoclassical theory of corporate investment is based on the assumption that management seeks to maximize the present net worth of the corporation. An investment project should be undertaken only if it increases the value of the outstanding shares. According to the neoclassical model, the cost of capital can be measured by a weighted average of the cost of different sources of financing.[13] This specification is empirically difficult, since expected capital gains are not observable, yet they are a key element in the return on equities. Management must be viewed as approving those projects expected to increase the firm's market value. The weighted average measure of the cost of corporate capital is simply an *ex post* estimate of the accuracy of those expectations.[14]

As an alternative approach to the link between the stock market and investment expenditure, the securities valuation model regards investment as determined by the ratio of the market value of the firm to the replacement cost of its physical assets. In Tobin's formulation this ratio q provides the link between the real and financial sectors as the ratio of the net return on real assets to the return on equity.[15] When q is greater than unity the value of capital in the stock market is higher than the cost of producing it, and investment is stimulated. When q is less than unity it is more attractive for firms to purchase control of existing corporations, or to repurchase their own shares, than to incur new investment.[16]

Unfortunately data do not exist to estimate annual values of q for the period 1920-1940. Goldsmith's data give estimates of the value of total physical assets for nonfinancial corporations for the years 1922, 1929, 1933, and 1939.[17] From these benchmark dates I estimated annual replacement values of total assets interpolating them from the price index for producer durables.[18] The following investment equation was estimated for the period 1920-39 and the two subperiods 1920-29 and 1930-39:

$$GPDI = \alpha_0 + \alpha_1 (TA/DPI)_t + \alpha_2 (SPI)_{t-1} + \alpha_3 (GPDI)_{t-1} \qquad (17.6)$$

where

$GPDI$ = Gross Private Domestic Investment, current dollars

TA = Total Physical Assets Nonfinancial Corporations, current replacement cost

DPI = Disposable Personal Income, current dollars

SPI = Stock Price Index, Standard and Poors

In view of the problem of serial correlation I performed a first order auto-regressive transformation, and ran the regressions using levels, lags, and first difference transformations of all the variables. The results are presented in Table 17-3.

For an investment demand equation the results are strongly encouraging. All variables are correctly signed, and, with the exception of the lagged dependent variable in four equations, all are significant. Investment spending clearly appears to be positively related to the level of stock prices in the previous year. For the period as a whole the elasticity of investment spending to the stock price index is 0.5, but it was less than 0.4 in the decade of the twenties and rose to 1.5 in the decade of the thirties. The index of stock prices plummeted by 75 percent from 1929 to 1933. If the coefficient on the lagged index of stock prices in the log transformation of the investment equation is regarded as plausible, this alone would account for most of the virtual cessation of Gross Private Domestic Investment over the same period, from $16 billion to less than $0.3 billion.

Very rough estimates of the value of q derived from Goldsmith's data suggest that it fell from a level of 1.5 in 1928 to about 0.5 at the end of 1932. While it is true that the ratio of the market value of the firm to the replacement cost of its capital is a measure of the average rather than the marginal expected return on capital, it is difficult to believe that such a fall could not have had a depressing effect on corporate investment decisions. As long as management is concerned about long run "fundamental" market value, it would not scrap investment plans in response to a highly volatile short run drop in stock prices. But in the depth of the depression it was precisely these "fundamental" values that were shaken by the debilitating erosion of investor confidence.

4.

The final question concerns the implications of the views expressed in *SMCCF* for our present understanding of the relationship between the stock market and

Table 17-3
Securities Valuation Estimates of Business Investment, 1920-39 (Annual Rates in Billions of Current Dollars[a])

Period	Transformation	Dependent Variable	Constant	Explanatory Variables TA/DPI	SPI(-1)	GDPI(-1)	$\bar{R}^2$	D.W.	Rho
1920-39	Levels	GDPI	34.24 (5.6)	-18.53 (5.7)	0.05 (1.4)	0.22 (1.7)	0.811	1.98	0.01
1920-39	Logs	GDPI	2.43 (1.8)	-6.6 (6.9)	0.50 (1.6)	0.26 (2.5)	0.879	1.88	0.01
1920-39	First Differences	GDPI	-0.18 (0.5)	-17.14 (4.1)	0.08 (1.8)	-0.07 (0.6)	0.744	2.34	-0.46
1920-29	Levels	GPDI	52.17 (6.7)	-29.36 (5.8)	0.07 (3.4)	0.04 (0.3)	0.944	2.24	-0.43
1920-29	Logs	GPDI	2.61 (8.0)	-3.54 (8.1)	0.37 (5.3)	-0.05 (0.5)	0.989	2.18	-0.47
1930-39	Levels	GPDI	23.07 (6.8)	-12.76 (8.7)	0.07 (1.8)	0.14 (1.3)	0.960	2.34	-0.71
1930-39	Logs	GPDI	-1.63 (0.5)	-5.81 (4.3)	1.49 (2.1)	0.10 (0.7)	0.898	2.25	-0.30

[a]Figures in parenthesis are t-statistics.

the economy. The *General Theory's* break with neoclassical economics is perhaps most clearly expressed in its treatment of investment. In chapter 11 of the *General Theory* the level of investment is tied to the relationship between the marginal efficiency of capital and the rate of interest. This is formally equivalent to the neoclassical notion, with the exception that for the neoclassicists the marginal efficiency of capital is governed by the physical productivity of capital goods, whereas for Keynes investment decisions are governed by the expected profitability of investment. For Keynes the uncertainty surrounding investment is not the uncertainty concerning its physical product, but rather the uncertainty concerning the realization of the value of its product as profits. This realization is uncertain because relative prices may change between the time of installation of capital goods and the time of the realization of its profits. Production takes time, and thus all investment necessarily includes a speculative component. In addition, the expected return on investment is a positive function of the current level of investment.[19]

In chapter 12 of *The General Theory* the treatment of investment loses even its formal resemblance to that of neoclassical economics. Investment is then viewed as an autonomous process, and depends critically on what Joan Robinson likes to call the "animal spirits" of entrepreneurs. The other side of this Keynesian break with the neoclassical tradition is the severing of the connection of investment to the intertemporal consumption decisions of households. Investment is viewed as both an autonomous and a self-sustaining process. Through its effect on the level of income investment is self-financing, that is, generates the funds required for its existence.

In *The General Theory* the level of savings is tied to the level of income, but is within the realm of individual consumption decisions. The neoclassical treatment of savings makes investment dependent on individual consumption preferences, and so contradicts the autonomous nature of the Keynesian investment process.

In contrast, the post-Keynesian treatment by Kalecki[20] and Kaldor[21] views savings as an element of profits realized by firms through the market sale of their commodities. Savings, viewed as an element of profits, are determined by the determinants of profits. The funds required for investment are thus removed from the consumption decisions of individuals to the pricing and expansion decisions of firms. In Kalecki's formulation the proportion of income saved is tied to profits and the degree of monopoly. Since saving is the chief component of profits realized by firms, the proportion of income saved is tied to the distribution of income between wages and profits.

In this manner, post-Keynesian economics eliminates the dependence of Harrod's growth process upon the intertemporal consumption decisions of individuals. The result of this elimination is, in turn, the disappearance of the knife-edge problem. The proportion of saving out of income is made subordinate to the requirements of the expansion of capital, and the latter is transformed into a process that is, in principle at least, self-sustaining. In Joan Robinson's words, the result of these steps is that "whatever I/Y (investment/income) may be, P/Y (profits/income) and therefore s (Savings/income) is equal to it; . . . an equilibrium growth rate may be anything between zero and g^*, the upper limit set by the minimum level of the real wage."[22] The self-reproducing growth rate becomes that rate which is consistent with the expansion desires of firms rather than that rate consistent with the consumption desires of individuals.

This treatment of accumulation as self-sustaining underlies the post-Keynesian break with neoclassical theory. However, since the process of accumulation is not viewed as determined by the preferences and needs of individuals as savers, the rate of capital accumulation is left undetermined in post-Keynesian economics. This is reflected in the multiplicity of possible growth paths in Joan Robinson's theory.[23] This element of indeterminacy is expressed in the connection of the rate of accumulation to the "animal spirits of entrepreneurs," factors which are intrinsically indeterminate.

Professor Kaldor's formulation of the valuation ratio offers a way out of this dilemma.[24] Even if firms rely primarily on internal funds to finance their investment expenditures, and so are able to free themselves from the discipline and scrutiny of financial markets, the decision of corporate managers to expand and accumulate capital necessarily flows through to the value of equities in household portfolios. If the valuation ratio remains unchanged, retained earnings will be reflected in a proportional appreciation of stock values and concomitant capital gains income to corporate stockholders.[25]

Here lies the importance of consumption out of capital gains. If household savers do not wish to undertake the amount of savings decided for them implicitly by their business managers, they have the option of undoing such saving by increasing their consumption expenditures and reducing the valuation ratio. All wealth must have an owner, and in market economies capitalists cannot be forced to hold a higher wealth-income ratio than they desire. This is the mechanism by which the wealth preferences of savers can control the rate of real capital accumulation, even if firms rely primarily on internal finance as in Kaldor's model.

This recognition of the role of equity markets in enforcing wealthowner preferences serves to validate in principle the neoclassical view that the rate of accumulation is governed by saver preferences. If business firms in total attempt to accumulate capital at a greater rate than household wealthowners desire, this will result in falling valuation ratios as households choose to realize their accrued gains by the sale of stock to finance consumption expenditures. The fall in valuation ratios must after some point serve to restrain net investment by business managers, since when the valuation ratio is substantially below unity it is cheaper for firms wishing to expand to buy out existing companies rather than to incur new investment to expand their productive capacity.

However, while the neoclassical concern with the problem of scarcity and the founding of accumulation on the time preferences of individuals is confirmed in principle by this view of the role of equity markets, the post-Keynesian view of accumulation as a self-sustaining process reflecting firm profitability and the animal spirits of business investors appears confirmed in practice over long stretches of time. Throughout the entire period of the twenties there is little evidence that household capitalists refused to validate the accumulation decisions of their hired managers. While the data are admittedly incomplete, it does not appear that the marginal propensity to consume out of capital gain income rose during the bull market of the late twenties. Wealthowners appear to have been willing to accumulate passively both the great bulk of savings made for them by their hired manager, and even the capital appreciation created by speculative forces.

The collapse of the stock market in 1929 put an end to this process of passive accumulation by wealthowners. This collapse of equity values had two chief effects for macroeconomic behavior. The first was the effect that lower wealth values and capital losses on equities had in reducing household consumption expenditures. Yet as stated above, perhaps due to the high degree of concentration of stock ownership, the data suggest that the effect of declining stock values on household consumption expenditures was relatively slight. While admittedly it is very difficult to distinguish empirically the wealth and income effects of a change in stock values from the psychological effects of falling or rising stock market values on consumer sentiment,[26] the data provide little supporting evidence for a large fall in consumption propensities due to wealth effects during the 1930s.

More important empirically was the impact of the fall in the valuation ratio on corporate investment spending. The speculative collapse in stock prices from a high of 250 in September 1929 (1926 = 100) to a low of 40 in June 1932 represented a fall of more than 80 percent. The resulting fall in corporate valuation ratios removed all desire on the part of corporate managers to expand their physical capital stock. Stock prices did not recover to their 1926 values until the end of 1935. While they rose to a high of 140 early in 1937, they fell again to a value below 100 at the end of 1937, at which level they remained until the outbreak of the Second World War. The low level of the valuation ratio throughout the thirties suggests a plausible explanation for the failure of corporate investment spending to revive, even in the face of unprecedented low interest costs of borrowing and ample bank liquidity. It was not until the postwar years that stock prices rose sufficiently to restore the valuation ratio back to the neighborhood of unity, a necessary step in order for business investment spending to become once again attractive to ultimate wealthowners and their business managers.

Notes

1. Fritz Machlup, *The Stock Market, Credit and Capital Formation,* William Hodge and Company, London, 1940.

2. Ibid., p. 27
3. Ibid., p. 49.
4. Ibid., p. 52.
5. Ibid., p. 270.
6. Ibid., p. 300.
7. Sir John Hicks, "The Hayek Story," in *Critical Essays in Monetary Theory,* Oxford, 1967, p. 203.
8. F. Machlup, "Hayek's Contributions to Economics," in *Essays on Hayek,* F. Machlup (ed.), New York University Press, New York, 1976. p. 29.
9. See Barry Bosworth, "The Stock Market and the Economy," *Brookings Papers on Economic Activity* (1975:2), pp. 257-300; Saul Hymans, "Consumption: New Data and Old Puzzles," *Brookings Papers on Economic Activity* (1970:1), pp. 117-26; Kul Bhatia, "Capital Gains and the Aggregate Consumption Function," *American Economic Review,* Vol. 26 (December 1972) pp. 866-79; John Arena, "Capital Gains and the 'Life Cycle' Hypothesis of Saving," *American Economic Review,* Vol. 54 (March 1964), pp. 107-111; Franco Modigliani, "Monetary Policy and Consumption," in *Consumer Spending and Monetary Policy: The Linkages,* Federal Reserve Bank of Boston, 1971, pp. 9-84; and Irwin Friend and Charles Lieberman, "Short-run Asset Effects on Household Saving and Consumption: The Cross Section Evidence," *American Economic Review,* Vol. 65 (September 1975), pp. 624-33.
10. Raymond Goldsmith and Robert Lipsey, *Studies in the National Balance Sheet of the United States,* Vol. I and II, National Bureau of Economic Research, 1963; and Robert Lampman, *The Share of Top Wealth-Holders in National Wealth,* National Bureau of Economic Research, 1962.
11. E.B. Cox, *Trends in the Distributional Stock Ownership,* University of Pennsylvania Press, 1963.
12. R. Lampman, ibid.
13. For a detailed development see Dale Jorgenson, "The Theory of Investment Behavior," in Robert Ferber (ed.), *Determinants of Investment Behavior,* National Bureau of Economic Research, 1967.
14. Charles Bischoff has done considerable empirical work with a cost of capital defined as the weighted average of the bond rate and the dividend-price-ratio. This measure ignores expected capital gains, but the inclusion of the stock market variable seems to improve the performance of the equation. "The Effect of Alternative Lag Distributions," in Gary Fromm (ed.), *Tax Incentives and Capital Spending,* Brookings Institution, Washington, D.C., 1971.
15. James Tobin, "A General Equilibrium Approach to Monetary Theory," *Journal of Money, Credit and Banking,* Vol. 1 (February 1969), pp. 15-29.
16. Charles Bischoff has estimated an empirical version of the model. "Business Investment in the 1970's: A Comparison of Models," *Brookings Papers on Economic Activity* (1971:1), pp. 13-58. See also John Ciccolo, "A Linkage

Between Product and Financial Markets-Investment and q," Essay III of unpublished Ph.D. dissertation (New Haven, Conn., Yale University, 1975).

17. Goldsmith and Lipsey, *Studies in the National Balance Sheet.*

18. *Long Term Economic Trends, 1860–1965.*

19. See A. Asimakopulos, "The Determination of Investment in Keynes's Model," *Canadian Journal of Economics* (August 1971), pp. 382-388.

20. M. Kalecki, *Essays in the Theory of Economic Fluctuations,* Farrar & Rinehart, New York. 1939.

21. N. Kaldor, "Alternative Theories of Distribution," *Review of Economic Studies,* Vol. 23, 1955-56.

22. J. Robinson, Harrod After Twenty-one Years," *Economic Journal* 80 (September 1970), p. 733.

23. Joan Robinson, *Essays in the Theory of Economic Growth,* MacMillan, London, 1962.

24. N. Kaldor, "Alternative Theories of Distribution."

25. See B. Moore, "Some Macroeconomic Consequences of Corporate Equities," *Canadian Journal of Economics,* Vol. 6 (November 1973), pp. 529-44.

26. F. Thomas Juster and Paul Wachtel, "Inflation and the Consumer," *Brookings Papers on Economic Activity* (1972:1), pp. 71-114.

18

Machlup on Economic Integration

Charles P. Kindleberger

Economic integration is perhaps not the most important topic that Fritz Machlup has dealt with in his long and illustrious career, but it has the distinction of being the most recent. As president of the International Economic Association, he gave an address on the "History of Thought on Economic Integration," at the Fourth World Congress of the Association held in Budapest in 1974.[1] That same year his Harms-Prize Lecture at Kiel was entitled "Integrationshemmende Integrationspolitik."[2] Inevitably reminding us of the parable of Christ feeding the multitude with two fish and five small loaves, there was enough left over from these efforts, and especially the first, to fill a book, which appeared in 1976 and which testified to what we all know of his characteristic energy and drive to work.[3] Finally, though I use the word provisionally, he retraced a small piece of this ground in his paper given at the Nobel Symposium on Interregional and International Trade in Stockholm in June 1976, entitled "Conceptual and Causal Relationships in the Theory of Economic Integration in the Twentieth Century."[4]

As the informed reader will surmise, Machlup's approach to economic integration, as to any subject he tackles, is multifaceted. He deals with the semantics of the subject. He has produced a far-ranging compendium of economic thought dealing with integration, covering four centuries and the literature in four languages. He of course subjects the topic to extensive economic analysis of his own. At an absolute disadvantage across the board, the law of comparative advantage induces me to neglect Machlup's contributions to the history of thought on economic integration. To the extent that the semantics and the analysis can be disentangled, moreover, I choose to focus on the former. Machlup's economic analysis of integration, as he himself indicates, amounts more or less to a textbook in international economics—an activity in which I may be forgiven for detecting diminishing returns. And semantics are, after all, close to the heart of Machlup's contribution to economics.

In Machlup's view, the theory of economic integration is coextensive with the theory of interregional and international economics. Integration is division of labor—a neat oxymoron, since integration is oneness and division is two-or-more-ness. Its essence is taking advantage of all opportunities for efficient transfers of mobile factors of production, that is labor and capital, and all opportunities for efficient division of labor, using "labor" in the Ricardian sense of all productive factors. On this definition, economic integration is underdetermined, since as Robert Mundell has shown, under certain specified conditions factor transfers can substitute for trade or trade can substitute for factor movements.[5] For the most part, Machlup's analysis deals with trade, rather than with factor movements. It would be possible to insist on first, all factor movements that are possible, and then trade to the extent of the remaining room for equalizing goods prices, on the assumption that factor movements would in the real world fail to achieve equalization of goods prices. But the fact that Machlup insists on the division of labor as the essence of integration indicates his concentration on trade. Factor movements substituting for trade constitute a division of labor only in a limited geographical sense, and not in the sense of specialization and exchange the expression normally implies.

Trade substituting for factor movements, or factor transfers substituting for trade, seems to imply factor-price equalization, and this has been suggested in the literature as a criterion of complete economic integration.[6] Machlup, however, rejects this measure, largely on the practical ground that it is difficult, perhaps impossible, to take adequate account of differences in quality of land, labor, and capital between countries in comparing factor prices, or of differences in risks, actual or perceived, in discounting yields on securities to measure the return to financial capital. This fastidiousness seems excessive, especially in the light of the liberties with data that the present generation of econometricians is forced to take and does take, on the whole, cheerfully. There are, to be sure, some questions that must be raised when factor-price equalization is chosen as the criterion for economic integration, but there are also some serious theoretical losses that result when it is rejected.

Factor-price equalization can be achieved by trade—under highly restrictive conditions which every graduate student learns to rattle off—linear homogeneous production functions of degree one, perfect competition in goods and factor markets, no transport costs, no factor reversals, more goods than factors, no complete specialization, and so on, and so on. It can also be achieved by factor movements. But there is a third possibility which involves neither trade nor factor movements. If skewness of resources is exactly offset by skewness of demand, goods prices may be equalized, and with the appropriate assumptions from the foregoing list, factor prices as well. This is surely not integration, and there is no division of labor, except in the trivial sense that each country specializes in minding its own business.

There is a fourth possibility. It involves no trade, and no movement of indigenous factors. Factor prices can be equalized between two countries in a multi-country world with movements at the margin of outside factors. Because such movements are marginal, they can be limited in size. In the Europe of the 1950s and 1960s, substantial progress toward factor-price equalization was achieved through the movement of American corporations, Euro-money and Euro-capital, and Mediterranean labor. Assume that German and French corporations are unwilling to establish subsidiaries in the other country, that German and French capital do not move from one country to the other, and that German and French labor show strong preferences for working within their own borders—conditions that accord somewhat loosely perhaps to the facts. If American corporations are prepared to move enterprise between Germany and France so as to equalize profits, if German and French capital move rather freely back and forth to the Euro-money and capital market, and if Mediterranean labor is ready to shift between Germany and France in search of higher wages, factor-price equalization can be achieved—or at least approached—without either trade or movement of French or German productive factors, and there is no integration. Things equal to the same things are equal to each other, but may remain at base separate and disintegrated. The division of labor is performed by outside factors, on a geographical shifting basis, and not through specialization and exchange.

Factor-price equalization is therefore an adequate criterion for economic integration when it is accompanied by oneness, that is, the unification of markets, for goods or factors. And when there is oneness or unification of markets, factor-price equalization has a generality as a criterion for economic integration which is unhappily lost in Machlup's rejection of it on operational grounds. Take a labor market. If blacks and whites are paid different wages, the labor market is surely not integrated. As wages for whites and blacks of the same skills, experience, credentials, or performance converge—the multiplicity of criteria underline the validity of Machlup's diffidence—the labor market may be said to be more integrated; as they diverge, less so. Women are integrated into the general labor market to the extent that they receive the same pay for the same work as men. Machlup's claim that the criterion is nonoperational has overtones of perfectionism. At the interregional or intraregional level, it is being used operationally, if not by economists at least by lawyers and judges in legal actions, every day.

It is true that factor-price equalization as a sole criterion of economic integration diverts attention from oneness, and oneness is the essence of integration. Given oneness, however, factor-price equalization is helpful in establishing a base of complete integration toward and away from which markets and economies may move. It has operational difficulties, but the same is basically true of all economic aggregates.

More or less oneness conveys a sense of paradox, and here Machlup misses a chance of semantic exploration—what others may choose to call hair-splitting. It is one, moreover, which has relevance to international economic policy, and particularly to the differences between British and United States views on tariff discrimination and customs union. The debate goes back to the discussions of the draft charter of the abortive International Trade Organization at Geneva and Havana in 1947 and 1948. The United States insisted that the exception to the rule of nondiscrimination for customs unions and free-trade areas must be all or nothing, go or no-go, yes or no, like pregnancy, rather than divisible by degrees. British negotiators maintained that it was illogical to insist that 100 percent discrimination in favor of a trade partner in a customs union or free-trade area was acceptable, whereas 99 percent was not. The American arguments that I recall from the period were admittedly unconvincing. It was feared that if a country started to discriminate less than totally with a trade partner, it might find itself sliding down a slippery slope of discriminating widely. Anything less than 100 percent discrimination was thought to be a positive feedback process, or habit forming, like eating peanuts. But some actions are habit forming; others are not. There is no evidence that I am aware of which would support the view that to discriminate 99 percent in favor of a country would start a country down the road to wicked trade practices.

It is true, however, that some relationships are divisible and other are integral. In undergraduate classes, I cite friendship as a relationship that can be measured by degrees, and marriage as one that is indivisible (of late this analogy has seemed less apposite). And occasionally, it has helped beginning students to fix the idea in mind when I recall a song of Sophie Tucker from the 1920s:

You gotta see Mama every night
Or you can't see Mama at all.
You gotta see Mama and treat her right,
Or she won't be there when you call.

And then the verse becomes quantitative:

If you want my company,
You can't fifty-fifty me.
You gotta see Mama every night,
Or you can't see Mama at all.

Oneness is of course oneness of markets. Adding one and one makes not two, but, with perfect integration, one. If we allow for degrees of integration, with more or less, rather than only integration-nonintegration as in the customs-union issue above, one and one may make one and a half. The law of one price states that in one market there is one price. As we have seen in early examples of *curiosa*—cases of factor-price equalization without oneness—there may be one price and separated markets. But there is an intermediate position: one price and markets which are neither merged, nor completely separate, markets, that is, which are joined. This is integration in the Machlup sense of division of labor. It is, however, both a semantic and an analytical question whether joined markets are as truly integrated as merged or added markets.

The point may be illustrated by an example I have discussed on an earlier occasion.[7] The San Francisco and New York capital markets can be joined in two different ways: one, by taking the excess demand for savings in San Francisco and transferring it to New York until rates of return are identical (or more realistically, diverge by some customary wedge); the other, by shifting San Francisco demanders and suppliers of savings both to New York and merging them with New York demanders and suppliers of savings available for use in California to arrive at a common demand curve, a common supply curve, and of course a common price and quantity. The first is the method used in trade, balancing off excess demand in one market against excess supply in the other until prices are equated. The second, which is a possibility only when transport costs are negligible, implies merger of markets rather than division of labor. In each case there is but one price, but the prices will be different. A California bond issue sold in New York to Californians and New Yorkers differs in kind from the same volumes of savings sold in two bond issues, one marketed in San Francisco and the other in New York. California savers are willing to accept a lower coupon rate on a bond issued in New York because of the increased liquidity inherent in such an issue, which will be traded in a much wider secondary market than that in San Francisco. Commodities may not be altered when separate markets are joined by trade, through equating the excess demand in one with the excess supply in another at a single price adjusted for transport costs. In today's world we do not add demand and supply curves in two or more countries to form single demand and supply curves. Something like this occurred in the seventeenth, eighteenth and nineteenth centuries when colonial goods were stapled first through Amsterdam and then through London. It may even be that the goods were improved in the stapling emporia through quality control, repacking and the like, and hence differed from goods directly traded, although the historical sequence from stapling to direct trade makes this unlikely. There may be an analogous phenomenon in labor migration, but it eludes me, unless one makes a distinction between a labor excess supply in one country that meets an excess demand in another and equalizes wage rates on a temporary basis that will later be reversed, and permanent migration where the immigrants are assimilated into the labor force.

Leaving aside the cases of commodities and labor, however, we can say of capital that oneness of price is compatible with two means of joining markets. And it would appear that a higher form of integration is achieved when the demand and supply curves in the two markets are added together, rather the excess supply in one country being matched against excess demand in the other.

Oneness of markets can be frustrated by more than governmental barriers, and within the category of barriers by more than merely tariffs, barriers to migration, and capital taxation or controls. Governments discriminate, but so do Nature and people. Governmental discrimination, moreover, derives not only from tariffs, but from non-tariff barriers (NTBs) such as taxation, state regulation, as in pure food and drug laws, pollution control, parochial standards of weights, measures, labelling, and the like. Machlup of course is fully aware of the necessity for integration to go beyond tariff elimination and to harmonize taxation, governmental benefits, and regulation of all kinds to achieve integration in goods markets. He is not equally disposed to take into account the separation of markets by discrimination on the part of Nature and of individuals.

For discrimination by Nature, let us consider an intellectual experiment of an attempt at integration between New Zealand and old Zealand, or, if you like, the country of Denmark rather than its most prominent province. Governments, let us assume, put aside their rivalry in the British butter market and prepare a customs union between the two countries, harmonize direct and indirect taxation, governmental benefits, regulations of all sorts. Assume that New Zealanders and the Danes are prepared to merge fully, but let us leave aside for the moment actual migration. Would this be integration? The two countries would make *"actual* utilization of all *potential* opportunities of [efficient transfers of productive resources and] efficient division of labor" (Machlup's italics, my brackets to eliminate indeterminacy), but the result would hardly be oneness. Nature has put the two countries in separate hemispheres, both longitudinally and latitudinally. Transport costs must overwhelm all but a very few potential opportunities for division of labor, and if these are all completely used, the degree of integration would be low.

Discrimination by people—whether as consumers or as producers—raises a further semantic-analytical question. Let us assume two countries that happen to be contiguous so that transport costs are low, with skewed resources, skewed tastes which offset the skewness of resources, identical goods prices, and factor-price equalization because of the presence of the condition posed by the assumptions of the factor-price equilization theorem. There is no division of labor. Is there potential for division of labor? It depends on whether tastes are exogenous or endogenous, whether we allow for demonstration effect, and the harmonization of tastes from frequent intercourse between the people of the two economies, or not. If people discriminate by tastes and demands, the potential opportunity for division of labor can quickly be exhausted without economic integration in a commonsense view of that term, that is, oneness of the economy. Integration does not require identical homothetic demand maps, any more than does the factor-price equalization theorem. It is enough that tastes are less skewed than resources in the portion of the map relevant for the before-trade after-trade comparison. But the more nearly identical are tastes, and the more skewed resources, the larger the opportunities for efficient division of labor, and for integration.

People may discriminate as consumers, but also as producers. On previous occasions I have referred to the fact that when the sovereigns of Belgium and the Netherlands cut the ribbons along their mutual border to signalize the readiness of the Belgium-Netherlands-Luxemburg (Benelux) governments to permit the movement of labor among the members, nothing happened. The

Dutch stayed on their side of the frontier and the Belgians on theirs despite differences in wages that might have been expected to lead to equalizing movements of labor. Cultural and political discrimination led to economic discrimination and prevented "efficient transfers of productive resources," if we define "efficient" in terms of Pareto-optimality without allowing for differences in the tastes of producers. It is possible to regard this as a second-best solution, one in which competition is less than perfect because producers discriminate, or in which nationalism is an argument in the objective function, along with economic well-being. "Potentiality" may be constrained by tastes or it may not be. If it is so constrained, one will have to conclude that all potential opportunities for efficient transfers of resources are actually utilized, but that few exist because of differences in tastes or the existence of nationalism. If we assume that the potential opportunities for efficient division of labor are limited for any reason—because of separation by Nature, separation by transport costs such as might arise from strong demands for services that are produced and consumed locally and not traded internationally, or separation by differences in tastes for goods, or strong attachment to the home country which makes migration intolerable, we shall have to conclude that Machlup's criterion for actual utilization of potential opportunities for efficient transfers or efficient division of labor can be met without achieving much in the way of oneness, which is the essence of economic integration.

Applying these notions to the European labor market throws light on what Machlup may mean by "potential." In 1973 and 1974, Switzerland, France, and Germany halted the immigration of further foreign labor. The evidence makes clear that the reasons for so doing were largely social, despite some protestation on part of West Germany that the move was dictated by the business cycle. The Swiss were worried about what they regarded as the threat to their national identity, or Swissness, as the proportion of the labor force represented by migrants reached one-third. Germany, with a lower proportion—close to 10 percent—nonetheless felt itself unable to assimilate 2,400,000 workers and their families, most of whom had no interest in learning the language or identifying with the German culture. Halting the immigration may be taken over the longer run to be inefficient, though the cost in the short run is zero or even a gain. The economics of the move to be sure are somewhat debatable. But there can be no doubt that halting immigration is an act of economic and social disintegration between Central and Northern Europe on the one hand and the Mediterranean and Eastern Europe on the other. The social potential for oneness is low; the economic potential larger. There rests an important question, however, whether such an economic potential may be said actually to exist when the social potential is so limited.

Thus far the argument has been conducted in static terms treating countries as units rather than aggregates. Machlup of course recognizes the dynamic aspects of the process of integration, and particularly the scale economies and decreasing costs, with which Scitovsky's name is associated. He also approaches disaggregation of national economies in recognizing backwash effects, emphasized by Myrdal. Freedom for factor movements may drain the cheap-labor countries of their best workers, and capital, so that the rich country gets richer and the poor poorer. This effect of complementarity among disaggregated units of an economy is noted, but it raises an interesting problem which even the rich and full contribution of Machlup does not fully explore.

Integration and disintegration can exist side by side. Take two economies which are themselves integral, but made up of closely related sectors, regions, industries, or other subsidiary parts. The theory of integration normally sums countries as integers, adding one and one to make one as in $X + Y = Z$. But if X and Y are aggregates, rather than simple units, the process of addition may be more complex.

In his book on the *Crédit Lyonnais,* Jean Bouvier notes that the bank held its breath, so to speak, as a new railroad joined a particular town more intimately to the rest of France, waiting to see whether the new connection would create new opportunities for growth and profitable banking in the town, or kill existing opportunities.[8] One unhappy village near Dijon was punished twice, first by the north-south railroad which brought in the better wines of Burgundy to destroy its viticulture, and secondly by a east-west railroad which introduced cheap, excellent beer from Alsace and ruined its attempt to build a brewing industry as a replacement for wine. Highly localized, idiosyncratic regions like western and southwestern France, southern Italy, eastern Bavaria, and peripheral Scotland, Northern Ireland, and Wales may be cut off and in effect abandoned by the efforts of the country to integrate with foreign countries; which stimulates mostly the portions of the country adjacent to the new partners.

At an early stage in mercantilism, national integration was provided by improved transport, removed internal barriers to trade, and movement of labor and capital, by the public goods of uniform justice, a single national money and capital markets, and the like. The countries we think of as ripe for international economic integration were themselves thoroughly disintegrated in the Middle Ages.[9]

International integration today has the effect of undoing some considerable part of the earlier national integration. If one regards countries not as units but as decomposable matrices, a question arises whether it is integration, disintegration, or both to unify certain of the mobile, transformable, or dynamic parts of the economy in one country with similar subunits abroad, whilst leaving other subunits in both countries to revert to their premercantilistic separate condition. Contemplate two couples, each with children. Is it integration, disintegration, or both if the handsome and rich husband in one couple runs off with the beautiful wife in the other, each leaving behind an average spouse and dependent children whom I hesitate to characterize. In the European case,

of course, the Social Fund and the Investment Fund were established to look
after the portions of the countries adhering to the Treaty of Rome which might
suffer from backwash effects—a sort of alimony in the extension of our elaborate
metaphor of friendship, marriage, and separation. It is nonetheless well to
remember that while integration is the addition of one and one to make one
$(X + Y = Z)$, when X and Y are decomposable matrices, the result may be
$X + Y = Z + x + y$, and it is better to analyze the case rather than to characterize
it as integration, disintegration, or both.

The problem with economic integration arises from the fact that the word
itself has positive overtones, or resonance. Just as there are persuasive definitions,
so are there "buzz words," which need merely to be spoken or written to evoke
an affirmative response. We all intuitively applaud weddings, deprecate separa-
tions and divorces. As the world becomes more complex, an increasing number
of cases involve the two simultaneously.

Is integration good? The United States has always thought so. That bigger
is better is a typical American view of life. The preamble to the European
Recovery Act of 1948—enacting the Marshall Plan into law, and written by the
Congress rather than by the Executive Branch of the government—urged a
United States of Europe so that the Continent could enjoy the benefits of a
wide market like that in the United States. Paul G. Hoffman's speech or October
31, 1948, echoed that same theme. Most of us intuitively feel a sense of loss
as we contemplate separatism in Quebec, devolution in Scotland and Wales,
independence movements in Brittany, the Basque country, and Catalonia. So
deeply felt are these sentiments that civil wars have proved to be among the
most devastating in history.

These attitudes are not without challenge today. E.F. Schumacher has
made many converts with the notion that smaller is better.[10] A number of
pundits interested in economic development are studying "decoupling" of
North and South as these terms are applied worldwide, with the thought that
independence is fraught with political tension and potential strife; to reduce
the division of labor internationally, leading to less dependence, is regarded
as conducive to peace. Johann Galtung, the Norwegian sociologist, equates
dependence with exploitation, and even interdependence with mutual exploitation—a suggestion I found fanciful until Martin Bronfenbrenner pointed out
that husband and wife can mutually exploit one another if he regards her as
a servant and she him as a meal ticket. I refuse to believe that all marriages are
like that.

Machlup's escape from this dilemma is a sound one, through the distinctions between Pareto-optimality and welfare economics on the one hand, and
between private and public goods on the other. The efficiency criteria of
Pareto-optimality are irrelevant as a guide to policy in a world of interdependent
welfare functions, where distributional criteria are paramount and one country
is made worse off by the gains of another, even when its own real income does

not decrease and may even increase. Integration that makes both parts of the
new whole richer may be intolerable if it widens the gap between them absolutely, even if the rate of gain in the poorer country is higher than that of the
richer.

For private goods, Machlup hypothesizes, the optimum area is the world,
whereas the optimum cultural, social, and political area appropriate for public
goods may be much smaller. (I would take exception to this for economic
public goods, like money, where I cling to the minority opinion that the
optimum currency area is the world.) For private goods, bigger is better, and
integration or the division of labor has a positive value, optimally on a world
bases, with perhaps half-way stops at customs union or free-trade areas. The
public goods of nationalism, cultural identity, local participation, and the like
flourish only on a smaller scale, with an optimal area, in a number of cases,
smaller than present countries if the separatist movements are to be taken
seriously, as presumably they should be.

In the clash between economics and the other social sciences, which is
likely to prevail in determining the scale of activities? Machlup, like Marx and
like most economists, including the writer, seems to think that in the long run
economic considerations will dominate, and lead to integration on a wider and
wider basis until it encompasses the world.

But if economic integration is a potential good, and political integration
a possible bad, perhaps it is time to stop using the word "integration" with its
multifarious overtones, semantic and otherwise, and to stay closer to the
analysis. This is a lesson which Machlup has often preached to the rest of us.

Notes

1. International Economic Association, *Economic Integration: Worldwide,
Regional, Sectoral,* London, Macmillan, 1976.

2. Published Kiel, Institute für Weltwirtschaft, 1974.

3. Fritz Machlup, *A History of Thought on Economic Integration,* to be
published by Macmillan, London.

4. To be published in *The International Allocation of Economic Activity.*

5. Robert A. Mundell, "International Trade and Factor Mobility,"
American Economic Review, 47, 3 (June 1957), pp. 326–35.

6. See for example, Gunnar Myrdal, *An International Economy, Problems
and Prospects,* New York, Harper. 1956.

7. C.P. Kindleberger, "European Integration and the Development of a
Single Financial Center for Long-Term Capital," *Weltwirtschaftliches Archiv,*
90 (1963), pp. 189–210.

8. Jean Bouvier, *Le Crédit Lyonnais de 1863 à 1882, Les années de
formation d'une de dépots.* Paris, SEVPEN, 1961.

9. See Fernand Braudel, *The Mediterranean and the Mediterranean World in the Age of Philip II,* New York, Harper and Row, 1972 (Torchbooks, 1975), Vol. I., pp. 384–85: "European countries were checkered by low-cost regions which were in every case separate worlds by-passed by the general economy. . . . What more backward and uncomfortable province could there be than Brittany? . . . There were similar regions in England."

10. E.F. Schumacher, *Small is Beautiful; Economics as if People Mattered,* New York, Harper and Row, 1973.

Bibliography

Editor's Note: A complete recent bibliography of Fritz Machlup's works can be found in *Selected Economic Writings of Fritz Machlup,* George Bitros, ed. (New York University Press, 1976). It is neatly categorized and contains references regarding reproductions and translations into and from foreign languages of Machlup's various writings.

The bibliography given below is limited to his writings cited in this volume. It consists of two parts: "Books and Monographs" and "Articles and Reports." Articles are refered to their original source even though in the volume the reference could have been made to a reproduction. Whenever references are made to specific articles published in books edited or co-edited by Machlup himself those articles appear in Part II of the Bibliography. The corresponding book would appear in Part I only if a specific reference is made to this book as a whole.

All items are listed in the order of their original appearance.

Part I: Books and Monographs

Die Goldkernwährung (Haberstadt: Meyer, 1925).

Die neuen Währungen in Europa, (Stuttgart: Enke, 1927).

The Stock Market, Credit and Capital Formation, (London: William Hodge and Company, 1940).

International Trade and National Income Multiplier, (Philadelphia, Pa.: Blakiston, 1943).

The Economics of Sellers' Competition, (Baltimore, Md.: The Johns Hopkins Press, 1952).

"An Economic Review of the Patent System," *Study No. 15 of the Subcommittee on Patents, Trademarks and Copyright,* Committee on the Judiciary, 85th Congress, 2nd Session, (Washington, D.C.: 1958).

Essays on Economic Semantics, (Englewood Cliffs, N.J.: Prentice-Hall, 1963).

International Monetary Arrangements: The Problem of Choice, (Princeton, N.J.: International Finance Section, Princeton University, 1964).

International Payments, Debts, and Gold, (New York: Charles Scribner's Sons, 1964).

Plans for Reform of the International Monetary System, Special Papers in International Economics, No. 3, (Princeton, N.J.: International Finance Section, Princeton University, 1964).

Involuntary Foreign Lending, (Stockholm: Almquist and Wiksell, 1965).

Maintaining and Restoring Balance in International Payments, (Princeton, N.J.: Princeton University Press, 1966).

Remaking the International Monetary System. The Rio Agreement and Beyond, (Baltimore, Md.: The Johns Hopkins Press, 1968).

Approaches to Greater Flexibility of Exchange Rates. The Bürgenstock Papers, (Princeton, N.J.: Princeton University Press, 1970).

Gendai Keizaigaku no Tembo (Views on Selected Topics in Modern Economics), Yasukichi Yasuba, ed., (Tokyo: Nihonkeizai Shimbunsha, 1971).

The Alignment of Foreign Exchange Rates, (New York: Praeger Publishers, 1972).

International Mobility and Movement of Capital, (New York, National Bureau of Economic Research–Columbia University Press, 1972).

Selective Economic Writings of Fritz Machlup, George Bitros, ed., (New York: New York University Press, 1976).

A History of Thought on Economic Integration, (London: Macmillan, 1977).

Part II: Articles and Reports

"Währung und Auslandsverschuldung," *Mitteilungen des Verbandes österreichischer Banken und Bankiers,* Vol. 10 (1928).

"Transfer und Preisbewegung," *Zeitschrift für Nationalökonomie,* Vol. 1 (1930).

"The Commonsense of the Elasticity of Substitution," *Review of Economic Studies,* Vol. 2 (1935).

"Further Notes on Elasticity of Substitution: Reply," *Review of Economic Studies,* Vol. 3 (1936).

"Why Bother with Methodology," *Economica,* N.S., Vol. 3 (1936).

"The Theory of Foreign Exchanges," *Economica,* N.S., Vol. 6 (November 1939) and Vol. 7 (February 1940).

"Eight Questions on Gold," *American Economic Reviews, Papers and Proceedings,* Vol. 30 (1941).

"Elasticity Pessimism in International Trade," *Economia Internazionale,* Volume 3 (February 1950).

"Issues in Methodology," *American Economic Review, Papers and Proceedings,* Vol. 42 (1952).

"Do Economists Know Anything?" *The American Scholar,* Vol. 22 (1953).

"Concepts of Competition and Monopoly," *American Economic Review, Papers and Proceedings,* Vol. 45 (1955).

"On Some Misconceptions Concerning Academic Freedom," *American Association of University Professors Bulletin,* Vol. 41 (1955).

"The Problem of Verification in Economics," *Southern Economic Journal,* Vol. 22 (1955).

"Relative Prices and Aggregate Spending in the Analysis of Devaluation," *American Economic Review,* Vol. 45 (June 1955).

"The Terms of Trade Effects of Devaluation upon Real Income and the Balance of Trade," *Kyklos,* Vol. 9 (Fasc. 4, 1956).

"Equilibrium and Disequilibrium: Misplaced Concreteness and Disguised Politics," *Economic Journal,* Vol 48 (March 1958).

"The Optimum Lag of Imitation Behind Innovation," in *Festkrift til Frederik Zeuthen,* (Copenhagen, Nationaløkonomisk Forening, 1958).

"Another View of Cost-push and Demand-pull Inflation," *Review of Economics and Statistics,* Vol. 42 (May 1960).

"Erfindung und Technische Forschung," in *Handwörterbuch der Sozialwissenschaften,* Vol. 3 (Stuttgart: Fischer; Tubingen: Mohr-Siebeck; Göttingen: Vandenhoeck & Ruprecht, 1960).

"Operational Concepts and Mental Constructs in Model and Theory Formation," *Giornale Degli Economisti,* Vol. 15 (1960).

"The Supply of Inventors and Inventions," *Weltwirtschaftliches Archiv,* Vol. 85 (1960).

"Comments on the 'Balance of Payments' and a Proposal to Reduce the Price of Gold," *Journal of Finance,* Vol. 16 (1961).

"Liquidité, internationale et nationale," *Bulletin d'information et de documentation,* Banque Nationale de Belgique, (February 1962).

"In Defense of Academic Tenure," *American Association of University Professors Bulletin,* Vol. 50 (1964).

"The Cloakroom Rule of International Reserves: Reserve Creation and Resources Transfer," *Quarterly Journal of Economics,* Vol. 79 (1965).

"Real Adjustments, Compensatory Corrections, and Foreign Financing of Imbalances in International Payments," in *Trade, Growth, and the Balance of Payments,* Richard Caves, Harry Johnson, and Peter Kenen, eds. (Chicago: Rand McNally, 1965).

"International Monetary Systems and the Free Market Economy," in *International Payments Problems: A Symposium* (Washington, D.C.: American Enterprise Institute for Public Policy Research, 1966).

"The Need for Monetary Reserves," *Banca Nazionale del Lavoro Quarterly Review* (September 1966).

"Operationalism and Pure Theory in Economics," in *The Structure of Economic Science,* Sherman Roy Krupp, ed. (Englewood Cliffs, N.J.: Prentice-Hall, 1966).

"World Monetary Debate—Bases for Agreement," *The Banker,* Vol. 116 (1966).

"Credit Facilities or Reserve Allotments?" *Banca Nazionale del Lavoro Quarterly Review,* No. 81 (June 1967).

"From Dormant Liabilities to Dormant Assets," *The Banker,* Vol. 117 (1967).

"Theories of the Firm: Marginalist, Managerial, Behavioral," *American Economic Review,* Vol. 57 (1967).

"Academic Freedom," in *International Encyclopedia of the Social Sciences,* (New York: Macmillan & Free Press, 1968).

"Liberalism and the Choice of Freedoms," in *Roads to Freedom: Essays in Honour of Friedrich A. von Hayek,* (London: Routledge and Kegan Paul, 1969).

"On the Alleged Inferiority of the Social Sciences," in *The Nature and Scope of Social Science. A Critical Anthology,* Leonard I. Krimerman, ed. (New York: Appleton-Century Crofts, 1969).

"Positive and Normative Economics: An Analysis of the Ideas," in *Economic Means and Social Ends: Essays in Political Economics,* Robert L. Heilbroner, ed. (Englewood-Cliffs, N.J.: Prentice-Hall, 1969).

"Homo Oeconomicus and His Class Mates," in *Phenomenology and Social Reality: Essays in Memory of Alfred Schultz,* Maurice Natanson, ed. (The Hague: Nijhoff, 1970).

"Academic Freedom," in *Encyclopedia of Education* (New York: Crowell Collier and Macmillan, 1971).

"Changes in the International Monetary System and the Effects on Banks," in *Banking in a Changing World* (Rome: Associazione Bancaria Italiana, 1971).

"The Faculty: A Body Without Mind or Voice," and "European Universities as Partisans," in *Neutrality or Partisanship: A Dilemma of Academic Institutions* (New York: Carnegie Foundation, 1971).

"The Role of Gold in the International Monetary System," *Economic Notes,* Vol. 1 (Monte dei Paschi di Siena, 1972).

"Exchange Rate Flexibility," *Banca Nazionale del Lavoro Quarterly Review,* No. 106 (September 1973).

"The Illusion of Universal Higher Education," in *The Idea of A Modern University,* Sidney Hook, Paul Kurtz, and Miro Todorovich, eds. (Buffalo, N.Y.: Prometheus Books, 1974).

"Situational Determinism in Economics," *British Journal for the Philosophy of Science,* Vol. 25 (1974).

"Between Outline and Outcome the Reform Was Lost," in *Reflections on Jamaica,* Edward M. Bernstein et al., Essays in International Finance, No. 115 (April 1976), International Finance Section, Princeton University.

"Hayek's Contributions to Economics," in *Essays on Hayek,* Fritz Machlup, ed. (New York: New York University Press, 1976).

About the Contributors

William J. Baumol
Princeton and New York Universities

John S. Chipman
University of Minnesota

Alfred W. Coats
University of Nottingham

Jacob S. Dreyer
U.S. Treasury Department

Robert Eisner
Northwestern University

Otmar Emminger
Deutsche Bundesbank

Dietrich Fischer
New York University

Gottfried Haberler
American Enterprise Institute

George N. Halm
Santa Rosa, California

Charles P. Kindleberger
Massachusetts Institute of Technology

Burton G. Malkiel
Princeton University

Basil J. Moore
Wesleyan University

Mark Perlman
University of Pittsburgh

Gerhard Prosi
Universität Kiel

Walter S. Salant
The Brookings Institution

Paul A. Samuelson
Massachusetts Institute of Technology

Robert Triffin
Yale University

Yasukichi Yasuba
Kyoto University

John Williamson
University of Warwick

About the Editor

Jacob S. Dreyer is an international economist at the Office of International Economic Analysis, Department of the Treasury. He was educated in Europe and the United States and earned degrees in law and economics. Dr. Dreyer studied under Professor Machlup at New York University where he received his Ph.D. degree in 1974. In 1974-1976 he taught at New York University and served as consultant to Federal agencies and non-profit organizations. He authored the book *Composite Reserve Assets in the International Monetary System,* several articles in professional journals, and a number of contributions to various volumes. His main research interests are in the areas of international economics, monetary theory, development economics, and comparative economic systems.

DATE DUE

~~AUG 0 0 1999~~	

MP 728